THE
EARLY MAPS
OF SCOTLAND
To 1850

THE
EARLY MAPS
OF SCOTLAND

To 1850

BY A COMMITTEE OF THE
ROYAL SCOTTISH GEOGRAPHICAL SOCIETY

THIRD EDITION

Revised and Enlarged

with A History of Scottish Maps *by*

D. G. MOIR

PUBLISHED BY
THE ROYAL SCOTTISH
GEOGRAPHICAL SOCIETY
EDINBURGH
1973

MEMBERS OF COMMITTEE

DONALD G. MOIR, F.R.S.G.S. (Convener).

Miss ANN YOUNG, M.A.

JOHN C. BARTHOLOMEW, M.A., F.R.G.S., F.R.S.E.

DAVID C. SIMPSON, M.B.E., B.SC., PH.D., F.R.S.E., F.R.S.G.S.

ROBERT L. SMITH, J.P., F.R.I.C.S.

Volume 2, to be published in 1975, will deal with the special maps of Scotland (road maps, canal maps, railway maps, geological maps, historical maps); charts; county maps; and town plans up to 1850.

Volume 2 will also contain corrections or additions to Volume 1. The Secretary of the Society will be glad to receive particulars of maps published up to 1850 and not included here, or of earlier editions of maps included, or other corrections.

CONTENTS

PREFACE

The first edition of 'The Early Maps of Scotland' was published in 1934 to commemorate the jubilee of the Society.

As a result of this publication details of many additional maps were received and a second edition was issued in 1936.

In recent years the interest in old maps has so increased that a third edition has been called for, and the opportunity has been taken to give fuller details and to include many more of the maps of Scotland.

The Committee hope that the introduction to the history of Scottish maps will stimulate interest, and encourage others to extend the research into the subject, particularly into the work of Scottish cartographers and map-makers.

The Committee wish to thank all those who have helped, and to place on record their indebtedness to many, in particular to Mrs. Muriel Barnett, Mr. A. D. Baxter, Mr. G. R. Crone, Mr Marcel Destombes, Mr. R. H. Fairclough, Miss Betty D. Fathers, Dr. J. B. Harley, Prof. Dr. C. Koeman, the late Dr. R. A Skelton, the Superintendent and Staff of the Map Room of the British Museum, the Librarians and staff of the National Library of Scotland, Edinburgh Public Library, Edinburgh University Library, Glasgow Mitchell Library, Glasgow University Library, Aberdeen University Library, Royal Geographical Society, Bodleian Library, and Cambridge University Library.

Special acknowledgment is made of the contributions by two former members of the Committee, the late Prof. S. T. M. Newman and Dr. A. B. Taylor.

ILLUSTRATIONS

ACKNOWLEDGMENTS

Map 1 is reproduced by courtesy of the Trustees of the National Library of Scotland; maps 2 and 11 by courtesy of the Trustees of the British Museum. Maps 3 and 4 are from the collections of the late Dr. John Bartholomew and the late Mr. D. Alan Stevenson respectively by kind permission of their owners.

THE OUTLINE OF SCOTLAND

1. Gerard Mercator 1595

In 1585 Gerard Mercator, the Flemish geographer and cartographer, published the first part of his famous *Atlas*. The third part, issued in 1595, contained Mercator's map of Scotland. This map was widely copied and on it were based most maps of Scotland in the next sixty years.

THE OUTLINE OF SCOTLAND

2. Robert Gordon 1654

In 1654 a completely new map of Scotland by Robert Gordon was published by the firm of Blaeu in Amsterdam. It replaced Mercator's and became the model for numerous maps issued over the next sixty years by Dutch, French and German cartographers and publishers. Its most distinctive features are the flat top of Lewis and the shape of the north coast.

3. Herman Moll 1714

By the end of the 17th century it was realised that the Gordon-Blaeu map did not fit with the more recent observations of latitude and longitude. Herman Moll's outline is apparently due in part to information supplied by John Adair from his surveys of the Scottish coasts around 1690 to 1710.

THE OUTLINE OF SCOTLAND

4. James Dorret 1750

In 1750 all previous maps were superseded by the large map of James Dorret who was able, through the Duke of Argyll, to make use of recent surveys. The north coast was corrected from Alexander Bryce's map of 1744, and Lewis was at last given its correct shape from the coastal surveys of Murdoch Mackenzie.

I—A History of Scottish Maps

INTRODUCTION

The principles of cartography were already known to the Greeks. In his *Geographia*, written in Alexandria about A.D. 150, Ptolemy expounds the fundamentals, drawing upon his own work and a critical study of his predecessors. The basis of his maps were the reports of travellers and their itineraries, checked against each other, which he inserted into the framework of one of the two projections which he devised. For some cities he used observations for latitude (or, more often, the length of the longest day), but there were no means at his disposal for determining longitude with great accuracy. The primitive maps of Britain were almost entirely based upon itineraries, supplemented by information derived from topographical writers.

The first improvements followed the introduction of the seaman's magnetic compass in the 12th century. By its use Mediterranean navigators were able to determine bearings with considerable accuracy. These, with distances estimated from their vessel's speed, enabled them to lay down a fairly correct coastline on seamen's charts ('portolan charts'). Since Scotland lay away from the main channels of trade the first reasonably accurate chart of the Scottish coasts, *c.* 1540, probably originated in the naval activities encouraged by James IV in the years 1500-13.

Ptolemy's maps were superseded through the cartographic advance which followed the Renaissance. The first separate engraved map of the British Isles was printed in Rome in 1546. Attributed to George Lily, an English exile, it gave a somewhat crude representation of Scotland. Then in 1595 Mercator published his greatly improved map of Scotland, based partly on the chart of 1540 (of which an engraved version had been published in Paris in 1583), and partly on information he had himself assembled and critically assessed.

Map production then developed in the Netherlands but the other Dutch cartographers were content to copy Mercator, until Joannis Blaeu, in 1654, published a map of Scotland by Robert Gordon, and numerous county maps, all based on the manuscript maps drawn by Timothy Pont from his personal surveys in the period around 1580 to 1600.

In the second half of the 17th century the maps of French cartographers began to supplant those published in the Netherlands. In 1665 Nicolas Sanson published in Paris a map of Scotland which was based, with some corrections, on the maps of Gordon and Pont. French scientists now applied themselves to the reformation of cartography, firstly in efforts to establish a method for the reliable calculation of longitude and, secondly, in the use of triangulation for the more accurate topographic mapping, and their methods were followed in other countries.

Attempts at a new survey of the Scottish coasts, and of some Scottish counties by an elementary form of triangulation, were made by John Adair of Edinburgh in the closing years of the 17th century, but he lacked the resources to carry through his projects and most of his manuscript material was never engraved and much was lost. Seemingly using some of Adair's manuscripts, Herman Moll, a Dutchman settled in London, produced in 1714 a new map of Scotland, the first map to break away from the Mercator and Gordon prototypes.

The 18th century was marked by more reliable observations of latitude and longitude with the help of improved instruments. A proper survey of the north coast in 1741-43 by Alexander Bryce, a trigonometrical survey of the Orkneys and Lewis completed by Murdoch Mackenzie in 1750, and assistance from the military surveyors then working in Scotland, all contributed to a much improved map of Scotland by James Dorret, published in London in 1750.

From this time English engravers, who had hitherto contented themselves with small maps of Scotland based on Dutch or French originals, now had a large map of Scotland which they could copy, and numerous maps based on Dorret's were published in London in the next 30 years.

From 1770 onwards more charts of the coasts, and numerous county maps based on accurate surveys became available for the improvement of the general map. These were used by John Ainslie, who himself made some coastal surveys in 1783, and several county surveys, for his map of Scotland published in Edinburgh in 1789, and by John Stockdale in 1806 in the largest map of Scotland yet produced ($3\frac{1}{2}$ miles to an inch).

Then in 1807 Aaron Arrowsmith prepared a map of Scotland on the scale of 4 miles to an inch, based on the maps of the Military Survey of 1747-55, supplemented by all the coastal charts, county maps, and local surveys then available. This large and detailed map served as the basis of maps of Scotland until the Ordnance Survey began their publications. In the 19th century Scottish cartographers and publishers produced numerous maps and atlases, notably the *Atlas* of Scottish counties by John Thomson in 1832, and the *Physical Atlas* of Keith Johnston in 1848.

1 Early Maps of Britain

The earliest representation of Scotland in the form of a map is in the map of the British Isles in the *Geographia* of Claudius Ptolemaeus, usually known as Ptolemy, the eminent Greek astronomer, mathematician and geographer, who lived in Alexandria from about A.D. 90 to A.D. 150. The oldest surviving manuscripts of the *Geographia* (or *Cosmographia*), were written in Greek in the late 12th or early 13th century; their contents include the latitude and longitude (as estimated by Ptolemy) of some 8000 place names in the known world along with 27 maps. Manuscripts of the *Geographia* brought to Italy in the early 15th century were translated into Latin and with the invention of printing in Europe it became widely circulated, first printed without maps at Vicenza in 1475, and then with 26 maps at Bologna in 1477, and in numerous later editions with 27 maps.[1]

In the map of the British Isles, Scotland is correctly placed to the north of England, but instead of extending northward it stretches eastward, with the west coast facing north. Apart from this east-west position, the outline of Scotland, although crude, is clearly recognizable, with the Moray Firth, Firths of Forth, Tay and Clyde clearly indicated. The map has 57 names of coastal features, native sites, and some Roman forts; the knowledge of the east coast and of the Galloway coast, both with a considerable number of place names, could have been acquired by the Romans between A.D. 80 and 83, during the first period of their occupation of southern Scotland, when their fleet sailed to the Orkneys and round Britain and their troops penetrated into south-west Scotland.

Students of Ptolemy's works have debated whether we have the maps as Ptolemy left them, or indeed whether he actually drew maps at all; the view most generally held is that the maps were originally drawn by Ptolemy but that they became separated from the text and that both underwent modifications in the course of the centuries.[2] It is certainly hard to believe that Ptolemy was responsible for the east-west orientation of Scotland; so eminent a geographer must surely have studied all the writings then available as well as questioned mariners and travellers concerning other countries, and would know the description of Scotland by Tacitus, the Roman historian, in his *Life of Agricola*, written about A.D. 98: 'Caledonia stretches a vast length of way towards the north . . . it sharpens to a point at the extremity and terminates in the shape of a wedge'. Attempts have been made by various scholars to show how the error in the position of Scotland occurred,[3] but the result, to quote Professor I. A. Richmond, 'is neither Ptolemy, nor any version of his work that ever in fact saw the light of day'.[4]

The Ptolemy maps created a wide interest in geography and cartography as edition after edition appeared, in Italy with copperplate maps, and in Germany from 1482 at first with woodcut maps. The limitations of the Ptolemy maps were recognized and in the 1482 edition published in Florence by Berlinghieri they were supplemented by four modern maps of Italy, Spain, France and Palestine, and in the Strasbourg edition of 1513 by 20 modern maps, the work of the eminent geographer, Martin Waldseemüller. Amongst numerous later editions was one by Gerard Mercator in 1578.

MEDIEVAL MAPS

Although the Ptolemy maps have the earliest origin, several other manuscript maps of Britain, or showing Britain, were in existence before the Ptolemy maps were brought to the knowledge of Western Europe in the 15th century. Of actual surviving maps the oldest is an anonymous world map of the late 10th century, generally known as the 'Cottonian Map', contained in a Latin manuscript in the British Museum. Scotland is very small and but vaguely defined; only three names are given—Camri (= Cumbria), Orcades, and a large island off the west coast named Tylen.[5] A later map of Western Europe by Giraldus Cambrensis, the Welsh churchman, dated about 1200, now in the National Library of Ireland, shows Scotland in the shape of an oval, with only three names—Scotia, Orcades, and Mare Scotie.

The conventional representation of the known world as a flat disc surrounded by the ocean was taken over by the Christian Church from late Roman cartography. This circular world map, oriented to the East (the Garden of Eden), held its place, with considerable amendments, until well into the 15th century. The best known of these world maps is in Hereford Cathedral and dates from about 1300; it bears an inscription that Richard of Haldingham created it.[6] In the map, England has the shape of an elongated oval, and connected with it by a narrow isthmus a smaller oval for Scotland, which has nine place names, not correctly placed. In other world maps of the time which survive, the scale is too small for any accurate delineation of Scotland.

MATTHEW PARIS

More detail than in the preceding maps is found in four maps of Britain which are part of manuscripts written in the 13th century

by Matthew Paris, a monk of St Albans, who died in 1259, three of them now in the British Museum (designated A, C, and D), and one (B) in Corpus Christi College, Cambridge.

In three of the maps (A, B, and C) the outline of Scotland is very similar, with the Solway Firth, the Firths of Clyde, Forth and Tay, clearly recognizable, but with the northern part of Scotland flattened out of recognition. Two of them (A and B) have each 28 place names in Scotland, and one (C) 20 names; as some names appear on one map but not on the others there is a total of 36 place names in all. The fourth map (D) is even less recognizable and has only 15 place names. Several of the names indicate the religious connection: Arbroath, Dunfermline, St Andrews, Icolmkile (Iona), Melrose, and Whithorn, were all sites of abbeys; Stirling Bridge, Queen's ferry, and Earl's ferry, would all be known to pilgrims and monks. The maps were probably based on the reports brought back by travelling monks; the many Normans who received lands in Scotland in the 12th century during the reign of David I had always clergy in their retinues.[7]

THE 'GOUGH MAP'

The earliest map of Britain with an approach to actuality is an anonymous manuscript map, dated about 1360, known as the 'Gough Map' (after Richard Gough, who was the first to publish an account of the map in 1780), and now in the Bodleian Library in Oxford. It is on two skins of vellum with a total size of $45\frac{1}{2} \times 22$ inches. It shows great progress in mapping since the Matthew Paris maps of the previous century and provides a remarkably accurate and detailed map of England and Wales on a scale of roughly 16 miles to an inch, with the rivers, road systems, and an abundance of place names, but Scotland, with exaggerated length and poor detail, has the shape of a thumb projecting northward from England. It is thought to have been an official map prepared for Edward I, preserved in some government office and may be the only survivor of several copies in use at that time in England for official purposes.[8]

The contrast between the relative accuracy of England and the defective shape of Scotland confirms what the place names show, i.e., that the compiler had access to reliable information for England and that Scotland was relatively unknown. Many of the place names in Scotland suggest a distinct connection with the routes of the expeditions of Edward I into Scotland, and persons on these expeditions could have supplied the information for the map. In the course of eight expeditions the English armies covered most of southern Scotland; and Edward I twice made extended journeys up the east coast to Elgin and Kinloss, the second in 1303-4 when he spent fifteen months in Scotland. This would account for some of the names on the map: Kildrummy, where Edward stayed on several dates; Monthe Colli (Cowie Mounth), the most easterly crossing of the Grampian range; Monthe Capell (Capel Mounth), another crossing; and Culross, mentioned in the King's intinerary of 1304.[9] The shape and size of the northern part of Scotland show a lack of knowledge of the country beyond the Moray Firth, the limit of the English expeditions. The map does not have the space for the names of all the places mentioned in the King's itineraries, and many places he visited were not recorded; to add to the difficulties of a comparison some names on the map are now indecipherable, and others have been rubbed off with use.

SIXTEENTH-CENTURY MAPS

No progress seems to have been made in the 15th century in the mapping of Britain, and little has survived from that period apart from the Ptolemy maps first printed in 1477, and the manuscript maps of Scotland only attached by John Hardyng to his *Chronicle*. Hardyng was in Scotland in the years 1418-21, and again in a later year, in a search for documents which might prove the sovereignty of England over Scotland from earliest times. He wrote three versions of his *Chronicle;* the first, completed in 1457 (a manuscript now in the British Museum), has a coloured diagrammatic map of Scotland with drawings of castles and towns, many of them incorrectly placed in relation to the others. It has no coastline to give a shape of Scotland. The two later versions have similar maps, but covering only the southern part of Scotland.[10] The *Chronicles* have an itinerary which shows that Hardyng was obviously recording from his personal knowledge of a large part of Scotland.

The 16th century saw the great advance in cartography, and the maps of Britain from that century fall broadly into two groups: (*a*) the older type, mostly manuscripts, showing little or no improvement in the cartography of Scotland, and (*b*) those, mostly printed maps, which show the remarkable progress in a short space of time from the imperfect outline of the 1546 map to the very detailed map of Scotland, with an abundance of place names, by Gerard Mercator in 1595.

The older type include a woodcut by Martin Waldseemüller in his 1513 edition of Ptolemy; a manuscript map by Pietro Coppo, a Venetian geographer, which was probably drawn about 1520 and shows Scotland as an island; and another manuscript, a marine chart, by Diogo Homen in 1558; all of them showing Scotland as roughly square in outline and with only few place names. Another manuscript by Aegidius Tschudi, the Swiss geographer, resembles

Ptolemy's map, except that Scotland is not bent so far to the east; but even before the date suggested for this map (*c.* 1552) other more accurate maps of Britain were being printed in Italy.

The first map of Britain to show an approximation to the true shape of Scotland is a manuscript map in the British Museum with an inscription beginning 'Angliae Figura', and drawn between 1534 and 1546. The outline of Scotland has some resemblance to the Ptolemy map (of which several editions had by then been printed), but 'Angliae Figura' has better detail and with the correct north-south orientation; it is like the Ptolemy map and the 'Gough Map' in its disproportionate north-south length—in all three the length of Scotland is equal to the length of England. The influence of the 'Gough Map' is seen not only in the length of Scotland but in the close resemblance in the shape of England and in its river system. It is the earliest map, apart from Ptolemy, to show latitude and longitude and to be drawn on a conical projection; the latitude of the Scottish mainland extends from 55° to almost 61°, an excess length of nearly 2°. The main features are well defined—the Firths of Forth, Tay and Clyde; Solway Firth and Moray Firth, Duncansby Head and Cape Wrath. Out of 91 place names 60 are found in Hector Boece's *History of Scotland*, printed in 1526, including the use for the first time of 'Grampius Mons' for the Grampians. Seventeen of the remaining 31 names are found on the 'Gough Map'; the conclusion that they were copied from it, or from a similar map, is reinforced by the position of some of the names on both maps, e.g., Kilwinning.[5]

Portolan Charts

One other type of manuscript map in use in medieval times was the sea chart for mariners. To guide them on their voyages seamen had written sailing directions known in Italian as 'portolani', and as the first charts to supplement the sailing directions were drawn by Italians, they are known generally as 'portolan charts'. These charts were drawn on single skins of parchment, sometimes quite large, to show the coastline with harbours, river mouths, rocks, shallows, currents, and every coastal feature likely to be important to a pilot. They were prepared with the aid of the magnetic compass which first came into use in the 12th century. Charts at first dealt solely with the Mediterranean and were comparatively accurate, but in charts of Western Europe the outline of the British Isles was very rough; portolan charts for the British Isles only are unknown.

The earliest known Mediterranean chart, the 'Carte Pisane', belongs to the latter part of the 13th century, and the earliest showing any part of Scotland, to the early 14th century, all Genoese or

Venetian charts. The oldest chart showing the whole of Scotland (as part of Britain), was produced by the Catalans of Majorca in 1325. Michael C. Andrews in 1926 listed 103 surviving charts of the 14th and 15th centuries which include Scotland or part of it, but the Scotland of these charts would be unrecognizable were it not for its name and situation and about a dozen place names.[11] Inaccurate as were these earlier forms, many of the charts of a century later were no better; they depict Scotland as rather square in shape; with irregular sides and almost separated from England by channels on the east and west which leave only a narrow isthmus in the middle joining the two countries. These portolan charts contributed very little to the mapping of Scotland.

The first chart which gives a reasonably correct representation of the shape of Scotland was the work of Battista Agnese, who worked at Venice from 1536 to 1564, and produced a large number of beautifully executed and splendidly ornamented charts. In his earlier charts Agnese gave the old squarish form of Scotland, but in his later work dating from 1553 to 1564, the outline of Scotland is completely changed and approximates to the correct shape, although with still a poor and incorrectly placed representation of the Hebrides, and with the Orkney Islands missing.[12] It is obvious that between 1545 and 1553 Agnese had seen a new map or chart of Scotland, or of Britain. Two new maps come into this period: (1) 'Britanniae Insulae', engraved and published in Rome in 1546 and ascribed to George Lily (see Chapter 2); and (2) a manuscript map, or more correctly chart, of the whole coast of Scotland, dating from 1540, a copy of which was obtained by Nicolas de Nicolay on his visit to England in 1546 (see Chapter 3). That Agnese saw the Lily map is known from the copy he made of it and included in his atlas of 1554; moreover, the place names on his own chart are taken from the Lily map in the form found there. But in its outline the later Agnese chart resembles the Nicolay map more than the Lily map, and this suggests the possibility that Agnese had seen a version of the manuscript map of 1540 described in Chapter 3.

2 The First Maps of Scotland

In a period of fifty years, between 1546 and 1595, the map of Scotland developed from a crude outline with a scattering of place names to a map full of detail, with rivers, lochs, mountains, and several hundred place names. The steps by which this development occurred are not easy to trace because the maps of that period which still survive do not provide a regular pattern of progression. Two manuscript maps which are recorded no longer exist (so far as is known), and there may well have been other unknown maps in the sequence. It was the multiplication of maps through engraving and printing which not only helped in their preservation but also, by their circulation, contributed to the progressive improvement in the mapping of Scotland.

In order of date the maps of Scotland of this period which have survived or have been recorded are:

1540   Alexander Lyndsay's map of Scotland known through the printed version of 1583, and two undated manuscript maps (one probably 1559). The 1540 original has not survived. These are described in Chapter 3.

1543   A map by John Elder known only from his letter describing the map.

1550   Clement Adams was paid £5 by the Privy Council of England 'for his charges and pains sustained about the new making of a plott (i.e., map) of Scotland'. This map is otherwise unknown.[1]

1559   'Carte de la Coste d'Escosse depuis Barwick jusques à Cruden faite en 1559': a manuscript in the Bibliothèque Nationale, Paris.

1559   A manuscript version, which has not survived, of Nicolay's engraved map of 1583 (see Chapter 3).

c. 1566   'Scotia': the first engraved map of Scotland alone; it is based on Lily's printed map of 1546 of the British Isles.

c. 1566   Laurence Nowell's manuscript maps of Scotland now in the British Museum.

1573   Abraham Ortelius: 'Scotiae Tabula', based on the map of the British Isles engraved by Gerard Mercator in 1564.

1578   Bishop John Leslie's two printed maps of Scotland, one based on Lily's map of 1546 and the second on the 1573 map of Ortelius.

1583   Nicolas de Nicolay's printed version of Alexander Lyndsay's map of 1540 (see Chapter 3).

1587   A map 'Iscotia' in a manuscript atlas by Joan Martinez, Spanish cartographer; this is based on Mercator's map of the British Isles of 1564.[2]

1595   Gerard Mercator's first map of Scotland alone, 'Scotia Regnum', and his larger map of two sheets 'Scotiae Regnum', all in the 1595 edition of his *Atlas*. (See Chapter 4.)

GEORGE LILY

The earliest printed map of Scotland alone, 'Scotia', c. 1566, is derived from a map by George Lily, which has the title 'Britanniae Insulae quae nunc Angliae et Scotiae regna continet cum Hibernia adiacente nova descriptio', and was the first map of the British Isles to be engraved on copper apart from the Ptolemy map. On it is the date 1546, the initials 'G.L.A.', generally accepted as standing for George Lilius Anglius (i.e. George Lily, an English exile in Rome), and the words 'Romae, Anglorum studio & diligentia', which suggest that other exiles had helped in the preparation of the map. The map has been described by Lynam as 'a landmark in the history of English cartography . . . his delineation of Scotland is so markedly superior to anything previous that it increases greatly the importance of the map'.[3]

Lily's delineation of England, and his place names, come substatially from the 'Gough Map', but the outline of Scotland is entirely new. Though still very imperfect, the outline is a great improvement on the Scotland of 'Angliae Figura' (which is about the same date); the length of Scotland is roughly correct in relation to its breadth and to the size of England. The map, on a modified conical projection and on a scale of about 29 miles to an inch, has north on the right and west at the top. Latitude and longitude are shown in the margin, with the mainland of Scotland extending from latitude 56° to 60°40' compared with the 54°40' to 58°39' of the Ordnance Survey. The east coast is reasonably well drawn, apart from a bulge at Arbroath, but the west coast from the Clyde to Skye is far from accurate, whilst the Hebrides are badly represented. The name of the engraver is unknown; his work is neat and the lettering clear. It is also the first map of the British Isles with a key to the different symbols used for archiepiscopal and episcopal sees, county towns, and castles.[4]

George Lily studied at Oxford and not later than 1535 became a member of the household of Cardinal Pole, an English exile in Venice. After the accession of Queen Mary to the English throne, and the restoration of Roman Catholicism, he returned to England in 1554 with Cardinal Pole, and died a canon of St Paul's and of Canterbury in 1559. In Italy Lily devoted much of his time to research into the history and geography of Britain and made contributions on these subjects to a description of Britain, published by his friend Bishop Paolo Giovio in Venice in 1548. In this book the Bishop provides confirmation of Lily's authorship of the map of 1546: 'By the same ingenious mind we behold a map of England, delineated with clearness and learning and engraved in copper in such a manner that it may be studied with this work to gain a more reliable and agreeable knowledge of that country'.

The map has no similarities with the chart of Scotland which Nicolas de Nicolay saw in 1546 (see Chapter 3), and one can only conjecture that it was drawn at Rome by Lily and his friends from information supplied by other exiled priests and by Scottish priests visiting Rome: the break between Scotland and the Church of Rome did not occur until 1550. Some geographical information was available to Lily in John Major's *History of Great Britain* printed in 1521 and in the *History of Scotland* by Hector Boece published in 1526. The large island 'Cumbra' next to Ila (Islay) on the map suggests both Major's 'greater Cumbra is another island, rich and large', and Boece's 'Not far from Islay lies Cumbra'; the position of Hirtha (St Kilda) also suggests Boece, who placed its latitude at 63°, far beyond Cape Wrath, and Lily has also taken the name of the mountains 'Grampius Mons' from Boece.

Although the influence of Boece might be seen in the place names —70 out of 105 could have come from his *History*—the additions from other sources, and the concentration of place names in the south and east of Scotland, suggest the work of priests who knew Boece's description in general and could add to it from personal knowledge of the routes to the shrines at Whithorn and Tain.

Lily's map provides an early example of the copying by other engravers which flourished widely for the next two centuries and frequently makes it difficult to distinguish between the original and the copy, where the copyist has not added his own name. Lily evidently brought the plate with him on his return to England in 1554, as in the following year the map was re-issued by Thomas Geminus in London with 'Romae MDXLVI' replaced on the plate by 'Londini, anno 1555 . . . T. Gemini'. At least nine copies, by different engravers, were published over the years 1549-89 at Antwerp, Venice, and Rome. In Lily's map west was at the top:

only two engravers followed this, all the others placing north at the top. Other minor differences occur in misspellings, omission of some names or of some of the five bridges in Scotland shown on Lily's map.

The map of Scotland alone which is copied from Lily's map has the title 'Scotia' and across the map 'Regno di Scotia'; its size is $10\frac{1}{2} \times 13\frac{3}{4}$ inches and scale about 40 miles to an inch, with north at the top. The map is undated and has neither the name of the engraver or publisher nor the place of publication. It is a careless copy of Lily and as it has mistakes which do not appear in other versions of Lily's map, it cannot be definitely attributed to any of the engravers of the copies mentioned above. Montrose is placed south of Arbroath; Rossia is placed too far south; Strebogi becomes Slermaggi; the 'Mons' relating to 'Grampius' is omitted; and eight of the place names on Lily's map are omitted, including Clyde and Lothian. A resemblance to the copy of Lily's map by Sebastian di Re in 1558 suggests that it may be derived from this map and not directly from Lily; one authority says that from its style it seems to be the work about 1566 of Paolo Forlani of Verona, who worked in Venice; the paper has a Veronese watermark of the period 1556-75.[5]

JOHN ELDER

One of the shadowy figures in this period is John Elder, who visited Rome in or about 1538 and refers to his 'countrymen then being in Rome',[6] and who prepared a map of Scotland which he sent to Henry VIII in 1543. This map was presumably prepared by Elder when resident in England; there is no known connection with the Lily map but the fact that such a map existed leaves open the possibility that some of the information was eventually passed on to Lily, or that other manuscript maps were then in existence. Elder's map is lost and only his letter, 'by John Elder, Clerke, a Redshank,' offering the map to King Henry, and making 'a proposal for uniting Scotland with England', survives. It is of interest in the description of the map:

'I can no les do, then offer this plotte [i.e. map] of the realme of Scotland unto your exsellent Maiestie, wherein your Highnes shall perceave and se, not onely the descripcion of all the notable townes, castels, and abbeis ther set fourthe, and situat in ther propir places, as they stand in every countie and schyre, withe the situacion of all the principall yles marched with the same, callid Orknay and Schetland, and of the out yles, commonly namede the Sky and the Lewys; but also your noble Grace shall se the cost [coast] of the same; the dangers lying therby, with every port, ryver, loigh, creke, and haven ther, so truely drawyn and set fourthe as my poore witt and lernynge can uttir and discerne.

'Which plotte, I have not maide by relacion of others, but in so moche (and please your Highnes) that I was born in Caitnes, which is the northe part of the said plotte, marched with the East yles of the same, callid Orknay; educatt, and brought up, not onely in the West yles of the same plotte, namede the Sky and the Lewys, wher I have bene often tymes with my frendis, in ther longe galeis, arryving to dyvers and syndrie places in Scotland, wher they had a do; but also, beinge a scholar and a student in the southe parts of it, callid Sanctandrois, Abirdene and Glasgow, for the space of XIIth yeares, wher I have travailde, as well by see as by land, dyvers times; by reason whereof, knowinge all the notable places ther every wher, with ther lordis and masters names and from thens unto the said countreth wher I was born, I am the bolder (pardon cravide) to offer the saide plotte unto your ex ellent Maiestie.'[7]

It is to be regretted that the map does not survive to confirm Elder's claim that he showed every port and river, all the towns and castles, and to show whether there was any common identity between Elder's map of 1543 and the original Alexander Lyndsay map of 1540, which, in the versions we know, shows all the ports but not the rivers, towns and castles. A John Elder is listed in the records of the University of St Andrews as a student there from 1533 to 1536.[8] Elder trained as a priest, a member of the collegiate church of Dumbarton. In 1544, described as the King's servant, he received an annuity of £20 from Henry VIII; was later with Hertford's army on its invasion of Scotland in 1545, and wrote a letter to Robert Stuart (former Bishop of Caithness), describing the arrival and coronation of Philip and Mary in 1554, in which he says he had then lived in England for 20 years. Here he was for a time tutor to Henry, Lord Darnley. He is probably the John Elder banished from England in 1556; he was in France in 1561. In 1562 it was said of him 'he has the wit to play the spy where he list'.[9]

CARTE DE LA COSTE D'ESCOSSE

On a manuscript map in the Bibliothèque Nationale in Paris the title 'Carte de la Coste d'Escosse depuis Barwick jusques à Cruden', and the date 1559, have been written on it by a later hand, but there is no reason to doubt the accuracy of the dating and so this is the oldest regional map of Scotland, covering the east coast from Berwick to Cruden and extending inland to Doune. The size is $17\frac{1}{4} \times 11\frac{3}{4}$ inches; scale about 8 miles to one inch.[10] It has 105 place names—more than three times the names on the Lily map for the same area, but many fewer than the Mercator map of 1564. It is a topographical map, with the inland names as numerous as the names on the coast. This map is of considerable interest in two respects: (1) the place names, with only one or two exceptions, all appear in Mercator's map of 1564; (2) the delineation of the coast in this 1559 map is quite different from Mercator's map of 1564, but resembles closely his maps of 1595, particularly in the two-sheet map of Scotland where the east coast and river system are remarkably like the 1559 map. The 1559 coastline and river system are followed almost exactly by Laurence Nowell in his map (see below), but Nowell has many more place names and omits several which appear on the 1559 map.

The map is possibly connected with the transport of French troops to Scotland in 1559 to help Mary of Lorraine, the Queen Regent, in her efforts in that year to quell the rebellion of the Reformers. It may have been based on Nicolay's manuscript map of the same year (see Chapter 3)—it is to be noted that the Inch Cape rock appears on this map and on Nicolay's map of 1583, but is not found on other maps of the period.

GERARD MERCATOR AND ABRAHAM ORTELIUS

The map of Scotland 'Scotiae Tabula' published by Abraham Ortelius in 1573 was copied from a map engraved by Gerard Mercator in 1564. Mercator (whose work is more fully described in Chapter 4), then residing at Duisburg in the Rhineland, published a large map of the British Isles, 35 × 50 inches, in eight sheets, on a scale of $14\frac{1}{2}$ miles to an inch, with the title 'Angliae Scotiae et Hibernie nova descriptio'. Only three copies of this have survived, in Rome, in Perugia, and in Paris, but a reproduction published in 1891 from a copy then in Breslau (unfortunately destroyed in 1945) is in several libraries. This map is an immense improvement on the Scottish part of Lily's map of 1564, with a much more accurate coastline, with more features in the interior, and with many more place names. In latitudes, and even more in longitudes, the eastern half of Scotland is reasonably accurate, but the western half north of the Clyde, and the Hebrides, are considerably distorted. It has been described as 'one of the most perfect cartographic works of the 16th century'; a recent writer calls it 'a landmark in the regional cartography of the British Isles . . . it makes a striking advance both in accuracy of outline and angular correctness and wealth of detail'.[11]

Mercator explains in a note engraved on the map that a friend offered him the draft of the map and asked him to engrave it. He was unwilling to refuse this friend and as it was such a perfect piece of work he decided to engrave it in the state he received it.

His biographer, Walter Ghim, Lord Mayor of Duisburg and a friend for forty years, says that the map was offered from England by a distinguished friend, again without naming him.[12]

Much speculation has centred on the identity of the friend. The most likely person is John Dee (1527-1608), a student at Louvain University from 1548 to 1550, under Gemma Frisius, the professor of mathematics, where he became friendly with Mercator, and after returning to Cambridge to teach mathematics, maintained a life-long correspondence with him. Dee was on the Continent from late in 1562 until some date in 1564, and early in 1563 travelled from Antwerp to Zurich.[13] He would surely visit his friend Mercator on the way and so could have been the bearer of the draft map offered to Mercator. It is generally thought that Dee himself was not the author of the map, but from whom he obtained it is unknown. Many names have been suggested; in the opinion of one writer only two of the candidates proposed deserve serious attention: Laurence Nowell, who between 1560 and 1566 drew maps of England and Wales and of Scotland (see below), and John Elder.

A comparison of the English portion of the map with earlier maps of England has produced no certainty as to the author, and what follows is confined to a consideration of the Scottish portion. It is true that some resemblances exist between the Nowell maps of Scotland and the Mercator map, including the great number of place names on both maps, far in excess of the names on Lily's map of 1546. But there are certain differences; the Nowell shape of Scotland is much more accurate than Mercator's map of 1564, and many place names on the north-west coast which are on the Nowell map are not on Mercator. More positive evidence that the Nowell map is not the basis of the 1564 map is found in Mercator's later map of 1595, which agrees closely with Nowell (and with Nicolay), most noticeably in Buchan, the north coast, the north-west coast, Mull and the Orkneys, all quite different from the 1564 map. This suggests that subsequent to 1564 Mercator had seen some version of the Nowell map, as well as Nicolay's printed map of 1583, and accepted the new outline for his later map of 1595.

There is more to support the view that Elder was the author of the Scottish part of the map. He was born in Caithness, and this could account for the number of place names in Caithness and the names given on the map to the currents in the Pentland Firth, 'the swell', 'the hoppers', and 'the boyer'. His visits to Skye and Lewis, and residence at the Universities of Aberdeen, St Andrews, and Glasgow, may be reflected in the more numerous place names in these localities. It could also be said that the map shows Elder's 'every port, river, loch, creek and haven', and the names of the earls given on the map suggest a connection with Elder's reference to 'their Lord's and Master's names'.   John Dee had a long association with Court circles and if Elder's map sent to Henry VIII in 1543 was in the Royal Library, Dee would almost certainly learn of it.   The map supplied to Mercator was of the British Isles; our knowledge of Elder refers only to a map of Scotland, so that someone would have to combine it with a map of England, and (presumably) re-draw the whole before it went to Mercator for engraving.   One feature of the engraved map which was to influence maps of Scotland for almost two centuries was the merging of Cape Wrath and Faro Head into one 'Cape Wrayght or Faro Head'.

LAURENCE NOWELL

Small manuscript maps by Laurence Nowell, of England, Ireland, and Scotland, are in the British Museum; one of Scotland is $7\frac{1}{2} \times 10\frac{1}{4}$ inches, a second and larger map is in two parts, each $7\frac{1}{2} \times 10\frac{1}{2}$ inches.[14] The text attached to the maps includes a short paragraph relating to some of the Western Isles, and a two-page extract from Ranulph Higden on Scotland.   The date of the maps is probably between 1561 and 1566.[15]

Nowell graduated at Cambridge in 1542, became an M.A. of Oxford, and for a time taught in a grammar school until he fled to Germany for religious reasons after the accession of Queen Mary. He returned when Elizabeth became queen, was made Archdeacon of Derby, and Dean of Lichfield in 1559.   Some time before 1563 he became tutor to the Earl of Oxford, and lived for a time in the house of Sir William Cecil in the Strand; in 1563 he wrote a letter to Cecil proposing to make a series of maps of English counties, a project he did not carry out.[16]   He died in 1576.

The smaller map is neatly drawn, crowded with place names in black or red, with the coastline coloured blue or yellow, and mountains greenish-grey.   It is marked off in squares, which may have been used in making a drawing for his larger map, which is twice the size but unfinished, with Scotland in two parts on two double pages.   It looks as if Nowell drew the larger map to provide more space for the place names; latitude and longitude are shown, the longitude with converging meridians, and with a surprising degree of accuracy.   Out of seven towns or capes the maximum error from Ordnance Survey figures for latitude is only 19 minutes; at one place the figures coincide.   The differences in longitude at these seven points are all between 1°01' and 1°43' (the latter accounted for by the omission from the map of the Cape Wrath promontory), so that if all were moved 1° to the east, the differences in longitude would be very small on a map of this scale.   The Nowell map in its latitudes and longitudes is in fact more accurate than Mercator's map of 1595 or Blaeu's map of 1654; and even Moll's map of 1714 shows greater errors in the north of Scotland. Considering its date, it is altogether a remarkable map, both in the detail of the coastline, and in the number of places names—*c*. 600, surely the accumulated result of the work of several persons. Not until Dorret's map of 1750 was more overall accuracy shown in the shape of Scotland.

The Nowell map resembles so closely the Nicolay map of 1583 in its outline of Scotland, that Nowell must have seen one of the manuscript versions—possibly the original seen by Nicolay in 1546 (see Chapter 3), but this does not explain the source of such relatively accurate figures for latitude and longitude, as these are not on the Nicolay map.

BISHOP JOHN LESLIE

The next printed map of Scotland in order of date, the map by Abraham Ortelius published in 1573, is described in Chapter 4. Then came two maps of Scotland, both bearing the name of John Leslie (or Lesley), and both engraved in Italy in 1578.

John Leslie (1527-96) a native of Inverness-shire, graduated M.A. at the University of Aberdeen, studied in Paris from 1549 to 1554, and on returning to Scotland served for a time as a parish priest, before becoming Professor of Canon Law at Aberdeen. He became a judge of the Court of Session and a member of the Privy Council in 1565, Bishop of Ross in 1566, and Queen Mary's adviser on ecclesiastical matters. On one of his visits to her during her imprisonment in England he was arrested on the charge of conspiring to place her on the English throne, but after a short imprisonment in the Tower was released on condition that he left Britain. He settled in Rome in 1575 in order to represent Queen Mary's interests at the papal court, and in 1578 published there a history of Scotland: *De origine, moribus, et rebus gestis Scotorum*, containing a map of Scotland 'Scotiae Regni Antiquissimi Accurata Descriptio'. In 1579 he was appointed to the diocese of Rouen, and died in the monastery of Guirtenburg, near Brussels, in 1596. He founded a Scots College at Paris and left money to found a Scots College at Douai.[17]

The map in his *History* is a small one, on the scale of *c*. 40 miles to an inch; it has a brief description of Scotland, with Leslie's name, in a cartouche. The outline of Scotland is copied, somewhat roughly, from Lily's map of 1546 or possibly from one of the copies of Lily because 'Mons' is omitted in relation to 'Grampius'. The place names are also to a large extent taken from Lily, with some omissions, but Leslie has added others in the north and north-west, places obviously known to him through his travels in the Bishopric of Ross. Like Lily he has noted 'Orcades Insulae XXXI', but he has left out two of the 31, and has named another of the islands 'Scetlandia', i.e., Shetland.

In the same year, 1578, Leslie prepared a larger map 'Scotiae regni antiquissimi nova et accurata descriptio', engraved at Rome by Natalis Bonifacius Sibenicensis (= Natale Bonifacio of Sebenico in Dalmatia). As the map is obviously copied from the Ortelius map of 1573, 'Scotiae Tabula', and also has west at the top, this suggests that Leslie had just seen this map and recognized that his smaller map was out of date. In his second map the correction or alteration of many of the place names, as well as additions and alterations in the shape of some of the Western Isles are no doubt the work of Leslie himself. Ortelius has 'St. Kylder' as a small island to the west of Lewis; Leslie copies this but adds 'Hirta' as a large island to the north of Lewis (although St Kilda and Hirta are both names, one English, one Gaelic, for the same island). Other differences appear in the Hebrides, where Leslie has added a large island 'Cumbra', which had appeared on Lily but not on Ortelius. 'Grampius Mons' disappears from the Lothians. An oval frame cuts through south-west Scotland and at the north separates the Shetland Islands from the Orkney Islands.

Only two copies of the larger map are known, and R. A. Skelton has pointed out that neither of these copies seems to have been printed in Italy as the watermark of each is associated with paper made or in use at Troyes, south-west of Paris. He suggests that when Leslie moved from Rome to Rouen in 1579 he took the engraved plate with him, and in support of this view draws attention to the copy in the British Museum which has printed strips added at the top and bottom of the map, the one at the top reading 'La Vraye et Entiere Description du Tresancien Royaume, Pays et Isles d'Escosse', and the bottom one containing a dedication to James VI, King of Scotland, dated Rouen, 20 August 1586.[18]

The production of maps in the earlier part of the 16th century had been mainly the work of Italian cartographers. Later in the century some Italian map-sellers began to bind for their customers collections of maps (of different sizes and no two collections alike). By the end of the century the work of map engraving, and the publication of atlases, was firmly established in the Netherlands.

3 Nicolas de Nicolay and Alexander Lyndsay

In the year 1583 a greatly improved map of Scotland on the scale of *c.* 21 miles to an inch was engraved and published in Paris. It gave a much better outline of Scotland than any previous map—an outline which was in fact more accurate than any later maps of the 17th century. It was a chart rather than a map, a coastline with all the capes, firths and ports named, some 200 names on the coast of the mainland and another 100 in the islands, but no inland features apart from 20 names of regions. Although the printed map is dated 1583 the author tells us that the original manuscript map was obtained by him in 1546, and so the map in its origin is earlier than Mercator's 1546 map of the British Isles, and possibly earlier even than Lily's map of 1546.

The map of 1583 accompanied a rutter (a book of sailing directions for seamen) with the title '*La Navigation du Roy D'Escosse Jaques Cinquiesme du nom, autour de son Royaume, & Isles Hebrides Orchades, soubz la conduicte d'Alexandre Lyndsay excellent Pilote Escossois. Recueilliée et redigée en forme de description Hydrographique, & representée en carte marine, et Routier ou Pilotage, pour la cognoissance particulière de ce qui est nécessaire & considérable à ladicte navigation,* Par Nicolay d'Arfeville, Seigneur du dict lieu et de Bel-Air, Daulphinois, Premier Cosmographe du Roy. . . . Paris: chez Gilles Beys 1583'. (*The Navigation of the King of Scotland, James fifth of the name, around his Kingdom and Isles Hebrides and Orkneys, under the guidance of Alexander Lyndsay, excellent Scottish Pilot*).

The title of the map is (translated): 'True & exact hydrographic description of the maritime coasts of Scotland Isles Hebrides & Orkneys . . . serving for navigation by Nicolay d'Arfeville, Daulphinois, first Cosmographer of the King, 1583'.

Nicolas de Nicolay was born in 1517 in the Dauphiné of France; he became seigneur (lord of the manor) of Arfeville in Bourbonnais and so was known also as Nicolay d'Arfeville. He travelled widely throughout Europe and the Middle East, wrote several narratives describing his journeys, and also published *De l'art de naviguer* translated from a well-known Spanish work. In 1544 he published a marine chart of Europe (on which Ortelius based his map of Europe in his first atlas of 1570), a chart of America in 1554, and a map of the Boulonnais (in northern France) in 1558. Appointed

19

'Géographe (or Cosmographe) du Roy' to Henri II, he was in 1566 commissioned by Catherine de Médicis, the Queen Mother, to prepare maps and geographical descriptions of the provinces of France, and most of his later years were spent in this work. He died in Paris in 1583.[1]

The rutter and map of Scotland published in 1583 were accompanied by a dedication to the Duc de Joyeuse, the French admiral, in which Nicolay relates how he acquired the book and map.[2] In the year 1546, he says, Lord Dudley, Admiral of England and later Duke of Northumberland, was in Paris in order to negotiate a peace treaty between England and France.[3] Learning of Nicolay's travels and of his map and geographical description of England (this has not been traced), Lord Dudley persuaded Nicolay to return with him to England, where he stayed about a year.

During his visit Nicolay was shown 'a small book written by hand in the Scottish language, containing the voyage of the King of Scotland, James fifth of that name, made around his kingdom and the isles of Hebrides and Orkneys, under the guidance of Alexander Lyndsay, an excellent pilot and hydrographer, with all the notable peculiarities worthy of being observed in such a voyage; together with the marine chart somewhat roughly made, in order to acquaint all subsequent mariners to whom it was expedient to make a similar voyage. And considering with what great industry this little paper had been written, I did not wish to part with it without retaining a copy, and on my return to France, at the accession of the good King Henry II to this crown, I got the said booklet translated into French with the assistance of the late Maitre Jehan Ferrier, a very learned Scotsman, and having made a fair copy of it with its chart, I presented it to his Majesty, who immediately sent it to Sieur Leon Strozzi, Prior of Capua, captain general of his galleys, and he and I also went with sixteen galleys, and other forces to besiege the castle of St Andrews.' Elsewhere Nicolay confirms that he was with this fleet to assist Regent Arran to avenge the death of Cardinal Beaton; one of the defenders taken prisoner by the French was John Knox.

In addition to the printed rutter of 1583, a manuscript version, now lacking the map, is in the British Museum.[4] This one is dedicated to the Cardinal of Lorraine, and was written in or about 1559 as the dedication contains a reference to Nicolay's new map of the Boulonnais published in 1558 as 'last year'. In this dedication Nicolay says: 'Being by chance at the court of King Henry VIII of England with his admiral, who has since died, there fell into my hands a number of notebooks containing the Navigation of Alexandre Lyndesay made by command of the King of Scotland James Fifth around his Island (which is his Kingdom), with all the notable

peculiarities that it was possible to notice in such a navigation, in order to instruct all the other mariners coming later to whom it was expedient to make a similar voyage. Considering with how much industry this little paper had been written, I did not wish to part with it until I had retained for myself a copy of it, which I have for a long time left neglected among my other memoirs, and indeed, Monseigneur, I had completely forgotten it if your reverence, by the gracious welcome that last year my new map of the Boulonnois received from you, had not encouraged me to employ myself in other similar designs. . . . Therefore, Monseigneur, I have worked to make this Chart and this Book of the Navigation of Scotland on the records that I have had of it for a long time, and I think that I have forgotten very little of it . . .'

Nicolay's statement concerning the book and map is confirmed by a letter of 23rd May 1547, from Odet de Selve, the French ambassador in London, to the King of France, in which he says that he sends the king some maps and a book of the navigation of Scotland, which he had received from a French painter (i.e., Nicolay). He explains that the original of the book was in the Scottish language, and has been taken by the painter to France; the translation has not been well done because it was done by a Scotsman who did not understand too well the French language.[5]   Dr Wotton, the English ambassador in Paris, took a less friendly view of Nicolay's activities; Nicolas, he said, has given the French king pictures of all the havens in England by means of which they may land easily their men that go into Scotland.[6]

There is one important difference between the dedication of 1559 and the dedication of 1583; in the former Nicolay describes the book as 'containing the Navigation of Alexandre Lyndesay made by command of the King of Scotland', in the latter as 'containing the voyage of the King of Scotland, James 5th . . . under the guidance of Alexandre Lyndesay'. Writing 12 years after his visit to England, Nicolay describes it as the voyage of Alexandre Lyndesay; writing 36 years after his visit he describes it as the voyage of the King himself. A possible reason for the map sent in 1559 to the Cardinal of Lorraine is that French troops were then being sent to Scotland to support Mary of Guise, sister of the Cardinal, and in 1583, there were plans for a French force to assist in putting Mary Stewart on the throne of England.

The navigation or voyage of James V which is referred to in the printed version is clearly the voyage of 1540 (described by Bishop John Leslie in his *History of Scotland* written in 1568-70), when the King, with several earls and other nobles, set out to subdue the unruly lords of the Western Isles. The Lord High Treasurer's

Accounts give the names of five vessels in the expedition, which left Leith on 12th June 1540.[7] English agents in Scotland writing in May 1540 rather magnified the size of the fleet. At first they reported 12 ships, later 16, including the King's ship *Salamander*; most of the nobility were to go, and between 3000 and 4000 men; Lord Maxwell had been named as Admiral of Scotland and the Master of Kilmaurs as Vice-Admiral.[8] The King visited Orkney, Skye, Lewis, Ross and Kintail and continued by sea to Dumbarton, where he left his fleet and rode to Edinburgh which he reached before 29th July (when he wrote to Henry VIII that he had visited the north and south isles),[9] while the ships returned round the north of Scotland and arrived in the Firth of Forth before 3rd August.[7]

The most cursory examination of Nicolay's map is sufficient to show that it could not be the product of one short voyage which lasted less than two months. The voyage ended at Dumbarton, but the map has the Ayrshire and Solway coasts accurately defined, and the details of the Orkney Islands, the west coast, Skye and the Hebrides can only be the result of surveys spread over many voyages and several years. The map could not have been made on the King's voyage, but it might have well been prepared to provide the King with an accurate guide for his voyage. He had reigned for 26 years and this was his first visit to the Hebrides; it was to be a display of the royal power, with Cardinal Beaton and a large retinue of nobles to support the King.

In both dedications Nicolay refers to Alexander Lyndsay, an excellent pilot and hydrographer. An entry in the 1609 catalogue of the library of Lord Lumley refers to: 'Alexander Lindesay his rutter of the sea, with Havens, roades, soundes, etc., from Humber Northwards rownde abowt Scotland', a manuscript in English, which may have been the original version or a copy of it; unfortunately this manuscript is lost.[10] Nothing more is known of Lyndsay: no one of that name can be traced in Scottish records as having any connection with the sea in or about 1540.

Nicolay's map marks a great advance in the cartography of Scotland. Not only is the shape of Scotland shown with considerable accuracy, but it is much more accurate than the later Gordon-Blaeu map of 1654 or the Moll map of 1714. Even the Mercator map of 1595 conforms less to the correct outline of Scotland, though the similarities between the Nicolay map and Mercator's map, both in respect of the outline of Scotland and in the choice of place names, are evidence that Mercator's map is based largely on Nicolay's map, or a version of it. In 1688 John Adair had a new plate of the 1583 map engraved by James Moxon for his *Description of the Sea-Coast and Islands of Scotland*, on the ground that it was the most accurate map, and in 1734 John Cowley recorded that when preparing his own map of Scotland he found Nicolay's map to be more exact than any other map.

Three versions are known: (1) the Nicolay engraved map of 1583, $15\frac{1}{2} \times 11\frac{1}{2}$ inches; (2) a manuscript variant of (1), also $15\frac{1}{2} \times 11\frac{1}{2}$ inches in the Deutsche Staatsbibliothek in Berlin; and (3) a smaller version, $8\frac{3}{4} \times 11\frac{1}{4}$ inches, in a manuscript *The Booke of the Sea Carte*, undated but belonging to the late 16th century, and now in the British Museum.[11] All three are charts, with considerable detail of the coasts and of the Orkneys and Western Isles, and with some 300 place names on the coasts, but inland only 20 names of districts. Dr A. B. Taylor has shown that the three maps have about 250 place names in common, but have also certain differences which point to an earlier common source, a manuscript map no longer in existence.[12] A copy of the rutter, in English, probably early 17th century, but without map, is in the National Library of Scotland.[13]

Accepting Nicolay's statement that the original of his map was drawn in 1540, the common ancestor of this and the two manuscript maps must have been an earlier map. Even for 1540 it is a remarkable production and shows quite an advanced skill in cartography. Those who carried out the survey of the coast must have known how to calculate the position of coastal features with considerable accuracy though neither latitude nor longitude is shown on the map.

No great maritime activity is recorded in the reign of James V prior to his voyage round the north of Scotland in 1540; it was his father who was the naval King. In the years 1493-98, James IV made at least four expeditions to the Western Isles, with him on occasion being two famous naval captains, Sir Andrew Wood and Robert Barton. The same king spent large sums in the years 1500-13 in building a Scottish navy, when timber was brought by sea from the northern parts of Scotland and ships were built on the Forth and the Clyde, and at least one ship was built in the Hebrides, all indicating a frequent movement of ships round the north of Scotland. The Treasurer's Accounts of this period record numerous purchases of compasses, and the need for surveys was met by the opportunities and the knowledge to make them. The flagship of the small Scottish navy of James IV was the *Great Michael*, and the list of the 300 men in her crew in 1513 contains an Alexander Lyndsay, the only one of that name traced in all this period as having a connection with the sea.[14] Was it he who learned on the *Great Michael* to chart the coast of Scotland, and lived to prepare a new chart for the voyage of James V in 1540? Whoever he was, he made a notable contribution to the cartography of Scotland.

4 Dutch Cartographers

Map publishing began in the Netherlands in the early part of the 16th century. Dutch supremacy on the seas and the distant voyages of Dutch mariners created an interest in maps which was met by a succession of notable cartographers and engravers, who began with the production of single maps and by the second half of the 17th century were producing atlases of over 600 beautifully engraved maps in 11 or 12 splendidly bound volumes, never since equalled in size or style, with separate editions for the text in Latin, Dutch, French, German and Spanish.[1]

A feature of the map trade of that time was the transfer of engraved map plates from one publisher to his successor in business, or by sale to another publisher, with the result that a map may have one publisher's name on it in one edition, and another name in a later edition. The maps in the Mercator *Atlas*, for example, were being published sixty years after Mercator's death, with his name deleted and replaced by one of his successors. It was also common to find the maps of one publisher copied by another publisher, sometimes so exactly that slight differences can hardly be detected, even although the original publisher tried to protect his work by obtaining a 'privilege' or copyright from the States-General for a period of years. This map trade in the Netherlands had its origin in the work of Gerard Mercator, who published his first map, of Palestine, drawn and engraved by himself, at Louvain in 1537, but the first to achieve fame through his production of atlases was Abraham Ortelius.[2]

ABRAHAM ORTELIUS

Abraham Ortelius, born in Antwerp in 1527, became an illuminator of maps, a dealer in books, maps, and antiquities, and then a cartographer, producing between 1564 and 1567, maps of the World, Egypt and Asia.[3] His fame rests on his publication in 1570 of his *Theatrum Orbis Terrarum*, described as 'the world's first regularly produced atlas'. Before this, an edition of Ptolemy's *Geographia* with 27 Ptolemy maps and 20 modern maps by Martin Waldseemüller had been published in 1513, a step towards the later atlases, and Italian mapsellers had bound to order collections of maps of different sizes, but it was Ortelius who saw the advantage of having maps all

24

the same size made specially for binding with accompanying text into a volume for general sale, and so began the great 17th-century development of atlases. His maps were not the result of his own research; he obtained the maps then available and redrew them at the size to fit his volume, making acknowledgment on the map or in the text to the author of the map he copied.

The first issue of the *Theatrum* in 1570, with Latin text, contained 53 pages of maps covering the world, and included a map of the British Isles based on Mercator's map of 1564. The success of the *Theatrum* called for a second Latin edition and an edition with Dutch text in 1571, and French and German editions in 1572.

In the 1573 edition Ortelius added 17 maps (also issued separately in an *Additamentum* or supplement for owners of earlier editions); these included his first map of Scotland alone, 'Scotiae Tabula', which remained unaltered throughout all later editions. It is 19 × 14 inches, on the scale of 20 Scots miles to an inch, with west at the top; it is based on Mercator's map of 1564, but because of the larger scale has more place names than in the Scotland part of Ortelius's earlier map of the British Isles. Also in this edition were maps of England and of Wales prepared from drafts which Ortelius had received from Humphrey Lhuyd of Denbigh in 1568. In the 1573 and later editions Ortelius printed the letter from Mercator commending the *Theatrum:* 'You deserve no small praise, for you have selected the best descriptions of each region and collected them into one manual, and that without diminishing the work of any, so that the complete and perfect works of all may be bought for a small cost, kept in a small space, and even carried about wherever we wish'.[4] When religious persecution threatened Ortelius in 1576 he took refuge for a short time in England, where he came to know William Camden and others interested in geography. Returning to Antwerp, he continued to produce expanded editions of the *Theatrum* until it had 117 map-sheets. After his death in 1598 publication was continued by his heirs up to 1601, when the *Theatrum* was taken over by Jan Baptist Vrients, who produced several editions. Vrients died in 1612 and the last editions of the *Theatrum* were published in 1612 by the firm of Plantin. The plates were not used again; by this time the *Theatrum* had been supplanted by Mercator's *Atlas*.

The only edition of the *Theatrum* with the text in English was printed in 1606 by John Norton, King's printer in London. Instead of the usual practice of printing the text first, the maps in this edition were printed in Antwerp and the sheets then sent to London to have the English text printed on the reverse, the only known instance of this being done in the 16th and 17th centuries.[5] This edition had 158 pages of maps, including maps of ancient geography which Ortelius had earlier published separately under the title of *Parergon*.

In 1577 a pocket-size edition of the *Theatrum*, the '*Epitome*', was produced by Philip Galle in Antwerp, with 72 small maps, including 'Scotia', size $3 \times 4\frac{1}{4}$ inches; new and expanded editions appeared up to 1602. A rival edition, with 133 small maps by the Arsenius Brothers, and text by Michael Coignet, appeared in 1601, the last edition in 1612. English editions of each which were published in 1602 and 1603 respectively, have been described by R. A. Skelton as 'the earliest world atlases to be published in England and the earliest world atlases with English text'.[5]

GERARD MERCATOR

Although Ortelius led the way in the production of an atlas by making use of the maps of other cartographers, the first and greatest of the Netherlands cartographers was Gerard Mercator (1512-94), 'the most famous cartographer after Ptolemy', who, in his world map of 1569, developed the method of projection still known as 'Mercator's projection', and who was the first to use the word 'Atlas' as the title of a volume of maps. Through his book, *Literarum latinarum*, published in 1540, he popularized italic script, which soon came into general use for engraving names on maps.[6]

Born in 1512 at Rupelmonde in Flanders, Mercator graduated in 1532 at the University of Louvain and later studied mathematics, becoming expert as a land surveyor, cartographer, and engraver. In 1544 he was in prison for four months for his religious beliefs as a Protestant, and so in 1552 he moved to Duisburg in Germany for religious freedom. In the Grammar School there he taught mathematics for a time; he was appointed Cosmographer to the Duke of Cleves, and continued his work on globes and maps. He published a six-sheet map of Palestine in 1537, a large map of Europe in 15 sheets in 1554, and his great map of the world in 24 sheets in 1569. His map of the British Isles has already been described in Chapter 2.

Through his knowledge of astronomy and mathematics he gave his work a strictly scientific basis, by checking the latitude and longitude of places, and testing the accuracy of the information he received, becoming recognized as the outstanding cartographer of his time. He was 73 years old before he published at Duisburg in 1585 the first part of his *Atlas*, with 51 maps of Western Europe, followed in 1589 with a second part with 22 maps of South-eastern Europe. A third part, with 27 maps, including one of the British Isles, seven of England, five of Ireland, and three of Scotland, was ready for publication when Mercator died in 1594; his son Rumold issued it in 1595. In the same year a complete volume with 107 maps was issued containing the three parts, with Gerard Mercator's name on the title page and the first use of the title *Atlas*, above which was an engraving of the Greek giant Atlas holding a globe.

The three maps of Scotland are: (1) 'Scotia Regnum', the whole of Scotland, $13\frac{1}{2} \times 16$ inches, on the scale of *c*. 25 miles to an inch; (2) a map of southern Scotland with no title; and (3) 'Scotiae Regnum', northern Scotland, these last two on the scale of *c*. 16 miles to an inch. The map of Scotland is a considerable improvement on the map engraved by Mercator in 1564, and marks another stage in the mapping of Scotland, becoming the basis of practically all maps of Scotland by other cartographers over the next 60 years. Mercator was obviously indebted to the map published by Nicolay in 1583 for his outline of Scotland; the resemblance in the river system to the manuscript maps of Laurence Nowell and the similarities in place names, e.g. Nowell has 'Loghaber Hills' and Mercator 'Logh Aber hills', suggest that Mercator had also seen a version of the Nowell map, or of the original from which it was compiled, but where or how he could obtain it is unknown. The place-names on the 1595 map are substantially taken from the 1564 map, with more added, and some corrections, such as the elimination of 'Grampius Mons' from southern Scotland.

Rumold Mercator died in 1599, and after one more edition of the *Atlas* was issued in 1602 the map plates were sold in 1604 to Jodocus Hondius. Hondius was born in Flanders in 1563 and trained as a draughtsman and engraver in Ghent, but in order to be free from religious persecution he lived in England from about 1583 to 1593, working as an engraver and instrument maker. He then settled in Amsterdam, engraving and publishing maps and globes.

After acquiring the plates of Mercator's *Atlas* he engraved 37 new maps (copied from various authors), and published an edition in 1606 with 144 maps, still describing it as *Gerard Mercator's Atlas* but with his own name on the title page as publisher. In the next five years three re-issues appeared, with the addition of only six maps over that period.

Jodocus Hondius died in 1612. The business was continued by his widow, and then by his sons, Jodocus II and Henricus, who were joined by their brother-in-law, Joannes Janssonius (1588-1664). Seven more maps were added in the 1619 edition of the *Atlas*. In 1629 Jodocus II died, and the remaining partners were stirred to activity by the appearance of a rival, Willem Janszoon Blaeu, who published his *Atlantis Appendix*, an atlas with 60 maps, in 1630. The Mercator *Atlas* was now rapidly expanded by Henricus Hondius and Janssonius; an edition in 1633 with French text had 238 maps, and an English edition in 1636 (the translation by Henry Hexham), had 195 maps. The 1638 edition with over 300 maps in three volumes had a new title, the *Atlas Novus* of Janssonius; from 1644 Mercator's name was dropped from the title page.

In 1646 Janssonius issued his Volume IV, with maps of England, and in 1659 expanded this volume with six maps of Scottish regions based on the maps in Blaeu's Volume V which had been issued in 1654. By 1658 the *Atlas Novus* had six volumes, and these were supplemented by maps of other cartographers to make up a 10- or 11-volume edition with over 600 maps, on sale between 1658 and 1662. It did not have the outstanding merit of the *Atlas Major* which Blaeu published in 1662. Henricus Hondius died in 1651 and Janssonius in 1664; the latter's heirs carried on the business for a time but no new editions of the *Atlas* were published. About 1680 the map plates were bought by P. Schenk and G. Valck, who used many of the plates but did not republish the *Atlas*.

The original maps of Scotland by Mercator were continued unaltered up to 1634. For the 1636 English edition Mercator's name was removed from the map of Scotland and it had a new vignette for the title 'Scotia Regnum'; the map of southern Scotland now had 'Amstelodami: Apud Henricum Hondium', and on the map of northern Scotland a new title 'Scotiae pars Septentrionalis' replaced the original 'Scotiae Regnum'. In the 1636 German edition and later editions Mercator's map of Scotland was replaced by a new map 'Scotia Regnum Amstelodami, Apud Joannem Janssonium', an almost exact copy of the map of Scotland published by Willem Blaeu in 1635 (see below). The Mercator maps of northern and southern Scotland were not reissued after 1638. When expanding the *Atlas* in 1630 Hondius added a new map 'A New Description of the Shyres Lothien and Linlitquo. . . . Be T. Pont', and in 1636 added 'Orcadum et Schetlandiae', another map by Pont (see Chapter 5). Six maps of Scottish regions were added in 1659 to keep pace with Blaeu, and all based on Blaeu's maps of 1654: (1) 'Extimae Scotiae pars Septentrionalis', (2) 'Scotiae Provintiae Inter Taum Fluvium', (3) 'Scotia Provincias intra Flumen Taum et murra fyrth sitae', (4) 'Lochabria', (5) 'Tabula Leogi et Haraiae', (6) 'Lorna, Knapdalia, Cantire (etc)', on scales varying from 6 inches to 8 inches per mile.[7]

In 1607 Hondius met the demand for a smaller atlas by the issue of the *Atlas Minor Gerardi Mercatoris a J. Hondio*, with 152 maps including three small maps of Scotland; (1) 'Scotia', (2) 'Scotiae tabula II' (southern Scotland), and (3) 'Scotiae tabula III' (northern Scotland). Nine editions (Latin, French and German) appeared up to 1621, after which the plates were sold to a London publisher and used for an English edition in 1635-39. Janssonius published a new edition of the *Atlas Minor* in 1628 with new maps including (1) 'Schotia', (2) 'Scotia Meridonalis', (3) 'Scotia Septentrionalis'; nine editions were issued up to 1651. A third *Atlas Minor* was produced in 1630 for Johan Cloppenburg, an Amsterdam bookseller; the maps included: (1) 'Scotia Regnum', (2) 'Scotiae Regnum', (3) and a map of southern Scotland without a title, all $7\frac{1}{2} \times 10$ inches, and still based on the original Mercator maps. There were several re-issues and later the plates of this edition were acquired by Henri du Sauzet, publisher in Amsterdam, who issued them in his *Atlas Portatif* in 1734.

WILLEM AND JOANNIS BLAEU

The finest Dutch atlases of the 17th century came from the firm of Willem and Joannis Blaeu, surpassing in extent and quality the *Mercator Atlas* of their rivals, Hondius and Janssonius. From a small volume of 60 maps in 1630 the Blaeus expanded their *Atlas* until in 1663 they had 600 maps in 12 volumes, each map beautifully engraved and decorated, to produce what was generally agreed to be the greatest and finest atlas ever produced.

Willem Janszoon Blaeu, born in 1571 in or near Alkmaar, studied astronomy and the art of globe making in Denmark under Tycho Brahe, the famous astronomer, and in 1596 began business in Amsterdam as a maker of globes and instruments. In 1608 he produced the first edition of his atlas of marine charts *Het Licht der Zeevaert*, which went through some 30 editions in the next fifty years.[8]

An extant letter from Blaeu shows that in 1626 he was planning a topographical atlas on a large scale, but he seems to have made little progress until he was able in 1629 to purchase 37 map plates from Jodocus Hondius II. Adding 23 plates of his own, he published in 1630 a volume of 60 maps with the title *Atlantis Appendix*, followed in 1631 by two editions with 98 and 99 maps. In 1635 he issued Volumes I and II of his *Theatrum Orbis Terrarum sive Atlas Novus* with 208 maps; these included his first map of Scotland, 'Scotia Regnum', 15×20 inches, on a scale of 20 miles to an inch. This map was based on Mercator's map of 1595; no new material was incorporated but it shows a higher standard of engraving.

Willem Blaeu died in 1638 but his ambitious plan was ably carried out by his son Joannis (or Joan), who in 1640 produced Volume III with 62 maps of Italy and Greece, and Volume IV in 1645 with 58 maps of England and Wales. Most of the maps of English counties were copied from John Speed's *Theatre of the Empire of Great Britaine*.

Volume V with maps of Scotland and Ireland, its compilation and publication in 1654, are described in the next chapter. Volume VI, with 17 maps of China and Japan, was issued in 1655. In between the publication of Volumes IV and V Blaeu produced a town atlas of the Netherlands, with 223 town plans in two volumes, and later he published town atlases of Italy with over 200 plans.

After issuing Volume VI of the *Atlas Novus* in 1655, with some 400 maps in the six volumes, Joan Blaeu began the preparation of his monumental *Atlas Major*, which appeared in 1662 in 11 volumes, with 3000 pages of Latin text and 593 double-page maps covering the entire known world—including 107 for Germany, 49 for Scotland, and 23 for America. A French edition with 598 maps in 12 volumes was issued in 1663 and again in 1667; a Dutch edition in nine volumes in 1664; a German edition in nine volumes in 1667; and a Spanish edition in ten volumes over the years 1658-72. The maps of Scotland and Ireland which were in Volume V of the *Atlas Novus* now formed Volume VI of the Latin, French and Spanish editions, and Volume V of the Dutch and German editions.

In 1672 the firm met with a catastrophe: one of the buildings where the *Atlas* was printed, and all the maps in stock there, were destroyed by fire, and most of the copper plates so damaged as to be useless for reprinting. There is no trace of the map plates of Scotland being used again after the fire. In 1673 Joan Blaeu died. His sons gradually sold off the remaining stock of plates and atlases and the firm was wound up in 1694-96.

The death of Joannes Janssonius in 1664 and of Joan Blaeu in 1673 brought to an end the great period of Dutch pre-eminence in cartography; some of the later Dutch publishers were excellent engravers but their maps were mainly copied from the earlier work of Janssonius or Blaeu, or from the more up-to-date maps of Nicolas Sanson or Guillaume De L'Isle of France, or even from their own contemporaries in the Netherlands.

LATER DUTCH CARTOGRAPHERS

Four maps of Scotland by four different Dutch publishers in the period 1680 to 1708 are so much alike that it is difficult to say which is the original and which are copied from it. Only one of them is dated (1708); where they appear in atlases there is seldom a date on the title page and the variations in the contents of the atlases add to the difficulty of fixing the order of publication. An atlas published by Nicolaus Visscher may contain some maps by De Wit; and Visscher's maps may be found in an atlas published by De Wit.

The four maps of Scotland so closely related are: (1) 'Scotia Regnum' by Frederick de Wit; (2) 'Novissima Regni Scotiae . . .

Tabula' by Carel (or Carolus) Allard; (3) 'Exactissima Regni Scotiae Tabula' by Nicolaus Visscher; and (4) 'Novissima Regni Scotiae . . . Tabula' by Pieter (or Petrus) Schenk. Each of these four publishers obtained a 'privilege' (protection against competition) from the States-General, and where the date of this privilege is known the map can be assigned to a later or an earlier date according to whether 'cum privilegio' appears on it or not. Professor Dr C. Koeman in *Atlantes Neerlandici* gives these dates of the privileges: Visscher 1682 and 1697; Allard 1683; De Wit 1689; Schenk 1695; but even with this guidance the dating of the maps is difficult.

Although the four maps resemble each other very markedly there are certain differences which place them clearly into two groups; in the first group are the maps by Frederick de Wit, Carel Allard and Pieter Schenk; in the second group are Nicolaus Visscher and the two German cartographers, Homann and Seutter (described in Chapter 6).

The first group have indications that some features of the map have been taken from Sanson's map of Scotland of 1665 (see Chapter 6); the Visscher map, by contrast, shows more indebtedness to Jaillot's revised version of the Sanson map. For example, Sanson, Allard, De Wit and Schenk have St Andrew, Skeer (modern Skene); all omit Loch Tummel and the Isle of May; Jaillot and Visscher on the other hand have St Andrews, Skeen, and show Loch Tummel and the Isle of May; Sanson and De Wit have Yedbrugk, whilst Jaillot and Visscher have Iedbrugh. Visscher makes the mistake in copying place names of placing Aberdour west of Inverkeithing, and this is repeated by Homann and Seutter, the two German map publishers. These are only examples; many others occur. In the first group (De Wit, Allard and Schenk), all three have the River Awe flowing out of the middle of the west side of Loch Awe; this, with other resemblances, makes it obvious that two of the three are copied from the third.

As to which of the three maps was the first, the evidence is inconclusive. Allard's map is 'Met Privilegie' and so after 1683; De Wit had two issues, one without and one 'cum Privilegio', so that one is earlier than 1689, and one later; Schenk's map is 'cum Privilegio' and therefore after 1695—one of Schenk's maps is in fact dated 1708. As between Allard 'after 1683' and De Wit 'before 1689', the balance of probability seems to favour De Wit. De Wit was a man of greater talent than Allard; he was engraving maps in or before 1659 when Allard was only 11 years old; the atlases published by Allard generally included some maps from De Wit's stock—his *Atlas Minor* in 1697 included De Wit's map of England along with Allard's own maps of Scotland and Ireland.

FREDERICK DE WIT

Frederick de Wit (1630-1706), born at Gouda, settled in Amsterdam, where he became one of the foremost engravers of maps. His earliest dated map is 1659. He apparently began the publication of atlases about 1680, as several have no mention of the 'Privilege' granted in 1689. De Wit engraved some 130 maps in all, and a number of sea charts. He also published a town atlas of the Netherlands and a town atlas of Europe, mostly from plates originally belonging to Blaeu or Janssonius, supplemented by some plates of his own.

His map of Scotland 'Scotia Regnum divisum in Partem Septentrionalem et Meridionalem' on the scale of *c*. 12 miles to an inch,[9] based on the 1665 map of Sanson with additional place names from the maps of Blaeu or Jaillot, was first published before 1689; a later edition mentions the 'privilege' which was granted to De Wit in 1689. The map has no lines of latitude and longitude, but the figures (with longitude based on Ferro) are given in the margins. It is included in several De Wit atlases issued around 1680; most of them have simply the title *Atlas*; but about 1690 he issued an *Atlas Major*. His widow, in 1710, sold the map plates to Covens and Mortier, who continued the publication of the *Atlas Major* for some time. An *Atlas Major* and an *Atlas Minor* with De Wit's name on the title page were issed by Christopher Browne in London *c*. 1706-10; these were made up from loose maps purchased from various Amsterdam map sellers, supplemented by Browne's own maps.

CAREL ALLARD

Carel (or Carolus) Allard (1648-1706) succeeded to the business of publisher and printseller founded in Amsterdam by his father, Huych Allard, and in 1683 obtained a privilege from the States of Holland for the maps he was then engraving. In 1697 he published an *Atlas Minor* with 100 maps, 27 of them by himself, and about 1705 issued an *Atlas Major* in three volumes with 521 maps, of which only 47 were his own. Both atlases contained his map of Scotland: 'Novissima Regni Scotiae Septentrionalis et Meridionalis Tabula', on a scale of *c*. 12 miles to an inch; 'met Privilegie' on it indicates a date after 1683. The map is almost identical with De Wit's map (see above). Carel's son, Abraham, sold off his complete stock in 1708.

NICOLAUS VISSCHER

The Visscher business was founded by Claes Jansz Visscher, (1587-1652), and was continued by his son Nicolaus I (1618-79), who published an *Atlas Contractus* between 1656 and 1677, with 54 maps. He was succeeded by Nicolaus II, who between 1682 (the date of his patent), and his death in 1702, issued several editions of a world atlas, the *Atlas Minor*, of which no two have the same number of maps. Nicolaus I and II were between them responsible for engraving over 170 maps, marked by their ornate decoration; in addition to making up atlases from their own maps supplemented by the maps of other publishers, they also sold their maps for inclusion in the atlases of other publishers.

Visscher's map of Scotland (on a scale of *c.* 12 miles to an inch), has in a very large and decorative cartouche 'Exactissima Regni Scotiae Tabula' and 'Cum Prvl. Ordin. Gener. Belgii Foederati', indicating a date after 1682. His map of England is dedicated to King William III, which would date it after 1689, and both maps may therefore be attributed to Nicolas Visscher II and dated *c.* 1690. Visscher has taken the outline of Scotland from Jaillot's edition of Sanson's map of Scotland (see next chapter), with some minor differences, and there is also substantial identity in place names with the Jaillot map, but Visscher has added many place names from the Blaeu regional maps, considerably more than De Wit added in his map.

PIETER SCHENK AND GERARD VALCK

The fourth of the maps of Scotland based on the Sanson/Jaillot maps was published by Pieter (or Petrus) Schenk (1660-1718), who had a partnership arrangement with Gerard Valck (or Valk) (d. 1726), both engravers and publishers in Amsterdam and connected by marriage. About 1690 they acquired the plates of the *Atlas Novus* of Janssonius, removed his name and substituted their own, and sold the maps separately. These included 'Scotia Regnum' and the nine regional maps of Scotland which were first issued in the 1659 edition of the *Atlas Novus*. Apart from this joint arrangement both published maps independently.

Petrus Schenk and his son, Petrus II (d. 1773), produced about 70 original maps and increased their stock by acquiring the plates of Nicolaus Visscher (and adding the name of P. Schenk, jun., on the maps). They published an *Atlas Contractus* about 1700, with different issues having up to 160 maps, an *Atlas of Saxony*, and other small regional atlases. Petrus Schenk's map, 'Novissima Regni Scotiae Septentrionalis et Meridionalis Tabula', on the scale of *c.* 12 miles per inch, has 'Cum Privil.', indicating that it was issued after 1695; a later issue is dated 1708. This map was copied from De Wit's map (see above).

Gerard Valck, printer, engraver and globe-maker in Amsterdam obtained a 'privilege' from the States of Holland in 1696. His son Leonhard (b. 1675), joined him in partnership and continued the business for some years after the death of Gerard in 1726. Their output of original maps was comparatively small, some 80 in all, of which over half have the name of Gerard only, the rest having both names. The map of Scotland 'Regnum Scotiae seu pars Septent' by Gerard and Leonhard Valk, on the scale of *c.* 12 miles per inch, is partly based on Visscher's map (and not, like Schenk, on De Wit's map), but the west coast is considerably distorted by a westward inclination of Galloway, Argyll and Skye. Lewis is more than 4° west of Cape Wrath (Faro Head on the map) instead of $1\frac{1}{2}$°; Kintyre is 2° west of Ayr instead of 1°; and Skye extends over $2\frac{1}{2}$° instead of 1°. This map was included in some editions of Valck's atlas *Atlantis sylloge Compendiosa*, first issued about 1702.

SMALLER MAPS

Several pocket-size atlases were on sale in addition to the *Epitome* of Ortelius and the small atlases of the Mercator-Hondius firm. In 1598 Barent Langenes, printer in Middelburg, published the *Caert-Thresoor*, an atlas of 169 small maps, including 'Scotia', $3\frac{1}{4} \times 4\frac{3}{4}$ inches, with Dutch text. From 1600 the atlas had the new title *P. Bertii Tabularum Geographicarum Contractarum*, and the 1616 edition published by Jodocus Hondius II had new maps of a slightly larger size ($3\frac{3}{4} \times 5\frac{1}{4}$ inches): 'Scotia' by Salomon Rogiers, 'Scotia Septentrion', and 'Scotia Australis'.

Pieter van den Keere (Latin = Petrus Kaerius), an engraver who took refuge in England for a time from religious persecution, engraved 44 maps of parts of the British Isles which were probably published between 1605 and 1610, although three of the maps are dated 1599. Six of the maps relate to Scotland; these are all based on Ortelius's map of 1573. In 1617 the 44 map plates were used in an edition of Camden's *Britannia* published by W. J. Blaeu, and then were acquired by George Humble in London (see Chapter 9).

In 1706 Daniel de la Feuille, a Frenchman who had settled in Amsterdam in 1683 as an art dealer and engraver, published the first edition, and in 1707 French and English editions, of *The Military Tablettes* which included his 'Carte Nouvelle d'Écosse', size 7×10 inches, with inset views of 14 Scottish towns and castles.

Several small maps of Scotland were published by Pieter van der Aa (1659-1733), bookseller and publisher in Leiden; they are of little cartographic value as they were frequently distorted to fit into a small page or part of a page. Three maps, 'L'Escosse', 'L'Ecosse

Meridionale' and 'L'Ecosse Septentrionale' (each 5 × 8 inches) appeared in his *Nouveau Petit Atlas* and other atlases about 1710 and in his *La Galerie Agréable du Monde*, a massive collection in 27 volumes of over 3000 maps, plans and views covering the whole world. A slightly larger map, L'Ecosse (9 × 12 inches), appeared in *Le Nouveau Théâtre du Monde* of 1713 and in the *Nouvel Atlas* of 1714.

COVENS AND MORTIER

After the death in the first quarter of the 18th century of Nicolaus Visscher II, Carel Allard, Frederick de Wit, Pieter Schenk I and Gerard Valck, many of their map plates were acquired by Pieter Mortier, a printer and publisher in Amsterdam. His eldest son Cornelis took over the business in 1719, and in 1721 was joined by his brother-in-law Johannes Covens. Neither partner was a cartographer or engraver, but with skilled engravers employed to alter old plates or copy maps, the firm of Covens and Mortier published numerous atlases and maps.

The maps of Scotland appearing in their atlases included: (1) 'Scotia Regnum', by F. de Wit, in their re-issue of his *Atlas Major*, (2) 'Regnum Scotiae' by Gerard and Leonhard Valck, along with the eight regional maps of Scotland which Valck and Schenk had taken over from the heirs of Janssonius, all issued about 1741 by Covens and Mortier in a *Nieuwe Atlas* in three volumes with 352 maps, (3) 'Scotia Tabula' by Nicolaus Visscher, with the name of P. Schenk, jun., added; in an edition around 1759 of their *Nieuwe Atlas*, in six volumes with 742 maps, (4) 'L'Ecosse' originally published by Pieter van der Aa, now re-issued with the name of Covens & Mortier on the map. The firm also re-issued Van der Aa's *Nouvel Atlas* (with the three maps of Scotland), firstly with Van der Aa's name retained on the maps and in a second issue with their name in place of Van der Aa.

Pieter Mortier was the grandson of French refugees and trained as a bookseller in Paris. His knowledge of the new maps of the French cartographer, Nicolas Sanson, led him in 1690 to obtain from the States of Holland a 'privilege' to copy and publish these maps on Amsterdam. So exactly were the Sanson maps and atlases copied in every detail, including the title and even the Paris address on the title page, that identification of some of the Amsterdam printings is difficult, unless they have the addition on the title page of the name of Pierre Mortier or Covens and Mortier. A 'Sanson' atlas published by Mortier *c.* 1708 contains 'Le Royaume d'Escosse divise en parties septentrionale & meridionale', Jaillot's revised version of the Sanson original (see Chapter 6). The firm also from

1730 issued atlases copied from those published in Paris by Guillaume De L'Isle, but these did not have a map of Scotland.

The firm maintained its great output of maps—25 different atlases are mentioned—throughout the 18th century and well into the 19th. But by this time the initiative in map production had passed to other countries.

5 Timothy Pont and Blaeu's Atlas of Scotland

In 1654 Joannis Blaeu published in Amsterdam Volume V of his *Novus Atlas* containing three general maps of Scotland, 46 maps of Scottish counties or regions, and six maps of Ireland. Thirty-six of the Scottish regional maps have the name of Timothy Pont as author, and a letter in Latin, dated 1648, from Robert Gordon to Sir John Scot of Scotstarvet printed in certain issues of the volume, describes Pont's experiences in making his survey of Scotland:

'Now at length, after many labours, after the loss of much time, and after such troubles as the mind shudders to remember, our Scotland worthily shows herself, and, among the other countries of the world, assumes her place in the great and famous Atlas of Joannis Blaeu, who is so renowned and so far before all others in this department of knowledge. Nor is she, as so often before, drawn by her writers from mere hear-say, deformed by wretched fables, contracted on scanty sheets, and quite unlike her real self; but as that talented young man Timothy Pont, the originator of this work, left her in his papers, the memory of which man, without the crime of the greatest ingratitude, neither can nor may be neglected. For, with small means and no favouring patron, he undertook the whole of this task forty years ago: he travelled on foot right through the whole of this kingdom, as no one before him had done; he visited all the islands, occupied for the most part by inhabitants hostile and uncivilised, and with a language different from our own; being often stripped, as he told me, by the fierce robbers, and suffering not seldom all the hardships of the dangerous journey, nevertheless at no time was he overcome by the difficulties, nor was he disheartened. But when, having returned, he prepared to publish the results of his labours, he was defeated by the greed of the printers and book-sellers, and so could not reach his goal. While awaiting better times, untimely death took him away'.[1]

Timothy Pont was the son of the Rev. Robert Pont (1524-1606), who held the highest offices in the Scottish church and in the law, a noted author of religious works and for many years minister of St Cuthbert's Church in Edinburgh, where there is a tablet to his memory.[2] Timothy was the eldest of Pont's eight children; the date of his birth is unknown, but as the records of the University of St Andrews show that he matriculated there in 1580 and graduated in or before 1583, we may assume that he was born in or shortly before 1565.[3] The first mention of his name occurs in 1574, when his father granted a charter of certain lands to him, a charter renewed in 1583.[4]

From the extent of Pont's surveys it seems likely that he began them immediately after graduation in 1583, possibly inspired by Christopher Saxton's *Atlas of England and Wales* published in 1579. In 1593, his father, who had been in receipt of an annuity of £160 Scots (= £13·30 sterling) from Edinburgh Town Council since 1585, in consideration of renouncing the Provostry of Trinity College,[5] assigned £140 of this annuity to Timothy, and thereby provided him with an assured, if small, income.[6] In this same year, Robert Pont, in the course of his duties as a Church Commissioner for the northern parts of Scotland, made an extensive tour of the Orkney Islands, and there is a strong presumption that Timothy accompanied him.[7] In June 1592, Lord Menmuir, who held the office of 'Master of the Metals' recorded a note: 'Robert Pont anent the lead of Orkney: to ask for his commission at his returning'.[8] Then Menmuir issued a commission to Timothy Pont, giving him full power to search out minerals and metals in the Orkneys and Shetlands and charging the inhabitants not to impede Timothy in his search—a very useful authority for a person making surveys.[9] That Pont made a map of the Orkneys is explicitly stated by James Gordon (referred to later). In July 1596, the Dean of Limerick, Dionise Campbell, who had been on a visit to Scotland, wrote to Sir Robert Cecil that he had heard that one Pont had travelled over the whole of Scotland and proposed to publish a 'perfect description', and the Dean had asked for one of the first edition to be sent to Cecil.[10] Pont's manuscript map of Clydesdale is dated 1596, the only map with a date.

Robert Pont's duties in the far north included the establishment of churches, and his hand can be seen in the next record of Timothy: his appointment as minister of the church at Dunnet in Caithness in 1600 or 1601, his brother Zachary being appointed about the same time to the neighbouring parish of Bower.[11]

In May 1605, Timothy collected personally the annuity due to him by the Town Council of Edinburgh when he produced his father's assignation.[12] It was possibly at this time that he gathered the material for his list of 348 towns, villages, estates, etc., of the district of Cunninghame in Ayrshire, printed in 1876 under the title of *Cunninghame Topographized*, and dated by the editor from internal evidence as compiled between 1604 and 1608; the notes accompanying the place names are no more than could have been collected in the course of a short visit, possibly staying with clergymen he had met at the Assembly or had met at the University when students together.[13]   Sir Robert Sibbald mentions a pedestrian expedition undertaken by Timothy in 1608 to explore the more barbarous parts of the country,[14] but this is probably a too literal reading of Robert Gordon's statement in his letter of 1648 that Timothy had undertaken this work 'forty years ago'.

Robert Pont died in 1606 and Timothy evidently began to think of leaving Dunnet. He was still minister there in 1609 when, for some reason which is not apparent, he was one of the applicants to the Privy Council in Scotland for 2000 acres in the forfeited lands in Ulster then being offered to Scots at the price of £100 for 500 acres. Seventy-seven applicants, including Timothy, were allotted lands, but the list of applicants was not approved by the Council in London, who cancelled the list, invited new applications and made fresh allotments, omitting Pont and many of the original applicants from the new list.[15]   On 7th December 1610, Timothy was still described as parson of Dunnet when he signed as witness to one of the Sutherland charters.[16]   This is the last record of him, now between 45 and 50 years of age; the list of ministers' stipends (salaries) is lacking for the years 1609 to 1613, and he must have left Dunnet before 1614 when another minister's name is recorded there.

Pont's later life is described briefly by Gordon in his letter to Scot: 'But when, having returned, he (Pont) prepared to publish the results of his labours, he was defeated by the greed of printers and booksellers, and so could not reach his goal. While awaiting better times, untimely death took him away'. Gordon was without doubt referring to 'A New Description of Lothian and Linlithquo. Be T. Pont', a map which bears Pont's dedication to James I, King of Great Britain and the imprint 'Jodocus Hondius caelavit sumptibus Andreae Hart', i.e., engraved by Jodocus Hondius at the expense of Andrew Hart, an Edinburgh bookseller who died in 1621.[17] Although the earliest known issue of this map appeared in the 1630 edition of the Mercator-Hondius Atlas,[18] the engraver, Jodocus Hondius, died in 1612, and the date of the map is therefore between 1603 (when James became King of Great Britain) and 1612. In the years 1605 to 1610 Jodocus Hondius was engaged in engraving in Amsterdam the plates of the maps for John Speed's *Theatre of the Empire of Great Britaine*, and it is possible that Pont learned of this atlas (it also has a dedication to King James and the inscription 'Jodocus Hondius caelavit'), and was encouraged to leave the Church in order to concentrate on preparing his maps for the engraver. The probable date of the Lothians map is therefore 1611 or 1612. It was apparently not revised before inclusion in the Mercator-Hondius Atlas in 1630, as it does not show Cramond Bridge built in 1619.

In the 1633 edition, when it next appeared, the names of Jodocus Hondius and Hart are erased and replaced by 'Henricus Hondius excudit'. A second finished map is also Pont's work; James Gordon, in comparing the latitudes shown on Pont's maps, says that 'Mr Timothie, in his Mapps of Lothian and Orkney doth not agrie with himself'.[19] The reference is clearly to a map of the Orkneys and Shetlands (first published in the 1636 edition of the Mercator-Hondius), and we may assume that after finishing the map of the Lothians, Pont then worked on the map of the Orkneys and that it was not engraved at the time because of the death of Jodocus Hondius. Robert Gordon speaks of the greed of booksellers and printers, but Pont may have found, as others did later, that Scotland did not provide a large enough market for maps to meet the cost of producing them.

At some unknown date Pont applied to James I, and was promised financial assistance, as shown by a note quoted later; he may have written to the King or Pont may have visited London about 1611— James would certainly lend a ready ear to a son of Robert Pont. Nothing later is known of Timothy; the date and place of his death are unknown, but the fact that in March 1614 the widow of Robert Pont collected from Edinburgh Town Council the arrears of the annuity which had been assigned to Timothy creates a strong presumption that he died between 1611 and 1614.[20] He would then be about 50 years of age, and Gordon's words 'untimely death took him away' would be fitting.

THE MANUSCRIPT MAPS

Of the manuscript maps left by Pont at his death, 36 sheets have survived (all now in the National Library of Scotland), varying in size from 8×7 inches to 25×14 inches, containing 60 maps or fragments of maps covering the greater part of the mainland of Scotland, along with one map of a small part of the Hebrides.[21] Central and northern Scotland are well covered, and we know from the published *Atlas* that manuscript maps, now lost, covered southern Scotland (Blaeu, the engraver, in 1631 acknowledged receipt of Pont's manuscript map of the Merce (Berwickshire)). These confirm the statement that Pont travelled over the whole of Scotland; if there is no evidence of mapping of some areas we may reasonably conclude, in the light of his careful mapping of the Hebrides and Orkneys, that the omissions are more probably due to lost manuscripts than to the absence of surveys by Pont. Out of 35 maps in the *Atlas* attributed to Pont, the original manuscripts for 28 have not survived, so that the total number left by Pont at his death was possibly more than twice the number which have been preserved. At least three possible causes account for the losses, (*a*) neglect for years by Pont's heirs, (*b*) losses at sea—Blaeu records 'lost by the violence of the stormy seas', and (*c*) a fire in the publisher's premises in 1672. Pont also left a substantial quantity of descriptive notes; these have not survived but some extracts from them in the writing of James Gordon are preserved in the National Library.

If we accept that the surveys of Scotland could be carried out only in the summer months between Pont's graduation in 1583 and his appointment to Dunnet in 1601, Pont must have surveyed the equivalent of two counties each summer. This was by any standard a most remarkable achievement; even though they were only compass traverses of the rivers and valleys, the work in tracing the courses of the rivers and of merely recording the vast number of place names was immense. And this was achieved, as Gordon tells us, at the cost of great personal hardship. Nearly two centuries later, when the military survey was carried out, some fifty men required eight years to do the survey, the winters being spent in drawing the maps.

Robert Gordon tells us that Pont's heirs (we do not know who they were, presumably his brothers and sisters), 'to whom he left his maps at his death, being men without knowledge of such things, neglected the whole matter, and the maps, being badly kept and carelessly, worn and moth-eaten, already were falling to pieces, and, fading away, were becoming illegible even to careful eyes. Then that most munificent Prince, James, King of Britain, being informed of these matters gave orders that they should be purchased from the heirs, and published. But alas! they went from bad to worse, for they fell into the hands of those whose purpose was to conceal them as though they were religious mysteries; and so again they lay hidden, though the keepers were changed. Then you [Sir John Scot], O famous man, born for the good of literature, regretting so great a loss, urged that they should be published; you took charge of the matter with especial care, and you inquired anxiously who could be got to assist in the production of this work, as yet incomplete. . . . Indeed I may say, without fear of contradiction and without flattery, that without thee, thee only, the world would yet have seen nothing of these maps, and, though produced with such great labour by their first author, they would evilly have perished . . .'.

In writing this Robert Gordon attributes more to Sir John Scot than the documentary evidence justifies. The maps were indeed kept by Pont's heirs, but there is no evidence that King James gave orders for their purchase, and, as letters show, the initiative for publication of the maps came not from Scot, but from Willem Blaeu, the map publisher in Amsterdam. The first reference to them after Pont's death is contained in the following letter from King Charles I, in February 1629, to Sir William Alexander, Secretary of State for Scotland, which shows that in or before 1628 they were bought from Pont's heirs by Sir James Balfour of Denmiln.[22]

'Whareas it was our late royall father's intentione to have caused give unto one Mr. Timothie Pont, deceased, some moneyis touardis his charges in the perfecting of the descriptione of that our antient kingdome, as by a noat [note] under his hand doethe appeir: Wee being noe les willing to further a purpos soe muche tending to the honour thereof, and seing . . . James Balfour, Esquire, hath, as wee are credibillie informed, cost [i.e. bought] these mappes and tabellis from the executouris of the said Pont, and is about to perfect and publishe the same, which will both require great panis and charges: Oure pleasoure is, tharefore, and wee doe heirby will and command that with all convenient diligence you pay or caus be payed unto the said James Balfour, his assignayis or servantis haveing his pouare, the soume of £100 sterling, and that out of the first of our rentis and casualities whatsoever of that our kingdome, resting, or which at ony time heirefter shal happin to rest due unto us and be in your hand: And for your soe doeing, etc.—Whitehall, the last of Februare 1629.'

Sir James Balfour (1600-57), of Denmiln in Fife, was a historian, antiquary, and a diligent collector of historical manuscripts. In 1628 he went to London to study heraldry, and in 1630, on his return to Scotland, was knighted and appointed Lyon King-of-Arms.[23] At his death his collection of manuscripts passed to the Advocates Library, now the National Library. It seems possible that among the papers which he bought from Pont's heirs was the note of the promised payment by James I, and that when he was in London he showed it to Charles I and spoke of his intention to publish the maps.

SIR JOHN SCOT

Balfour's connection with the maps was brief; Sir John Scot's was lasting and important. Scot (1585-1670), born in Fife, acquired the lands of Scotstarvit in 1611; he held the important offices of Director of Chancery, Lord of Session, and Privy Councillor, but was deprived of these offices in 1652 when Cromwell was in power.[24] Before 1626 Scot had been in correspondence with Willem Blaeu of Amsterdam about printing a volume of Latin poems by Scottish poets, which was eventually published in 1637 with the title *Delitiae Poetarum Scotorum*. Fifteen letters from Willem Blaeu and his son Joannis Blaeu to Scot, covering the years 1626 to 1633 and 1641 to

1657, which have survived, explain Scot's connection with the maps and show the progress of the *Atlas*.[25]

The earliest letter, written by Willem Blaeu to Scot on 12th August 1626, refers to the volume of poems, and then asks for the arms of ancient Scotland, and the arms of Scot himself, to be inserted on a map of the Orkneys and Shetlands. No clue is found in the correspondence as to how Blaeu obtained a draft of this map, which was almost certainly the work of Timothy Pont (see page 40); from the details Blaeu gives it is clearly the map included in the *Atlas* of 1654 which bears a dedication to Scot by Willem Blaeu (who died in 1638). A similar map, with the same appearance and with the same geographical details but about one-fifteenth smaller, was engraved by Henricus Hondius and included in the 1636 edition of the *Mercator-Hondius Atlas*; certain minor differences suggest that this was copied from Blaeu's map (which was ready in 1630 although not included in his *Atlas Novus* until 1654), and not the Blaeu map copied from Hondius, whereas the map of the Lothians, referred to earlier, was first engraved by Hondius and later copied by Blaeu.

In the second letter from Blaeu, dated 28th October 1626, he acknowledges the illustrations of the arms and continues: 'Meanwhile if you have any other maps of Scotland or of the surrounding islands, I beg you to deign to send them to me; for I am contemplating the publication of an *Atlas* (*Theatrum Geographicum*)'. Two years later, on 12th September 1628, when Blaeu sent a proof of the map of the Orkneys and Shetlands to Scot, coloured except for Scot's arms, which had been lost during the engraving, he repeated: 'I am putting in hand the geographical work . . . and since scarcely anything is available on the Kingdom of Scotland, I request you to have any maps that may be found anywhere forwarded to me'. Another two years passed, and then on 3rd September 1630 Blaeu wrote: 'Here at length are the maps of the Orkneys which will, I hope, please you. I shall have proof of this if you receive particulars of Scotland from your friend at your honour's intercession . . .'. This friend was no doubt Sir James Balfour, with whom official duties would bring Scot into frequent contact; evidently Scot had learned between 1628 and 1630 of Balfour's acquisition of the Pont manuscripts and had told Blaeu about them.

Balfour may still have had thoughts in 1630 of publishing the maps himself, because it was not until 17th June 1631 that Blaeu acknowledged receipt of the first of Pont's maps: 'Your letter, with that of Master Balfour attached, and the map of the Merce, which I have received, place it beyond my power to express how much you will have put posterity in your debt here and elsewhere, when, as I intend, I shall have put the work into more finished form with your help and—through you—that of Master Balfour and other friends. I will send you, as requested, copies of the completed map and of that of the Orkneys, and that quickly. For your services to me, which I cannot repay, I give you my thanks. Meanwhile, if I can do anything for you here, I shall be while I live the most devoted servant of you and yours.'

Balfour is referred to again ('Salute Master Balfour for me') in a letter from Blaeu in 1633 but is not mentioned subsequently; a gap in the surviving correspondence (the next letter is dated 1642) leaves us to surmise what took place over the next ten years. From Blaeu's 'Address to the Reader' printed in the 1654 *Atlas* we learn that 'Scot collected these and other maps and sent them over to me, but much torn and defaced. I brought them into order and sometimes divided a single map . . . into several parts. After this Robert and James Gordon gave this work the finishing touches . . . and added thereto, besides the corrections in Timothy Pont's maps, a few maps of their own.' The maps passing between Amsterdam and Edinburgh went in vessels sailing to and from Campveere (now Veere), the port of entry for Scottish goods into the Netherlands; Samuel Wallace, the deputy Conservator of the Scottish staple at Veere, is frequently mentioned as the intermediary for letters and maps.

ROBERT GORDON

It is apparent that Blaeu had not proceeded far with the work of engraving when he found the manuscripts, with sometimes two or more maps, or overlapping maps, on the same sheet, too confusing for the preparation of correct maps. Scot enlisted the services of Robert Gordon (1580-1661) of Straloch in Aberdeenshire, a graduate of the University of Aberdeen, who had also studied in Paris, described by a contemporary as 'one of the ablest men in Scotland in the mathematical faculties',[26] and by Blaeu as 'doyen of geographers'. Gordon's interest in maps dated from his youth; an astrolabe with his name, the date 1597, and one of its tablets with the latitude of Straloch, still exists.[27] He himself said in his letter in 1648 to Scot: 'Truly I had spent my life from my earliest years in these studies, yet I had no thought beyond my own pleasure and did not intend to prepare anything for publication'. He twice mentions talks with Timothy Pont on topographical matters, and though he lived far from Edinburgh, obviously his qualifications for revising the maps were known to Scot. When the French Secretary of State asked in 1648 for a map of Scotland the French ambassador in Edinburgh replied: 'In all Scotland there is no person but Robert Gordon of Straloch able to make such a map as you order me to send to you, and he has even studied more specially the inland part of the Kingdom than the sea-board. . . . I have tried, through one of his most intimate friends, to comply with your order, but in vain.'[28]

Robert Gordon began the revision before 1636, as this date appears on a manuscript map by him of Edrachillis 'gathered out of Mr. Timothie Pont his papers', and it took him until 1648 (by this time aged 68) to complete the work (except for the map of Scotia Antiqua done in 1653), with some assistance from his son, James Gordon, the parson of Rothiemay.   It would appear that Gordon did not receive all Pont's manuscripts but only those which Blaeu could not decipher.   Gordon's comment in his letter of January 1648 that 'I wish it had been allowed me to unfold all the writings of our Timothy . . . before they had known the hand of the engraver; there were many things to change, to add, to remove', can only mean that Blaeu had engraved some maps from the original manuscripts, probably some or all of the maps of southern Scotland and of the Hebrides, for which Pont's original drafts have not survived.   Sixty-one sheets of various sizes of the Gordon drafts of maps have been preserved; dates on some of them indicate the progress with the work —Strathearn 1637, Aberdeen, Banff and Moray 1640, Caithness 1642, Nithsdale 1644, and two of Fife and Kinross by James Gordon, both dated 1642.   Some of the maps are noted as compiled from Timothy Pont's papers; Robert Gordon's remark quoted above about his own studies indicates the possibility that some of the other maps had been drawn by him before he was asked to revise Pont's manuscripts.   Although he nowhere tells us whether these studies included personal surveys, he could hardly have amended and supplemented Pont's manuscripts to the extent he did unless he had a wide knowledge of Scotland, and the large number of his manuscript maps which have no evident connection with the engraved maps suggest that some were his own independent work.

In 1641, the King, Charles I, was in Scotland, and when shown proofs of some of the maps wrote to Gordon: 'Trustie and weill beloved We greitt yow weill Haveing laitly sein certane cairttis [maps] of divers schyres of this our ancient kingdome sent heir from Amsterdam To be correctit and helpeitt in the defectis thairof And being informed of your sufficiencie in that airtt And of your Love bothe to Learning and to the creditt of your natioune We have thairfoir thoucht fitt heirby earnestly to intreitt you to taik so mutche paines As to reveis the saidis cairttis And to helpe thame in sutche Thingis as yow find deficient thairintill That they may be sent back by the directour of our chancellarie to Holland Quhilk as the samyne will be honorabill for your sellf So schall it do ws guid and acceptable service. And if occasioun present we schall not be unmyndfull thairof. ffrom our paleice of Halyruidhouse the aucht day of October 1641'.[29]

A letter of 10th March 1642 from Joan Blaeu to Scot confirms that these maps were proofs: 'I have learnt from Master Wallace, that, when the King was in Scotland, your Honour showed to his Majesty those proofs of maps which I had sent to you for correction. They were exceedingly imperfect, and so are these, a little more elegant but still lacking for completion the ornament, titles, mile scales, and some other details. . . . Many maps are still lacking to us, as I gather from the maps of G. Mercator, as noted below—Sutherlandia, Strathleith, Assynshire, Rossia, Cogyouth, Ardmanoth, Strathcarron, Loquhabria, Lorna, Bread Albayn, Argadia, Perthia, Athole, Strathamunde, Stratherne, Gourea, Angusia, Mernia, Badenochia, Menteith, Lennos. Would that there were some hope of recovering these!' If we take this list as complete (Blaeu had taken these names from the two-sheet map of Scotland in Mercator's *Atlas*), it means that at this stage Blaeu had in hand or completed 40 of the regional maps and only five more were added later—Lennox, Sutherland, Lorne, Braid-Allaban, and Extima Scotiae.

The engraved maps were to be accompanied by geographical descriptions, and for this purpose the General Assembly of the Church of Scotland in 1641 agreed on the motion of Sir John Scot that some person in every presbytery should prepare such a description, but when Scot renewed his request in 1643 'it was not so much regarded',[30] and ministers' names are attached to only two descriptions—Galloway by John Macleland and the Lothians by William Forbes, although Blaeu in his 'Address to the Reader' acknowledges contributions also by others—Boner, Lauder, and William Spang, minister of the Scots Kirk at Veere.[31]

A gap of three years now occurs in the correspondence. These were troubled years in Scotland; the Civil War began in 1642 and the campaigns of Montrose took the royalist armies several times through Aberdeenshire. The conflict in Scotland seems to have been the reason for Sir John going to the Netherlands in September 1645; Thomas Cunningham, the Scots Conservator at Veere writes of him as 'being fled, as the most part of the well affected were constrained for a time to do'.[32] A letter from Blaeu to Scot at Veere implies that Scot's visit was not pre-arranged: 'I rejoice that you have so happily escaped both the war and the afflicted city (the pestilence was then raging in Edinburgh). I am glad that I shall have the opportunity of seeing you. For there are some things concerning the maps of Scotland about which I would fain confer with you. . . . I have already supplied the proofs of the maps to Master Wallace, and shall shortly forward the seventh, for all except three or four are finished, apart from some details in them which we can discuss in person. For I hope to see you in Amsterdam.' Scot, in a letter to Robert Gordon of 2nd September 1645, accounts for his visit by saying: 'Being resolved to see my friends in the Low Countries in this idle time for learning', and goes on to say that a Dunkirk ship had taken James Gordon's map of Fife from a Leith ship, so it was fortunate that James had kept a copy; he had also learned that all the maps in Blaeu's hands had now been printed, and that Blaeu was hourly expecting the rest from Gordon to finish the work.[29] Scot spent over two months in Amsterdam, helping Blaeu with the maps and the descriptive text to accompany them; according to Blaeu, Scot 'had such an excellent memory that, without any chart or book, he drew the shapes of areas, the places, boundaries . . . the cities, the rivers, and many other things of this nature'. On 29th November 1645 he was at Veere on his homeward journey—the Covenanters were again in power and the Estates of Zealand provided an armed vessel to protect Scot from the danger of pirates on the voyage[33]—when Blaeu sent him for amendment a draft of the Preface as received from Casper Barlaeus (who had presumably been consulted so as to ensure the correctness of the Latin text), along with two copies of maps which required correction by Gordon. Blaeu referred again to the maps still wanted to complete the *Atlas*, saying that Gordon formerly wrote that he had maps of various districts in Sutherland, Ross, Inverness, Perth, Angus, and that he believed the map of Sutherland by the Earl of Sutherland to be in the Earl's possession. It seems from Blaeu's list that he had received very little from Gordon in the years 1642-5 (a period when Gordon was much occupied in the political activities in Aberdeenshire through the duties placed on him by the head of the Gordons, the Marquis of Huntly, and so Blaeu now says 'but if the completed versions of the others cannot be had, the volume must be finished'. Blaeu in his 'Letter to the Reader' says that 'The works of Gordon would have progressed further had not the Civil War which sadly shook Scotland hindered the work'.

The importance of Robert Gordon's work was recognized by the Scottish Parliament in January 1646, when they renewed an earlier Act exempting him from all public burdens in consideration of his 'pains and travail in revising and correcting the maps of this Kingdom'; an exemption which was repeated in May 1646 when he was declared to be free 'from all quartering or other public burdens whatsoever to the end he may more freely attend to perfect that work . . . of helping and correcting the several maps of this Kingdom', and again confirmed in December 1649.[34]

In August 1646 Gordon sent Samuel Wallace at Veere, for transmission to Blaeu, a packet, the contents of which are not specified. Wallace, writing to Gordon in March 1647, said that Blaeu had been occupied with printing the two volumes of his *Town Atlas of the Netherlands*, but with that now completed he would take no other work until the maps of Scotland were finished. The map of Fife was 'for the most part performed'. Wallace conveyed an urgent request from Blaeu for all available material, 'aither for supplie, ornament, decore, or illustratione', and added that as both Scot and Gordon were now of advanced age, it was all the more necessary to ensure that 'a famous and honourable work may be brought to light in our days'. (He also mentioned that James Gordon had been asked by the magistrates of Edinburgh to draw a plan of the city—a plan which Blaeu writing in March 1649 described as already finished, and waiting for the city arms.)[35]

Blaeu had in 1645 published Volume IV of his *Novus Atlas*, with maps of England and Wales, and evidently thought that the volume of Scotland would follow soon, as in March 1647 he applied to the Scottish Parliament, saying that his father and he, for seventeen years past (i.e. from 1630) had been concerned in the printing of maps of Scotland, and as the work was ready to go to press, he asked them to request the English Parliament to grant him a privilege for England as already given by His Majesty for Scotland, for he would be ruined if other printers copied his maps.[36]

A sense of urgency was shown by Blaeu from 1645 and it was no doubt the pressure from him which made Gordon decide to complete his work by preparing two maps on smaller scales to cover the remaining parts of Scotland—one map with the title 'Braid-Allaban, Atholia, Marria Superior, Badenocha, Strath-Spea, Lochabria, (etc)' covering west-central Scotland and the other 'Extima Scotiae Septentrionalis ora (etc)', covering northern Scotland. These maps on a scale of approximately 5 miles to an inch are markedly different from the maps of Southern Scotland on scales between 1 and 2 miles per inch; the material was available as the surviving manuscripts show, but evidently not the time to prepare maps on the larger scale. Gordon also prepared the map of Scotland, 'Scotia Regnum', which was completed about this time as it bears a dedication to James, Duke of Hamilton, who died in 1649. In January 1648 he wrote to Scot the letter, quoted above, printed in the *Atlas*, its terms indicating that Gordon now regarded his work on the maps as finished.

In March 1649 Blaeu informed Scot that he was already beginning Scotland and intended to finish it that year if only the descriptions were supplied, but adding that he feared that Scot might be impeded by other more urgent business. Scot was still Director of Chancery, and the execution of Charles I in January 1649 brought more anxieties and problems; in March 1652 he was deprived of his official posts and later fined £1500 by Cromwell. Then in 1652 war broke out between Britain and Holland, and for a period of five years from 1649 to 1654 there is no record of progress with the *Atlas* except that Robert Gordon's map of 'Scotia Antiqua' is dated 1653.

In the beginning of 1654, even before the peace treaty between Britain and Holland was signed in April, Blaeu began preparations for publication. In February Scot obtained from Colonel Robert Lilburne, then in command of the Commonwealth forces in Scotland, a letter to Cromwell saying that Scot had been responsible for an exact map of Scotland now being printed in Amsterdam, that he, Lilburne, had seen copies of the map and found them very useful for the army.[37] With this letter Scot went to London, combining an application to Cromwell for a privilege for Blaeu's maps with an appeal against his own fine; in a petition dated 29th April he says: 'I came here a month since to procure your favour for the printing in Holland by John Blaw of maps of Scotland and Ireland. I also showed my wrongs in being deprived of my offices in Scotland . . .'.[38] Cromwell granted the 'privilege', which is dated 14th June 1654; but Scot was less successful in his own affairs although a year later his fine was cancelled. Blaeu also received privileges from the Netherlands and the Empire on 10th June and 11th August, respectively, and Volume V of the *Atlas Novus* was at last published in 1654 after 25 years in preparation; in editions with the text in Dutch, Latin, French and German, all dated 1654.

Robert Gordon's own views of his work are contained in his letter to Scot printed in some copies of the volume: 'I wish he [Pont] had been fated to outlive his own works, and from them to draw the hoped-for honours and the due rewards, and not that I, as a substitute for him, should have laboured in this duty with abilities less than his. Conscious of my own weakness, I have greatly shrunk from this project. Truly, I had spent my life from my earliest years in these studies, yet I had no thought beyond my own personal pleasure, and did not intend to prepare anything for publication. . . . So, if anything at all faulty should appear in this edition, let it be held as due to the evil of the times, and not to my want of care. For it must be acknowledged that these labours, which demand leisure and equanimity, have fallen on most unfavourable times. Yet I wish it had been allowed me to unfold all the writings of our Timothy, to drink them in with the eye before they had known the hand of the engraver. There were many things to change, to add, to remove, which now await a second edition. Now whatever work is here, it is necessary that we should all say that it is yours, that you are the real parent and the true nurse; you brought these maps out of darkness; they were restored on your authority; you, as my fugleman, dispelled from me the slothfulness of declining years. When I lay hidden in distant lands and far from home, you procured me the favour of great and renowned friends, who helped me, and by exhortation urged me to do this work, without whose assistance my mind would have despaired, nay, even now would be despairing. . . . Robert Gordon, Aberdeen, 24th January 1648.'

In 1655 Blaeu completed his *Atlas Novus* with Volume VI containing maps of China and Japan. On 19th July 1655 he sent to Scot by sea the six-volume *Atlas* with this written on the flyleaf of Volume I: 'In the fifth you will find the preface changed and an epistle of Gordon's added. A similar copy I have sent to the Lord Protector and Secretary Thurloe. And if you have any other points for a second edition, either things to be added or things to be changed, I beg you will supply them.'

In the final stages the first copies of Volume V had been put together in some haste, and we find Blaeu in December 1655 again asking Scot if he can get the Gordons to send him what is lacking in the volume and promising to send Gordon's copy of the volume when the opportunity occurred. He also enclosed a verse as dedication to Scot, which he proposed to include in the preface; the fact that it appears in copies with the title-page dated 1654 shows that these copies were not made up and bound until 1656 or later. In March 1656 Scot sent him Gordon's description of Aberdeen and Banff; a year later Blaeu said he was now printing this in Spanish (this edition has 1654 on the title page but was not published until 1659), and would print it in the other languages in all the editions. In the last surviving letter, undated but apparently written in July 1657, Blaeu says that he is sending fifty copies of the plan of Edinburgh, coloured, and that the two copies of the volume of Scotland, are coloured and ready for binding in red or black vellum, according to Scot's preference.[39]

Blaeu now began the preparation of his expanded *Atlas Major* and in 1662 issued the Latin edition in 11 volumes, Scotland (with Ireland) forming Volume VI. The text was re-set with some alterations and corrections, Robert Gordon's description of Aberdeen and Banff added, ships were inserted on 28 of the maps and compass roses on some. Scotland formed Volume VI also in the French edition of 1663 and the Spanish edition of 1658-72; it was Volume V in the Dutch and German editions of 1664 and 1667, respectively. There was no later reprint; many of the plates were probably destroyed or badly damaged in the fire at one of the Blaeu printing works in February 1672.

The manuscript maps in the possession of Robert Gordon passed to his son, James Gordon, the parson of Rothiemay, who gave them to Sir Robert Sibbald when the latter was planning a 'Scottish Atlas' in 1683. In 1707 Sibbald wrote that he had all the maps of Pont and of the two Gordons. After Sibbald's death in 1722 they were acquired by the Advocates' Library, now the National Library of Scotland.[40]

THE 'ATLAS'

The first part of the *Atlas* consists of certain preliminary items:

(1) Blaeu's address to the Reader, either the shorter version on three pages or the longer version of four pages;
(2) Blaeu's dedication to Sir John Scot;
(3) Robert Gordon's letter to Scot of February 1648;
(4) the States-General's privilege dated 10th June 1654;
(5) Oliver Cromwell's privilege dated 14th June 1654;
(6) the Imperial privilege dated 11th August 1654;
(7) Andrew Melvin's poem on the topography of Scotland;
(8) George Buchanan's 'Dialogus';
(9) a catalogue of Scottish Kings;
(10) Robert Gordon's 'Adnotata' on the antiquities of Scotland.

All the editions contain one of the versions of Blaeu's address to the Reader; the States-General's privilege; Andrew Melvin's poem and Gordon's 'Andotata', but one or more of the other items may not be included. Cromwell's privilege, for example, was of value in 1654 when he was Protector, but was omitted in 1662 after the Restoration of Charles II. Other differences in the make-up of the preliminary items (e.g., the omission in some copies of the dedication to Scot and Gordon's letter to him), were no doubt associated with political circumstances at the time and the market for which the volume was intended, these variations being possible as the maps and the text sheets were not bound until ordered.

The maps comprise two maps of Scotland, ancient and modern, and 46 maps of Scottish countries or regions; a map of Britain based on Ptolemy and six maps of Ireland are also in the volume. Both maps of Scotland have Robert Gordon's name, 'Scotia Antiqua' and 'Scotia Regnum'; minor differences occur between the two maps in the outline of Scotland. Considering the work which went into the making of the *Atlas*, and all the material available to Gordon, his map of Scotland is a disappointment. One might have expected an improvement on Mercator's map of 1595, but Gordon's outline of Scotland is markedly less accurate in many respects, although the interior is much improved and more detailed and the number of place names vastly increased. The more noticeable errors are the shape of Lewis, with its flat top, the distortion of the north coast, and the bend in the Great Glen, all features copied by cartographers for the next ninety years. In place of Mercator's 'Cape Wrayght or Faro head', Gordon has only 'Farro Head', and so Cape Wrath disappears from the maps of Scotland for a century. Here Gordon was apparently misled by Pont's manuscript of the north coast which ends just west of Durness with an unfinished line going NNW to 'Faro Head'. By taking this line as the western end of the north coast, Gordon cut off the north-west corner of Scotland, although part of it is shown on another of Pont's manuscripts and a more accurate outline is given in the engraved map of 'Strathnavern', which shows the coast extending westward beyond Faro Head. The westerly distortion of Galloway is not reconcilable with the separate maps of Galloway and Ayrshire; and the region of Arisaig and Morven in 'Scotia Regnum' is less accurate than in the map of the Hebrides—or even in Gordon's own map of 'Braid-Allabain' Only Kintyre and Duncansby Head are a marked improvement on Mercator. Possibly Gordon, still working under pressure from Blaeu, did not have copies of all the regional maps beside him for comparison when he drew his map of Scotland. His letter to Scot refers to a period 'When I lay hidden in distant lands and far from home you procured me the favour of great and renowned friends, who helped me, and by exhortation urged me to this work', and this absence from home—neither date nor place is known—may explain some of the discrepancies. The map is graduated for latitude and longitude, overall more accurately than Mercator, but the latitudes do not coincide with those of the regional maps.

THE REGIONAL MAPS

Out of 46 regional maps, 36 are attributed to Pont, three are by Robert Gordon and one (Fife) by James Gordon. There is evidence elsewhere that other two (Lothians and Orkneys) are by Pont, and he is certainly the author of the map of Lewis and Harris, as his name appears on the smaller scale map of the Hebrides. The separate maps of East and West Fife are presumably both by James Gordon; the remaining map, Sutherland, is attributed to the Earl of Sutherland by Blaeu in one of his letters. Latitudes are marked on five maps: 'Lothians' and 'Orkneys' by Pont; 'Aberdeen', and 'Extima Scotiae' by Robert Gordon; and 'Fife' by James Gordon. James Gordon says that the latitudes in the maps of Lothian and the Orkneys are Timothy Pont's. If that is so then Pont was remarkably accurate in his calculations as his latitudes are more accurate than the latitudes in the maps of Scotia Regnum, Extima Scotiae, and Fife. For example, Pont has 55°46' for Edinburgh, and Gordon 56°12'—the correct latitude is 55°57'. Even more remarkable is the northernmost point in the Orkneys—59°24' according to Pont against the correct figure of 59°23'. The coverage of Scotland is very uneven. Out of 46 regional maps 29 cover southern Scotland and Fife, 9 the Hebrides and Orkneys, leaving only 8 maps to cover central and northern Scotland, more than half the country. The reason is apparent from the correspondence quoted above; 40 maps had been completed between 1631 and 1642 from (presumably) the more legible manuscripts; a large part of Scotland was still to be covered and Blaeu was anxious to publish the *Atlas*, so Gordon, having prepared maps of Aberdeen and Moray, completed the work by two smaller scale maps covering central and northern Scotland ('Braid Allabain' and 'Extimae Scotiae').

In what was presumably the first lot of county maps to be engraved (southern Scotland), different symbols distinguish churches, castles, mansion-houses, villages or 'farm-towns', hamlets, mills, woods and policies, the difference in the shape of some of the symbols e.g., in 'Teviotia' and 'Mercia', suggesting a different engraver. Other maps vary in the use of symbols, e.g., in 'Carrick' the symbol for a mansion-house is much used, but in 'Kyle' a small circle is in greater use. 'Braid-Allabain', one of the later maps, shows haste in the engraving, as a small circle suffices for everything except a few towns. This is not found in the maps of English counties in Volume IV of the *Atlas*, all of which show a considerable use of different symbols.

The loss of so many of the Pont manuscripts, and the lack of any proofs of the maps, make it impossible to arrive at any precise knowledge of the extent of Gordon's work, but judged from the years he spent on it, and the large number of his manuscript maps which have survived, it was substantial. The dating of the information contained in the engraved maps presents some difficulty. Pont made his surveys around 1585 to 1600, so that where the maps (probably the Hebrides and most of southern Scotland), were engraved by Blaeu direct from Pont's manuscripts they reflect the same period. Where the maps were based on drafts prepared or revised by Gordon they may include information up to 1647, so that these maps reflect a period half a century later than the earlier ones. It has been shown by J. C. Stone that the engraved map of 'Aberdeen and Banff' has 12 place names which are neither on Pont's nor Gordon's manuscripts;[41] presumably they were added by Gordon when checking the engraved proof and some of them may indicate new buildings.

E

6 French Cartographers

The first French cartographer of note was Oronce Finé of Briançon who, in the early 16th century, published four separate world maps and a map of France. Nicolas de Nicolay (see Chapter 3) drew maps of several parts of France between 1560 and 1583, and contemporary with him were several French geographers and cartographers, whose work was largely confined to the mapping of France and French provinces, represented in the atlases of France, *Le Théâtre Françoys* by Maurice Bouguereau in 1594, and the *Théâtre Géographique du Royaume de France* of Melchior Tavernier in 1634. Then came the period of Dutch supremacy, and it was only when Dutch maps began to go out of date, and Janssonius and Blaeu were becoming less active, that the initiative in the production of new maps passed to the French. Even then the Dutch map publishers prolonged their hold on the market by copying and publishing in Amsterdam maps by the French cartographers, Sanson, Jaillot, and De L'Isle.[1]

NICOLAS SANSON

A century of French pre-eminence in cartography was begun by Nicolas Sanson (1600-67), who has been named 'the father of French cartography', and 'the founder of geography in France'. Born in Abbeville, he moved to Paris in 1627, and with the publication of a map of ancient Gaul attracted the attention of Louis XIII, who appointed him 'Géographe ordinaire de Roy'. Sanson's atlases were not made on the systematic method of the Mercator and Blaeu atlases; they were collections of maps, frequently without a title page, and with varying contents. Sanson's first atlas, with 100 maps (the earliest dated 1632), was issued in 1654; a second, with 113 maps, in 1658 had a title page, *Cartes Générales de Toutes les Parties du Monde*, and a list of contents; later issues had 147 and 181 maps. Sanson also issued small quarto-size atlases separately for Europe, Asia, Africa, and America, and published in all some 300 maps, as well as a number of geographical works.[2]

Sanson was primarily a geographer, always testing his material for accuracy and bringing a more scientific approach to cartography; his maps are more reliable, if less ornate, than the Dutch maps and less crowded with place names; the work of his engravers is invariably clear and neat. His maps were widely esteemed and were copied by Dutch, German, and English publishers. In his first map of the British Isles, issued in 1641, Scotland was based on Mercator's map of 1595. In 1665 he published a new map of the British Isles and his first maps of Scotland alone: (1) 'L'Escosse Royaume', a single sheet map on the scale of *c.* 30 miles to an inch, and (2) 'L'Escosse deça le Tay' and 'L'Escosse dela le Tay', two sheets covering Scotland on the scale of *c.* 14 miles to an inch. The larger map is described in the cartouche as 'tirées de toutes les Cartes particulières qu'en ont faict Timothee Pont, Robert Gordon à Straloch, etc.', and numerous differences between Sanson's map and Gordon's map of 'Scotia Regnum' show that Sanson prepared a new and better outline based more on the county and regional maps in Blaeu's *Atlas* than on Gordon's map. The influence of the regional maps is seen particularly in the coastline of Galloway and of the Moray Firth, but in adopting Gordon's inaccurate north coast from 'Extima Scotiae', and the misshapen island of Lewis, for lack of other sources of information, Sanson unwittingly perpetuated errors which were prominent features of maps of Scotland for almost a century. He gave a slightly better orientation to Scotland, but still left Aberdeenshire too far to the east. His latitudes show a difference between north and south Scotland more correct than Gordon's map. It has been said of Sanson that he worked with too much haste and this may explain the omission of Isle of May, the Bass, and Ailsa Craig, and the many misspellings of the place names often quite unrecognizable, which also show the substantial use of the regional maps.

After the death of Nicolas Sanson in 1667, the business was continued for a time by his sons Guillaume and Adrien but they soon transferred the management of it to Alexis Hubert Jaillot (*c.* 1632-1712), who had trained as a sculptor and later developed an interest in maps and engraving. He published his first map in 1669, and was appointed 'Géographe ordinaire du Roy' in 1675. With the large amount of material left by Nicolas Sanson, he began about 1677 to revise the original maps and prepare new ones on a larger scale, with the titles in large cartouches, keeping always the name of Sanson on the maps, and describing his large atlases, first issued in 1681, as *Atlas Nouveau, contenant toutes les parties du Monde . . . par le Sr. Sanson.* The greater accuracy of these up-to-date maps gave them a wide sale; they were copied exactly in every detail and sold as Sanson maps and atlases with the Paris address on the title page, by Pieter Mortier, map publisher in Amsterdam from about 1690 onwards, and some English publishers either copied the maps or used them as a basis for their own maps because of the Sanson reputation. The title of the *Atlas Nouveau* was changed to *Atlas Francois* in 1695, with 115 maps. Jaillot was also the publisher in 1693 of *Le Neptune Francais*, a volume of marine charts prepared in cooperation with J. D. Cassini and other members of the French Académie des Sciences.

Jaillot's map of Scotland with the title 'Le Royaume d'Escosse . . . presenté a Monseigneur le Dauphin par le Sr. Sanson, Géographe du Roy', has additional text at the top: 'Dressé sur les memoires les plus nouveaux par le Sr. Sanson . . . à Paris, chez H. Jaillot'. In fact Jaillot, although adopting Sanson's outline in general, has compiled his map from the regional Pont-Blaeu maps and produced a map which follows the originals more closely and quite noticeably in the shapes of the lochs, the lines of rivers, more forests, the addition of the Isle of May and Bass Rock, and with numerous differences from the Sanson map. The slightly larger size of the map—about 13 miles to an inch as against Sanson's 14 miles— has allowed Jaillot to add more place names taken from Blaeu's regional maps, many of them, as in Sanson's map, misspelt by the engraver. The map is on two sheets; curiously, the southern sheet has lines of longitude on a conical projection and the northern sheet on a cylindrical projection. Some copies of the map are dated 1696, others are undated; as it was copied by the Dutch publishers De Wit, Allard and Visscher, it must have been issued not later than 1680. After Hubert Jaillot's death in 1712 the business was continued by his son Bernard (d. 1739), and his grandson, also Bernard (d. 1749), and then by others until 1780, all of whom continued to publish the atlases but with no new maps.

Contemporary with the Jaillots were two other French cartographers who produced maps of Scotland, Nicolas de Fer, and Jean Baptiste Nolin. Nicolas de Fer (1646-1720), published a large number of maps and several atlases from 1693 onwards, but although he was appointed 'Géographe du Roi' his maps were noted more for their profuse ornamentation than for their geographical accuracy. His map of Scotland is merely a distorted version of Sanson's map on a smaller scale.

Jean Baptiste Nolin (1657-1725), engraver in Paris, published several atlases and very decorative maps, mostly based on the work of other cartographers. One of these, Padre Vicenzo Maria Coronelli, Cosmographer of the Republic of Venice, obtained a privilege to publish his maps in France and transferred this to Nolin under an arrangement to supply Nolin with drawings. Nolin's map of Scotland 'Le Royaume d'Escosse', on the scale of *c*. 13 miles to the inch, has on it a statement that it was drawn by P. Coronelli, with corrections and additions by Nolin based on the work of

Sieur de Tillemon, the pseudonym of a French geographer, Jean Nicolas de Tralage. The map has nothing original; it is in fact based on Sanson's map of 1665. It is dated 1689 and has a dedication to James, Prince of Wales; a later issue dated 1708 has this altered to James III, King of England, Scotland and Ireland (when Queen Anne was on the throne). Nolin also published a smaller map, 'Royaume d'Ecosse', on the scale of c. 40 miles to an inch.

SCIENTIFIC CARTOGRAPHY

For over fifty years the maps of French cartographers and engravers were largely based on the work of Nicolas Sanson, who had taken much of his material from the maps of the Dutch cartographers. Then in the latter part of the 17th century the French took the lead in the application of a more scientific basis to cartography, first by the development of methods for the more exact calculation of the latitude and longitude of places on the earth's surface, and later, in the 18th century, by their progress in the technique of triangulation.

It had been relatively simple from early times to calculate the latitude of any place as the equator provided a definite base-line midway between the poles; meridians, however, which run from pole to pole, are indistinguishable and no reliable method had yet been found of measuring the east-west distances. Ptolemy had chosen the Canary Islands (the westerly limit of the known world) for the prime meridian; the Dutch map-makers chose, at one time or another, the Canary Islands, the Azores, the Cape Verde Islands, and the Peak of Teneriffe. In 1634 Louis XIII of France by decree fixed the island of Ferro (now Hierro), the most westerly of the Canary Islands, and this was generally adopted until, for British maps, it was replaced by the meridian of London from 1676.

French scientists now studied this problem of longitude. The Académie Royale des Sciences was founded in Paris in 1666 for the purpose of astronomical observations and their applications to the problems of geography and navigation, and in the preparation of maps and charts. Here Jean Dominique Cassini (1625-1712), a distinguished Italian astronomer who had been encouraged to transfer his studies to Paris, decided that calculations by reference to the movements of Jupiter's satellites provided the surest method of determining longitude.

Great attention was also given to an alternative method, sometimes known as 'transport of chronometers'. By comparing local time, with the time on a clock showing Paris meridian time, the longitude east or west of this meridian could be calculated. (A difference of one hour equals approximately 15° longitude.) However it was not until late in the 18th century that a sufficiently accurate and sturdy chronometer was perfected by John Harrison (see Chapter 9). Other problems which occupied the astronomer-surveyors were the figure of the earth, and the length of a terrestrial degree. To solve these, French expeditions were sent to Lapland and to South America.

The French also gave their attention to a more accurate mapping of France. The method of survey by triangulation had been described in a book by Gemma Frisius, a Flemish mathematician, in 1533, and this had been put to practical use in a survey of Bavaria by German surveyors around 1560.[3] It was recognized that triangulation was the only method which would result in correct mapping, and in 1669 the astronomer Abbé Jean Picard made a start on the triangulation of France by measuring, by means of triangles, an arc of the meridian passing through Paris, using a greatly improved quadrant. A new survey of France from this base line, and a new map published in 1693, showed so much alteration from older maps of France that a complete triangulation of France was begun in 1733 by Jacques Cassini and his son Cesar François Cassini, Comte de Thury (son and grandson of Jean Dominique). The large and very detailed map prepared from this survey, the 'Carte de Cassini' comprised 182 sheets on the scale of 1 : 86,400 = 1 inch to 1·36 miles.[4]

The work of Jean Dominique Cassini and his fellow scientists was put to practical use by Guillaume De L'Isle (1675-1726), who had studied under Cassini. De L'Isle's influence on Scottish mapping was indirect, as he produced only a small map of Scotland, but with his maps in general he set new standards of accuracy, basing his maps on the latest reliable information he could obtain, so that he became outstanding both as a geographer and cartographer. In 1702 he published a map of the British Isles; it is described as 'England taken from Speed; Scotland taken from Timothy Pont, and Ireland from Petty, the whole corrected from various observations'. Even with the small scale of the map the outline of Scotland is seen to be a considerable improvement on Blaeu, Sanson, or Visscher; the longitudes are more accurate, and the island of Arran has the north-south axis last found in Mercator's map of Scotland and in the 1635 map of Blaeu.

De L'Isle was succeeded by his son-in-law Philippe Buache, who (following the example of a Dutch engineer) showed depths on his charts by under-water contours; later French engineers applied this method to heights on land. Not all the French cartographers sought to emulate De L'Isle; in 1746 Georges Louis le Rouge (d. 1778), a military engineer, published a map 'L'Écosse', on the scale of 10 miles to the inch, described as 'according to the new observations published in London in 1735 by Bowles'. (Bowles was a London map publisher.) It is in fact a close copy of Visscher's map, with occasional mistakes in the small circle indicating the hamlet or village. Le Rouge also issued a smaller map 'Le Royaume d'Écosse', scale *c*. 35 miles to an inch.

ROBERT DE VAUGONDY

The Sanson tradition was continued by Gilles Robert de Vaugondy (1688-1766), who inherited the cartographic material of the Sanson family, and by Gilles' son, Didier (1723-86), who became a partner with his father not long after 1740. Sometimes the name on the map is simply 'par le Sr. Robert' or 'M. Robert'; where the names of both are given the form is usually: 'Par M. Robert, Géographe ordinaire du Roy et par M. Robert de Vaugondy, son fils, Géographe ordinaire du Roy'. Their *Petit Atlas* was first issued in 1748; an *Atlas Portatif* in 1748-49. Their *Atlas Universel* completed in 1757 with 103 maps has a lengthy preface concerning the geography of the various countries, and a chapter on projections, which indicate the extensive researches they had made to obtain accuracy in their maps.

The *Atlas Universel*, the result of seven years work, has a map of Scotland 'Le Royaume d'Écosse divisé en Shires ou Comtes' on the scale of *c*. 16 miles to the inch, dated 1751. Of it Robert says in the preface: 'We have availed ourselves for Scotland of the new map published in 1745 by Mr. Elphinston: we did not have in time the one which appeared five years later in four-and-a-half sheets and in two sheets by Dorret, engineer of the Duke of Argyll. But the comparison we have made of the two maps has shown the former to conform well enough, with only a few corrections required for the map we publish.'

Jacques Nicolas Bellin (1703-72), who became Hydrographer to Louis XV, and a Fellow of the Royal Society of London, was responsible for the production in the Department de la Marine of maps and charts for the use of the French navy and merchant shipping; these included an *Atlas Maritime* in 1751, volumes and charts of all known coasts throughout the world, and several smaller atlases and geographical works. Bellin's larger map of Scotland dated 1757 is merely part (two sheets) of his five-sheet 'Carte Réduite des Isles Britanniques', (included in his *Hydrographie Française*), sheet 3 being 'Partie Méridionale de l'Écosse', and sheet 4, 'Partie Septentrionale'. The map, which is on the scale of 11 miles to an inch, is obviously taken from James Dorret's map of 1750, with more emphasis on the coastline and only a selection of the place names because of the smaller scale (and some oddities in the selection). Bellin's smaller map of Scotland appeared in his *Essai géographique sur les Isles Britanniques* in 1757 and in his *Le Petit Atlas Maritime* in 1764.

Two small maps of Scotland were published by Rigobert Bonne (1727-94); his *Atlas Moderne ou Collection de Cartes*, included his 'Carte du Royaume d'Écosse' dated 1771, on the scale of 37 miles to an inch; on it he describes himself as Mathematics Master. On a later and slightly larger map, the 'Carte d'Écosse', which appeared in his *Atlas Encyclopédique* published in 1788, he is described as 'Engineer-Hydrographer of the Navy'. Both maps are based on Dorret's map.

Other small maps of Scotland published in Paris in the later part of the 18th century, and all based on Dorret's map were: (1) 'L'Écosse' on the scale of 35 miles to an inch, with a description of Scotland forming columns of text on each side of the map, by M. Brion = Louis Brion de la Tour (*c.* 1768-1823), engineer and geographer to the King, in 1766; (2) 'Isles Britanniques—Quatrième Carte—Écosse', scale 34 miles to an inch, engraved by P. F. Tardieu. Small maps by J. D. Barbié du Bocage (1790), and by E. A. Philippe de Pretot (1770), give very poor representations of Scotland.

In 1783 Cesar François Cassini de Thury, then responsible for the triangulation and mapping of France, proposed to the Royal Society of London that a trigonometric survey should be made between London and Dover to connect with the French survey, and so establish exactly the difference in latitude and longitude between the observatories of Paris and Greenwich. The English survey carried out by Major-General William Roy in 1787 for this purpose was followed in 1791 by the establishment of the Ordnance Survey of Britain and the beginning of a complete triangulation of the British Isles (see Chapter 10).

7 German Cartographers

The map production which flourished in Germany in the 15th and 16th centuries began in 1472 when the earliest printed map, a crude diagrammatic woodcut representing a world map, appeared in a book. It was followed in 1475 by the first printed regional map, a map of Palestine, and then in 1482 by an edition of Ptolemy's *Geographia* printed in Ulm. In 1492 a notable globe was made at Nurnberg by Martin Behaim before the discovery of America and therefore showing the apparently short distance between the Azores and the East Indies.[1]

The German cartographer, Martin Waldseemüller (who first named the new world America), has already been mentioned in connection with the maps he prepared for an edition of Ptolemy's *Geographia* published at Strasbourg in 1513. Sebastian Munster's edition of Ptolemy, published at Basle in 1540, contained a new map 'Anglia: Nova Tabula' (extending north to Edinburgh), obviously derived from the 'Gough Map' or a variant of it.

In 1563 Philip Apian prepared a map of Bavaria after a six-year survey in which he applied the elementary form of triangulation described by Gemma Frisius. And although Mercator belongs to the Netherlands it was at Duisburg that he published his best works: the map of Europe in 1554, the map of the British Isles in 1564, his map of the world on Mercator's projection in 1569, and the first edition of his famous *Atlas* in 1595. At Cologne between the years 1572 and 1617 Georg Braun and Frans Hogenberg published in six volumes over 360 plans and views of towns, the *Civitates Orbis Terrarum*, although it was mainly the work of Flemish engravers.

Then came the century of Dutch supremacy, and only when the age of the great masters of Dutch cartography had passed was there a revival in Germany, notably in Nurnberg, where engraving had been recently established. Johann Baptist Homann (1664-1724) first did work as an engraver and cartographer for other publishers (his first map was engraved in 1690), and then set up his own publishing office in 1702. His maps had soon a large sale and in 1707 he produced his first Atlas, the *Atlas Novus*, of 40 maps, including one of Great Britain. Several atlases followed, including his *Grosser Atlas*, first issued in 1716 with 126 maps, and expanded in later editions. In 1715 Homann was appointed Geographer to the Emperor, Charles VI.[2]

Most of Homann's maps were copied from Visscher, Sanson, De L'Isle, and others, sometimes acknowledged on the map, sometimes not; but at the same time he understood the need for a correct scientific basis for his maps, devoting considerable time to research, as well as making use of the research of others, and incorporating this in some new maps of Germany and of the continents. He was the first German cartographer after Mercator's time to carry on systematically the production of maps and atlases. Bagrow says 'Homann ranks next in greatness to Mercator among German cartographers, for he contributed much to the development of German regional cartography and published atlases of the highest quality'.[1]

His map of Scotland, 'Magnae Britannia Pars Septentrionalis qua Regnum Scotiae . . . accurate tabula ex archetypo Vischerano desumta exhibetur imitatore Johan Bapt. Homann', is an almost exact copy of Visscher's map, including the style of lettering and the positioning of the place names; even the two elaborate cartouches are copied with only minor differences. One mistake in the copying is that Visscher's Pert (Perth) is Fert in Homann. Unlike Visscher, Homann does not have lines of latitude and longitude across the map, though the same figures as in Visscher's map are noted in the border. The main difference between the two maps is in the delineation of the hills and mountains; the shading in Homann's being much lighter. At least two states of the map are to be found; an early one with no mention of privilege and one 'cum privilegio', published after 1729, the year when the privilege was obtained.

Homann died in 1724 and was succeeded by his son Johann Christoph Homann (1703-30), who bequeathed the business to his brother-in-law, J. G. Ebersperger, and his friend J. M. Franz, on condition that it was carried on under the name of 'Homannische Erben' (Homann's Successors), and in this name it continued the publication of atlases until the beginning of the 19th century.

Matthäus Seutter (1678-1756), born in Augsburg, learned map engraving under Homann in Nurnberg, and on returning to his native town set up his own business there shortly after 1707. His output was noted for quantity rather than quality; a catalogue of 1748 lists some 330 maps, town plans, etc., and by 1760 the number had increased to nearly 500 items. He made up several atlases from his maps; an *Atlas Geographicus* in 1725 with 46 maps, an *Atlas Novus* which eventually had 292 maps, a *Grosser Atlas* expanded in later years to two volumes, and several special and regional atlases. Although most of the actual maps were engraved by Seutter himself, the decorative work was usually done by other engravers, some of whom also engraved the maps, especially in Seutter's later years.[2]

Seutter's maps were mostly copied from the Dutch and French cartographers, in style and size closely following Homann. The map of Scotland 'Nova et accurata, totius Regni Scotiae, is a copy of Visscher's map, similar to Homann's map but with 'Pert' copied correctly. It has a new cartouche with the title and new panel with the scale; the lettering is in general bolder, and the mountains are more clearly defined, but copied less exactly, with the result that breaks occur here and there in a line of hills. The lines of latitude and longitude omitted by Homann in his copy have been restored; the map has on it the name of And. Silbereysen an engraver. The title of the map includes mention of Seutter as Imperial Geographer, an honour conferred by Emperor Charles VI about 1740; 'cum grat. et priv.' dates it after 1740-42, when the privilege was granted.

Seutter died in 1756 and left his business to his son Albrecht Carl and his two sons-in-law, one of whom, Tobias Conrad Lotter, born in Augsburg in 1717, continued the Seutter business until his own death in 1777, when his son Matthäus Albrecht continued it for a time. The two Lotters were content to repeat the old maps without improving them in the light of the more scientific principles of cartography now widely accepted. Lotter reissued Seutter's map of Scotland, substituting his own name in the form 'Tobiae Conradi Lotteri' in the title.

THE 19TH CENTURY

In the 19th century German cartographers gave the lead in the construction of thematic maps to show the distribution of natural phenomena. The geographer, Carl Ritter, in 1804-06, supplemented his geographical textbook on Europe with six maps dealing with products, inhabitants, and physical geography. In 1812 the volumes by Alexander von Humboldt relating to his travels and studies in America were accompanied by an *Atlas geographique et physique du Royaume de la Nouvelle Espagne*, with maps to illustrate the distribution of natural phenomena.

Humboldt communicated his ideas to Heinrich Berghaus (1797-1884) for 'an atlas of the physical geography, somewhat after the style of the attempts I made in the Atlas relating to my travels'. Berghaus, born at Cleve in 1797, founded in 1839 a school for cartography and geography at Potsdam, and after working on the maps from 1827, issued in sections over the years 1837-48 his famous *Physikalischer Atlas*, designed 'to portray lucidly all important phenomena in the sphere of geophysics'. The *Atlas*, when complete, had 93 maps covering meteorology and climatology, hydrography, geology and terrestrial magnetism, plant geography, zoological distributions, anthropology, and ethnography. This atlas greatly influenced A. K. Johnston of Edinburgh (see Chapter 12) in the development of atlases of physical geography. Another contribution to cartography was made by Adolf Stieler (1775-1836), working at Gotha, where he produced a map of Germany in 85 sections and several atlases, and between 1816 and 1828 issued the 56 sheets of the first edition of his *Hand-Atlas*, which proved immensely popular and was expanded and kept up to date by successive issues.

The development of this atlas was mainly due to Augustus Petermann (1822-78), who had trained at the geographical school of Berghaus at Potsdam, and then spent two years, 1845-47, in Edinburgh assisting A. K. Johnston in the preparation of his *Physical Atlas*. From 1847 to 1854 Petermann lived in London and in 1850 produced an *Atlas of Physical Geography*. In 1849 he published a map of the British Isles showing the distribution of the population on the basis of the 1841 census, and in 1852 similar maps of England and of Scotland based on the 1851 census, as well as a cholera map of the British Isles. In 1854 Petermann was invited by the firm of Perthes of Gotha, publishers of the Stieler *Atlas*, to become director of their geographical institute, where he developed the atlas and founded *Petermanns Geographische Mitteilungen*.[3]

8   John Adair

In the year 1680 or early 1681, John Adair, mathematician in Edinburgh, was asked by Moses Pitt, bookseller in London, to prepare maps of Scottish counties for a *Great Atlas* in 12 volumes of which Pitt had already published two volumes. Adair applied to the Scottish Privy Council for financial assistance, 'as', he said, 'a revision of Blaeu's maps was very necessary and there must be a survey of all the shires, which could not be done without much expense and much time', and as evidence of his ability to do the work he submitted to them his new map of Clackmannanshire. The Council, on 4th May 1681, gave Adair authority 'to take a survey of the whole shires of the Kingdom, and to make up mapps thereof, describing each shire, royal burgh, and other towns considerable, the houses of the nobility and gentry, the most considerable rivers, lochs', etc. They appointed a committee to give him instructions from time to time, promised to pay him £100 over two years out of fines imposed by them, and asked the nobility, gentry, sheriffs and burghs to give him every encouragement and assistance.[1]

Adair then printed an 'Advertisement anent the Surveying of all Shires of Scotland and making new mapps of it', to announce that he was now engaged on the map of West Lothian, and would shortly proceed to survey Mid Lothian and East Lothian, and invited all the nobility and gentry, magistrates and clergymen, all learned, observing and curious persons to send information on a great variety of subjects to him at the Post Office in Edinburgh.[2]

The year or place of birth of Adair, and what surveying he had done before 1681, are unknown; the only earlier reference to him is in 1676 when he (along with John Ogilby, author of the road book *Britannia* published in 1675) was with Robert Hooke, curator of experiments at the Royal Society, in London.[3] Assuming that Adair was by this time at least 25 years old, this would give the year of his birth as 1650 or earlier.

Adair at first made rapid progress with the county maps, judged by the dates on the surviving maps. He began with West Lothian in 1681, then surveyed and made maps of Mid Lothian and East Lothian, the latter completed in 1682. 'The Mappe of Orkney' is also dated 1682, though this does not seem to have been from an actual survey by Adair.

But his arrangement to provide Moses Pitt with maps was soon stopped. Sir Robert Sibbald (1641-1722), a Scottish physician and botanist, had plans for a geographical description of Scotland, and through the influence of his patron, the Earl of Perth, was appointed a physician to King Charles, and 'His Majesty's Geographer for Scotland', and by his patent, dated 30th September 1682, was authorised to prepare a geographical description and to compile maps. Sibbald thereupon issued in 1683 'An Account of the *Scottish Atlas or the Description of Scotland, Ancient and Modern* ... to be published presently by Sir Robert Sibbald', in which he announced that the King had commanded him to publish an exact description of Scotland with maps 'and, that the maps may be exact and just, the . . . Privy Council in Scotland gave commission to John Adair, mathematician and skilful mechanic, to survey the shires'; and that Adair 'by taking the distances of the several angles from the adjacent hills, had designed most exact maps . . . and hath lately made an Hydrographical Map of the River of Forth geometrically surveyed . . . and he is next to survey the shire of Perth, and to make two maps thereof, one of the South side, and another of the North'.[4] The *Atlas* was to have about seventy maps, one edition with Latin text, another with English text. The statement that Adair was commissioned to survey the shires in order to prepare maps for Sibbald's *Atlas* is misleading; Sibbald's patent prohibited anyone else from publishing maps except with Sibbald's permission, but Adair's commission preceded Sibbald's appointment by well over a year. As will be seen later, Adair's association with Sibbald was not a happy one. Sibbald's work was published in 1684 with the title *Scotia Illustrata sive Prodromus Historiae Naturalis*; it had no maps.[5]

Soon came the first sign of the financial difficulties which were to handicap Adair throughout the rest of his life; in 1682 he was in debt to merchants and failed to meet their bills on the due dates.[6] He continued his surveys, completed 'The Hydrographicall Mappe of Forth', and also 'The Mappe of Straithern, Stormont & Cars of Gourie', both dated 1683. 'The East Part of Fife' is dated 1684; 'A Mapp of the Countrie about Stirling', 1685, and the 'Firth of Clyde', 1686. A general map of the south-west of Scotland, from the Solway to the Clyde, is dated 1686, but this is not the result of a survey, as the Solway coast and features in Galloway so resemble Pont's 'Galloway' that Adair has obviously copied it. His own survey of the Solway coast was not made until 1695. In May 1686, he complained to the Privy Council that out of the £100 promised in 1681 he had received only £50 in 1682, and asked for payment of the balance as he had been engaged on the surveys since 1681 with great expense.[7] The Council ordered the Treasurer to pay the outstanding £50 and then, in the following month, the Scottish Parliament passed an 'Act in favour of John Adair, Geographer' to provide for, firstly, a charge of 1s Scots per ton on all Scottish vessels, and 2s per ton on all foreign vessels, entering Scottish ports (1d and 2d sterling), for defraying the cost of hydrographical surveys, these being 'most necessary for navigation and may prevent several shipwrecks' and, secondly, instructions to the sheriff of each county to collect money from the owners of property at the request of John Adair when he came to make a survey of their county, adding that 'one or two knowing men in each parish' were to be appointed to go along with Adair to help him in making his survey; and finally, when the maps and charts were completed, the Privy Council was recommended to have them printed.[8]

What prompted Adair to embark on surveys of the coast is not clear. It could have been the difficulties over county maps with Sir Robert Sibbald which came to a head later, or the more urgent need for accurate coastal charts and the apparent ease of financing their cost through the tunnage dues, but Adair must have known at this date (1686), of the coastal survey of Britain in progress since 1681 under Captain Greenvile Collins, unless he assumed that Collins would confine his survey to the coasts of England.

Promptitude in carrying out the instructions of Parliament was not a feature of the time and in September 1686 we find Adair complaining to the Privy Council that the collectors of customs were slack in exacting the tunnage dues, which the masters of ships were generally unwilling to pay. The Privy Council thereupon gave instructions that the Act was to be enforced so that John Adair 'be not frustrat in what was allowed to him'.

Adair's next step, in the summer of 1687, was to visit the Netherlands to examine the work of engravers and the methods of printing maps;[9] he did not return until February 1688, when, at the Council's request, he induced James Moxon, an engraver, to return with him. Moxon in fact engraved only one map, which is dated 1688, a copy of Nicolay's map of 1583 of the coastline of Scotland; either lack of money or delays in getting drafts of other maps made Moxon leave Edinburgh for London, and the rest of Adair's maps for his *Description of the Sea Coast* (not published until 1703), were engraved by James Clark, an engraver employed in the Scottish Mint in Edinburgh. Adair had, when passing through London in February 1688, no doubt renewed his contacts with those interested in maps; he was elected a Fellow of the Royal Society on 30th November 1688.[10]

In February 1690 Adair again appealed to the Privy Council saying that he had spent over £300 sterling, had surveyed the Firths of Forth, Clyde and Tay and brought from abroad instruments of great value, but by the negligence of the Collectors had received hardly one-third of this sum. On examining his progress and his maps, the Council reported that he had drawn charts of the Firths of Forth, Tay and Clyde, with their adjacent coasts; that they had also seen maps of eight counties already drawn, with several parts of other counties, and that they had requested Adair to change the dedication of some of his maps. Collectors were again instructed to collect and hand over the dues, but they in turn petitioned the Privy Council for powers to make the skippers and landed proprietors pay. And so it went on.

In the next year, 1691, Adair was freed from any commitment to prepare maps for Sir Robert Sibbald. In a petition to the Privy Council Adair said that he was obstructed and hindered from carrying out surveys and preparing maps 'by the envy, malice and oppression of Sir Robert Sibbald who, upon pretence of a private pact and contract, exorted from (him) by Sir Robert, contrary to the public interest of the nation and in manifest defraud of the Act of Parliament and Act of Council, took the petitioner bound not to survey any shire or part thereof nor to enter into any other conditions or bargains for surveying and making up maps of any shire or part of the same without the said Sir Robert his general advice and consent and he should not give copies of these maps to any other person without the said Sir Robert his special permission and that under a severe penalty . . . and the said Sir Robert neither can nor will meet the expenses . . . '. Sibbald, in his *Autobiography*, says that he employed John Adair for surveying and paid him a guinea for each 'double' of the maps he made; that Adair got much money from the county people and an allowance from the public funds; yet he, Sibbald, received nothing except one year's salary of £100 sterling as the King's physician.[11] The Privy Council, having examined the contract between Sibbald and Adair, declared Adair free from it, instructed him to proceed with the maps notwithstanding this contract, and commanded Sibbald not to impede Adair in any way.

Through this dispute Adair had lost valuable years. He could not resume his arrangement to supply maps to Moses Pitt, as Pitt was bankrupt, and in 1689-91 in prison for debt after publishing only four volumes of his *Atlas*. A new proposal in 1691 to get 600 or 700 subscriptions for county maps of £1 each brought less than £100, not enough to proceed with the engraving.

In August 1692, six years after passing of the Act to finance Adair from 'tunnage' levies, the Privy Council, reporting on his progress, found that he had completed charts of the east coast from the Scarheads to Buchanness, and of the Forth, Tay and Clyde, in ten separate maps, and all that he had received from the 'tunnage' money for his expenses and travel in six years had not exceeded £120 sterling, although his expenses had exceeded twice that amount. He had also completed 12 county maps: two of East Lothian, one each of Midlothian, West Lothian, Stirling and Menteith, Clackmannan, Perth, the lowlands of Angus, two of Fife, a map of southwestern Scotland and another of Cunningham and Renfrew, and for all this he had so far received only £50 of the £100 promised him in 1681. His outlay in instruments expressly made for this work had alone been nearly £100, and he had paid £70 to Mr Moxon, the engraver he had brought from Holland, besides all the expenses of himself and a servant in surveying. By all this, Adair said, he 'hath broken his fortune, lost his time and run into debt'. It would cost at least £700 sterling besides the engraving, to complete and publish the county maps, but if he could have £200 now, the county maps of the Lothians (three), Fife (two), Stirling, Perth, and Clackmannan, and all the ten charts could be ready for the engraver by the end of the year (1692).[12] The Privy Council appointed a committee to consider ways and means of meeting Adair's expenses but little was achieved, as two years later, in July 1694, Adair, in making another request for money, said that the Act of 1686, which imposed a charge on owners of property, had never been put into force, and what he had spent (£200), was three times more than he had received from the tunnage levy. A committee appointed to consider his claim reported in November 1694, that he had ten coastal charts 'which are most exact and useful for navigation, describing many errors upon the coasts whereby ships have been frequently lost', and ten land maps finished, and another four land maps almost ready, and these 24 maps would make up the first volume of the *Scots Atlas*. Engraving would cost £10 per map, paper for 500 copies £150, printing £80, plus £100 already paid for printing press and copper plates, made a total of £570. As Adair had already spent £300 more than he had received, the committee proposed to take more stringent action to collect the tunnage money.

In April 1695, Adair again appealed for funds as he planned a survey that summer of the coast and country of the Solway Firth. In an effort to meet Adair's outlays, Parliament in July 1695, increased the 'tunnage' levies from 1s to 4s Scots on Scottish vessels and from 4s to 16s Scots (4d and 1s 4d sterling) on foreign vessels, but they introduced a complication by deciding that the amount collected was to be shared between Adair and Captain John Slezer, a Dutchman long settled in Scotland, who had published a volume of views of Scottish towns, colleges, castles, and other buildings under the title of *Theatrum Scotiae*.[13] This had exhausted his own money

F

and he now asked the Privy Council to meet the cost of a second volume.

In December 1695 Adair made still another appeal for payment, saying that he had nine sea charts ready which, with their descriptions, would make up the first part of the work. As only four of the charts had been engraved (one by James Clark is dated 1693) the sum of £200 sterling would soon be necessary for engraving the other five, buying paper and printing them with their descriptions; if this sum were paid before the middle of January, Adair said, he would undertake to have the first part printed and published by Whitsunday (May) 1696. The Privy Council Committee accordingly signed an order in February to the Collector of taxes to pay £200 to Adair (and £100 to Slezer).

In the summer of 1696 he was surveying on the west coast, i.e., the Firth of Clyde. In August when making another petition for payment of his outlays, he began to show his impatience with the Privy Council: 'it is thought very hard, that John Adair should spend so much of his time, undergo so much travel and hardship, yea, and frequently run the hazard of his life, and only get back his bare disbursements, and that not without difficulty; and truly he hath met with so much trouble, debate, and groundless clamour in this affair already, not only from strangers but also from those concerned in the Act, that if such methods be not taken as may free him from that hereafter, and let his work go . . . he is most willing to resign his interest in the Act'. In December he was again pressing for payment and reported that, on the advice of members of the Royal Society, he had ordered a large quadrant to be made in London which would cost over £80, and that the set of large printing letters and part of the paper had arrived from abroad; the Privy Council thereupon ordered payment to him of £378 10s sterling.

Adair spent the summer of 1697 in surveying the approaches to the Clyde. The following winter was again occupied in claims for payment; the skippers of Borrowstounness and Queensferry had complained that the levy was too heavy as the Scottish ships had made great losses during the war, to which Adair replied that all he had received from the tunnage was £200, and explained the delay in publishing: 'the only stop of publishing that part is want of more hands to engrave, a fault not to be laid at John Adair's door'. Adair does not say why Clark could not engrave all the maps as they were finished. Captain Slezer also appealed for some payment to himself 'having brought himself and his family to trouble' and said that Adair had received more than he admitted and that he had not kept his promise made in December 1695, when he received the £200 he requested, that he would have the first volume ready by

May 1696. All Adair had to do, said Slezer, was to send the drafts to London and he could have had 300 volumes printed nearly two years ago for less than £150. At a later date Slezer claimed that Adair had got £628 out of the tunnage from November 1695 to January 1698 without publishing 'one sheet of his pretended atlas'.

In February 1698 the Privy Council investigated the claims of Adair and Slezer and found that Adair had prepared charts of the east coast from Sunderland Point to Buchanness, including the Firths of Forth and Tay, the rivers at Montrose and Aberdeen, and of the Firth of Clyde from Ailsa to Bute, together with maps of the three Lothians, Stirling, Clackmannan, Fife, Strathearn, and the Carse of Gowrie, some parts of Angus, Ayr, Renfrew, and Clydesdale, and that his total outlays to date, including the cost of instruments, printing press, copper plates, letters, engraving, and paper, had been £16,727 Scots of which he had at different times received £10,215.

His statement of expenditure included these payments in respect of maps, charts, instruments and other items (in Scots pounds: 12 = £1 sterling):

Two maps of East Lothian	£340
A map of Midlothian	320
A map of West Lothian	260
A map of Stirlingshire	340
A map of Clackmannanshire	160
Two maps of Fife	600
A map of Strathearn, Stormount & Carse of Gowrie	460
A general map of the West of Scotland	400

(He added a note that great parts of several shires—Angus, Ayr, Renfrew and Clydesdale, had been surveyed.)

A second list covered his sea charts:

1. A map of the coast from Sunderland Point to St Abbs Head	£300
2. A map of the Firth of Forth to Queensferry	560
3. A map of the River Forth	110
4. A map of the River and Firth of Tay	320
5. A map of the coast from Red Head to Aberdeen	260
6. A map of Aberdeen and the adjacent country	160
7. A map of the Town and Water of Montrose	140
8. A map of the Firth of Clyde from Ailsa to Bute	300
9. A general map of the coast from Sunderland to Buchanness	—
10. A general map of the coast and islands of Scotland (cost of engraving Nicolay's map)	88

His expenditure also included:

1. A telescope—16 feet long   £72
2. A large azimuth compass for navigating the Isles   160
3. Mathematical instruments   900
4. Journeys to the Meikle Bin above Kilsyth, the hills above Dumbarton, Saline Drum, and the Ochil Hills   130
5. Journeys 'to several great hills towards the west sea to make observations for joyneing the mapps of the west and east coasts'   120
6. Paper and ink from Holland for the 'Description'   1700
7. A small printing press   130
8. To Moxon the engraver brought from Holland by the Council's order   800

Other expenditure included the cost of the ten months' visit by Adair to London and Holland to buy the instruments, and examine the work of engravers and the methods of printing maps, at a cost of £1000; and the expenses of Adair and his servants in surveys over six summers. Against a total expenditure of £16,727 Adair had received £10,215 6s, from fines and tunnage dues, leaving a sum of £6511 14s, owing to him. (The sterling equivalents are £1394 payments, £851 receipts: balance £543.)

The figures for receipts and payments are somewhat confusing. In another petition Adair states that before February 1698 he had received £7,536 Scots (£628 sterling), but confirms that the amount due to him at 15 February 1698 was £6,511 Scots.

Adair's plans for 1698 were to finish the survey of the Firth of Clyde and then survey the Western Isles 'being that part of the work most desired by seamen'. His estimate of £450 (sterling) for the cost of the Western Isles survey was accepted by the Privy Council, which gave instructions in February 1698 that this sum (and also £100 to Captain Slezer) should be set apart from the available tunnage dues, but as these amounted to only £608 3s, the Council said that Adair could get nothing of the arrears owing to him until his return from the west coast, by which time more money would have come in from the tunnage. The £450 was not forthcoming in May, but 'so forward was Mr. Adair to pursue the voyage that he borrowed the money and went off with the first fair wind' (most of this sum seems to have been paid by August 1698).

He hired a ship, the *Mary* of Leith, and with a Highland pilot, six seamen and a doctor, spent the summer of 1698 on surveys of the west coast of Ross, Skye, and the Western Isles from Lewis to Uist. When Captain Slezer later alleged that he had charted an unnecessarily large vessel, Adair contemptuously replied that Slezer 'understands no more of shipping or sea affairs than a shepherd', for no seaman who ever was in those seas and saw the dangers would say that they were to be attempted in anything but a vessel of good size. Even with the ship they had, they were three times driven ashore through storms, 'but the Captain who sits at home knows nothing of such trouble and hardships'. The total cost of the survey was £518 8s, including £195 for hire of the *Mary* of Leith, and £42 for his family's expenses for six months; from it Adair prepared *A Journal of the Voyage made to the North and West Islands of Scotland, by John Adair, Geographer, in the year 1698* consisting of fifteen full pages, seven charts and two sheets of views of the coasts. These were to form Volume 2 of his work, but were never published. (In 1723 they were all handed over to the Exchequer by Mrs Adair.)

Adair returned over the hills of Ross to Inverness and Edinburgh, and to more disappointments over finance. In March 1700, when submitting an account of his expenditure in the 1698 voyage to the Western Isles, he pointed out that although a year and a half had passed since he returned he had still received nothing of the earlier balance of £542 7s sterling due to him, so that the summer of 1699 had been lost, and if the money were not provided the summer of 1700 would also be lost. Another year passed with no progress; in a petition in March 1701 he said that since he returned at the beginning of November 1698, three years ago, during which time he could have finished a true survey of the whole coast and islands, he could never get any part of what was due to him, except £20 sterling, nor one sixpence from the fund to carry on his work, notwithstanding the many applications he had made for payment. His claims to what money was available were disputed by Captain Slezer, each submitting memoranda urging his own claims and disputing the other's claims; Captain Slezer, in pressing his claims, pointed out that in November 1694 Adair had said that he had 10 sea maps and 14 land maps ready with the related descriptions almost exactly done, but when in February 1698 Adair gave the Privy Council an account of his work, it appeared that no progress had been made since November 1694. Adair's reply to this was that the money promised in 1694 had never been received as the fines had never been exacted, except in the counties of Edinburgh and Inverness, and even then all the money collected hardly paid the charges of collection.

In 1701 Adair proposed, if the arrears were paid, to proceed with the survey of the Solway Firth and coasts of Galloway, and evidently did so (then or later) as four charts of these coasts are on a list dated 1713. In his *Scottish Historical Library* published in 1702, Bishop Nicolson records that the first volume of Adair's surveys was ready and that 'in the second part he designs us an instructive journal of a voyage he made to the North and West Islands in the year 1698; several of the maps intended for this are now ready for engraving, and the rest in good forwardness'.[14]

At long last, in 1703, appeared *The Description of the Sea Coast and Islands of Scotland*, a volume containing the general chart of Scotland, dated 1688 and engraved by James Moxon; along with five larger scale charts of the east coast from Sutherland Point to Aberdeen, engraved by James Clark. The general chart of Scotland is merely a copy of Nicolay's map of 1583, adopted by Adair because (he said) 'it cannot be expected that the author should make a general map of the Kingdom before he had occasion to survey the several parts'.

The publication of this volume seems to have encouraged Parliament; Adair's work was inspected and he was ordered to finish the sea maps first and the land maps after, and in August 1704 they passed another 'Act for an Imposition on Foreign Ships that come into this Kingdom, for bearing the charges of finishing the maps and *Description of the Sea Coasts and Isles*, etc.', the money now increased to 12s Scots = 1s sterling per tun, to be used for various purposes including payments to Adair for his finished maps and for his expenses in completing his charts and descriptions of the coast and islands, and his land maps, the imposition to be in force for five years, but again Adair was only to have a share in the money and not the whole of it.[15] They found that from August 1695 to August 1698 the total tunnage collected had been £21,339 Scots, of which Adair had received £12,840 = £1070 sterling, and Slezer £4800, but they could not get reliable figures from 1698 to 1703. Writing in or about 1704 Adair said that even if the £7000 due to him were paid he would still have no payment for his own time and work. Difficulties were still experienced in collecting the tunnage money and when Adair tried himself to organize the collection of the levies he was no more successful.

In August 1706 he was surveying the coasts of the Shetlands.[16] He was apparently there again in a later year as his manuscript chart of the Orkney and Shetlands has a note 'magnetic variation 11 degrees West', which could apply to a year as late as 1715.[17] The Union of the Parliaments in 1707 ended both the Parliament and the Privy Council of Scotland, and also reduced the income from tunnage dues as English ships were no longer classed as 'foreign'. The Collector of the dues at Irvine reported in 1711 that since the Union 'none pay'd excepting one of whom I had 4 shillings; the rest refused absolutely alleadging that by the Treaty they had the same privilege of navigation here as in England'.[18] Some time after this Adair applied to the Admiralty in London, and in a letter of 2nd June 1713 to the Secretary of State, the Earl of Mar, indicated his progress and his problems:[19]

My Lord
    I had the Honour of yours, and as your Lordship required, An account of the surveys, I have made, or drawn, out of the Coast, and Islands of Scotland (which are not printed) is sent; The Surveys of the South and West coasts and Firth of Clyde, are in the greatest forwardness, an so wil require the least time, and expence to finish them.   They are very necessare for carrying on trade, and with the discriptions wil make a compleit part or Volume, which in my humble opinion, wil pleas better, and be of greater use, than the publishing separated maps.
    My Lord Ther is a considerable sum of Debursed money resting as wil appear by precepts of Privy Council, and Thesauring and stated accounts, And I never had one farthing for pains, which the Parliament, did truly consider, and designed a full recompence as appears by their Act the 26 of August 1704, But the English and Irish Ships, after the Union, not paying the dewty then imposed, all was frustrated; However if the Government shall think fit, to appoint a fund to finish the part above proposed, I shal let all my claims stand, til that be done.
    And as to the Survey of ye West and North West Islands, The Islands of Orkney and Zetland, which wil require the constant attendance of a good vessel and pinnance, if these be furnished by the Government and a suitable number of seamen to manadge them, my proper expence will not be great.
    My Lord, I never doubted of the Subscriptions for the Survey of Clackmannanshire, and Country about Stirling, but having gone to East Lothian, about the end of March, to Finish some work I had on hand there, the weather in April proved so very cold, that soon after I was attacked in my right arm, and hand, by a Rhewmatick pain, which not only hindered my being West long agoe; but also this returne which in all dewty should have been made sooner; I am now much better, so shal set about the work with all diligence, and doe my best to recover any time that is lost.

I hope your Lordship wil pardon this from
My Lord Your Lordships most Humble and most
Obedient Servent   John Adair.

Along with the letter he gave a detailed list of 19 coastal charts not printed; these were six from his 1698 voyage (five of parts of

North Uist, Harris, Lewis, Scalpa, Canna and Rum, and the coast of Wester Ross, and one of part of Orkney); five of the coast from Aberdeen to the River Spey; three of the Firth of Clyde coasts; four of the Solway Firth coasts, and a general map of the coast from Carlisle to the Clyde; but of these 19, only 14 were 'drawn out', the other five being described as only 'surveyed'. He said that the map of the coast from Carlisle to the Clyde could not be finished until Arran, Bute, Kintyre, etc., had been surveyed, and this would require the help of a sloop and pinnace for four or five months. The Clyde volume of eight charts could be finished in 12 months at a cost of £600 sterling; another volume with charts of the coast from Aberdeen round the Moray Firth could be ready in five or six months at a cost of not more than £250 sterling. He added that considerable progress had been made in the survey of the Orkneys and Shetlands which could not be put on paper until the rest were surveyed, but owing to the bad and dark weather he could not estimate the time required nor the cost.

In March 1714 he is described in a document relating to Customs establishments in Scotland as 'Geographer for Scotland'.[20] Illness affected his work in the following year—he was probably now in his sixties—as Alexander Pennecuick's *A geographical and historical description of the Shire of Tweeddale*, published in 1715, contains a note saying that the map of Tweeddale was not ready by reason of Adair's indisposition and inability to travel owing to severe gout, but that he intended to do it as soon as his hands and feet were again capable of a survey of the county, and describing him as 'the best and fittest geographer to make a survey'. As no copy of this map exists it was presumably never completed. His map of the north of Scotland, the Orkneys and Shetlands, which might be as late as 1715, has already been mentioned. What seems to have been his last work is a rough map of southern Scotland, not so neat as his earlier work, undated but on it is recorded the battle 'Sheriffmuir 1715'; noticeable are the differences in the Solway coast from his earlier map of 1686. He died in the Canongate, Edinburgh, on 15th May 1718; the only asset recorded in his will being 50s sterling still owing to him for tunnage dues. His rival for the tunnage money, Captain Slezer, fared no better; he died in the Abbey of Holyrood, a sanctuary for debtors.

Mrs Adair, after much difficulty, and only as the result of a personal visit to London in 1723, obtained a Government pension of £40 per annum on condition that she handed over to the Exchequer Office in Edinburgh all her husband's maps and papers.[21] The 'Inventory of the Maps and Papers delivered by Jean Adair, Relict of Mr. John Adair, Geographer, F.R.S., to the Right Honble the

Barons of Exchequer, in pursuance of a Warrant from the Lords Justices, dated 21st June 1723', comprises 39 items:

Printed—11 maps: (1-6) in the *Description of the Sea Coast*, published in 1703; (7) Strathearn, Stormount and Carse of Gourie; (8) Turnings of the Forth; (9) South of England/English Channel; (10) Nova Scotia Tabula (in Buchanan's *History*); (11) Parish of Tranent.

Manuscripts—28 maps: (12-20) *A Journal of the Voyage made to the North and West Islands of Scotland in 1698*, and accompanying charts; (21) Firth of Clyde; (22) Solway Firth; (23) South part of Galloway; (24) Aberdeen and adjacent coast; (25-27) three maps of the inland counties of south-central and south-west Scotland; (28-33) 6 manuscripts of the charts printed in the *Description* in 1703; (34) Map of West Lothian; (35) Clackmannan; (36) Mouth of Don and part of coast at Aberdeen; (37) Galloway coast at Whithorn; (38) Clyde at Greenock and Port Glasgow; (39) Brassa Sound and Island.[12]

Mrs Adair certified this was a complete account of every map and survey left by her husband, and that she had not given away any, or any copies, since his death. It is presumed that all the maps and charts which she deposited in the Exchequer Office were destroyed in a fire there in 1811.[22] Some of the manuscript maps which have survived are not in her list, e.g., the maps of Mid Lothian and East Lothian and the draft of the map of Scotland engraved in 1688, and must have left Adair's hands during his lifetime. There is always the possibility that some may have been extracted from the Exchequer Office between 1723 and 1811, but when it is noted that most of the surviving maps relate to the earlier years 1681 to 1689 there is a possibility that these are the duplicate maps which Adair provided at a guinea each to Sir Robert Sibbald, until the arrangement was stopped in 1691. As there are twice duplicates amongst the surviving maps Adair may well have made others.

Adair achieved little in relation to the thirty years he spent on his surveys. He was unfortunate in being dogged by financial difficulties almost from the start, and this delayed his work time and again. He was also unfortunate in his connection with Sir Robert Sibbald, whose contract bound Adair from 1683 to 1691 not to give copies of his maps to anyone else and who paid him only one guinea for each map. The failure to get enough subscribers to pay for county surveys was a complaint to be echoed by other surveyors a century later. What is not clear is why Adair made so little progress with the engraving of his maps and charts. His expenditure in 1687-8 in spending ten months in London and the Netherlands in buying plant and paper, and in bringing Moxon the engraver from Holland, shows an ambition or an optimism which was not justified. Adair was evidently more interested in using the money for actual surveys than in the engraving and publication of the maps and charts and seemed to want first to make a complete survey of the coasts of Scotland. Slezer was not unreasonable in saying that all Adair had to do was to send the drafts to London and get them engraved there, but sending them to London was even unnecessary when James Clark was available in Edinburgh. The charts published in 1703 show that Clark was capable of excellent work, and it is strange that Adair did not have more engraved by him—or did Clark have to wait too long for payment for his work? The accuracy of the maps and charts which have survived show that more money spent on engraving would have produced a much greater contribution to the mapping of Scotland.

9 English Cartographers

The art of engraving was introduced into England in the middle of the 16th century and the first map engraved by an Englishman was a map of Palestine in 1572 by Humphrey Cole, a maker of mathematical instruments. About the same time a young Yorkshire land surveyor, Christopher Saxton, was engaged by Thomas Seckford, an official at the court of Queen Elizabeth, to make a survey of England and Wales; for his assistance the Privy Council issued a warrant instructing the local officials that he was to be 'conducted into any towre, castle, highe place or hill to view that countrey, and that he may be accompanied with ii or iii honest men, such as do best know the countrey, for the better accomplishment of that service . . .'. The survey took nine years and the result was the publication between 1574 and 1578 of 34 superb county maps; in 1579 a map of England and Wales, a frontispiece portrait of Queen Elizabeth, and an index were added to form the first county atlas of England and Wales and the first atlas of the kind for any country. Some of the maps were by English engravers; others by Protestant Flemish refugees who had settled in England and made a distinctive contribution to the development of engraving in England. Later editions of the atlas with various alterations on the map plates appeared at intervals over the next century, and the plates, without text, were last reprinted about 1770.[2]

Saxton's method of surveying and the instruments he used are not recorded, but he no doubt knew the principle of triangulation, first described forty years earlier, and there was available to him a textbook in English published in 1571 by Thomas Digges, *A Geometrical Practise named Pantometria*, which described surveying, determination of longitude, compass variation and mathematical instruments, including an early form of the theodolite.[2]

WILLIAM HOLE

The first map of Scotland to be engraved in England was by William Hole, a well-known portrait engraver who flourished 1600-46, for inclusion in the 1607 edition of Camden's *Britannia*, the first edition with maps; it contained maps of England, Scotland and Ireland—all based on Mercator's maps of 1595—and 54 maps of English and Welsh counties, most of them based on Saxton's maps. The map of Scotland ($10\frac{1}{4} \times 12\frac{3}{8}$ inches; scale about 33 miles to an inch), is copied from Mercator's one-sheet map of 1595, but is more crudely drawn, and has fewer place names. The maps were reprinted without text on the back in the English editions of 1610 and 1637 which now had the title of *Britain*. An abridged Latin edition of *Britannia* in 1617 had four small maps covering Scotland which are described under Blaeu; a re-issue of the same text in 1639 had three by Salomon Rogiers (see Chapter 4).

JOHN SPEED

The second county atlas of England and Wales was the work of John Speed (1552-1629), historian and antiquary, who in 1611 published in London *The Theatre of the Empire of Great Britaine*, a volume of maps which formed the first part of his *The History of Great Britaine*. The title page is dated 1611, but the date 1612 appears on two later pages. The *Theatre* contains 67 maps of which 56 are maps of English and Welsh counties; the others include a map of Scotland dated 1610. Speed based his county maps mainly on the earlier maps of Saxton, and others, but revised by Speed from his own travels throughout the country. The maps were engraved in Amsterdam, some by Jodocus Hondius, some by his assistants, but all the printing was done in London.

Speed's map of 'The Kingdome of Scotland', is a close copy of Mercator's two-sheet map of 1595, even to the extent of placing 'Grampian Mountains' alongside Loch Ness, on practically the same scale (*c.* 20 miles to an inch), and with a few additional place names and changes in spelling. In panels on each side of the map are the figures of King James and Henry, Prince of Wales (on the left), Queen Anne and the Duke of York (on the right). The popularity of the atlas called for frequent reprints, with new dates on the map of Scotland in 1650 and 1652, the latter having figures of a Scottish man and woman and a Highland man and woman, in place of the Royal figures, as being more appropriate in the Cromwellian era. The last edition of the *Theatre* as such appeared in 1676; the map plates thereafter passed through several hands but no later issue of the map of Scotland can be identified.

In 1627 the publishers of the *Theatre* issued a pocket edition: *England Wales Scotland and Ireland described* by John Speed, with 63 maps. Six maps of parts of Scotland are printed from the plates engraved by Pieter van den Keere in the years 1599-1605 (see Chapter 4), which had been used by Willem Blaeu in his 1617 edition of Camden's *Britannia* and later acquired by Speed's publisher. For the 1627 issue the titles were re-engraved in English (e.g., 'Scotiae pars Orientalior' on the original plate was altered to

'The Eastern part of Scotland'), and a new map added 'The Kingdome of Scotland' on the scale of 80 miles to an inch, based on Speed's larger map. This atlas was re-issued several times up to 1676.

About 1670 John Overton (1640-1713), printseller in London, published an atlas of maps of the British Isles, with county maps of England and Wales mostly supplied from the plates of Speed or Blaeu, but with a new plate 'The Kingdome of Scotland', an exact copy of Speed's map without date or imprint and without the panels of portraits on each side. Overton also copied Frederik de Wit's map 'Scotia Regnum' and issued it with the title 'The Kingdom of Scotland divided into the North and South Parts'.

RICHARD BLOME

The Dutch pre-eminence in map production in the first half of the 17th century, with the French later entering the field with the maps of Nicolas Sanson, left little scope then for the development of cartography in England. In 1673 a new period of activity began with the publication of *Britannia or a Geographical Description of the Kingdoms of England, Scotland and Ireland*, by Richard Blome (d. 1709), a publisher and compiler of illustrated books. He drew on existing publications to a large extent in compiling the books; *Britannia* has been described as 'a most entire piece of theft out of Camden and Speed', the former for text and the latter for the maps.[3] Its 50 maps include 'A Mapp of the Kingdome of Scotland', a somewhat crudely drawn copy of the map in Speed's *Theatre*. Blome also published *Speed's Maps Epitomiz'd*, a volume of maps of the English counties on a smaller scale than in *Britannia*; and *A General Description of the Four Parts of the World* (1670) based on Nicolas Sanson's works.

Britannia was also the title given by John Ogilby to the first road book of England and Wales published by him in 1675. Before this date roads had not been shown on maps of Scotland (except on two county maps in Blaeu's *Atlas* of 1654), but Ogilby's work brought out the importance of roads and in 1679 'A New Map of Scotland with the Roads', on the scale of 13 miles to an inch, was published by Robert Greene (fl. 1674-85), mapseller in London. Apart from the roads it is copied from Sanson's map of 1665, with the Isle of May, Bass and Ailsa Craig added; the place names are substantially from Sanson, with a few more added from Blaeu's maps. The roads shown are in the south and east of Scotland; although too generalized to give the exact line of the road, they serve to indicate the routes of the main highways of the period.

ROBERT MORDEN

A new edition of Camden's *Britannia* published by Edmund Gibson in 1695 contained 50 maps by Robert Morden, geographer, cartographer, and mapseller in London from about 1650 until his death in 1703. The maps of English counties were based on earlier maps of Speed; the map 'Scotland', is a close copy of Robert Gordon's 'Scotia Regnum' in Blaeu's *Atlas*, even to the place names, their position on the map and the style of lettering. Morden also published an *Atlas Terrestris*, and *The New Description and State of England* in 1701, the latter having 55 maps of England and Wales smaller than those in *Britannia*.

Morden began a new development in geographical textbooks with the publication of *Geography Rectified* in 1680. The second edition in 1688 contained maps, including a small map of Scotland 'Scotiae Nova Descriptio', on the scale of *c.* 70 miles to an inch. The same map appeared in later editions, and also in Patrick Gordon's *Geography Anatomiz'd or The Geographical Grammar*, first published in 1693.

JOHN SELLER

A small map of Scotland by I. (i.e. John) Seller, on the scale of *c.* 60 miles to an inch, appeared in Seller's *Atlas Terrestris* about 1689, in his *A New System of Geography* in 1690, and again in his book *Camden's Britannia Abridged* published in 1701. John Seller (fl. 1658-97), cartographer, mapseller and instrument maker, was appointed Hydrographer to the King, and in 1671 published *The English Pilot*, a volume of marine charts. Some of the charts were printed from old Dutch plates bought by Seller, others were copied from Dutch charts, but the volume met a demand and numerous later editions appeared with altered or new plates.

GREENVILE COLLINS

The need for a proper survey of the sea coast of Britain was apparent, and in June 1681 Captain Greenvile Collins, an experienced naval officer, was chosen by the King to make the survey. The Admiralty provided a vessel, and Charles II promised substantial financial assistance. Samuel Pepys, then Secretary of the Navy, was instrumental in Collins being made a Younger Brother of Trinity House. The work, frequently held up through lack of the promised financial help, continued until 1688, and the results were published in 1693 in *Great Britain's Coasting Pilot*, with charts of the entire coast of England, a few of Irish harbours, one general chart and eight detailed charts of the east coast of Scotland from Berwick to the

Orkney and Shetland Islands, 48 charts in all. Two of the Scottish charts have the date of engraving, 1688 and 1689; on the chart of the approaches to Dundee is engraved 'The Sea Coast from Fiffnesse to Montros was Surveyed by Mr. Mar, an Injenious Marriner of Dundee'. Although the charts came under some criticism for inaccuracy, 11 later editions of *Great Britain's Coasting Pilot* were issued, the last in 1792.[4]

HERMAN MOLL

An entirely new map of Scotland, with an outline differing from all previous maps, was published in 1714 by Herman Moll (fl. 1678-1732). The date and place of Moll's birth are unknown; he is generally described as of Dutch origin and is first mentioned in 1678 as associated in London with Moses Pitt, who was then engaged on his project of a world atlas.[5] Two of his early maps signed 'H. Mol' appear in *A New System of Mathematicks* by Sir James Moore in 1681. A chart engraved by him for Greenvile Collins *Coasting Pilot* is dated 1686, and in 1688 he engraved John Adair's map of 'The Turnings of the Forth'. He had therefore considerable experience of engraving and of maps before he began his own publications with a textbook *A System of Geography*, issued in 1701 with 43 maps, including a small map of Scotland on the scale of *c.* 50 miles to an inch.

Moll was very industrious and with his great output of maps and atlases from Devereux Court in the Strand had by far the largest share of the English market in the first quarter of the 18th century. His atlases include: *Atlas Manuale*, with 43 maps (1709); *Atlas Minor*, with 62 maps (1729); *A New and Compleat Atlas*, with 27 maps (1708-20); *The World Described*, a large atlas with his largest maps, 30 two-sheet maps each about 23 × 39 inches (1709-1720); frequent re-issues are indicated by changes in the names of the publishers. In 1724 he issued *A New Description of England and Wales*, a county atlas of 50 maps, in 1720 a county atlas of Ireland, and in 1725 a county atlas of Scotland; and added to all this the production of many separate maps and many smaller maps for book publishers.

His best and largest map of Scotland, on a scale of 12½ miles to the inch, has the title 'The North Part of Great Britain called Scotland, with Considerable Improvements . . . According to the Newest and Exact Observations', by Herman Moll, Geographer, 1714. The map is dedicated to John, Earl of Marr, one of her Majesty's Principal Secretaries of State. The map is flanked by views: (left) Aberdeen, Edinburg Castle, Sterling Castle, Dunotyr Castle, The Bass, Channery Town, (right) Edinburg, Glascow, St. Andrews,

Sterling, and Montrose, all copied from Captain John Slezer's *Theatrum Scotiae* (published in 1693), with minor changes.

Moll's map, though still far from accurate, gives a much better outline of Scotland than in the maps of Gordon or Sanson. The north coast has been improved and the far north-west corner extended to include Cape Wrath, even if still named Faro Head; the west coast is considerably straightened, and Arran is given its correct north-south axis instead of east-west as shown by Blaeu and Sanson. But the Gordon-Blaeu shape and position of Skye and the Western Isles are substantially maintained, with some alterations in their shape, whilst the north-east region of Aberdeen and Banff is much too contracted. Moll made no personal surveys, so far as known; he says in his county atlas of Scotland, that he made use of 'Gordonius a Straloch, Tim. Pont, and John Adair, late Geographer for Scotland, who surveyed the coast'. The north coast of Scotland in Moll's map, quite different from the maps based on the Gordon-Blaeu outline, bears so much resemblance to one of Adair's manuscript charts than even without this acknowledgment it is clear that Moll had obtained some of the information for his map from Adair.[6] Their association dates certainly from 1688, when Moll engraved Adair's map of the River Forth, and probably from an earlier date as both had associations with Moses Pitt in London. So much of Adair's manuscript material has not survived that we cannot tell whether Moll owed much or little to Adair; curiously, Moll did not take the outline of the east coast from Adair's printed charts—nor from the charts published in 1689 by Greenvile Collins in his *Great Britain's Coasting Pilot*. The place names on Moll's map were taken from the regional maps in Blaeu's *Atlas*, the choice sometimes falling on names of little importance. There were several editions of the 1714 map printed in London, and at some date after 1727 George Grierson, a map publisher in Dublin, copied the map, exact in every detail except that the illustrations in the panels on each side of the map were engraved and printed in reverse.

Although Moll's outline of Scotland is best seen in his large map of 1714, the same general outline on a much smaller scale (43 miles to an inch) appeared in a map 'The North Part of Great Britain by Herman Moll' which was included in a volume *Fifty Six new and accurate Maps of Great Britain* published in 1708. Moll's new outline of Scotland can therefore be dated not later than 1708. Another small map of Scotland by Moll on the scale of *c.* 29 miles to an inch was first issued in 1718.

Moll's county atlas of Scotland, *A set of Thirty Six New and Correct Maps of Scotland Divided into Shires*, published in 1725, has a short description of Scotland by John Adair, a small map of

Scotland on the scale of 29 miles to an inch, a map of 'Scotia Antiqua', and 34 small maps of counties or parts of counties, most of them about $10\frac{1}{2} \times 7\frac{1}{2}$ inches. The maps in a second edition of the atlas in 1745 had roads added.

Moll's map of 1708 was the basis of 'A New Mapp of Scotland' by Sutton Nicholls about 1710. 'A New Mapp of Scotland' by Thomas Taylor in 1715 was a close copy of Moll's map of 1714; these both had roads, with mileages, shown as straight double lines between the main towns. The demand for maps at this period led to more copying: 'A New Map of Scotland according to Gordon of Straloch, Revis'd and Improv'd by I. Senex, 1721', was actually copied from Visscher's map; and a map on two sheets by Andrew Johnston in the 1722 edition of *Camden's Britannia* is a copy of Senex's map even to the note that many place names are added from Blaeu's county maps (although more place names seem to have been omitted than added). Robert Gordon's map of 1654 was also the basis for a military map (still in manuscript) of Scotland prepared in 1731, on the scale of $6\frac{1}{2}$ miles to an inch, by Clement Lempriere, a draughtsman at the headquarters of the Corps of Royal Engineers at the Tower of London: 'A Description of the Highlands of Scotland, the Situation of the Several Clans . . . as also the Roads of Communication'. It gives the numbers of men in 31 clans, inset plans of Fort William, Fort Augustus, and Fort George, and the military roads made by General Wade; only a few towns are named. Although based on the Gordon-Blaeu map, Arran is given its correct north-south axis, the north-east region of Aberdeen and Banff is more accurately drawn, and, notably, for the first time the Great Glen is shown correctly as a straight line.[7]

JOHN COWLEY

The substantial differences in the outline of Scotland between the maps of Gordon, Adair (i.e., his 1688 version of Nicolay's map), Moll, Inselin of Paris, Sanson, and Senex, were illustrated by John Cowley on his map of 1734 entitled 'A Display of the Coasting Lines of Six General Maps of North Britain shewing the Disagreement among Geographers in their Representations of the extent and situation of the Country'. It was accompanied by a pamphlet by Cowley, *An Explanation of Four Several Maps*, in which he comments on the substantial differences of latitude shown by these six geographers in respect of certain prominent coastal features, differences up to 60 miles in the position of certain places and even the best far from accurate in latitude or longitude, or in the outline of Scotland. He points out that Nicolay's 1583 map of Scotland (re-published by Adair in 1688), was more accurate than any of the

G

six later maps.[8] Cowley himself prepared another map with the title 'A new Map of North Britain, with the Islands thereunto belonging', with latitude and longitude shown, on the scale of approximately 20 miles to an inch. For this map Cowley prepared a new outline of the west coast from Ayrshire to Skye which was based partly on Adair's survey of the Firth of Clyde and partly on a map made for the Duke of Argyll from recent estate surveys of Ardnamurchan and Loch Sunart. For the rest of Scotland Cowley took his coastline from the Nicolay map of 1583, i.e., the 1688 edition in which Adair had added lines of latitude. For all Cowley's claims his map is not an overall improvement on Moll's map of 1714, and it still has the bend in the Great Glen copied from earlier maps.

The misshapen outline of the north coast of Scotland which had appeared on the Gordon-Blaeu map of Scotland in 1654 and on numerous later maps, was finally corrected by the Rev. Alexander Bryce, minister in Thurso, who made a survey (with three assistants) at the request of the Philosophical Society of Edinburgh.[9] His map, based on a series of triangles and on observations in the years, 1741-2, was published by the Society in 1744 with the title 'A Map of the North Coast of Britain from Row Stoir of Assynt to Wick in Caithness by a Geometrical Survey'. This map finally cleared up the confusion which had persisted for two centuries about the most north-westerly point in Scotland, which in some maps had been called 'Faro Head' and in others 'Cape Wrayght (Wrath) or Faro Head'. Bryce showed that there were two capes: Faro or Farout (modern Faraid) Head, and seven miles west of it, Cape Wrath, and so corrected a distortion which had affected so many earlier maps.

JOHN ELPHINSTONE

A military engineer, John Elphinstone, was responsible for a considerable improvement in the map of Scotland with his 'A New & Correct Mercator's Map of North Britain', on the scale of $13\frac{1}{3}$ miles to an inch, engraved by T. Kitchin, and published in London on 6th March 1745 by A. Millar, who dedicated it to the Duke of Cumberland. John Elphinstone, born in 1706 in Midlothian, was the eldest son of the 9th Lord Elphinstone. In 1743 he published a map of Great Britain (the Scottish part is rather inaccurate), and in 1744 entered the Corps of Royal Engineers as a Practitioner Engineer (= P. Engineer on his map), the year in which he published a 'Map of the Lothians' based on Adair's surveys. He was with the Duke of Cumberland in 1746 at Culloden, when he prepared a plan of the battle; he died in 1753.[10]

On the map faint lines indicate the main differences from the maps of Moll and Senex. A note on the map says: 'As the Geography of this map differs greatly from all others hitherto published; it's necessary to observe that the Authorities for the Alterations are Mr. Adair, Sr. Alexr. Murray of Stanhope, Captn. Bruce, Willm Edgar, Alexr Bryce, and Murdoch Mackenzie, &c., so that it must be as correct as possible till a New Survey of the Whole is made . . . The Projection is Mercator's or Wright's and due Regard is had to the Oblate Spheroidical Figure of the Earth without wch all maps however just in other particulars are faulty. This being the first attempt that I know of to correct an Error of projection which affects above ⅔ of the Globes Surface'.

This map shows a considerable improvement on earlier maps. The north coast is based on Bryce's map of 1744, the east coast from Berwick to Aberdeen on Adair's printed charts, and the Clyde and south-west Scotland probably on one of Adair's manuscript maps. The reference to Murray of Stanhope is to Cowley's map of 1734; Bryce published a plan of Loch Sunart in 1733; and William Edgar was responsible for a map of Peeblesshire in 1741 and for some manuscript maps of small parts of the Highlands. Murdoch Mackenzie began a hydrographic survey of the Orkney Islands in 1743, but, though he may have helped Elphinstone, the Orkney Islands in this map are based on the chart of Greenvile Collins. Elphinstone's west coast shows some improvement on Moll, although still far from accurate; whilst Skye and the Hebrides are taken from Blaeu's map of a century earlier because no proper survey had yet been made there. Curiously, Elphinstone still shows the bend in the Great Glen, although Lempriere in 1731—and presumably other military engineers on the spot—knew it as a straight line. A second issue of the map, still dated 1745, has the battlefield of Culloden (1746) marked.

Elphinstone's map was severely criticized by one of his contemporaries, Thomas Jefferys. 'The projection of a land map should certainly be drawn according to the gradual declension of the meridians; but Mr Elphinstone's being made on Mercator's projection, which was designed merely for sea charts, the whole surface of Scotland is distorted, and the geography needlessly confounded. His longitude from Fero and Paris are both computed wrong; the former is a degree too much, and the latter a degree too little . . . The making his longitude from Paris preferable to London is a gross absurdity in a map representing part of an island where London is the metropolis'.[11] The map is more accurate than the criticisms suggest; the longitude is generally a degree too far east, but this is fairly consistent over the map and not an unusual error at that time; latitude on the other hand is remarkably accurate, with errors usually of only one or two minutes, except for the north coast, where he has taken the latitudes from Bryce's map with its errors of nine and ten minutes. The map has other errors: Selkirkshire is misnamed Roxburghshire, many rivers are nameless and two wrongly named. Possibly some of the errors were due to the inexperience of the engraver, Thomas Kitchin (then aged 27); this was the first of many maps of Scotland engraved by him, and Elphinstone's larger map (below) does not have these defects.

Elphinstone prepared a much larger map in 1746 on the scale of 7 miles to the inch: 'A New Map of North Britain done by order of the Duke of Albemarle', who was appointed Commander-in-Chief in Scotland in August 1746. This is still in manuscript (in the British Museum), never having been engraved. Numerous improvements can be seen in the map, especially the north, but the west coast, Skye, Lewis and the Great Glen are still the same as in his map of 1745; lines of longitude are on the meridian of London. The island of Eigg, correctly placed south-east of Rum in his 1745 map, is now placed, incorrectly, north-east of Rum. At the top of the map are illustrations of the Castles of Edinburgh, Stirling, Dumbarton and Blackness, a view of the Corriyarick Pass and a plan of the battle of Culloden; and in a large decorative cartouche with the title are Lists of the Highland Clans in Rebellion and of the Clans who were for the Government, accompanied by figures of Lord Lovat and of a Highland chieftain, both in chains.

EMANUEL BOWEN

Emanuel Bowen (fl. 1714-67) engraver and printseller in London, had the distinction of holding appointments as Geographer to George II of Britain and as Engraver to Louis XV of France. His large output included *A Complete System of Geography* covering the whole world in two volumes extending to over 2000 folio pages, with 70 maps. In *The Large English Atlas* (1760 and later editions), and *The Royal English Atlas* (c. 1763 and later editions up to 1828), both county atlases prepared in association with Thomas Kitchin and others, most of the maps were drawn and engraved by Bowen; they show his liking for much detail, large ornamental cartouches for the titles, and long legends with geographical and historical information.

Bowen engraved for *The Complete System of Geography* 'A New and Accurate Map of Scotland compiled from Surveys and the most approved maps and charts' on the scale of c. 38 miles to an inch. On it he has engraved a long explanation that, as most maps of north Britain hitherto published were very erroneous, he had rejected them in all parts where there were better authorities to follow and names Alex Bryce, J. Cowley, and Murdoch Mackenzie's 'proposals and specimen for the survey of the Orkney Islands'. Notwithstanding these claims for it the map gives a very distorted outline, with the north of Scotland slanted to the east and numerous other defects. This map is the same size as other maps in *A Complete System of Geography*, and was apparently the map intended for that book, but Bowen must have soon realized its defects, possibly on seeing Elphinstone's map of 1745, and substituted a larger map, which folds into the book, based on Elphinstone. This second map has also the title 'A New and Accurate Map of Scotland' but with 'or North Britain' added. It follows closely the 1745 map of Elphinstone, including his roads and the bend in the Great Glen, but it is on a conical projection and, partly because of the smaller scale, is inferior to Elphinstone's map. Bowen's third and larger map, on the scale of 16 miles to an inch, is again described as 'A New & Accurate Map of Scotland or North Britain', but with the addition in the title of 'exhibiting the Kings Roads'. It was published in February 1746, between the battles of Falkirk (which is marked), and Culloden (not yet fought). It has the imprint 'Printed & Sold by Tho. Bakewell', with his dedication to the Duke of Cumberland. Bowen again gives a long description of the sources he consulted and refers to astronomical observations fixing the position of Faro Head at 58°17′ 'whereas in most other maps tis placed in latitude 59°17′ or higher'—a statement which is not in fact true. The roads shown on the map are merely straight lines between towns with no attempt to give the actual course of the road. Emanuel Bowen was succeeded by his son, Thomas, whose name appears on the 1750 edition of 'A New & Accurate Map of Scotland'.

Another small map of Scotland, on the scale of 41 miles to an inch, was issued in 1749 by Thomas Jefferys (1695?-1771), a well known chart and map publisher of the mid-18th century who became geographer to the Prince of Wales, afterwards George III. He acquired a high reputation for the excellence of his numerous maps and charts of North America, and in his later years he and his staff surveyed and engraved maps of several English counties.

MURDOCH MACKENZIE

Although John Adair made coastal surveys of parts of the Orkney Islands and of the Western Isles his draft charts were never engraved and it was not until the surveys of Murdoch Mackenzie were published in 1750 and 1776 that the correct shape and position of the Western Isles were at last known.

Murdoch Mackenzie, Senior, whose work and methods made a notable advance in hydrographic surveying, was born in 1712, possibly a grandson of a former bishop of Orkney. George

Chalmers, author of *Caledonia*, says that he had before him a certificate dated 19th November 1742 from Colin Maclaurin, Professor of Mathematics in Edinburgh, of the qualifications of Mackenzie 'to take a geometrical survey'.[12] His survey of the Orkneys was a private venture but he received help from the Admiralty with the loan of a theodolite, plane table, and chain. The exactness and thoroughness of his survey is evident from his description of his surveying procedure.

First he had beacons built on the summits of the higher hills and eminences. He then measured a base-line on the Loch of Stenness, when it was frozen over, by fixing poles in the ice and measuring by an iron chain the distance between them, 3¾ miles. Having determined the exact direction of the base-line by compass, he measured with a theodolite the angles from the ends of the base-line to the visible beacons, then the angles between all the beacons, then the angles from the beacons to all headlands, bays, houses, etc., until a complete triangulation had been made and the distances calculated. He next went round the coast and compared the actual positions of the various features with his protraction, filling in his chart, and finally from a boat checking the coastal features, and recording depth of water, channels, shoals and rocks. The whole process was repeated on each island, except that only on the island of Sanday was another base-line measured. Finally he checked the north-south measurement of the whole by calculating the latitudes of North Ronaldsay and Kirkwall with the use of Rowley's quadrant (his latitude for Kirkwall is 58°58′, against a correct figure of 58°59′). Mackenzie's speed of work and the limitations of the instruments then available, resulted in inaccuracies in his charts, but when published in 1750 his *Orcades, or a Geographic and Hydrographic Survey of the Orkney and Lewis Islands*, with eight charts, five of the Orkneys and three of Lewis, all engraved by Emanuel Bowen, six of them on the scale of 1 mile to an inch, showed an immense improvement in the mapping of these islands. The most noticeable difference was in the north of Lewis, where the flat top of earlier maps was at last replaced by the pointed shape which appears on modern maps. His general chart of the Orkney Islands includes the north coast of Scotland copied from Alexander Bryce's map of 1744, but with Bryce's error of nine minutes in the latitudes of Duncansby Head and Cape Wrath reduced to an error of one minute.

Mackenzie was now commissioned by the Admiralty to make surveys of the west coast of Britain and the coast of Ireland. For his survey of the west coast of Scotland he measured a base-line over three miles long on the sand between the islands of South Uist and

Benbecula, and linked the Hebrides with the mainland by compass triangulation. Nineteen charts of the Hebrides and west coast from Lewis to the Solway Firth, were prepared between 1753 and 1757 on the scale of one inch to a mile, and followed by ten years of surveys of the coasts of Ireland, the whole eventually being engraved and published in 1776 with the title *A maritim survey of Ireland and West Coast of Great Britain* Vol. 1, Ireland, Vol. 2, West Coast of Scotland. Although the charts were a great improvement on earlier maps, Mackenzie does not seem to have carried out the same detailed triangulation he had employed in his survey of the Orkneys, as the islands of Islay and Skye are far from accurate, the north-south length of the island of Arran on his chart is only 14 miles instead of the correct length of 20 miles, and other inaccuracies are very noticeable. A writer in 1851 said that Mackenzie's charts were 'considered at the time entitled to credit, but recent Admiralty surveys have proved them to be exceedingly erroneous'.

In 1774 Mackenzie published his *Treatise on Maritim Surveying*, a work on his surveying methods, and in the same year was elected a Fellow of the Royal Society. Mackenzie was succeeded in the Admiralty position by his nephew Murdoch Mackenzie, jun., but the latter's surveys were confined to the coast of England.

JAMES DORRET

All earlier maps of Scotland were superseded in 1750 by the largest and best map yet produced: 'A General Map of Scotland and Islands thereto belonging: From New Surveys, the Shires properly divided & subdivided, the Forts lately erected & Roads of Communication or Military Ways . . . by James Dorret, Land Surveyor', published in London in April 1750. All that is known of Dorret are some brief references connected with his employment with the third Duke of Argyll. The first mention is in 1744, when, described as 'Valet to the Duke of Argyll', he was made a burgess of the Burgh of Inverary at the same time as other servants of the Duke, the occasion being the new Duke's first visit to Inverary since inheriting the Dukedom in 1734.[13] There is mention of Dorret only two or three times carrying out duties for the Duke; he must have left the Duke's services in 1755 as the Duke in that year advertised for a valet. He describes himself on the map as a land surveyor, but no maps or plans by him have been traced apart from his three maps of Scotland. On one of the maps, dated 1751, the inscription is 'James Dorret, delin et sculp', i.e., drawn and engraved, but no other mention has been found of James Dorret as an engraver.

The map of 1750 is on a scale of 4 miles to an inch, the largest scale yet used for a map of Scotland, in four large sheets and two small sheets, 71 × 53 inches in all, with lines of latitude and longitude, the latter on the prime meridian of Edinburgh. Writing in 1757 about this map in the preface to his *Atlas Universel*, Robert de Vaugondy says: 'Although this map (Elphinstone's) is valued, the one which appeared in 1750 in four and a half sheets and in two sheets by Dorret, engraver to the Duke of Argyll, exceeds the preceding one in all respects. It was planned in manuscript in very great detail, drawn by order of and at the expense of this Duke, one of the richest, most enquiring, and one of the most learned noblemen of England. To realize the full cost of a similar work it is sufficient to know that the Duke of Argyll, not merely gave himself the trouble of revising personally the proofs of this map, but moreover he passed them on to some engineers and landed proprietors in order to assure himself of the position of places and of the spelling of names.' Gough records that the map 'was copied from particular MS surveys taken at the expense of the Duke of Argyll, who revised the whole, and procured the best information both of the names and situation of places'.[14] Aaron Arrowsmith, writing of it in his *Memoir* of 1809, says 'It long remained the standard map, nor was its reputation unmerited, being on a larger scale and better constructed, than any former map'.

Not only is Dorret's 1750 map generally more accurate than Elphinstone's but for the first time Lewis and Skye are shown with some degree of accuracy, and no longer has Lewis the flat top seen on every map since Robert Gordon's 1654 map of Scotland. Dorret must have seen Murdoch Mackenzie's chart of Lewis before it was published in 1750, as the outline of Lewis is practically identical. Mackenzie's survey came no further south than Loch Resort with the result that Dorret's map, and all the maps based on Dorret, show a large bay in place of the western half of North Harris. Dorret has corrected Elphinstone's shortening of northern Scotland; most of the west coast, and the shape of North and South Uist, Mull, Islay and Kintyre are much improved, but in view of Dorret's access to sources of information, it is curious that this map still has the bend in the Great Glen. Dorret's employer, the third Duke of Argyll, was for many years the virtual ruler of Scotland until his death in 1761, and no doubt was able to obtain for Dorret all the latest information required for the map; when Vaugondy says that 'he passed (the proofs) on to some engineers' he may be referring to the very likely possibility that the Duke was able to consult the engineers then engaged on the military survey of northern Scotland. Vaugondy's further statement that the Duke sent the proofs to some landed proprietors in order to assure himself of the position of places and of the spelling of the names, no doubt explains why in some parts of the map place names are crowded in at all angles as if they had been added later, an explanation which may also account for the relatively poor quality of the engraving, which looks from the variations in the lettering as if more than one engraver had beeen employed. The statement by another French writer in 1786 that 'the map was no longer on sale, the King of England having bought the plates',[15] is not improbable, because in 1745 the Army complained that they had no proper map for their campaign in Scotland and this was the first large scale map to supply the need. This may also account for Dorret producing a small map in April 1751: 'A correct Map of Scotland, from new surveys' on the scale of 10 miles to an inch ('James Dorret, delin et sculp'). His name is also on a third and still smaller map dated 1761, on the scale of 14 miles to an inch: 'An accurate Map of Scotland drawn from all the particular surveys hitherto published with many additional improvements, by James Dorret, Land Surveyor'. Unlike the two earlier maps, which had no publisher's name, this one has the imprint 'Printed for & sold by Robt. Sayer, Map & Print Seller, at the Golden Buck in Fleet Street'.

THOMAS KITCHIN

Thomas Kitchin (1718-84), engraver and publisher in London, and Hydrographer to the King, was responsible for a large output of maps engraved for atlases, books and magazines, over a period of more than thirty years. He contributed maps to *The Small English Atlas* (1749) jointly with Thomas Jefferys; to *The Large English Atlas* (completed in 1760), and *The Royal English Atlas* (*c.* 1763), jointly with Emanuel Bowen. In 1773 he issued his *General Atlas* with large four-sheet maps, finely engraved and decorated with large cartouches; this atlas was re-issued several times up to 1810. He engraved more than a dozen maps of Scotland, in addition to a small atlas of county maps and a series of county maps published in the *London Magazine* over the years 1763-81. One of his early works as engraver was John Elphinstone's map of Scotland in 1745, and from it he produced in 1749 'Geographiae Scotiae, being new and correct Maps of all the Counties and Islands in the Kingdom of Scotland'. This atlas has 32 maps, each about $5\frac{3}{4} \times 6\frac{1}{2}$ inches, along with a small map of Scotland, all clearly based on Elphinstone's map; the maps have an identity of place names, and the same network of roads in general, except that Kitchin has added a few names from Moll's county maps of 1725, and some additional roads in the Lothians. A second edition was published in 1756.

Kitchin's larger maps of Scotland were all based on Dorret's map of 1750; his largest and best was 'A New and Complete Map of Scotland and islands thereto belonging', on the scale of *c.* 7 miles to the inch, in four sheets, which was issued in his *General Atlas describing the whole Universe*, first published in 1773. There is nothing original about this map; it has exactly the same lines of latitude and longitude as Dorret, the same roads and, on the left-hand side, the same list of 'Names of the most remarkable places in Scotland', but owing to the smaller scale space has not been found for all the place names on Dorret's map.

ANDREW AND MOSTYN ARMSTRONG

The work of Andrew Armstrong, and his son Mostyn James, in connection with county maps is described in Chapter 11; they come into the sequence of maps of Scotland through Captain Armstrong's map of 1775: 'A New Map of Scotland with the distances on the post & other roads in measured miles', on the scale of 15 miles to an inch, which first appeared in Bowles's *Universal Atlas* of 1775-80. The map is based on Dorret's small map, but is carelessly drawn with many mistakes and omissions; roads are shown but not many towns. Mostyn Armstrong published in 1777 *A Scotch Atlas or Description of the Kingdom of Scotland*, comprising two maps of Scotland, a map of the environs of Edinburgh, and 27 maps of Scottish counties, each about $7\frac{1}{2} \times 5\frac{1}{2}$ inches. Each map shows roads and is accompanied by a short description of the county. According to Richard Gough 'Armstrong's *Scots' Atlas* is little valued; his pretension to actual survey is entirely chimerical: he copied others, ingrafting mistakes of his own, and run over the Counties in a strange cursory manner. This *Atlas* is indeed more neatly engraved than Kitchin's *Geographiae Scotiae*: which yet is better esteemed, though erroneous. Armstrong has attended to his own and the engraver's profit more than that of the public or their information'.[14] Notwithstanding Gough's strictures it was a useful publication and was re-issued in 1787 and 1794.

Several maps of Scotland with the imprint of Bowles as publisher were issued by a firm of print and mapsellers established about 1700 by Thomas Bowles in St Paul's Churchyard, London. Thomas had two sons, Thomas (d. 1767), and John (1701-79), and the latter had a son, Carington (1724-93). After Carington's death the business was carried on under the name of Bowles and Carver until 1832. Two maps were first issued in 1782; 'Bowles's New Pocket Map of Scotland' (a later edition had the title 'Bowles's New One-Sheet Map of Scotland'), on the scale of 14 miles to an inch and described as 'laid down from the original survey of James Dorret, Geographer, with the addition of new roads and other modern improvements'; and 'Bowles's New and Accurate Map of Scotland' (later called 'Bowles's New Four Sheet Map') on the scale of 7 miles to an inch.

Dorret's map of 1750 was also the basis for 'A New Map of Scotland or North Britain' by Marcus Armstrong in 1782, on four sheets on the scale of 7½ miles to an inch, which was included in *A General Atlas* by Thomas Kitchin. Prominence is given to the roads and mileages. Nothing is known of Marcus Armstrong, who describes himself on the map as 'Geographer'. The map was re-issued in 1790 with substantial alterations, with a new title 'A New and Correct Map of Scotland or North Britain', and with the name of Lieut. Robert Campbell (another unknown cartographer) in place of Marcus Armstrong. The main alteration was the improvement of the Western Isles in accordance with Mackenzie's charts published in 1776.

Campbell's name is on a second and smaller map issued in 1790 with the title 'A New Map of Scotland or North Britain', on the scale of 14 miles to an inch, published in *A General Atlas* by Robert Sayer. This is in fact Sayer's original plate of Dorret's map of 1761 reworked with minor alterations (not incorporating the revision of the Western Isles made on the larger map), and with the addition of many more roads. The 1794 editions of both maps have the imprint of Laurie and Whittle, who took over Sayer's business when he retired in 1794.

LONGITUDE

The studies of the French scientists of the problem of calculating longitude, described in Chapter 6, were followed up in Britain, where an expanding sea-borne trade and a growing navy made accurate calculations of great practical importance. These depended on the reliability of the chronometer carried on the ship; the requirement was a clock which would maintain accuracy over a long period and would not be affected by the variations of temperature, climatic conditions, or the motion of a ship. The British Parliament passed an Act in 1714 to provide a reward of £10,000 for any device that would determine the longitude within one degree of accuracy, £15,000 if within 40 minutes, and £20,000 within 30 minutes (two minutes of time), and a permanent commission—the Board of Longitude—was set up and for fifty years examined all the ideas and tested all the clocks and watches submitted for the reward. Eventually the full reward was paid to John Harrison, a Yorkshireman, for his marine chronometer, on which he had worked for forty years, after five of his clocks, each one an improvement on the previous one, had been tested on lengthy voyages (his second one was used by Captain Cook on his second voyage), and the error in time reduced to a few seconds over ten weeks.[16]

GEOGRAPHICAL GRAMMARS

A feature of the 18th century was the proliferation of geographical 'grammars', all with maps, mostly small. *Geography Anatomiz'd or the Geographical Grammar*, first issued by Patrick Gordon in 1693, went to over twenty editions, with maps of Scotland by Morden in 1693, by Senex in 1722, and by Bowen in 1754. Herman Moll included one of his maps of Scotland in his *A System of Geography*, first published in 1701. Emanuel Bowen's voluminous work *A Complete System of Geography*, published in 1747, had two maps of Scotland. It was followed in 1749 by Thomas Salmon's *A New Geographical and Historical Grammar*, also with maps and some thirteen editions.

The most successful of all these 'grammars' was William Guthrie's *A New Geographical Historical and Commercial Grammar*, first issued in 1770. Guthrie was born at Brechin in 1708; his most ambitious work was a history of Scotland, in ten volumes, completed in 1767. Some twenty-four editions of his *Grammar* were published up to 1843; the earliest editions had maps by Kitchin; later ones had maps by Russell, and from 1785 onwards the *Grammar* was supplemented by *The Atlas to Guthrie's System of Geography*.

JOHN CARY

At the end of the 18th century and for the long period of fifty years a dominant figure in England in map production was John Cary (*c.* 1754-1835), who produced work of the highest quality, artistic engraving with the minimum of decoration, combined with the use of the latest geographical information.[17] His name as engraver first appears on a canal plan of 1779; by 1783 he was in business as 'map and printseller' in the Strand, and in 1787 issued his first atlas (of English counties), the *New and Correct English Atlas*. He published in all ten atlases (of which there were numerous editions), and a large number of separate maps, charts, plans, road books and globes, the engraving being done by himself in the earlier years and by his staff in his later life. A notable production was his 'New Map of England and Wales with part of Scotland', on the scale of 5 miles to an inch, issued in 1794 in 81 sheets, 13 of which cover southern Scotland. In 1832 Cary completed an even larger map, his 'Improved Map', on the scale of 2 miles to an inch, in 65 sheets, of which 8 cover southern Scotland.

Cary's first map of Scotland appeared in Richard Gough's 1789 edition of Camden's *Britannia*, a two-sheet map: 'The South Part of Scotland' and 'The North Part of Scotland', on the scale of *c.* 12 miles to an inch, with longitude based on London. The map is essentially a copy of Dorret's map of 1750, and was re-issued by Cary in his *New British Atlas* of 1805, although by this date Dorret's map had been superseded by John Ainslie's map of 1789.

Cary used the 1800 edition of Ainslie's large map as the basis for his 'A New Map of Scotland from the latest authorities', dated 1801, on the scale of 8 miles to an inch, in four sheets, later forming Sheets 7 to 10 of his *New Universal Atlas* first published in 1808. This has the Ainslie revisions of Angus and Kirkcudbright, but not of South Uist, supporting the view that Ainslie's South Uist was not revised until William Bald's survey of 1805; the choice and spelling of place names also indicate similarities with Ainslie. This is the first map of Scotland with the prime meridian of Greenwich.

A reduction of his four-sheet map appeared in 1809 with the title 'Cary's New Sheet Map of Scotland', on the scale of 11 miles to an inch; smaller maps appeared in his *New Elementary Atlas* in 1813. In 1821 the firm's name became G. and J. Cary (George was a son), and in this name the business continued until about 1850 when the plates and stock of maps and atlases were acquired by G. F. Cruchley.

JOHN STOCKDALE

Three maps of Scotland, one on the scale of $3\frac{1}{2}$ miles to an inch, another 4 miles to an inch, all appeared in the years 1806 and 1807. The first was by John Stockdale (1749-1814), born in Cumberland, and originally a blacksmith, later a porter to a bookseller in Piccadilly, and eventually in business himself as a book publisher and bookseller in Piccadilly, He was the publisher of the *New British Atlas* of 1805, with maps by John Cary, and of a large variety of books. In 1806 he issued a large map of Scotland in 12 sheets, and in 1809 a map of England and Wales in 20 sheets, both the work of S. J. Neele, the engraver. Stockdale died in 1814, aged 65.

His 'Map of Scotland from the latest Surveys', dated 1st January 1806, the largest scale map of Scotland ($3\frac{1}{2}$ miles to one inch on 12 sheets each $24 \times 26\frac{1}{2}$ inches) published before the one-inch Ordnance Survey, marks a further step in the improvement in the map of Scotland. Neele (who had already engraved at least ten smaller maps of Scotland) has made use of Ainslie's map to a certain extent, but generally he has gone to the county maps where these were available. Fifeshire, for example, is based on Ainslie's 1801 map of Fife and Kinross and not on his map of Scotland; Kirk-cudbright and Wigtown are also taken from his county maps. The island of Islay is taken from George Langland's 1801 map of Argyllshire and not from Mackenzie's charts which were followed by Ainslie. For Ayrshire, on the other hand, Neele has taken the roads and place names from Ainslie's map of Scotland, and not from Armstrong's 1775 map of Ayrshire, with the result that Ayrshire seems much less populated than in reality, and the same applies to certain other counties where county maps were not available.

WILLIAM FADEN

In the following year, 1807, another map of Scotland was published by William Faden (1750-1836), who took over the business of Thomas Jefferys on the latter's death in 1771. Faden was carto-grapher, engraver and publisher, and became Geographer to the King (George III) and to the Prince of Wales; his productions have been described as 'the finest maps being engraved anywhere in the world at this time'. From the material left by Jefferys, augmented with new material he collected, Faden produced a valuable *North American Atlas* with 34 maps in 1777, and a *General Atlas* in 1778 with beautifully engraved maps. His output was prolific; his catalogue, about 1822, listed over 350 items, maps, atlases, plans, charts and globes. He acted for the Ordnance Survey as publisher of the earliest one inch to the mile maps, beginning with Kent in 1801.

On 4th June 1807 Faden published 'A Map of Scotland drawn chiefly from the Topographical Surveys of Mr John Ainslie and from those of the late General Roy'. Dedicated to George Chalmers, the scale was 7 miles to an inch, and longitude on the meridian of Greenwich. The map provides a good example of Faden's excellent hill shading. The reference to the surveys of General Roy is puzzling. It does not apply to the map provided by Roy for his 'Military Antiquities', as a comparison of the maps will show. The obvious reference is to the Military Survey of Scotland, which Aaron Arrowsmith discovered in the King's Library in 1805 and copied in 1805/6. A possible explanation is that in 1805/6 Faden learned of the discovery of these maps (as Geographer to the King he would have access to the library), and used them in preparing his map of Scotland. The map shows some improvements on Ainslie's map of 1789 but it is not so accurate as Stockdale's map of 1806. The main defect is in the north-east of Scotland, where Aberdeen is placed 14 minutes (i.e., 8 miles) too far west, so that the coast from the Tay to Buchanness does not have the correct north-east alignment.

AARON ARROWSMITH

Faden's map of 4th June 1807 was very soon superseded by Arrowsmith's map of 25th June 1807, which remained the standard map for the next fifty years. Aaron Arrowsmith (1750-1823), born in Co. Durham, moved to London in 1770 and worked for a time as a land surveyor. In 1790, when he set up in business as a map publisher, he issued a large chart of the world on Mercator's projection, showing all the new discoveries, and followed this by many large scale maps of North America, Africa, the Pacific and Australia, keeping these up to date by incorporating all the latest information obtained from explorers about their discoveries. His atlases included a *New General Atlas* in 1817 and an *Atlas of Southern India* in 18 sheets in 1822. Arrowsmith's maps earned a reputation for their high standard of accuracy and clarity; his large output made him the leading British map publisher of the late 18th and early 19th centuries.

His 'Map of Scotland constructed from Original Materials obtained under the authority of The Parliamentary Commissioners for making Roads and building Bridges in the Highlands of Scotland', marks another stage in the mapping of Scotland; in a *Memoir* printed in 1809 to accompany the map, he describes the origin and construction of the map. In 1803 an Act was passed appointing Commissioners 'for making roads and building bridges in the Highlands of Scotland'. The Commissioners found themselves in difficulties because of the lack of accurate maps and their Secretary, John Rickman, learning that Arrowsmith was then compiling a large map of England, invited him to add a new map of Scotland to his work. Arrowsmith soon found that existing maps of Highland road surveys were inaccurate, but, to quote his own words 'was not a long time left in despair of accomplishing a map of Scotland', through the discovery of the Military Survey of northern Scotland deposited in the King's Library (see Chapter 10). In August 1805 Arrowsmith, with several assistants, began to copy it on transparent paper. For southern Scotland he collected all the county maps which had been produced up to that time, and with the help of other documents had prepared a drawing of the whole, when he learned by chance from General Sir David Dundas that the Military Survey had also covered southern Scotland. This was found and a copy of it was made in March and April 1806.

Arrowsmith verified the scale of the Military Survey (1000 yards = 1 inch), and next fixed the positions of more than 60 places throughout Scotland, of which the latitude and longitude had been ascertained by astronomical observations made by individuals whose accuracy could be relied on. He then completed the coastline from the nautical charts of John Ainslie, Murdo Downie, Alex. Bryce, Murdoch Mackenzie and Captain Huddart. For the Western Isles, which had not been covered by the Military Survey, Arrowsmith obtained plans already made of all the larger islands, except South Uist. From the Duke of Argyll he obtained maps of Tiree and Coll, and a volume of plans of all his farms in Mull; others provided maps of Islay, Jura, Colonsay, Oronsay, and Arran. He also examined a number of estate plans, including some of the forfeited estates. Arrowsmith lists in all some 100 maps and plans which he had used in compiling the map. From various sources he also obtained particulars of the variation of the magnetic needle at different places from 1688 to 1806 so as to arrive at true north in all these maps. Arrowsmith adopted the meridian of Greenwich, with 69·16 miles as the common measure of a degree of latitude on the meridian, arguing that the difference between southern Scotland and northern Scotland was not perceptible.

Arrowsmith applied to the actual production of the map the same meticulous care he had taken in drawing it. He had special large size sheets of paper made so as to avoid numerous junctions (the map is on four sheets each $37 \times 29\frac{1}{2}$ inches); and so that the lettering and style of work would be the same throughout, one individual, John Smith, was employed to do the engraving.

The map has a great mass of detail, much of which is obscured by the over emphasis on relief shown by the heavy hachuring in the style of the early Ordnance Survey maps. More place names are given than in any earlier map of Scotland. The latitude and longitude of the principal features on the coast do not yet quite show the accuracy of the later Ordnance Survey, but the differences are small. The islands of Lewis, South Uist, Barra and Raasay contrast with the rest of the map by their lack of detail; in his *Memoir* Arrowsmith mentions that a survey of South Uist had been completed since his map was compiled (it was in fact done by William Bald in 1805), that this would be incorporated in the next impression of the map, and that a survey of Lewis was now being made. In some other respects Arrowsmith's map is defective, e.g., the relative latitudes of Ballater and Braemar (4' difference instead of 2') despite all the care he exercised in making it. The cost of the first 500 copies came to £2050, apart from the cost of copying the Military Survey and other maps.

The map had its critics. In 1837 the Wernerian Society, Edinburgh Town Council and the Royal Society of Edinburgh joined in petitioning the Treasury for the resumption of the Ordnance Survey of Scotland on the ground that the best existing maps and charts of

Scotland were so defective. They had unfavourable comments to make on Arrowsmith's map:

'The errors in Arrowsmith's Map of Scotland, which has the reputation of being the best we possess, are so numerous and important, as to render the construction of a geological map of the Country on which dependance can be placed an impracticable undertaking; while its erroneous positions of our coasts and islands present the most formidable obstacles to navigation. The form and position of headlands, and even of considerable islands, in this map and in our best charts, are erroneously given; and sometimes dangerous rocks and whole islands are totally omitted. For example, the distant rocks of the Stack and the Skerry, off the northern coast of Sutherlandshire, as well as the island of St. Kilda, are totally omitted in Arrowsmith's map, while the important islands of Barra and Rona are misplaced, both in latitude and longitude.'

JOHN ARROWSMITH

On Aaron Arrowsmith's death in 1823 he was succeeded by his sons, Aaron II and Samuel. His nephew, John Arrowsmith (1790-1873), who had been trained in the business, decided to set up on his own, and in 1834 issued his *London Atlas of Universal Geography*, generally regarded as the best atlas of the time, with revised and improved editions up to 1858. His attention to accuracy of detail is emphasized in the preface, in which he explains that in the construction of the maps over several years, he had compared and critically examined more than ten thousand sheets of maps, charts, plans, etc., and had ascertained the most correct astronomical observations of latitude and longitude.

His map of Scotland, dated 1834, on the scale of 12 miles to an inch, is based on his uncle's map of 1807, with some corrections, but with Lewis, Harris, Islay and Tiree still defective, and with Cape Wrath still 4 minutes of longitude too far east. It was apparently with some reason that John Pinkerton wrote in his *Modern Atlas* of 1815: 'In Scotland, at present, there are only three or four places fixed by astronomical observations. Spots on the South Seas are far more accurately ascertained than cities in Great Britain.' Arran is still too short and misplaced on Arrowsmith's map, although Thomson's county map of Bute, dated 1823, gives the correct size and shape of Arran, as does Sidney Hall in his map of Scotland of 1828. Many of Arrowsmith's place names have obviously been taken from the maps in Thomson's *Atlas of Scotland*, not always the best choice. Arrowsmith's main interest was in the mapping of the developing continents and for his work he received the Patron's Medal of the Royal Geographical Society in 1863.

H

Between 1820 and 1850 maps of Scotland multiplied. They were mostly the work of engravers, copying from existing maps. James Wyld (1790-1836), re-issued Faden's map of 1807, and his son, also James, issued a smaller edition on the scale of 11 miles to an inch in 1840 with the title *Scotland with its Islands.* Amongst other engravers in London, Sidney Hall was responsible for much careful and exact work; his numerous maps of Scotland included one on the scale of 10 miles to an inch for A. & C. Black's *General Atlas.*

MARINE SURVEYS

The surveys of the Scottish coast, so essential for a correct outline of Scotland, have been very fully described by A. H. W. Robinson in his book *Marine Cartography in Britain,* and in his article in the *Scottish Geographical Magazine* on 'The Charting of the Scottish Coasts'.[19]

Although the east coast had been surveyed by Collins and Adair in the closing years of the 17th century, Murdo Downie recorded that in 1788, when appointed Master of H.M.S. *Champion* on the Leith station, he could find 'no chart published of the East Coast of Scotland that could in any degree be relied upon'. He accordingly made new surveys and eventually published his charts in a volume in 1792 with the title *The New Pilot for the East Coast of Scotland.* The Master at Trinity House in Leith praised them 'as more correct . . . and more complete than any directions of that part of the coast they have yet seen'.

The west coast of Scotland, with the hundreds of islands all with indented coasts, presented much greater difficulties than the east coast. Murdoch Mackenzie's charts of 1750 and 1776, and their defects, have already been described. In 1781 and 1790 Captain James Huddart prepared charts from new surveys which he made of the west coast, but he made only partial corrections of Mackenzie's charts. An accurate survey of the west coast and islands was too large an undertaking for a private survey, and it was not until the official surveys of the Admiralty Hydrographic Department that reliability was achieved. Beginning with the Shetlands in 1825, Admiralty surveyors were continuously at work, and a steady stream of accurate charts became available to the map makers.

10 The Military Survey of Scotland, 1747-55

In 1724 King George I instructed Lieutenant-General George Wade to inspect the state of the Highlands of Scotland; in his report Wade referred to the difficulties encountered by the regular troops for lack of roads and bridges in their movements between their barracks at various points in the Highlands. Some of these barracks, or forts, had been built by Oliver Cromwell to maintain his rule in Scotland; others had been added at different times after 1688.

Immediately following his report General Wade was appointed Commander-in-Chief for Scotland and one of his first requests in 1725 was for money 'for mending the Roads between the Garrisons and Barracks, for the better communication of his Majesty's troops', as well as for repairing existing barracks and building new ones. Several maps or plans of the roads dated 1725 and onwards, which, one may reasonably assume, must have been prepared for Wade in connection with his work on the roads and on the forts, are preserved in the National Library of Scotland, in the British Museum, and in the Public Record Office. Between 1725 and 1740 (when he left Scotland on promotion) Wade was responsible for making 258 miles of road, most of this on the route of existing tracks but some of it entirely new; his roads ran from Fort William to Inverness, Dunkeld to Inverness, Crieff to Dalnacardoch, and Dalwhinnie to Fort Augustus by Corrieyairack.[1]

Wade was succeeded in 1740 by General Clayton but the supervision of the road work devolved on a Mr (later Major) Caulfield, and over thirty manuscript maps of the roads constructed under him survive from the years 1746-54.

The 1731 manuscript map of Scotland by Clement Lempriere, referred to in Chapter 9, shows the military roads made up to that date. An engraved map, by R. Cooper, 'A Map of the King's Roads made by His Excellency General Wade in the Highlands of Scotland' was probably issued between 1740 and 1745; a somewhat similar engraved map by Andrew Rutherfurd of date 1745, 'An exact plan of His Majesty's great roads through the Highlands of Scotland', shows the position occupied by General Cope each day on his way to Inverness.

The Jacobite Rising of 1745, and the pursuit of Prince Charles' army brought out the need for better maps. In a letter of December

1745, General Hawley, on his way to take command of the Government troops in Scotland, wrote: 'I am going in the dark; for Marechal Wade won't let me have his map; he says that his majesty has the only one to fellow it. I could wish it was either copied or printed, or that his majesty could please lend it to me'.[2] He may have been referring to Lempriere's map of 1731, the only large scale map then in existence and not printed. The printed map of John Elphinstone was available and was in fact used, but the scale (13 miles to an inch) was clearly too small for military purposes.[3] Some larger scale maps of areas around Aberdeen are associated with the Duke of Cumberland, who encamped there for nearly six weeks with his army in the spring of 1746, as well as a map of the country between Aberdeen and Inverness for the Duke's march with his troops from Aberdeen to Culloden. Some of these were drawn by William Edgar, an Edinburgh land surveyor who was with the army in 1745-46.

Military needs emphasized the lack of adequate maps and in 1747 the Military Survey of Scotland was begun. Official records have not survived, but Aaron Arrowsmith in the *Memoir* published by him in 1809 relative to his map of Scotland printed information which he obtained from officers who had taken part in the survey, and the two men concerned with the Survey at its inception, David Watson and William Roy, have both left brief references to its origin.

Arrowsmith in his *Memoir*, says that he enquired into the history of the Military Survey from persons still living in 1805-06 who had been actively engaged in it. From them he learned that 'immediately after the Rebellion of 1745, it was determined, probably at the suggestion of the Duke of Cumberland, to survey the Northern Highlands of Scotland, a tract, then little known and hardly accessible, and in which that Rebellion originated. The Survey was put under the direction of General Watson, Quartermaster-General of Scotland, and in 1747 the late General Roy, then a young man, commenced the operation in the neighbourhood of Fort Augustus, and for two years was singly employed on the work. The specimens of his progress were so satisfactory, that it was determined to extend the Survey over the whole of the north of Scotland and in 1749 and 1750 several of the junior engineers were put under General Watson's orders; to wit, Lieutenants Debbeig, Manson, Howse, Williams, and William Dundas . . . Each surveyed his allotted district, Lieutenant Roy being the principal distributor of the whole, and Mr. Paul Sandby the chief draughtsman of the Plan, which occupied the winter months at Edinburgh, and where the connection of the summer work of the several surveyors was often the subject of mutual discussion'.[4]

William Roy, who became so closely associated with the Military

Survey that the map prepared from it is usually referred to as the 'Roy Map', thus describes the origin of the Military Survey: 'With a view to the commencement of arrangements of this sort [i.e., building military forts and constructing roads], a body of infantry was encamped at Fort Augustus in 1747, at which camp my much respected friend, the late Lieutenant General Watson, then Deputy Quartermaster-General in North Britain, was officially employed. This officer, being himself an engineer, active and indefatigable, a zealous promoter of every useful undertaking, and the warm and steady friend of the industrious, first conceived the idea of making a map of the Highlands. As Assistant Quartermaster, it fell to my lot to begin, and afterwards to have a considerable share in, the execution of that map; which being undertaken under the auspices of the Duke of Cumberland, and meant at first to be confined to the Highlands only, was nevertheless at last extended to the Lowlands; and thus made general in what related to the mainland of Scotland, the islands (excepting some lesser ones near the coast) not having been surveyed.'5

The references by Roy and Arrowsmith to the Duke of Cumberland and Lieutenant-General Watson are confirmed by the terms of a 'Memorial' sent about 1770 to the Treasury by John Watson, brother of General Watson (who had died in 1761), claiming arrears of pay and expenses incurred by Watson in the survey. Written so soon after the survey, and undoubtedly conveying information supplied by General Watson himself, this is the most authentic statement of the origin of the survey.

'That when his Royal Highness the late Duke of Cumberland in the beginning of the year 1746 marched with the King's Forces on account of the Rebellion which then prevailed in the North of Scotland, he and the generals under his command found themselves greatly embarrassed for the want of a proper Survey of the country. And on his Royal Highness's return to London, after quashing of the Rebellion and restoring the peace of Government, he stated the inconvenience and want of such a survey to the late King his royal father and the principal servants then employed by His Majesty. The inconvenience was perceived and the resolution taken for making a complete and accurate survey of Scotland, and of the coasts, creeks, rivers, islands, etc. thereof, and the Memorialist's brother, then a Lieut-Colonel, serving in Scotland as Deputy Quartermaster-General, at a pay of only 10 shillings per day burdened with the usual deductions, was employed under orders from his Royal Highness the late Duke to take the chief direction thereof and to carry the same into execution as soon as possible.

'Pursuant to these orders the Memorialist's brother in the year

1747 commenced the Survey on a very large but useful plan and scale, as appears by the Survey itself. He had several Deputies and Surveyors employed under him, and he continued in the constant execution of that service till the year 1755 inclusive, when the Survey was finished. Every year during that time making reports to his Royal Highness the late Duke and his Majesties' Servants of the progress he had made which always had their entire approbation, and produced fresh orders to go on with the work, which he did with much punctuality and care till it was finished. This obliged him to many journies and long attendance in the Highlands and other places of Scotland, and exposed him to very great and unavoidable expences in the charge of servants, guides, interpreters, and other ways.

'That for seven months of that time the Memorialist's brother paid three temporary assistants—Dundas, Pleydell, and another, at the rate of 5 shillings per day each, amounting to £157. 10s., which is still owing and unpaid by the Government. The other under-surveyors were paid annually their full established allowance, by bill and warrant from the War Office, on the Paymaster-General of the Forces, and were paid out of the Contingencies and extraordinary expences of the Army. But in these annual issues no charge was made for the said three temporary Surveyors. Nor for Mr. Roy on account of his constant labour in finishing the reduction of the Survey under the directions he received.' The Memorial was accompanied by a statement of the money expended by Colonel Watson during the survey, 'which engrossed and employed the (Colonel's) whole time and his deputy surveyors for 8 years 6 months, 1747 to 1755', this confirming that the survey was begun in the early summer of 1747. The account is mainly for keep of horses and Watson's own pay and expenses; the amount for Roy is not stated.[6]

The possibility of such a survey must have been discussed between the Duke and Lieutenant-Colonel Watson when both were in camp at Fort Augustus from May to July 1746 (the fort had been destroyed by the clansmen on the side of Prince Charles Edward and rebuilding was now undertaken). The Duke left Fort Augustus in July for London and apparently took an early opportunity of obtaining approval from the King and the War Office for the Survey.[7] We do not know how Watson came to employ William Roy—whether Watson employed Roy specifically for the survey (Watson was in Edinburgh in 1747 supervising reconstruction at Edinburgh Castle), or whether he had engaged Roy as civilian Assistant Quartermaster and then discovered his abilities—Roy's own statement quoted above rather implies the latter.

William Roy was born on 4th May 1726 at Miltonhead near Carluke in Lanarkshire, the son of an estate factor. He attended the parish school and then the grammar school at Lanark.[8] Nothing more is known of his education (although his brother James graduated at the University of Glasgow and became a clergyman), but two suggestions have been made about his early training or experience before becoming assistant quarter-master to Colonel Watson (a civilian post), though evidence to support them is lacking. George Chalmers, in *Caledonia*, published in 1810, says that Roy was employed in the Post Office in Edinburgh (in what capacity he does not say, but the most likely employment would be as a surveyor of the post roads).[9] R. A. Skelton suggested that Roy may have been working as a civilian draughtsman in the Ordnance office for some years before 1747; this would explain how he met Colonel Watson and why he was entrusted with the survey.[10] If it seems curious that Roy, a civilian clerk, was put in charge of the mapping we may firstly surmise that Roy had acquired some knowledge of surveying, and the preparation of estate plans, in his father's office— certainly the few maps which can be identified as his own work show a natural ability for drawing with very neat workmanship, and if he had further experience in making road surveys for the Post Office mails he would be well qualified for the survey planned by Colonel Watson. A second reason for Roy carrying on the work himself was no doubt the shortage of engineers; the Board of Ordnance in a report to the King in April 1748 said that only four engineers were available to carry on the works in Scotland—Morrison, Bramham, Gordon and Archer.[9] The plans of the military roads show that all four were engaged on superintending the construction of roads—Morrison and Gordon on the road from Stirling to Fort William, Bramham and Archer on the road from Blairgowrie to Braemar. The King approved an increase in the establishment of engineers, and several practitioner engineers were appointed, although only one of them, Hugh Debbeig, is named as working (at some date) on the survey. A letter dated April 1748, is quoted by Whitworth Porter conveying the Duke of Cumberland's command 'that the two engineers who are gone down to help Watson in his survey are to have 5/- a day', but these were not engineers, they were the draughtsman Paul Sandby, and John Manson. The reference by Arrowsmith, quoted above, to Lieutenants Debbeig, Manson, Howse, Williams, Dundas, and Roy is misleading in describing them as lieutenants; in fact none of these six held the rank of lieutenant during the Survey. Debbeig was appointed to the Corps of Engineers as a practitioner engineer in 1748; Manson in 1749, and Williams in 1753, but engineers at that time did not hold army rank. William Dundas and Roy were civilians, as were apparently also the three named by General Watson as temporary assistants—David Dundas, Pleydell, and 'another' (probably Charles Tarrant), whose remuneration was paid (for a period at any rate) by Watson personally.[7, 11]

The work of the surveyors is thus described by Arrowsmith: 'Each of the surveyors was attended by a non-comissioned officer and six soldiers as assistants; one carried the theodolite; two measured with the chain; two for the fore and back stations, and the remaining one acted as batman, or attendant on the party. As these parties encamped, they were enabled to penetrate into every recess of the Highlands: the summer months were spent in the field, and the finished work was every year carried by General Watson to London for inspection.

'The courses of all the Rivers and numerous streams were followed to the source, and measured; all the Roads, and the many Lakes of salt-water and fresh were surveyed, as well as such other intermediate places and cross lines as were found necessary for filling up the country; and intersections being taken to the right and left, ascertained innumerable minute situations. Each Surveyor kept a field-book and a sketchbook; in the first he inserted the angles and measurement of his stations, also the intersections made from each, with his own remarks. In the second, which was of sufficient size, he delineated his stations and the face of the country, which was then much less inclosed and woody than at present, and favourably featured for a military sketch. The instruments used in the Survey were plain theodolites of seven inches diameter, or three and a half radius, with common sights unfurnished with telescopes; and chains of 45 or 50 feet in length.'

The six work parties, with commendable speed, completed the survey of the Highlands (except the islands) in the years 1749-52, as far south as the line of Edinburgh-Glasgow, and it was then decided (to quote Arrowsmith) 'to extend the operation over the South of Scotland also, and at this time Lieutenant Dundas (now General Sir David Dundas), was added to the number of Surveyors being placed immediately under the tuition of General Roy, by whom the whole line of the coast, and the southern Border was accurately surveyed and measured. The present Lieutenant-General Tarrant was also employed as a draftsman, as was Lieutenant-Colonel Pleydell towards the conclusion of the Survey'. Paul Sandby (1725-1809) described as 'the chief draughtsman of the plan (he later became a noted water colour painter) worked in the Edinburgh drawing office from 1748 to 1751 in preparing the original protraction of Northern Scotland. He returned in 1753 and was responsible for the reduced map on one-quarter the scale (1 inch to 4000 yards), an unfinished map with the topography completed but only a few place names.'[12]

The main survey work was completed in 1754, fortunately so because in the same year war broke out between Britain and France in North America, and in 1755 Colonel Watson was recalled to London to work on plans to prevent a possible French invasion of southern England, while Roy was left in charge to complete the map. By the end of 1755 more troops and more engineers were required for the war; on 23rd December Roy, William Dundas, David Dundas and Charles Tarrant were brought into the Corps of Engineers at the lowest rank of practitioner engineer, and all later received military rank—Roy becoming a lieutenant in January 1756.[11] In 1756 Colonel Watson, Roy and David Dundas were all engaged in surveys of the south coast of England in connection with measures against an invasion, and several plans and sketches by Roy and Dundas of south coast areas are preserved in the British Museum.[7] (Of the men mentioned by Arrowsmith, five in later years became Generals—Watson, Debbeig, Roy, David Dundas and Charles Tarrant.)

After completion of the Survey in 1755 most of the maps remained with General Watson until his death in 1761, when they were handed over to the King for the Royal Library, 'consisting (according to Arrowsmith) of a fair copy of the north of Scotland as far as Edinburgh and Glasgow, with an unfinished reduction on a fourth of the larger scale; and the original Plan of the south of Scotland, of which no fair copy was ever made. In the fair copy of the north of Scotland the Mountains and Ground appear shaded in a capital style by the pencil of Mr. Paul Sandby, subsequently so much celebrated as a landscape draftsman. The Outlines were drawn and other particulars inserted under the care of (Colonel) Watson by sundry assistants.' The original protraction of the north of Scotland was in the possession of the Duke of Cumberland, probably handed to him by Colonel Watson when the fair copy was made; on the Duke's death in 1765 it also was placed in the Royal Library.

After 1763, when the peace treaty was signed with France, Roy (now Deputy Quarter-Master General with the rank of Lieutenant-Colonel) borrowed from the Royal Library the maps which had been deposited there in 1761 after Watson's death with a view to reducing them and publishing an improved map of Scotland. Roy proposed to the King in 1763, that a proper triangulation and survey of the whole of Britain be made, and the material of the military survey incorporated, but these proposals were not carried out and the only map prepared by Roy (or for him by Thomas

Chamberlain, chief draughtsman in the Ordnance office at the Tower of London under Roy's supervision) was a map of Scotland, engraved by J. Cheevers and dated 1774, the 'Mappa Britanniae Septentrionalis Faciei Romanae' which was printed in Roy's *The Military Antiquities of the Romans in North Britain,* published in 1793.[13] At some date after May 1787 the five rolls of the unfinished reduction by Paul Sandby were handed by Roy to Thomas Chamberlain, with instructions to prepare a further reduction on the scale of 1 inch to 6 miles. This was uncompleted at Roy's death on 1st July 1790, and in October 1790, Chamberlain sent the two maps to General David Dundas, Roy's executor, with this note (still attached to the larger map): 'Mr. Chamberlain presents his respects to Gen. Dundas and have herewith sent the Plan of Scotland being in five parts which Mr. C. had of the late Gen. Roy—also the Plan in two parts that Mr. C. was reducing therefrom. There is wanting in the unfinished plan to compleat it several towns, roads and part of the heights.' Dundas then handed over these maps, in two boxes, to the King in person in 1793 to be deposited in the Royal Library.

In 1805, when Arrowsmith was commissioned to prepare a new map of Scotland for the recently appointed 'Commissioners for making Roads and building Bridges in the Highlands of Scotland', he learned of the map of the Military Survey preserved in the King's Library and received permission to copy it as a basis for his new map. He did not know that the map he saw then in the Royal Library was only the original protraction of the north of Scotland which had been in the possession of the Duke of Cumberland; and he had laboriously compiled a map of southern Scotland from existing county maps and other documents when General Sir David Dundas, in the course of a visit in the beginning of 1806 to see the progress of the new map, told Arrowsmith of the maps he had deposited with the King, in two boxes, and on enquiry these were found unopened since left in the Royal Library in 1793.[14]

In 1828 all the maps of the Military Survey were transferred from the Royal Library to the British Museum.[13] In this collection is a manuscript map which is not accounted for in any of the records of the time. It is a beautifully executed map of Scotland, in 21 sheets, complete with rivers, mountains, roads, villages, place names, etc., on the scale of 1 inch to 4000 yards, i.e., the same scale as Paul Sandby's unfinished reduction. The lettering and style of drawing are different from Sandby's map, and we are left with no indication of the authorship or the date of the map. It has one marked difference from the other maps; it is oriented to true north whereas the others are all oriented to magnetic north. The possibility that it was prepared under Roy's instructions in the period 1770-90 (when the maps were in his possession), with a view to the publication of a larger map of Scotland than the small 'Mappa Britanniae Septentrionalis', is rather negatived by the fact that it was not in the two boxes of maps handed in by Sir David Dundas, nor would it have been necessary for Roy to give Paul Sandby's unfinished map to Chamberlain for the preparation of a reduction if this complete map had then been available.

Roy, writing in 1785, expressed his view of the main map produced from the Military Survey: 'Although this work, which is still in manuscript, and in an unfinished state, possesses considerable merit, and perfectly answered the purpose for which it was originally intended; yet, having been carried on with instruments of the common or even inferior kind, and the sum annually allowed for it being inadequate to the execution of so great a design in the best manner, it is rather to be considered as a magnificent military sketch than a very accurate map of a country. It would, however, have been completed, and many of its imperfections no doubt remedied; but the breaking out of the war of 1755 prevented both, by furnishing service of other kind for those who had been employed upon it.'[4] Sir Charles Close described it as 'little more than an elaborate compass sketch'.

It has imperfections in that it is not based on triangulation from an exactly measured base, shows neither latitude nor longitude, is oriented to magnetic north, and has some distortion and other errors here and there, not surprising in a hurried work covering the Scottish mainland in eight and a half years. But the speed of work has the advantage of presenting a picture of Scotland at a particular stage in its development, for little change would occur between 1747 and 1754, and as a cartographic work it fully justifies Roy's adjective of magnificent. The scale of 1 inch to 1000 yards—$1\frac{3}{4}$ inches to a mile—is large enough to provide remarkable detail; solid red for houses and other buildings; outline red for formal gardens; brown for roads; a darker brown for place names; blue/green for water; green for woodland; yellow for cultivated land; buff for moors; and the hills by shades of grey wash, with brush strokes in the direction of the slope, strokes of darker colour indicating the steeper slopes. The road system is remarkably accurate, and so is the position of villages and hamlets, although, as a comparison between the 'field sheet' and the 'fair copy' of northern Scotland will show, the number of red dots for a hamlet or farm is not necessarily the number of buildings. The delineation of arable ground is probably accurate; the actual field boundaries shown in the Lothians and other areas where the new methods of farming had been introduced

are not to be relied on. Place names often indicate the local pro-
nunciation rather than the correct spelling.

The completed reduction, authorship unknown, in 21 sheets on the
scale of 1 inch to 4000 yards, i.e., a quarter the scale of the original
survey map, and oriented to true north, is a remarkably fine map of
excellent workmanship. Towns, villages and hamlets are coloured
red; water pale blue.

Throughout the 19th century the scales preferred by the Ordnance
Survey were 1 : 63360 and 1 : 10560; recent years have seen the
advantages of the scale of 1 : 25000, which is not so far from the
scale of 1 : 36000 of the original map of the Military Survey.

ORDNANCE SURVEY

The Military Survey of Scotland had ended in 1755. William Roy,
who had been so active in the Survey and who was first given
military rank in 1756, had by 1781 reached the rank of Major-
General. At various times he had proposed a complete triangulation
of Britain (to which the original map of the Survey would be adapted),
but there was insufficient interest in his proposals and then from
1776 to 1783 the American war left no men for surveys. When in
1783 Cassini de Thury, director of the Paris Observatory, proposed
that a trigonometric survey should be made to link the Observations
of Paris and Greenwich through Calais and Dover the Royal Society
of London asked Major-General Roy to undertake the work. For
the purpose of maximum accuracy Roy asked Ramsden, the instrument maker, to make a new three-foot theodolite (this took
three years), a base was measured on Hounslow Heath, and the
trigonometrical connection was completed in 1788.[5] Roy died in
1790 without seeing any further development of his proposals, but
they were put into effect in the following year by the appointment
of two officers 'to carry on the Trigonometrical Survey' and so the
Ordnance Survey came into existence on 10th July 1791. Surveying
was started in the south-east of England, and the first four sheets
of the one inch to the mile map, covering Kent, were published by
W. Faden on 1st January 1801.

In 1809 the work of the primary triangulation was extended to
Scotland, then suspended for three years, and resumed in 1814. In
1817 a new base-line was measured on Belhelvie Links, north of
Aberdeen. In 1820 operations were again suspended, and resumed
in 1821 in the Orkneys, Shetlands and Hebrides. In 1824 all the
surveyors were required for the more urgent survey of Ireland for
valuation purposes and the work in Scotland was suspended,
except that a detailed survey of the counties of Ayr and Wigtown
begun in 1819 was continued until 1827.

Dissatisfaction with the lack of progress in Scotland was expressed by Sir Roderick Murchison at the meeting of the British Association in Edinburgh in 1834. This producing no result, the Edinburgh Town Council, the Royal Society of Edinburgh, and the Wernerian Society joined in petitioning the Treasury in 1837 for a resumption of the Survey on the ground that the best existing maps and charts of Scotland were so defective: 'in some charts the large island of Arran is laid down as six miles from Bute, in others as nine miles, and in a third as twelve miles distant from the island. Phadda Island Light in charts is placed at 16′ N. of Ailsa Craig, whereas its true distance is only 10′20″. These last are serious errors at the entrance of so important a river as the Clyde'.

In reply the Director-General of the Survey, Colonel Thomas Colby, explained in a report to the Treasury, that the suspension of the trigonometrical survey of Scotland had arisen from the urgent demand for the townland survey of Ireland, for which trained officers were necessary, that the funds available for the surveys were adequate only for the Irish and English surveys, but if he received another £800 to £1000 per annum he could train two officers to recommence the principal triangulation of Scotland in 1838, and this proposal was approved by the Treasury. From 1838 the work of triangulation of Scotland was continued until completed.

In 1844 the detailed survey of the county of Wigtown was begun; it was completed in 1850 and engraved on the six-inch scale in 38 sheets. The survey of Kircudbrightshire was begun in 1845 and completed in 1850. In July 1846 the survey of Lewis was begun when the proprietor agreed to pay part of the cost. The survey party from Wigtown were transferred to Midlothian in 1850 and thereafter the work went on steadily.[15]

11   Estate Surveyors and County Maps

During the 18th century the appearance of the Scottish countryside underwent great changes, which gave a new impetus to mapping. Prior to 1700—and in fact until much later in most parts of Scotland —farming of the land was carried on by the old 'infield' and 'outfield' system, where the 'infield' was the better land around the village or farm 'toun', more frequently manured and bearing crops every year, whilst the 'outfield' was the poorer land beyond the 'infield', usually of greater extent, seldom manured and used mostly for grazing, but with partial crops of oats where the situation and quality of the soil rendered some cultivation possible.   Both infield and outfield were shared between the tenants in long narrow strips or 'rigs' on the runrig system, these strips being re-allocated among the tenants annually or every second or third year.   These were open fields, with no permanent enclosures.   The forests which had once flourished had been cut down to provide timber for building or for fuel, and generally, but more particularly in southern Scotland, the visitor noted an absence of trees and saw a somewhat barren landscape.

The Scottish Parliament had in the latter part of the 17th century passed several Acts to encourage enclosures and the planting of trees, along with the straightening and fencing of the boundaries between estates.   An Act of 1695, 'Anent lands lying run-rig', referred to their great disadvantage and authorized the consolidation of holdings; another Act of the same year referred to the disputes which arose over individual rights in common lands and gave permission for such lands to be divided between those who had the rights.   The increasing cattle trade with England; the introduction of the potato and turnip; the improvements in farming methods introduced from England after the Union of 1707; all served to emphasize the need for a change from the runrig system of open fields to larger and enclosed fields, from which better and heavier crops could be obtained; regular four-sided fields, square or oblong, to facilitate cultivation, and to suit with the new methods of husbandry.   The change was a gradual one, slow in the first half of the 18th century, by 1750 becoming more widespread, and extending rapidly in the second half of the century.

For this change plans of the farmlands or of the estate were required, frequently two plans, one of the existing allocation of land and one of the proposed new lay-out of roads and fields. The earlier land surveyors employed for the purpose had no qualifications beyond a knowledge of measurement and drawing; we find plans by gardeners, mathematicians and schoolmasters.[1] Soon land measurers and land surveyors appeared, men often with a practical knowledge of the new farming methods who were able to advise the landowner on the best lay-out of the new fields and so the local amateur gradually gave way to the professional.[2] Whereas earlier maps of Scotland had been on a broad canvas, the new class of land surveyors supplied the detailed map, showing individual houses, fields and roads, all to exact scale, several of the surveyors gradually increasing the extent of their surveys and developing skills in cartography which resulted in the excellent county maps of the late 18th century.

It is not within the compass of this brief account to name the numerous land surveyors or to describe the great number of estate plans which they produced in the 18th century, as this volume concerns only the few who progressed to the extent of county surveys and county maps which were used in the mapping of Scotland. The nature of an estate survey to make ready for the change to the new methods of farming may be seen in *Selections from the Monymusk Papers*, concerning the estate of Monymusk, when its proprietor, Sir Archibald Grant, one of the pioneers of agricultural improvement in Scotland, in 1726 brought an English farmer, Thomas Winter, to introduce improved farming methods, which involved him in making plans of the farms.[3] The *Survey of Loch Tayside 1769*, describing a survey of the estate of the Earl of Breadalbane, shows the length of time and cost of a survey; of interest is the fact that while the survey of the two parts took 146 days and 140 days, it required another 90 days and 108 days respectively to draw the plans.[4] Illustrative of the experiences of surveyors is the note by John Home in his *Survey of Assynt* that the purchase of spirits 'for the use of self and assistants who led the chain to enable them to endure the fatigue of wading through lochs and mosses from morning early till late at night was by experience found necessary'.[5]

FORFEITED ESTATES SURVEYS

A second group of plans relates to the 'Forfeited Estates', the estates of those, mostly Highland chiefs, who fought for Prince Charles Edward in the Rising of 1745, and under Acts of Parliament forfeited their estates.[6]

In 1755 Commissioners were appointed to manage the forfeited estates, to have the land surveyed and proper plans of it made, and to see that the income derived from the estates was used solely for the 'purposes of civilizing the inhabitants upon the said estates and other parts of the Highlands and Islands of Scotland, the promoting amongst them of the Protestant religion, good Government, Industry and Manufactures and the Principles of Duty and Loyalty to His Majesty (etc.)'. One of the Commissioners was Lieutenant-Colonel David Watson, who had just completed the military survey of Scotland, and at the first meeting of the Commissioners on 23rd June 1755 he produced a draft of 'Instructions for the Surveyors to be employed in taking plans of the annexed forfeited estates', which with some minor amendments was approved by the Commissioners on 30th June. Colonel Watson had not wasted time; at this second meeting he introduced William Cockburn of Kelso, a land surveyor who was immediately engaged to make a survey of the Estate of Perth, payment to be 10s 6d, a day for Cockburn and 5s, a day to each of three surveyors assisting him. Each 'theodolite', i.e., each surveyor, was given the assistance of five soldiers (a corporal and four others), and a guide to show him the boundaries of the estate.

At subsequent meetings other surveyors were appointed: Peter May, a land surveyor in Aberdeen, was to survey the estates of Lovat and Cromarty with five assistants and one theodolite; John Lesslie of Liberton, described as 'gardener and land surveyor', to survey the estate of Strowan, and several other surveyors for other estates. Peter May asked for 13s, a day for himself and five assistants when on survey; John Lesslie's rate was 11s 8d. (John Lesslie in 1777 received 20 guineas from the Commissioners towards the cost of printing a new method of calculating areas.) For living expenses when on survey a surveyor was to get for himself and five assistants 30s weekly as an advance of his total remuneration.

They were all instructed first to make a reconnaissance of the whole estate to ascertain its general features; then 'When the Surveyor has made such Observations on the lying of the Estate, in order to prevent errors in connecting or joining together the several separate surveys, he ought particularly where the estate is very extensive, to fix from a long Base measured with the greatest accuracy some of the most remarkable objects within the estate, such as the tops of hills or any other thing that is conspicuous. These distances being found by Trigonometry and truly laid down, will be of the greatest service in joining the whole together and will preserve the true figure of the estate, without which in the course of many surveys, and a multiplicity of short stations, it would be impossible to prevent errors from creeping in.'

The 'Instructions' then go on to lay down that the boundaries of each farm must be accurately surveyed, with the exact extent shown of arable land, meadow land, woodlands, bogs and lakes, with the acreage of each area entered in a book referring to the plan; the Surveyor must also describe the nature of the woods, say whether the bogs can be drained and whether the land can be improved, and record on the plan any limestone or other minerals. He must show the exact courses of all rivers and rivulets so that the smaller bends are noted; must mark the state of the roads, and suggest where new roads would be more convenient and where bridges are necessary. All villages, farm or cott houses, and all enclosures were to be inserted; some indication must be given of the heights of the hills, and sketches of the hills and hilly ground should be made in a manner to distinguish these on the plan.[7]

COUNTY MAPS

Only a few of the estate surveyors extended their work to cover a whole county. The development of county maps began around 1735 when Richard Cooper engraved three maps of the Lothians—East, Mid, and West Lothian—on scales of $1\frac{1}{4}$ to $1\frac{1}{2}$ inches to the mile from the manuscript maps left by John Adair from his surveys in 1681-82. Not only were these maps already sixty years out of date, but they showed few roads and these only on general lines; hills were not accurately placed, and there was a general lack of detail and accuracy in respect of villages and other features. John Elphinstone in 1744 published 'A New & Correct Map of the Lothians from Mr. Adair's observations', on the scale of 2 miles to an inch, but although he describes it as 'This Map of the Three Lothians in one sheet wherein the mistakes of these already published in three separate sheets are set to rights, the true meridian is here expressed instead of that by the needle . . .', it is in fact a close copy of Cooper's three maps with no obvious improvement, with just as many misspellings, and not correctly aligned to true north.

WILLIAM EDGAR

The first, after Adair, to undertake county surveys was William Edgar, who in 1741 published 'A New and Correct Map of the Shire of Peebles or Tweeddale', engraved by Richard Cooper in Edinburgh, on the scale of almost an inch to a mile. It is still a sketch and not an exact delineation of the physical features, villages and roads; it has the prime meridian through Edinburgh (St Giles Cathedral), and only one minute of error in the latitude of Peebles. In 1742, Edgar describing himself as an architect, prepared a plan of Edinburgh, the first new plan for a century, for William Maitland's *History of Edinburgh*. Several manuscripts of unpublished maps by Edgar survive: 'Loch Lomond with the country circumjacent'

I

1743; 'Stirling-shire and Clackmannan-shire' 1743; a map of Perthshire in 1746, and a map (undated) combining his 'Tweeddale' (Peebles-shire) with the Firth of Forth and part of Midlothian taken from Adair's papers. In 1745 Edgar was employed by the Government in mapping the King's Road between Dumbarton and Inveraray; in 1746 he was with the Duke of Cumberland's army on the march from Aberdeen to Inverness, and several unsigned maps of areas around Aberdeen may be his work. According to Gough 'Mr. Edgar was a very faithful geographer, and did more shires, but his friends could not find his papers after he had accompanied the Duke of Cumberland in 1745 and died of fatigue in the Highlands in the beginning of the year 1746'.[8]

NEW SURVEYS: JOHN LAURIE

The first detailed survey, the pioneer of the reliable county map, was shown in John Laurie's map: 'A Plan of the County of Midlothian: from an Actual Survey made & drawn by John Laurie, 1763', engraved by Alex. Baillie of Edinburgh on the large scale of two inches to a mile. It is unusual in having south at the top. Roads, including minor roads, are drawn with fair accuracy, as also hamlets, villages and towns; plantations are rather generalized; the heights of hills are given but with considerable errors. Laurie published a smaller map in 1766 with north at the top: 'A Plan of Edinburgh and Places adjacent from an Actual Survey . . . by John Laurie, Geographer', engraved by Baillie on the scale of $1\frac{3}{8}$ inches to the mile. This also gives the roads and other features with substantial accuracy. It shows what are supposedly field boundaries of the arable land, but these do not appear to be actual boundaries as they are not in agreement with estate plans of the period. This 1766 map was re-issued in 1786, in 1811 and again in 1822, with Laurie's name removed and only minor alterations, principally in the New Town of Edinburgh.

The next county map in order of date was 'A Map of Roxburghshire' in 1770 by Matthew Stobie, on four sheets, on the scale of one inch to a mile, the first use of this scale in Scotland for county maps. Roads are roughly aligned; no enclosures are shown and the representation of the hills is rather inadequate.

ANDREW AND MOSTYN ARMSTRONG

In 1771 appeared the first of several Scottish county maps by Captain Andrew Armstrong and his son Mostyn James: 'The Map of the County of Berwick taken from an actual survey', and drawn on the scale of one inch to a mile. Andrew Armstrong had been a lieutenant in the army who retired on half-pay in 1763; in 1768 he published a map of the County of Durham, and one of the County of Northumberland in 1769. For the latter he received 50 guineas from the Society of Arts in London under its scheme, introduced in 1759, offering grants up to £105 for an accurate trigonometrical survey of a county and a map on the scale of at least one inch to one mile, a scheme which helped to establish this scale as the most useful one for county maps.[9]

The Armstrongs' map of Berwickshire conforms to the standards of the time (hills inadequately represented, no enclosures, and with the network of minor roads incomplete), as also did their 'Map of the Three Lothians', which has a note that the latitude and longitude were taken from observations by the Rev. Mr Bryce. The map is a substantial improvement on earlier maps of the Lothians; the line of the coast and the roads are better shown; positions in West and Mid Lothian are relatively accurate, but part of East Lothian is slightly out of position. Along with the map was published 'A Companion to Capt. Armstrong & Son's Map of the Three Lothians', giving a list of the towns, villages, landowners' residences, and subscribers. There were 292 subscribers at one and a half guineas each, so that the Armstrongs were assured of £460 from sales before they began the survey.

The Armstrongs then made a survey and map of Ayrshire; the map was drawn on the scale of an inch to a mile but a reduction on the scale of $3\frac{1}{8}$ miles to an inch was engraved and published in 1774 and the larger map then issued in 1775. According to Thomson 'the proprietors in the county saw the error of this map to be so great, that various efforts were made to have a new one, or to get this improved, which never met with suitable encouragement'. Comparison of the map with the map of the Military Survey shows the omission of some farms and minor roads, suggesting that the Armstrongs had not given enough time to their survey; the indications are that only one year, i.e., one summer, or at most two, were given to the actual survey, and, by comparison with other surveys of the period where the actual time spent on the survey has been recorded, this was quite inadequate. The errors of latitude and longitude are no greater than could be expected of the time; not much error in latitude but up to 15 minutes too far east in longitude; orientation is to true north.[10]

The County of Peebles was next surveyed by the son Mostyn John Armstrong, whose name alone appears on the 'Map of the County of Peebles or Tweeddale', published in 1775. His 'Companion to the Map of the County of Peebles' has a description of the Armstrongs' methods in making a county survey. Their textbook was Murdoch Mackenzie's book on *Maritime Surveying*; in accordance with his methods they first measured a base line with a chain, and went on to make a complete triangulation, before filling in the details of the physical features and settlements.

In 1776 Mostyn Armstrong published 'An Actual Survey of the Great Post Roads between London and Edinburgh', from surveys by his father and himself; in 1777 *A Scotch Atlas* (see Chapter 9), and 'Armstrong's Actual Survey of the Great Post Roads between London and Dover'. In 1775 or 1776 they left Scotland to engage in surveys of the counties of Lincoln and Rutland. Mostyn died in 1791 and Captain Armstrong in 1794.[11]

OTHER COUNTY SURVEYS

Other county maps of this period include 'A Map of the Shire of Lanark taken from an actual survey' by Charles Ross and engraved in 1773, on the scale of an inch to a mile. It is similar in style to the maps by Stobie and Armstrong; with the roads roughly correct, hills not adequately defined, and groups of trees shown to indicate plantations but no enclosures shown. Ross also published a map of Dunbartonshire in 1777. A marked improvement in surveying and mapping is seen in the 1776 'Map of Kincardineshire', engraved from a survey in 1774 by William Garden, land surveyor in Laurencekirk. This is one of the best examples of the estate surveyor applying his careful measurements to a county map. The roads are shown with complete accuracy; meticulous work is shown in delineating the enclosures and plantations, and there is sufficient identity between the field boundaries on this map and those on the modern Ordnance Survey maps to suggest that Garden's map is a very accurate picture of the county in 1774.

JOHN AINSLIE

The outstanding surveyor of the time, both in respect of the quality of his work and the large number of maps and plans he produced, was John Ainslie. Born in Jedburgh in 1745, we find him in the years 1765-71 gaining experience as a surveyor under Thomas Jefferys, Geographer to King George III, and taking part in county surveys of Bedford, Buckingham, Yorkshire, Cumberland, and Westmorland.[12] He returned home after Jefferys' death in 1771 and in the same year produced his first Scottish work 'A Plan of Jedburgh'. Richard Gough said of it: 'This Plan is accurately Survey'd, the Engraving the first of J. Ainslie's performance which is very bad both it and the printing'. In 1772 he engraved the reduced version of Armstrong's 'Map of Berwickshire', and in 1773 published a 'Map of Selkirkshire' from his own survey. This map followed the style of Edgar and Laurie in its generalizations, but Ainslie's next county map, 'Fife and Kinross', published in 1775, has the roads more exactly drawn and the enclosures carefully shown. In 1777 or 1778 Ainslie settled in Edinburgh as a stationer and land surveyor; and some ten years later went into partnership with his brother James in the New Town. This partnership lasted only two or three years; James kept the stationer's business and John continued his practice as a land surveyor. He died in Edinburgh in 1828.

The financial returns from his work up to 1784 seem to have been rather meagre, as in that year he applied to the Commissioners for the Forfeited Estates, explaining that his county maps had all been published by subscription but some of the subscribers had dropped out and other sales of the maps were few or none. He applied for assistance and asked if the Commissioners would buy some of his maps. They agreed to buy 25 copies of each (including 'Geographical Games of Europe' and 'Geographical Games of Scotland'), at a total cost of £98 15s—the plan of Edinburgh was 1s 6d and the map of Fife 31s 6d.[13]

His maps of Scotland in 1782 and 1789 are described in the next chapter. His surveys of the counties of Angus and Kirkcudbright showed up errors in existing maps of Scotland, and he was able to make corrections of these counties in the 1800 edition of his large map of Scotland.

The estate plans he prepared are too numerous to mention here, but quite exceptional are the volumes of plans prepared by him in 1789 for the Eglinton estate in Ayrshire—the Barony of Ardrossan, 25 plans; the Barony of Dreghorn, 8 plans; the Barony of Robertson, 16 plans; the Barony of Stone, 6 plans; the Barony of Kilwinning, 7 plans; and the Barony of Eglintoune, 12 plans.[1] He prepared and engraved a plan of Edinburgh about 1780, with a second edition in 1801, and a new plan in 1804 towards the cost of which the town council contributed £20.

In 1802 Ainslie published *The Gentleman and Farmer's Pocket Companion and Assistant*, as a guide to surveying, and then in 1812 published his *Comprehensive Treatise on Land Surveying*. It has chapters on The Chain, The Cross Staff, The Plain Table, The Sextant, Protractors and Parallel Rulers, Circumferenter, Theodolite; other chapters on County Surveying, Military Surveying, Reducing Plans, Delineating Plans, and so on. In county surveying he puts the basic requirement: select and measure a base line, go from hill to hill.

LATER SURVEYORS

Several other county surveys were made in the period 1780-1825 and maps published on the scale of one inch to a mile (or larger):

Perth and Clackmannan by James Stobie in 1783; Berwickshire by John Blackadder in 1797; Haddington by William Forrest in 1801; Argyll by George Langlands & Son in 1801; Dumfriesshire by William Crawford in 1804; Lanarkshire by Forrest in 1816; Midlothian by James Knox in 1816; Stirlingshire by J. Grassom in 1817; and the counties of Aberdeen, Banff and Kincardine by James Robertson in 1822. Of these, three were commended by Thomson in the Introduction to his *Atlas of Scotland* (1832). Of Blackadder's map of Berwickshire he says: 'This was considered the best map of the Counties when published, and the name of Blackadder stood high in the estimation of the proprietors in the county, for his attainments as a surveyor, and the care he took to make his plan remarkably minute and accurate'. James Stobie's map of Perthshire he described as one of the best county maps of Scotland, but his highest praise was given to the map of Haddington-shire (East Lothian) by William Forrest, 'a land surveyor of great experience, and no less industry' who spent two years on the survey: 'The masterly manner in which this map is executed is at once a memorial of industry, skill and enterprise, seldom found in one individual. The noblemen and Gentlemen's domains, the towns and villages, with the roads, the parish boundaries, the sea coast, the woods and the rivers, are presented on paper as if reflected in a glass.' No Ordnance Survey map, with all its accuracy, could justify greater praise.

TAYLOR AND SKINNER'S ROAD MAPS

Although volumes of strip road maps of England and Wales had been popular since first published by John Ogilby in 1675, a similar volume for Scotland did not appear until 1776, when George Taylor and Andrew Skinner, surveyors in Aberdeen, published *Taylor & Skinner's Survey and Maps of the Roads of North Britain or Scotland*, dedicating it to John, Duke of Argyll, Commander-in-Chief of the Forces in Scotland. It contains 'A General Map of the Roads of Scotland' dated 1778, on the scale of 23 miles to an inch, and 61 plates, generally $18 \times 7\frac{1}{4}$ inches, each divided into three strip maps of the roads on the scale of one inch to a mile, giving in all over 3000 miles of roads. Several engravers were employed on the maps—Pyle, Barber, T. Bowen, Terry, Roberts, Luffman, Taylor; the dates on the plates are spread over the period from June 1775 to February 1776.

The survey cost £306, engraving and binding 3000 copies £487, paper, expenses of distribution and allowances to booksellers £640, a total of £1433. The subscriptions at 10s 6d did not amount to 2000, a possible revenue of less than £1050, and Taylor and Skinner applied to the Commissioners for the Forfeited Estates in July 1775 and July 1776 for financial assistance, pointing out that in the reign of Charles II, Ogilby had received Government assistance. In July 1778 they thanked the Commissioners for generous assistance already given, and reported to the Commissioners that 1457 copies remained unsold and that they still owed £220 for printing costs. In July 1779 they still owed £150 and requested a further grant.[14]

Taylor and Skinner also published 'A Survey of the Great Post Roads between London, Bath and Bristol' in 1776; 'A Map of the County of Louth' in 1777, and 'Maps of the Roads of Ireland' in 1778. Richard Gough says of them that they 'published proposals, and got many subscribers, for taking a survey, and making a large map of this county (Perthshire), which has never been hitherto done. These surveyors neglected the scheme for a more lucrative employ of publishing the roads of Ireland: since that was finished they have gained some office in the army in America, and have quitted that project'.

Some years later a smaller version, described as *Taylor & Skinner's Survey of the Roads of Scotland on an Improved Plan . . . with the New Roads*, etc. was produced by Thomas Brown, bookseller and map publisher in Edinburgh. It contained 176 pages, each with a double strip map 6 × 3 inches on the scale of 6/10 inch to a mile; engraving was done in Edinburgh by Paton and D. Lizars.

In Cambridge University Library is a manuscript roadbook by George Taylor, 'Sketches of the Roads in Scotland', dated at Aberdeen 1785. It has 103 maps meticulously drawn and coloured, with written descriptions of the towns and villages on the route, and notices of the owners of country mansions, all in very neat italic script.[14]

12 Scottish Cartographers and Map-makers

The mapping of Scotland had brought no success to Timothy Pont in 1610, it had reduced John Adair to poverty in 1710, and it was to bring John Thomson to bankruptcy in 1830. A survey of the country was too great for one man's effort and too costly to be met by revenue from sales, but the production of maps, developed as part of an engraver's business to meet a specific need, could be a commercial success.

So it happened in Scotland. The development began in the second half of the 18th century, in an age of notable progress in Scottish culture. The Scottish Universities had entered upon a period of great expansion, with distinguished professors and talented lecturers giving them a reputation throughout Europe. The Scottish contributions to architecture, painting, and literature, in that period were all outstanding. The growth in cultural interests, and increasing prosperity, created a demand for books—an Edinburgh bookseller's catalogue of 1793 had over five thousand titles.[1] It is indicative of the search for knowledge that the *Encyclopaedia Britannica* originated with Edinburgh citizens who published the first edition in 1771. These books were frequently illustrated by engravings of portraits or landscapes, providing employment for several engravers working at this time in Edinburgh. It was not difficult for these engravers to turn from their portraits and landscapes to the engraving of maps, using as a basis for their work James Dorret's maps of 1750 and 1751, supplemented as time went on by the new county maps, and replaced in 1789 by the new map of Scotland by John Ainslie, and it, in turn, by the map by Aaron Arrowsmith in 1807.

Some Edinburgh engravers had worked on maps before this time; James Clark, who engraved charts for John Adair around 1693; Richard Cooper, portrait engraver, who about 1735 engraved several county maps, including three maps of the Lothians from manuscript maps left by Adair, and Alexander Baillie, who engraved a map of Midlothian in 1763.

The beginning with maps of Scotland was made with small maps engraved for books by some of the Edinburgh engravers: Hector Gavin, with a map of Scotland in 1767 for Salmon's *Grammar*; Daniel Lizars, who began a long connection with maps, with his

small map of Scotland in the *Scots Almanack* of 1782; and Andrew
Bell (1725-1809), co-founder of the *Encyclopaedia Britannica* and a
noted portrait engraver, with a map of Scotland in 1785 for James
Anderson's *Account of the Present State of the Hebrides*. All three
had previously engraved town plans of Edinburgh: Gavin in 1763,
Bell in 1773, and Lizars in 1778.[2]

JOHN AINSLIE

In 1789 all earlier maps of Scotland were rendered out of date by
the publication of a large map by John Ainslie, land surveyor and
engraver, whose work on estate plans and county maps is described
in Chapter 11. In 1783 he produced his first map of Scotland:
'Ainslie's Travelling Map . . . showing the distances from one stage
to another', which was copied from, and is on the same scale as, the
1761 map of James Dorret, with two improvements. (1) The Great
Glen is shown as a straight line—this follows J. Bayly's map of
1777, and (2) the Solway Firth coastline has been considerably
altered following Ainslie's survey of Wigtownshire in 1781-82. The
map has relatively few place names, no rivers, and only occasional
indications of mountains, the emphasis being on roads and mileages.

In 1784-85 the versatile Ainslie surveyed the east coast of Scotland
from Berwick to Duncansby Head and prepared a General Chart
on the scale of 4 miles to an inch, issued in 1785, and three separate
charts on the scale of 2 miles to an inch, published in 1786.[3] Ainslie
also prepared a chart of the south-west coast from Saltcoats to
Whitehaven, including Arran, in six sheets for the Commissioners of
Customs, partly from a survey by Ainslie from Saltcoats to Wigtown
Bay, and partly from other charts.

His 1789 map has the title 'Scotland Drawn and Engraved from
a series of angles and astronomical observations by John Ainslie,
Land Surveyor'; a map in nine sheets on the scale of 4 miles to an
inch—the same scale as Dorret's map of 1750—with longitude
based on Edinburgh, and, alongside, a table of distances between
61 towns. The main improvements in Ainslie's map, compared with
Dorret's map, were in the straight line of the Great Glen and in the
Hebrides, where Ainslie has made use of the charts of the west
coast and Hebrides published by Murdoch Mackenzie in 1775-76 for
more correct outlines and details of Skye, North and South Uist,
Mull, Jura and Islay. The northern part of Lewis had been corrected
by Dorret from Mackenzie's 1750 charts; Ainslie now corrected the
rest of Lewis and Harris from the 1776 charts. It is not obvious
where Ainslie got the coastline of the mainland from Skye to Cape
Wrath, as it does not follow either Dorret or Mackenzie, and the
same applies to the shape of Arran—which is corrected in his own

chart of the south-west coast. The east coast in the map of Scotland coincides, apart from minor details, with his own chart published in 1785.

The 1789 edition of the map was published by John and James Ainslie, Booksellers and Stationers, St Andrew Street, Edinburgh, and William Faden, Geographer to the King, London.[4] In a later edition 'with improvements till 1800' the Ainslie name is replaced by Thomas Brown, North Bridge Street, Edinburgh. The 1800 edition shows several alterations from the first edition, apart from the addition of a number of place names throughout Scotland. (1) The counties of Angus and Kirkcudbright have been redrawn, as a result of the surveys of these counties made by Ainslie in 1794 and 1796 respectively, and the publication of his separate maps of these counties. (2) On some of the maps South Uist has been redrawn. William Bald, who was an assistant to Ainslie, prepared a map of South Uist in 1805, and the most likely explanation is that after this survey, the plate with South Uist was altered without the date on the map being altered. Later editions of the map were published up to the 11th edition in 1840.

Ainslie published a third map of Scotland in 1792 'Scotland by John Ainslie, Land Surveyor', on the scale of c. 16 miles to an inch, based on his larger map of 1789 but with fewer place names.

JAMES AND ROBERT KIRKWOOD

The Kirkwoods were primarily engravers, who brought to engraving a high degree of skill. James Kirkwood (1745/6-1827), first in business as a watchmaker and engraver in Perth, moved to Edinburgh in 1785-86. He engraved plans of Perth in 1774 and 1792, and in 1795 a map of Glasgow and its environs. In 1799 his son Robert became a partner, and in 1801 they were the engravers of William Forrest's large map of Haddingtonshire, a map 48 × 58 inches on the scale of 2 inches to a mile. In 1804 they published a 'Travelling Map of Scotland' on the scale of 11 miles to an inch, and several plans of Edinburgh from 1815 to 1829, of which the most interesting is their 'Plan and Elevation of the New Town of Edinburgh', dated 1st October 1819, showing the elevations of all the houses and buildings in pictorial form. They also engraved small maps of Scotland and parts of Scotland for travellers' guide-books, three of the town plans (Ayr, Glasgow, and Kilmarnock) in Wood's *Town Atlas*, as well as railway and canal plans.

THOMAS BROWN

Thomas Brown was in business as a bookseller and map publisher from c. 1786 until his death in 1820, for most of the time at No. 1

North Bridge. He published a *General Atlas* in 1801, a *New and Elegant Classical Atlas*, several plans of Edinburgh between 1793 and 1820, and seven editions of a *Guide to Edinburgh* from 1790 to 1820.

Brown's publication of maps of Scotland began in 1791 with 'A New & Accurate Travelling Map of Scotland with the distances between each stage in Measured Miles', on the scale of 10½ miles to an inch, a map copied from Dorret's map of 1750. Later, about 1795, he published 'A New and Correct Map of Scotland reduced from Mr. Ainslie's Nine Sheet Map', on the scale of 7½ miles to an inch. This is a somewhat careless copy of Ainslie's map of 1789 as St Mary's Loch is omitted, and both Arran and Bute are taken from Dorret and not from Ainslie. A third map, 'A New and Accurate Map of Scotland with the Roads', on the scale of 19 miles to an inch, and based on Ainslie and engraved by Gavin and Son, was included in Brown's *Atlas of Scotland* (see below), and in *A General Atlas* in 1801. In 1806 appeared 'A Travelling Map of Scotland including all the new and intended roads, bridges and canals', drawn by Paton and engraved by D. Lizars, on a scale of *c.* 11 miles to an inch. This map has Arran and Bute from Ainslie, with longitude based on Edinburgh; no mountains are shown, and only a restricted number of place names.

Brown's *Atlas of Scotland, being a new set of County Maps from Actual Surveys* is undated. In addition to a map of Scotland, described above, it has 25 finely engraved maps of the counties (some plates have two counties), each with the title 'A New and Accurate Map of ——Shire', four of them engraved by T. Clerk, the others by Gavin & Son. The maps are mostly 11 × 13 inches, on scales varying from 2 to 8 miles per inch; altogether a much better atlas than those by Kitchin in 1749 and Armstrong in 1777.

W. H. LIZARS

William Home Lizars (1788-1859) son of Daniel Lizars, showed talent as a painter and two paintings which made his reputation, 'Reading the Will' and 'A Scotch Wedding', were exhibited at the Royal Academy in London and are now in the Scottish National Portrait Gallery. On his father's death in 1812 he took over the engraving business.

His maps of Scotland were small ones (*c.* 15 to 18 miles per inch) for guide books. About 1820 he engraved the maps for a small volume of 53 sectional maps of Scotland, on the scale of 7 miles to an inch, published with the title of 'Travelling Map of Scotland' by Peter Hill, a well-known bookseller in the old town of Edinburgh. This map was re-issued some years later by Oliver and

Boyd, a firm of printers in Edinburgh, with the title 'Oliver and Boyd's Travelling Map of Scotland'.

Between 1826 and 1850 Lizars engraved several plans of Edinburgh for the annual directories, several county geological maps, and in the years 1834-39 the series of Scottish county maps which are contained in the volumes of *The New Statistical Account of Scotland* published by William Blackwood & Sons and completed in 1845. These county maps, along with a map of Scotland, were also issued as a separate volume in 1838 with the title *Blackwood's Atlas of Scotland*, in two sizes, quarto and octavo, with a revised edition in 1853.

W. H. Lizars' brother Daniel, who had been his partner, left the partnership in 1819, and in 1823 started business on his own account as a bookseller in Princes Street, Edinburgh. From this address he issued *The Edinburgh Geographical and Historical Atlas*, first published in monthly numbers about 1827; the maps, engraved by W. H. Lizars, included a map of Scotland on the scale of 12 miles to an inch. There were two later re-issues of the *Atlas* by W. H. Lizars.

GALL & INGLIS

The firm of Gall & Inglis originated in a printing business set up by James Gall in Edinburgh in 1810. The son, James Gall, who became a partner in 1838 resigned in 1847 to become a minister of the Church of Scotland, but has left his mark on cartography by devising three projections—the Stereographic, the Isographic, and the Orthographic. Gall's Stereographic Projection is still in use in some atlases to-day. About 1851 they published *The Edinburgh Imperial Atlas*; it includes a map of Scotland on the scale of 16 miles to an inch.[5]

JOHN LOTHIAN

John Lothian, originally a bookseller at 41 St Andrew Square, later described himself as a map publisher and geographer.

In 1825 he published 'Lothian's Plan of the City of Edinburgh and its Vicinity', engraved by Geo. Bartholomew, with a second edition in 1829. His *County Atlas of Scotland* first issued in 1827, contained a map of Scotland on the scale of 33 miles to an inch, and 33 county maps, each about $9\frac{1}{2} \times 7\frac{1}{2}$ inches. A second edition was issued in 1830 and a third in 1835; the maps in 1835 had lines of latitude and longitude added, additional place names and other minor alterations. The maps were also sold separately or as a set, folded, in three small boxes.

A supplement to the *Atlas* was a series of six maps 'exhibiting Scotland at the time of the Romans' forming 'a work which may be had either separately or along with the *County Atlas* as an Appendix'.

Lothian also issued in 1846 *The People's Atlas . . . revised by J. Lothian*, containing 46 maps, including a map of Scotland on the scale of 19 miles to an inch.

JOHN THOMSON

Born in 1777, the son of an Edinburgh merchant, John Thomson apparently set up as a bookseller in Hunter Square, Edinburgh, in 1807, the earliest record of John Thomson, junior & Co., booksellers. In 1824 he moved to St Andrew Square in the New Town.

One of his early publications was *The Traveller's Guide through Scotland and its Islands* first published in 1798 (9th edition, 1829). His first atlas, *A New General Atlas*, was issued in 1817 and re-issued in 1821, 1828, and 1829. He also published *A New Classical and Historical Atlas*, a folio volume of 50 maps, *The Edinburgh School Classical Atlas*, *The Cabinet Atlas*, and the *Edinburgh School Atlas*, and separate large maps of Europe, Africa, Asia and America of four sheets each.

For the production of *A New General Atlas* in 1817, Thomson apparently got others to share the cost, as it was described on the title page as printed by G. Ramsay in Edinburgh for John Thomson & Co., Edinburgh; Baldwin Cradock & Joy, London; and John Cumming, Dublin. An introductory chapter has the title 'Memoir of the Progress of Geography'; this is followed by 'A Summary of Physical Geography' and a gazetteer of over 4000 place names. The large folio atlas has 81 double-page maps and charts, mostly about $19\frac{1}{2} \times 23$ inches, the largest atlas printed or published in Scotland up to that date. The work of engraving was shared between several engravers in Edinburgh and London, and the dates on the maps run from 1814 to 1817; N. R. Hewitt of London was the engraver of the map 'Scotland', on the scale of $12\frac{1}{2}$ miles to an inch and dated 1st April 1815. This map is a close copy of Arrowsmith's map, even to the shape of Bute and the relative positions of Ballater and Braemar, and in the lines of latitude and longitude. In the second edition of the *Atlas* in 1821 the number of maps was increased to 81 by redrawing several on a larger scale on two sheets. 'Scotland', again engraved by Hewitt, is on the scale of $9\frac{1}{4}$ miles to an inch, with several corrections, including the rectification of the Ballater/Braemar positions, and some slight improvement in relation to latitudes and longitudes, but the redrawn Western Isles are less accurate than in the earlier map. Later editions with the same map of Scotland were issued in 1828 and 1829.

Thomson's most ambitious work was his *Atlas of Scotland*, containing maps of each county on a larger scale than previously attempted except some in Blaeu's *Atlas* of 1654. The first prospectus was issued in August 1818 and within a short period the number of subscribers exceeded 1200. For most counties existing county maps were used as a basis, new maps being drawn from them and revised by land surveyors and other local persons; on many of the maps are four to seven names of persons who had checked the map, and attested the accuracy of the work. Some of the maps were engraved directly from existing maps—the map of Dunbartonshire is a close copy by S. Hall of Wood's map of 1818; the map of Haddington is a reduced but close copy of William Forrest's map of 1799. For the county of Edinburgh Thomson used the actual plates of Knox's map of 1812, with certain alterations to fit the map into the size of the *Atlas*. For some counties new surveys were made; for Ayrshire, William Johnson resided three summers in the town of Ayr so that he could more easily examine the plans of the different estates made available by the proprietors and check them from personal surveys. For Fife, Alexander Martin, land surveyor, made a new survey over the years 1822-26; the County of Sutherland was surveyed at the expense of the Countess of Sutherland; and John MacKinlay made a survey of Bute. Engravers both in Edinburgh and London were employed and the work spread over eleven years, two maps being dated 1820 and the last three dated 1830. They were in fact sold loose as they became available.

In the Preface Thomson wrote: 'Since that period (i.e. 1818), the work has been continually in progress, but the great difficulty of finding assistants, materials, and making the necessary surveys, have retarded the completion much longer than anticipated. The Publisher will now take leave of the ATLAS OF SCOTLAND—a Work which he never would have undertaken, had he known the difficulties to be encountered, the great number of people to be employed, the advance of capital, and the time necessary to carry through such an arduous undertaking, which required at least one surveyor to each county to correct the drawings, and find respectable names to guarantee their accuracy.'

Before the *Atlas* was finished Thomson found himself in financial difficulties; he could no longer meet the expenses of the work and on 20th April 1830, signed a petition of bankruptcy. The Trustee for the creditors decided to complete the *Atlas* and had to make payments to Thomas Clerk, engraver, in order to obtain the plates and 700 copies of the map of Nairn and Elgin; and to William Johnson, the draughtsman, and Robert Menzies, the engraver, who would not complete the map of Inverness-shire until paid. Attempts by the trustee to sell the complete stock were unsuccessful and when a public sale was held in April 1831, Thomson as 'John Thomson & Co.' bought the stock of atlases, maps, and plates for £1800, payment to be in three instalments and guaranteed by his friends.[6] It is recorded that even then large outlays were necessary to complete the *Atlas of Scotland*. A title page had been printed for the Trustee and dated 1831; it was replaced by one dated 1832. 'Printed for John Thomson & Co., Edinburgh; Baldwin & Craddock, London; and John Cumming, London', and with an index dated 1832 the *Atlas* was at last completed.

It has 58 maps, mostly 20 × 26½ inches, on scales between 1 and 2 miles to an inch (with the county of Edinburgh in four sheets exceptionally on the scale of almost 1½ miles to an inch), resulting in the largest and most detailed map of Scotland prior to the Ordnance Survey. The styles of engraving vary: Hewitt in 'Linlithgow' emphasizes the hills; Butterworth in 'Fife' almost ignores them.

Thomson continued to trade from 1832 to 1835 but financial difficulties persisted and on 16th May he signed a petition of bankruptcy for a second time. In November 1835 he could find no guarantors to assist him in another arrangement with his creditors, and the Trustee thereupon decided to sell off the plates and stock. Thomson & Co. are last on record in 1837 as 'Stationers and publishers of the Atlas of Scotland'. The plates of the *Atlas of Scotland* were later acquired by W. & A. K. Johnston, who re-issued it about 1855 in cooperation with William Blackwood & Son and others, with the names of all the surveyors and engravers removed from the maps and replaced by Johnston's name. Lines of railways and new roads were added to the maps, and for the county of Roxburgh a new map was drawn by N. Tennant.

ADAM AND CHARLES BLACK

The publishing firm of Adam and Charles Black was founded in 1807 when Adam Black (1784-1874) opened a bookshop at 57 South Bridge Street, Edinburgh. His nephew Charles became a partner in 1834. From 1827 to 1899 Black's were the owners and publishers of the *Encyclopaedia Britannica*, and in 1851 they acquired the copyright of all Sir Walter Scott's works.

In 1840 the first edition of Black's *General Atlas* was issued, a folio volume of 54 maps, engraved by Sidney Hall of London but printed by Constable in Edinburgh. The map of 'Scotland', on the scale of 18 miles to an inch, was based substantially on Arrowsmith's map, but with some corrections, e.g., Jura, and with a slight bend given to the Great Glen. The *Atlas* proved very popular and twelve editions were issued up to 1876—from 1844 with a larger map of Scotland by Sidney Hall on the scale of 10 miles to an inch. The 1882 edition had new and much improved maps by John Bartholomew. Black's published also *A School Atlas* in 1851, a

Pocket Atlas in 1852; an *Atlas of North America* in 1856, and *A Modern Atlas* in 1874. A plan of Edinburgh was issued in *Black's Economical Guide through Edinburgh* in 1839 (3rd edition, 1843). Black's *County Atlas of Scotland* with title page dated 1848, and maps dated 1847, was a re-issue of the county atlas first published by John Lothian in 1827.

In 1862 they were the publishers of the most accurate map of Scotland so far issued, a map drawn and engraved by John Bartholomew, on 12 sheets on the scale of 4 miles to an inch, which superseded all earlier maps and remained the standard map until the issue of the Ordnance Survey maps. It was also issued in atlas form as *Black's New Atlas of Scotland*.

W. & A. K. JOHNSTON

The business of W. & A. K. Johnston was founded in Edinburgh in 1825 by William Johnston (1802-88), who had learned engraving and printing with Lizars and Kirkwood. In May 1826 he was joined by his brother Alexander Keith Johnston (1804-71), who had also been trained as an engraver. In 1830 their first maps appeared in *A Traveller's Guide*. In 1833, 1834 and 1851, they published plans of the city of Edinburgh.

It was A. Keith Johnston who developed the production of maps and atlases. In 1843, after five years' work, he produced *The National Atlas of Historical, Commercial and Political Geography*. It contained 41 general maps, most of them engraved by Keith Johnston himself, an ethnographic map of Europe by Dr Gustaf Kombst, and four maps of physical geography by Heinrich Berghaus, professor of geography at Berlin, these last as a result of Keith Johnston's travels in Germany and Austria and an arrangement made then with Berghaus. In the Preface Professor Berghaus wrote: 'I now submit to the friends of Geography in Britain four sheets of my Physical Geography, which differ from those of the German edition, in being much larger and more complete. Should these be appreciated, I shall, in conjunction with my friend Mr. A. K. Johnston, gladly continue them . . . Of the German edition, which enjoys a very extensive circulation wherever the language is known, fifty maps have been published up to this time'. (Berghaus began the preparation of maps of physical geography in 1827 and published them in 1837-48). The four maps in Johnston's *Atlas* includes Humboldt's isotherms and the geographical distribution of food plants.

The *Atlas* includes a map of 'Scotland' by A. Keith Johnston, on the scale of $12\frac{1}{2}$ miles to an inch, engraved on the high standard of the work of W. & A. K. Johnston. A note engraved on the map says that several points on the west coast have been corrected from recent astronomical observations by W. Galbraith, and others have been checked from the Ordnance Survey, while rectifications have been made in the interior of the country from recent surveys. Improvements may have resulted from the corrections, but Ardnamurchan is less correctly drawn than in Arrowsmith's map and neither Islay nor Jura is correct. The *Atlas* was re-issued with a title page dated 1846; later editions appeared in 1850 and 1854.

Keith Johnston continued his interest in physical geography and the arrangements with Berghaus made possible Johnston's publication in 1848 of *The Physical Atlas . . . illustrating the Geographical Distribution of Natural Phenomena . . . based on the Physikalischer Atlas of Professor H. Berghaus (etc.)*. The *Physical Atlas* contained 30 maps and charts in four divisions: geology, hydrology, meteorology and natural history, each $19\frac{1}{2} \times 23$ inches, with a lengthy descriptive text. Fifteen of the maps were designed by Berghaus and were now issued on an enlarged scale with additions; the other 15 were drawn by Keith Johnston from information supplied by distinguished scientists; including a 'Palaeontological Map of the British Islands', on two large sheets, from the sketches and notes of Professor Edward Forbes, F.R.S.; and 'Glacier Systems of the Alps' from the surveys and sketches of Professor J. D. Forbes. The *Atlas* was reissued in 1850 with changes in colours on some of the plates. A second edition in 1856 had the shorter title *The Physical Atlas of Natural Phenomena*; six of the original maps were replaced by new ones, and of the seven new maps was one to show 'The Geographical Distribution of Health and Disease'. A smaller atlas by Johnston, with the same title, was issued in 1850 with Blackwood's name as publisher.

The third of the large atlases coming from this firm was *The Royal Atlas of Modern Geography*, dedicated to Queen Victoria, first issued in 1861, with 48 maps, each $17\frac{1}{2} \times 22\frac{1}{2}$ inches. Every sheet of this atlas was examined by the Prince Consort before publication. 'Scotland' by Keith Johnston, appeared on two sheets, 'Northern' and 'Southern', on the scale of 10 miles to an inch. This map shows a considerable improvement on the map of Scotland in his 1843 *National Atlas*. All the maps are very clear and beautifully engraved; they were revised with every new edition—usually involving the addition of new railways in Scotland, but with more extensive changes in those countries where exploration was bringing new information. In the 1873 edition a 'North Polar Chart' was added as a preface.

Keith Johnston's work was recognized by his appointment as 'Geographer to the Queen in Scotland', and by other honours.[8]

K

JOHN BARTHOLOMEW & SON

The association of the name Bartholomew with maps goes back to the 18th century when in 1797 George Bartholomew (1784-1871) started his apprenticeship as a map engraver with Daniel Lizars. Lizars had himself been a pupil of Andrew Bell, a famous engraver and co-proprietor of the original *Encyclopaedia Britannica*, the maps for which were later destined to be produced by the firm of Bartholomew. George's name appears as the engraver of Lothian's plan of Edinburgh in 1825. His son John I (1805-61) is reputed to have started the family business in 1826 and he was responsible for the engraving of the first directory plan of Edinburgh in that year. John II (1831-93) trained under his father and worked for a time under Dr. Augustus Petermann, the famous German geographer and cartographer. It was not until 1860 under his own management that the firm established their own printing works. John George (1860-1920) joined his father and in 1883 took control of the business.

The early work of the firm included the maps for *Black's School Atlas* in 1853, for the 1860 edition of *Black's General Atlas*, and for a large number of atlases in succeeding years. John Bartholomew II was the engraver of Black's 'Map of Scotland' (1862), on the scale of 4 miles to the inch, in 12 sheets, a map excelling in the standard of engraving and its general clarity, and printed with brown hill shading. However, it was J. G. Bartholomew who developed the commercial use of the portrayal of relief by contours and layer colouring. This was first used in Baddeley's *Guide to the Lake District* in 1880 and was later generally adopted for the well-known Bartholomew 'Half-Inch' Series of Maps, which thus acquired the distinction of being the first topographical series in any country to make use of the layered system of colouring. Other major works have included *Atlas of Scotland*, 1895; *Atlas of Meteorology*, 1899; *Atlas of England & Wales*, 1903; *Atlas of World's Commerce*, 1907; and *Atlas of Zoogeography*, 1911.

The outstanding *Times Atlas of the World*, the work originally of J. G. Bartholomew, was first produced in 1921, followed by a five-volume edition in 1955-59, and later editions in English, Dutch and German, with maps equalling in size, if not in number, the great Dutch atlases of the 17th century. It is not without interest that these atlases, coming from the small country of Holland, should have their modern counterpart, the *Times Atlas*, from another small country, Scotland.

SCOTTISH CARTOGRAPHERS AND ENGRAVERS

BIOGRAPHICAL NOTES

ADAIR, John

Adair is first mentioned in 1676 when he was in London, in the company of Robert Hooke, whose *Diary* records the meeting. In 1681 he first appears in Scottish records, in the Register of the Privy Council. His wife was Jean Oliphant, described by a descendant as the daughter of James Oliphant, W.S., and the granddaughter of Lord Oliphant (Edin. Univ. Liby., MS. LA 1011). In 1688 Adair was living 'in the Grassmarket near the muse well' (SRO Reg. Deeds DAL LXIX, p. 935). On 15th April 1697 he bought a 'back land', i.e., a tenement flat on the south side of the Canongate (Edin. Univ. Liby., Laing Charters, no. 3079). One of the witnesses to the deed was James Clark, engraver at the Scottish Mint. He was made a Burgess of the Canongate on 30th September 1699. He died on 15th May 1718. (See Chapter 8.)

AINSLIE, John

Born in Jedburgh on 22nd April 1745, the son of a writer (i.e. lawyer). On 27th October 1776 he married in the Tolbooth Church, Edinburgh, Christina Caverhill, daughter of a Jedburgh merchant. Ainslie first appears in the Edinburgh Directory in 1778 as stationer and land surveyor in Parliament Square. He moved to the New Town in 1788 and appears in the Directory for 1788-90 as a partner with his brother in the business of John and James Ainslie, booksellers and stationers, 4 St Andrew Street. John's first wife, Christina, had presumably died and he had remarried before 1788, as the property in St Andrew Street (occupied on 1st January 1788), was in the names of John Ainslie, land surveyor, and Mary Lookup, his spouse. She may have been the sister of James's wife, Agnes Lookup, daughter of a Jedburgh architect, whom he had married on 11th June 1787. The business partnership was a short one; the Directory for 1790/92 shows John Ainslie, land surveyor, Rose Street, and James Ainslie, stationer, at 4 St Andrew Street. The next Directory entries are for John Ainslie, land surveyor, 8 South Hanover Street, and Mrs Ainslie, bookseller, 11 East Rose Street. Presumably James had died and Mrs Ainslie carried on the stationer's business from 1796 in South Hanover Street until about 1812. In the 1793/94 Directory John Ainslie's address is given as 8 South Hanover Street; the property was actually acquired for occupation on 4th April 1789. In 1800 John Ainslie moved to 28 Nicolson Street; his second wife may by then have died as she is not named in the title deeds. He was at 28 Nicolson Street until 1810, at 31 Nicolson Street in 1810/11, and from 1811 at 58 Nicolson Street, where he died on 29th February 1828. His estate of £8976 7s 6d went to his daughters Catherine and Mary.

ARMSTRONG, Andrew

Although the name Armstrong is associated with the Scottish Border counties the fact that Andrew Armstrong's first two maps were of Durham and Northumberland (1768 and 1769) suggests that he may have been born in the North of England. In the Army list of 1761 he is entered under the 32nd Regiment of Foot as Lieut. Andrew Armstrong, appointed 31st August 1756. In 1763 this regiment was reduced and from that year Armstrong is entered up to and including 1796 as a lieutenant on half pay, although, except on his map of Northumberland, he always describes himself as Captain. His only address in Scotland was care of John's Coffee House. After completing the map of Peeblesshire in 1775 he and his son Mostyn John moved to Norfolk and in November 1776 they announced proposals for a survey and large scale map of Norfolk—a project never completed although Mostyn published the *History and Antiquities of the County of Norfolk*. Captain Armstrong surveyed Lincolnshire in 1776-78 and published a map of it in 1779 and in 1781 a map of Rutland. Mostyn became an ensign in the Norfolk Militia, later lieutenant; he describes himself as County Surveyor on a plan of Great Yarmouth dated 1779; he died on 11th December 1791. (See references to Chapter 11.)

BARTHOLOMEW, George

Born in Edinburgh in 1784 he was apprenticed as an engraver with D. Lizars in 1797. In 1806 he is entered in the Edinburgh Directory as engraver at 3 Richmond Street, later No. 33, until 1816. From 1823 to 1842 he was at 6 Leopold Place, then at Gayfield Place (later Haddington Place), and died at 6 Salisbury Place, Edinburgh, on 23rd October 1871, aged 87.

BARTHOLOMEW, John I

Born in Edinburgh in 1805, the son of George Bartholomew, John trained as an engraver and is usually credited with founding the family firm around 1826. The first entry in the Edinburgh Directory for John is in 1830 as engraver at 4 East St James' Street. In 1838 he was at 21 Broughton Street, in 1846 at 13 Union Street, and in 1860 at 4a North Bridge, with printing works in Carrubber's Close. In 1860 the firm's name became John Bartholomew and Son. He died on 9th April 1861 at Grange Bank Cottage, Morningside, aged 56.

BARTHOLOMEW, John II

Born in Edinburgh on 25th December 1831, son of John I, apprentice draughtsman and engraver with his father and then was in London from 1853 to 1856 as assistant to Dr Petermann. He became a partner with his father in 1860. In 1870 the business was moved to 17 Brown Square (where the Dental Hospital now stands), and in 1889 to Park Road. He died on 29th March 1893 on a visit to London.

BARTHOLOMEW, John George (1860-1920)

Born in Edinburgh in 1860, son of John II, he started in his father's drawing office at the age of 16. He immediately concentrated on perfecting the method of showing map relief by contours combined with layer colouring, which was first shown at the Paris Exhibition of 1878 and eventually became universally accepted. During his time expansion of the business required a further move in 1911 from Park Road to Duncan Street. In 1884 he was one of the original founders of the R.S.G.S. and was one of their Honorary Secretaries from inception until his death. In 1905 he was awarded the RGS 'Victoria Medal' and made LLD of Edinburgh in 1909. He was appointed Geographer and Cartographer to King George V.

BELL, Andrew (1726-1809)

Engraver in Edinburgh; an apprentice of Robert Cooper, Senior, his work was chiefly book illustration. He and Colin McFarquhar founded the *Encyclopaedia Britannica*, published 1768-71, for which Bell engraved the plates for the first edition. He died on 10th May 1809 at Lauriston Lane, aged 83. His portrait is in the Scottish National Portrait Gallery.

BLACK, Adam (1784-1874)

Born in Edinburgh on 20th February 1784, son of an Edinburgh builder, and educated at the High School and Edinburgh University, he was apprenticed to a bookseller for five years. He then went to London for two years and returned in 1807 to start his own business as a bookseller at 57 South Bridge, opposite the University, removing in 1822 to larger premises at 27 North Bridge, and in 1851 to No. 6 North Bridge. In 1827 he acquired the copyright of the *Encyclopaedia Britannica* and published the seventh edition in 21 volumes over the years 1830-44; he also acquired the *Edinburgh Review* and later the copyright of Sir Walter Scott's works. The firm became Adam and Charles Black in 1834 when he took his nephew Charles into partnership. Adam Black was twice Lord Provost of Edinburgh (1843-48), and from 1856 to 1865 M.P. for the city. He died on 24th January 1874, aged 89; a statue of him is in East Princes Street Gardens.

BLACKWOOD, William (1776-1834)

Born in Edinburgh in 1776, he was apprenticed to a bookseller in Edinburgh at the age of 14. After experience in London he returned to Edinburgh in 1804 and began business on his own account at 64 South Bridge. In 1816 he moved to 17 Princes Street, and in 1830 to 45 George Street. In 1817 he founded the *Edinburgh Monthly Magazine*, a title later altered to *Blackwood's Magazine*. (F. P. Tredrey, *The House of Blackwood*; Mrs Oliphant, *William Blackwood and his Sons*.)

BROWN, Thomas (1764-1820)

James Brown (presumably the father of Thomas) was in business as a bookseller in Parliament Close before 1773; in 1786 the name was changed to T. Brown. From 1789 until his death Brown's shop was at 1 North Bridge, east side, where, as a bookseller and publisher, he issued guide-books, maps and atlases. He was admitted a burgess of Edinburgh on 2nd November 1786, when he was described as an engraver. He married Elizabeth Swinton. He died in his house at Gayfield Square on 7th August 1820, aged 56, and was succeeded in the business by William Swinton (q.v.). He left personal estate of £2532 18s 11d.

CLARK, James

Engraver at the Scottish mint, engraved a portrait of Charles II for a 1681 edition of Acts of Parliament of Scotland, and five maps for John Adair's *Description of the Sea Coast* published in 1703, a map of Scotland (in the 1727 edition of *Buchanan's History*), and of Roman Camps in Scotland for Gordon's *Itinerarium Septentrionale*. He died in 1718. His wife's name was Katharin Cave. His moveable estate consisted of £300 for stock and instruments and £16,794 due to him (both Scots £s).

CLERK, T. (fl. 1804-1838)

Engraver in Edinburgh at 265 High Street 1811-23, and at 22 St James' Square, 1829-38. Engraved several maps for John Thomson's *General Atlas*, of 1817, and also maps of Scotland in 1820 and 1832. Engraved a map of Soils of Perthshire 1810, for Morison's *Guide to the City and County of Perth*; a map of Dunbartonshire by John Wood, 1818, and several plans of Scottish towns.

COOPER, Richard (*c.* 1705-1764)

Believed to be of English birth, Richard Cooper settled in Edinburgh as a youth and is credited with the 'real beginning of a school of engraving' in the city. One of his pupils was Andrew Bell (q.v.). He engraved portraits of many well known persons. In 1744 he engraved Bryce's map of the north coast of Scotland and in 1759 a plan of Edinburgh; about 1735-40 he engraved three maps of the Lothians from John Adair's manuscripts, Edgar's map of Peeblesshire 1741, plans of Leith and Peterhead, and several charts 1730-44.

EDGAR, William

Son of John Edgar of Wedderlie, apprenticed on 25th December 1717 to George Riddell, wright in Edinburgh, and admitted burgess and guild brother 23rd March 1736. On 13th February 1729 he borrowed £180 Scots from his sister Marion, on 24th September 1729 500 merks Scots from his mother, and, on 15th July 1738, £7·50 sterling from Alexander Arthur, tailor in Edinburgh. Edgar went with the Duke of Cumberland's army for survey work in 1746 and died on 23rd July 1746 at Fort Augustus as a result of fatigue. On 14th October 1746 Arthur, in respect of his loan, got title to Edgar's only asset—a plan of Edinburgh valued at £5 sterling, the price agreed between Arthur and William Maitland, who wanted the plan to illustrate his *History of Edinburgh* (published in 1753). But Edgar's sisters, Marion and Jean, lodged a claim for the sums due to them (the Mother having died on 30th September 1729), and the Court decreed that the plan must be put up for public sale on 27th January 1748, when it was bought by Maitland for £16 sterling. In a libel action by Maitland on 10th June 1748 against George Frazer, who had been acting for the sisters and who had alleged that Maitland used unfair methods to secure the plan for £16, it was stated that Edgar originally gave the plan to Maitland in 1744 to get it engraved, that it was returned after Edgar's death, and that John Elphinstone had made a reduced copy of it. (Register of Testament 1701-1800 (Scottish Record Society); and Scottish Record Office: CS238/M/1/120.)

GALL & INGLIS

James Gall is first on record in 1808 as a printer in Potterrow, Edinburgh. In 1842 the firm name became James Gall & Sons, Niddry Street; in 1849/50 it was changed to Gall & Inglis, booksellers, publishers and printers, 38 North Bridge.

GAVIN, Hector I

Born in Berwickshire on 7th May 1738. He was in business as an engraver from before 1774 in Parliament Close until his death, and a visit to his workshop there in 1776 is described in *A Memoir of Thomas Bewick*. He engraved a plan of Edinburgh in 1763, maps for Salmon's *Grammar* in 1767, a map of Berwickshire in 1772, and a map of Scotland for

Guthrie's History in 1772 and, with his son, county maps for *Brown's Atlas of Scotland.* He was elected a burgess of Edinburgh on 25th April 1782 and died at his house at Croft an Righ, Holyrood, on 7th July 1814.

GAVIN, Hector II
Son of the former, born on 5th October 1784 at Croft an Righ, Edinburgh, was apprenticed to Andrew Bell, engraver. Between 1814 and 1852 he had no less than eight different addresses. He was elected Burgess of Edinburgh in 1811 and Guild Brother in 1818, and became Governor of the Merchant Company in 1837. He married Marion Walker on 11th November 1814. He died at 7 Buccleuch Place, residence of his married daughter, on 1st March 1874, aged 89.

GELLATLY, John
Engraver, copper-plate printer and lithographic printer, was born in Forfar in 1802 or 1803. He appears in the Edinburgh Directory for 1826 as engraver and printer at 8 West Register Street, later No. 44; in 1843 at 1 George Street and from 1846 at 26 George Street. In 1851 he had in his employment twelve men and eight apprentices. He married Jemima Brydere. He died at 14 Scotland Street on 26th April 1859, aged 56.

GORDON, Robert
Born at Kinmundy, Aberdeenshire, on 14th September 1580, the second son of Sir John Gordon of Pitlurg, Banffshire. He was educated at Marischal College (University of Aberdeen), and in 1598 went to Paris to complete his studies, returning in 1600 on the death of his father. On his marriage in 1608 he bought the estate of Straloch in Aberdeenshire. (Straloch is 10 miles north of Aberdeen). In later life he was much concerned with the political affairs of George Gordon, Marquis of Huntly. He died in August 1661 in his 81st year. His portrait by Jameson is in the hall of Marischal College.

GORDON, James
Born 17th May 1617. Fifth son of Robert Gordon of Straloch. He was educated at the University of Aberdeen, graduating in 1636. In 1641 he was appointed pastor at Rothiemay. He drew plans of the cities of Edinburgh (1647) and Aberdeen (1661). He died on 26th September 1686.

HILL, Peter
Born in Dysart, Fife, in November 1755. He is entered in the Edinburgh Directory of 1786 as bookseller at 160 Nicolson Street, from 1788 to 1816 in Parliament Close. Robert Burns was a customer and a correspondent of Hill. Hill was admitted a Burgess and Guild Brother on 18th September 1794, and became City Treasurer and a Bailie of Edinburgh. His catalogue for 1793 shows a large business; it has 205 pages with 5372 items, including several atlases and numerous maps. From 1816 the shop address was 204 High Street, when Hill is also described as Collector of Cess. In 1817 the business name became Peter Hill & Co.; after a move in 1821 to 32 Princes Street, the business from 1823 was in the name of Peter Hill, junior. In 1780 Peter Hill married Elizabeth Lindsay; he died at 7 Randolph Place, Edinburgh, on 10th January 1837.

JOHNSTON, Alexander Keith

Born on 28th December 1804 at Kirkhill near Edinburgh, and educated at the High School and University. In 1820 he was apprenticed to Kirkwood & Son, engravers, and in 1826 joined his brother William to form the firm W. and A. K. Johnston. William was active in public affairs, A. K. developed the cartographic work. He became an honorary member of many foreign geographical societies, received the degree of LL.D. from Edinburgh University in 1865 and the Patron's Medal of the Royal Geographical Society in 1871, and was appointed Geographer to the Queen. He died at Ben Rhydding Hydropathic in Yorkshire on 9th July 1871.

JOHNSTON, Sir William

Son of Andrew Johnston, an Edinburgh merchant, born 27th October 1802 and educated at the High School, William Johnston trained as engraver and printer with Kirkwood and Son and W. and D. Lizars. He started business on his own account on 25th December 1825 at 6 Hill Square, and altered the business name to W. and A. K. Johnston on his brother becoming a partner in May 1826. The business was then moved to 160 High Street; an office was opened in 1835 at 107 George Street, and in 1837 office and works were combined at 4 St Andrew Square. Finally in 1879 the firm moved to the large Edina Works near Easter Road. Sir William was elected a burgess of Edinburgh on 28th July 1828 and guild brother on 11th April 1839. He was Lord Provost from 1844 to 1851, and died at Kirkhill House, Gorebridge, on 7th February 1888.

KINCAID, Alexander

Described in the Edinburgh Directory for 1773/74 as His Majesty's printer and stationer, in the Cowgate. He was elected a burgess and guild brother on 11th September 1776. The last entry is in the Directory for 1777/78. He prepared a plan of Edinburgh engraved by John Beugo in 1784. He published a *History of Edinburgh*; *The Travellers Companion through the City of Edinburgh*; and *A New Geographical Historical and Commercial Grammar* which has a small map of Scotland.

KIRKWOOD, James

Born in 1745 or 1746, James Kirkwood was licensed in 1771 as a clock and watchmaker in Perth. He was admitted a Freeman of Perth Hammermen in 1772. His first known engraving is the plan of the town of Perth for James Cant's *The Muses Threnodie* in 1774. In 1785 or 1786 he moved to Edinburgh and began business as an engraver in President's Stairs (Parliament Square). He was admitted a burgess and guild brother on 2nd November 1786. James retired in 1814 but returned when his son Robert (q.v.) died in 1818. At that time the business premises were at 19 Parliament Square; this property and his stock of plates were destroyed in the 'Great Fire' of 15th-17th November 1824, whereupon the business was moved to 11 South St Andrew Street in the new town. James died on 19th January 1827, aged 81. The business was continued by Robert Kirkwood II who died on 4th February 1843.

KIRKWOOD, Robert I

Born in Perth in December 1774, the son of James Kirkwood. On 28th January 1796 he married Janet Mitchell. In 1799 he became a partner with his father; and on 1st April 1801 was admitted burgess and guild brother. He died at Arniston Place on 14th or 15th November 1818. Some of his work: 'Travelling Map of Scotland 1804', 'Map of Kincardineshire 1813'.

KIRKWOOD, Robert II

Partner 1823 to 1843 (d. 4th February 1843). Succeeded by H. A. Kirkwood, who gave up business about 1851.

LIZARS, Daniel (Senior)

Born in Edinburgh on 6th November 1754, son of John Lizars, shoemaker. He was apprenticed to Andrew Bell, engraver, and first appears in the Edinburgh Directory in 1776 as engraver in Bishop Land Close. On 22nd July 1785 he married Margaret Home. He carried on business at various addresses in or adjoining Parliament Square until his death on 6th December 1812. He engraved many portraits and historical subjects. His personal estate included value of Lizars' *General Atlas* plates £125.

LIZARS, Daniel (Junior)

Brother and partner of W. H. Lizars; the partnership between them terminated in 1819 (NLS. Adv. MS. 3029 f. 9-10). Daniel set up as a bookseller at 61 Princes Street in 1823 (apparently with his brother's help), and shortly thereafter begun the issue in monthly parts the maps (engraved by W. H. Lizars) of the *Edinburgh Geographical and Historical Atlas*. The business was moved to 5 South St David Street. The last Directory entry is in 1832. The *Atlas* was re-issued by W. H. Lizars.

LIZARS, William Home

Son of Daniel, was born on 4th May 1788, and was apprenticed to his father as an engraver. His interest was in painting and he made his reputation as a portrait painter with his 'Scotch Wedding' and 'Reading of the Will', exhibited at the Royal Academy in London in 1812. He is entered in the Edinburgh Directory from 1810 to 1812 as historical and portrait painter, but on his father's death he had to devote himself to the business of engraving and printing, first at Parliament Stairs and from 1817 at 3 St James' Square. He was admitted burgess on 15th April 1828. He married Henrietta Wilson. His residence latterly was at Old Saughton House, but his death occurred in Galashiels on 30th March 1859. His personal estate amounted to £8219 5s 3d including stock of £1016 at 3 St James' Square.

LOTHIAN, John

Born in Edinburgh in 1805 or 1806, he first appears in the Edinburgh Directory in 1824 as bookseller at 41 St Andrew Square. He gave up this business about 1833 and is in the 1834 Directory as map publisher at 37 George Square (the house of his brother Alexander Lothian, advocate). From 1835 to 1839 John Lothian was at 21 Atholl Crescent; in 1840 he is described as geographer at 2 Baxter's Place, then in 1844 at 3 Abercromby Place. He died on 11th May 1846; his total personal estate, valued at £95, consisted of a three-fourths share in copyright, copper plates and sheets on hand of maps and atlases published by him.

MCINTYRE, Archibald
In business as an engraver at 3 East Rose Street from 1793 to 1811/12. Engraved a map of Scotland for T. Brown in 1793, and a small plan of Edinburgh 1793.

MENZIES, John
Born in Edinburgh 1780 or 1781, first appears in the Edinburgh Directory as an engraver in 1804. He was admitted burgess on 8th January 1806. In 1819 the firm name became J. and G. Menzies, the address at that time 201 High Street.

MURPHY, W.
Born in Edinburgh 1800 or 1801. He appears in the Edinburgh Directory as an engraver and printer at various addresses—from 1826 to 1829 at 209 High Street; 1830-42/43 at 62 Thistle Street; 1843-50 at 170 High Street; 1851-53 at Roxburgh Street. He was admitted burgess on 30th October 1839. In 1832 he engraved the maps of a small atlas of Scotland.

OLIVER (Thomas) and BOYD (George)
Thomas Oliver first appears in the Edinburgh Directory in 1799 as printer in North Richmond Street. He moved to the Nether Bow in 1802 or 1803, and in 1807/08 was joined by George Boyd to form the firm of Oliver and Boyd. In 1820 they are described as publishers and wholesale booksellers in Tweeddale Court, High Street.

SCOTT, Robert
Born in Lanark on 13th November 1777, Robert Scott was in business as an engraver in 1799 at Post Office Stairs, Parliament Close, and from 1825 at 65 Princes Street. He was admitted burgess on 5th July 1806. He was responsible for many engravings, both of Scottish landscapes and of portraits, most of them for books. He also engraved some small plans of Edinburgh 1805-36, a map of Scotland in 1825; and maps of English counties for *A New & Comprehensive Gazetteer of England and Wales*, first published in 1833/34. He died on 31st January 1841.

SWINTON, William
Born in 1794 or 1795, William Swinton was apprenticed to bookseller Thomas Brown (q.v.), probably his uncle, on 20th December 1808. He was admitted burgess on 12th June 1820; and succeeded to Brown's business at 1 North Bridge on the latter's death on 7th August 1820. In 1823 Swinton moved to 60 Princes Street (the same address as Peter Hill & Co.) where he is described as artists' fancy stationer. He died on 9th July 1832, aged 37.

TAYLOR, George, and SKINNER, Andrew
The first record of George Taylor is in 1772 when he prepared a plan of Banff and neighbourhood; in 1773 he made a plan of the city of Aberdeen and adjacent country. He and Andrew Skinner, described as surveyors in Aberdeen, were subscribers in 1775 to Armstrong's map of Peeblesshire.
Andrew Skinner appears in the Edinburgh Directory from 1776/77 to 1780/81 as land surveyor at Kincaid's land, Cowgate; this was probably a useful address when they were making applications to the Forfeited Estates Commissioners in the years 1775 to 1779 for financial assistance. The British Museum has a manuscript map of New York and Staten Island, dated 1781, drawn by George Taylor and Andrew Skinner.

THOMSON, John

Born in Edinburgh on 18th October 1777, was the son of John Thomson, merchant. He was admitted a burgess of the city on 18th August 1807 and guild brother 15th June 1809. The first mention in the Edinburgh Directory of John Thomson, Junior & Co., booksellers, Hunter Square, is in 1807. Binding shops in Fleshmarket Close were added in 1809. In 1824 Thomson moved to 41 St Andrew Square, later 32 St Andrew Square. For over 20 years his business as publisher of atlases prospered, but the cost of production of the *Atlas of Scotland* over the years 1822 to 1830 ruined him, and on 20th April 1830 he applied for sequestration as a bankrupt, with liabilities of £14,453 and assets of £9969. The assets included property at 9 and 11 Ann Street, 15 Stafford Street, Lynedoch Place, South Queensferry, and in St Andrew Square; the creditors included booksellers and engravers, the largest debt being £2530 to Cowan and Co. for paper. At this date five sheets of the *Atlas of Scotland* (one of Elgin and Nairn and four of Inverness-shire) were unfinished; the creditors therefore agreed to pay Thomas Clerk, engraver, £530 for the plates and 700 sheets of the map, and to negotiate with Robert Menzies, engraver, for the plates of Inverness-shire. In December 1830 Thomson made a proposal to the creditors to take over the stock of stationery and atlases on certain terms, his friends to be guarantors for payment, but the proposal was not accepted. As no purchaser was found a public sale of the stock was made on 7th April 1831, when it was bought for £1800 by 'John Thomson and Company', i.e. John Thomson, and his friends who were guaranteeing payment of the price. Eventually this was paid, although the third instalment was not paid on the due date, and in July 1834 the bankruptcy proceedings were wound up.

Thomson was still having financial difficulties and on 16th May 1835 he went bankrupt for a second time. In November Thomson offered to settle with his creditors by a payment of 2s per £, but he could find no guarantors, and the Trustee decided to sell off the stock of atlases and plates. (These were acquired by W. & A. K. Johnston who issued an edition of the *Atlas of Scotland* in 1855.) After his second bankruptcy Thomson makes only one more appearance in the Edinburgh Directory, in 1837/38, as John Thomson & Co., stationers and publishers of the *Atlas of Scotland*, 2 Rose Court. By this time even his house at 16 Stafford Street had been sold to meet his debts. (SRO CS 235/Innes Mack T/1/40; and CS 236 McNeill T/13/10.)

NOTES AND REFERENCES

Chapter 1

1. See Edward Lynam, *The First Engraved Atlas of the World* (Jenkintown, 1941); and R. A. Skelton, 'Introduction' to the facsimile edition of the *Cosmographia* of Claudius Ptolemaeus, Bologna 1477 edition (Amsterdam, 1964).
2. See Leo Bagrow, *History of Cartography*, revised and enlarged by R. A. Skelton (London, 1964). For the history of cartography in general see G. R. Crone, *Maps and their Makers*, 4th edn. (London, 1968); R. V. Tooley and Charles Bricker, *A History of Cartography* (London, 1969); R. V. Tooley, *Maps and Map Makers*, 4th edn. (London, 1970).
3. E.g. T. G. Rylands, *The Geography of Ptolemy elucidated* (Dublin, 1893); Erik Polaschek, 'Ptolemy's Geography in a new light', *Imago Mundi*, vol. XIV (1959), pp. 17-37.
4. I. A. Richmond, *Roman and Native in North Britain*, p. 133, 1958.
5. G. R. Crone, *Early Maps of the British Isles*, A.D. 1000-A.D. 1579 (RGS Reproduction of Early Maps) (London, 1961). The map *c.* 1154 by the Arab geographer, al-Idrisi, is even less recognizable and has no place names (described and illustrated by D. M. Dunlop in 'Scotland according to al-Idrisi', *Scot. Hist. Review*, vol. 26 (1947)).
6. G. R. Crone, *The World Map of Richard of Haldingham in Hereford Cathedral*, Royal Geographical Society (London, 1954).
7. *Four maps of Great Britain designed by Matthew Paris about A.D. 1250*, British Museum (London, 1928). The map is attributed to a Benedictine monk—J. B. Mitchell, 'The Matthew Paris Maps', *Geog. Jnl.*, vol. 81 (1923).
8. E. J. S. Parsons, *The Map of Great Britain circa A.D. 1360 known as the Gough Map* (Oxford, 1958).
9. Henry Gough, *Itinerary of King Edward the First* (Paisley, 1900).
10. BM, Lansdowne MS 204 and Harleian MS 661. The map in the Bodleian Selden MS B. 10 is reproduced in *National Manuscripts of Scotland*, part II (Edinburgh, 1870), and Richard Gough's *British Topography* (1780), Vol. ii. For a study of the *Chronicle* see C. L. Kingsford 'The first version of Hardyng's *Chronicle*', *Eng. Hist. Rev.*, vol. 27 (1912).
11. Michael C. Andrews, 'Scotland in the Portolan Charts', *Scot. Geog. Mag.*, vol. 42 (1926).
12. H. R. Wagner, 'The Manuscript Atlases of Battista Agnese', *Papers of the Bibliographical Society of America*, vol. 25 (1931).

Chapter 2

1. *Acts of the Privy Council of England*, new series, Vol. III, 1550-52, p. 183. For Clement Adams (1519?-1587), a graduate (M.A.) of Cambridge and a schoolmaster, see DNB, vol. 1. He 'cut' the wood block for an English edition of Sebastian Cabot's Map of the World. An Englishman, Markes Brown, received 40s in June 1548 for a map of the coast about the River Tay. *Acts of the Privy Council of England*, new series, vol. II, 17th June 1548 (London, 1890).

2. Illustrated, and described by A. B. Taylor, in 'Some Additional Early Maps of Scotland', *Scot. Geog. Mag.*, vol. 77 (1961).
3. Edward Lynam, *The Map of the British Isles of 1546* (Jenkintown, 1934). For George Lily (1500?-1559), see DBN, vol. 33.
4. The first map engraved in England to bear an explanation of signs was Norden's Map of Middlesex, 1593. E. M. J. Campbell, 'The beginnings of the characteristic sheet to English maps,' *Geog. Jnl.*, vol. 128 (1962).
5. (a) Marcel Destombes: The 1546 Map of the British Isles by Mercator (MS). (b) M. C. Andrews: 'Notes on the earliest known printed map of Scotland.' *Scot. Geog. Mag.*, vol. 35 (1919), p. 43.
6. John Elder, *The Copie of a letter sent in to Scotland* (etc.), printed London, 1555; also in *The Chronicle of Queen Jane*, ed. J. G. Nichols, Camden Society, 1850.
7. BM, Royal MS 18. A. 38, printed in *The Bannatyne Miscellany*, vol. 1 (Edinburgh, 1828), and in *Letters and Papers, Henry VIII*, vol. XVIII, pt. 2, p. 285.
8. *Early Records of the University of St. Andrews*, Scot. Hist. Soc., 1926; *Acta Facultatis Artium Universitatis Sancti Andree*, 1413-1588, ed. by A. I. Dunlop. Scot. Hist. Soc., 1964.
9. These references to John Elder are in (i) *Letters and Papers, Foreign and Domestic, Henry VIII*, vol. XIX, pt. 1, pp. 176 and 616, 1544; (ii) ib. vol. XX, pt. 2, p. 545, 6th October 1545; (iii) *Acts of the Privy Council of England*, New Series, vol. II, p. 114, 12th August 1547; (iv) ib. vol. V, p. 266, 3rd May 1556; (v) *Calendar of the State Papers relating to Scotland*, vol. 1, p. 602, 9th February 1561-62.
10. Marcel Destombes. 'La plus ancienne carte regionale de l'Ecosse,' in *Gazette des Beaux-Arts*, 1971, p. 305.
11. R. A. Skelton, 'Mercator and English Geography in the 16th Century', *Duisburger Forschungen*, Band 6 (1962), pp. 158-170. Walter Reinhard provides a detailed study of the map in *Zur Entwickelung des Kartenbildes der Britischen Inseln bis auf Mercator's Karte vom Jahre 1564* (Zschopau, 1909; reprinted Amsterdam, 1967).
12. Walter Ghymnius: 'Vita Gerardis Mercatoris' in Mercator's *Atlas*, 1595 and later editions; and see A. S. Osley, *Mercator, a monograph on the lettering of Maps* (London, 1969).
13. *John Dee*, by Peter J. French (London, 1972), pp. 36-7.
14. BM, Cottonian MS Domitian A XVIII, ff. 98v-99r, 104v-105r, 106v-107r.
15. R. Flower, 'Laurence Nowell and the Discovery of England in Tudor Times.' *Proc. Brit. Academy*, vol. XXI (1935), p. 47. For Nowell, see DNB, vol. 41.
16. BM, Lansdowne MS, 6, Art. 54. Printed in *Original Letters of Eminent Literary Men*, ed. Ellis, Camden Society, 1843.
17. For Bishop John Leslie, see DNB, vol. 33. Leslie wrote part of his history in Scots in 1568-70; this version was first published in 1830 as *The History of Scotland*, by John Lesley (Bannatyne Club, Edinburgh).
18. R. A. Skelton, 'Bishop Leslie's Maps of Scotland, 1578', *Imago Mundi*, vol. VII (1951) p. 103.

Chapter 3

1. (a) M. R. Hervé, 'L'Oeuvre Cartographique de Nicolas de Nicolay' in *Bull. de la Soc. de Géog. du Comité des Travaux hist. et scient.* (Paris,

1956). (*b*) E. G. R. Taylor, *Tudor Geography* (London, 1930), pp. 59-63. (*c*) For Nicolay see *Biographie Universelle*, vol. 30.
2. The Duc de Joyeuse became Admiral of France in 1582.
3. Robert Dudley (1502?-1553), appointed Warden of the Scottish Marches and Great Admiral of England 1542; Ambassador to France 1546; created Duke of Northumberland 1551; executed for high treason in 1553. See DNB.
4. BM, Harleian MSS 3996.
5. *Correspondance Politique de Odet de Selve*, ed. by Germain Lefevre-Pontalis (Paris, 1888).
6. *Calendar of State Papers, Foreign, Edward VI*, 1547-53 (London, 1861).
7. *Accounts of the Lord High Treasurer of Scotland*, vol. VII (Edinburgh, 1907), p. 353—'departing of the Schippis the xij day of Junii'; p. 359—return of the guns to the Castle, 3-6 August. Cardinal Beaton sailed on the *Mary Willoughby*; *Rentale Sancti Andree*, ed. R. K. Hanny, Scot. Hist. Soc. (Edinburgh, 1913).
8. *Letters and Papers, Foreign and Domestic, Henry VIII*, vol. 15 (London, 1896), Nos. 632, 634, and 709.
9. R. K. Hannay and D. Hay, *The Letters of James V* (Edinburgh, 1954).
10. Catalogue of the Library of John Lumley, MS 0.4.38 in Trinity College, Cambridge, and BM, Add. 36659.
11. (*a*) Berlin, Deutsche Staatsbibliothek: MS Hamilton 38. (*b*) BM, Add. MS 37024. *The Booke of the Sea Carte*.
12. A. B. Taylor. 'Name Studies in 16th century Scottish maps,' *Imago Mundi*, vol. XIX.
13. NLS, Adv. MS 33.2.27, item 29.
14. *Accounts of the Lord High Treasurer of Scotland*, vol. IV, p. 504.

Chapter 4

1. This chapter owes much to *Atlantes Neerlandici*, 5 vols. (Amsterdam, 1967-71), the bibliography of atlases published in the Netherlands, compiled by Professor Dr Ir. C. Koeman. These volumes are invaluable for the study of Dutch map production and biographies.
2. The personal names are the Latinized form used in their atlases; their own Flemish or Dutch names were: Mercator = Kramer; Ortelius = Ortels; Hondius = d'Hondt; Janssonius = Janssen or Janszoon. W. J. Blaeu was originally Willem Janszoon; he added the name 'Blaeu' between 1613 and 1617 to avoid confusion with the firm of Janssonius.
3. For Ortelius see: Professor Dr Ir. C. Koeman, *The History of Abraham Ortelius and his Theatrum Orbis Terrarum* (Lausanne, 1964).
4. Also printed by J. H. Hessels ed., *Abraham Ortelii . . . Epistolae* (Cambridge, 1887): letter No. 32, 22nd November 1570.
5. R. A. Skelton, Bibliographical Note to facsimile editions (Amsterdam, 1964 and 1968) of the *Theatrum* of Ortelius (Latin edition, 1570; English, 1606).
6. A. S. Osley, *Mercator, a monograph on the lettering of maps* (London, 1969).
7. R. A. Skelton, *County Atlases of the British Isles 1579-1703* (London, 1970), p. 66.
8. Professor Dr Ir. C. Koeman, *Joan Blaeu and his Grand Atlas* (Amsterdam, 1970).
9. Scales given here are approximate, they may not necessarily agree with what scale is shown on the map.

Chapter 5

Much of this chapter appeared in the *Scot. Geog. Mag.*, vol. 84 (1968): 'New light on the first atlas of Scotland' by D. G. Moir and R. A. Skelton.

1. This translation from the Latin is by C. G. Cash, in 'The First Topographical Survey of Scotland', *Scot. Geog. Mag.*, vol. 17 (1901).
2. For Robert Pont see DNB, vol. 46. Timothy is usually referred to as the eldest son, but elsewhere Zachary is described as Pont's 'apparent heir'.
3. St Andrews University MS Records: Acta Rectorum Session 1580/81 UY/305/2/f. 9 and Faculty of Arts bursar's book UY/412/f. 62r, 1583.
4. MS Feu Charters of Kirklands, vol. II, p. 173. 10th July 1574. Scottish Record Office.
5. MS Inventory of the Charterhouse of Edinburgh, vol. 5, pp. 161-4 (1585) (City Archives).
6. Edinburgh Town Council MS Records, vol. IX, p. 412, 21st February 1593 and 29th June 1593.
7. *Acts and Proceedings of the General Assemblies of the Kirk of Scotland*, Part 3 (Edinburgh, 1845), p. 812.
8. (a) R. W. Cochran-Patrick, *Early Records relating to Mining in Scotland* (Edinburgh, 1878), pp. 48/9. (b) Act anent the Mines, *Acts of the Parliaments of Scotland* 1592, *c.* 31 (vol. III, p. 556) appointing John Lindsay, parson of Menmuir Master of Mines.
9. NLS, Adv. MS 19.1.24 f .33. See 'A note on Timothy Pont's Survey of Scotland', by I. A. G. Kinniburgh, *Scot. Studies*, vol. 12 (1968).
10. *Calendar of the State Papers relating to Ireland*, 1596-97, p. 40, 20th July 1596.
11. Books of Assignation and Modification of Stipends. 1607-15. MS Scottish Record Office ref. E.47/9.
12. Edinburgh Town Council MS Records, 29th May 1605. Vol. XI, p. 337.
13. *Cunningham Topographized* by Timothy Pont, ed. J. S. Dobie and James Dobie (Glasgow, 1876). Printed from an MS in the handwriting of Sir James Balfour; original by Pont is unknown. Also printed as *Topographical Account of the District of Cunningham* (Maitland Club, Glasgow, 1858).
14. Sir Robert Sibbald MS *De Historicus Scotis*, p. 2. NLS, MS 33.3.18.
15. *Register of the Privy Council of Scotland*, vols. VIII, p. 330 and IX p. lxxxi. Pont's guarantor was Alex. Borthwick of Nether Laich—presumably meant for Nether Leny, residence of Borthwick and his wife Margaret Pont.
16. *Origines Parochiales*, vol. 2, pt. 2, p. 789 (Edinburgh, 1855).
17. (a) W. Cowan: 'Andro Hart and his Press.' *Edin. Biblio. Soc.*, No. 1, 1892-93. (b) Hart's Will, printed in the *Bannatyne Miscellany*, vol. II, p. 241 (Edinburgh, 1836).
18. *Atlantes Neerlandici*, vol. II, p. 369 (Amsterdam, 1969).
19. *Geographical Collections relating to Scotland made by Walter Macfarlane*, ed. by Sir A. Mitchell and J. F. Clark, vol. II, p. 510. Scot. Hist. Soc. (Edinburgh, 1907).
20. Edinburgh Town Council, MS Records, vol. XIII, p. 298 (25th March 1614).
21. A full list of the maps was compiled by C. G. Cash and printed in the *Scot. Geog. Mag.*, vol. 23 (1905), 'Manuscript Maps by Pont, the Gordons, and Adair'.
22. *The Earl of Stirling's Register of Royal Letters*, ed. C. Roger, 1885, vol. II, p. 510.

23. For Sir James Balfour, see DNB, vol. 3.
24. For Scot see T. G. Snoddy, *Sir John Scot, Lord Scotstarvit* (Edinburgh, 1968); and DNB, vol. 51.
25. MS Letters from W. J. Blaeu and Joannis Blaeu to Sir John Scot. NLS, Adv. MS 17.1.9.
26. Sir Thomas Urquhart, *Tracts* (Edinburgh, 1774), p. 125.
27. This astrolabe is in the Royal Scottish Museum, Edinburgh, (Tech. 1947.27). See A. S. Cumming, Gordon of Straloch's Astrolabe, *Scot. Geog. Mag.*, vol. 42 (1926).
28. *The Diplomatic Correspondence of Jean de Montereul*, ed. J. G. Fotheringham. Scot. Hist. Soc., 1899, p. 417.
29. The Straloch Papers in *The Miscellany of the Spalding Club*, vol. 1 (Aberdeen, 1841).
30. *The Letters and Journals of Robert Baillie*, Bannatyne Club, Edinburgh, 1841; (*a*) 20th August 1641, vol. 1, p. 368; (*b*) 22nd September 1643, vol. II, p. 88; also *Extracts from the Synod of Fife*, Abbotsford Club, 1837, p. 131.
31. Rev. William Spang was minister of the Scots Church at Veere, 1630-53. Sir James Hope in his Diary (*Miscellany of the Scot. Hist. Soc.*, vol. IX, 1958) records that on a visit to the Netherlands in March 1646 Spang showed him maps 'of the most part of the Shyres of Scotland but not yet perfected'. John McClellan or McClelland was minister at Kirkcudbright from 1638-50; William Forbes, minister at Innerwick, 1640-46; James Bonar, minister at Maybole.
32. *The Journal of Thomas Cunningham of Campvere*, 1650-54, ed. by E. J. Courthope, p. 130. Scot. Hist. Soc. (Edinburgh, 1928).
33. *The Historical Works of Sir James Balfour of Denmylne and Kinnaird: The Annales of Scotland* (Edinburgh, 1824).
34. *Acts of the Parliaments of Scotland*; 1646, vol. VI, i, 637b; 1649 VI, ii, 172a.
35. This plan engraved by Blaeu is rare in its original state, but the re-issue by F. De Wit *c*. 1690 is less rare.
36. Act in favour of John Blaeu, 12th March 1647. *Acts of the Parliaments of Scotland*, vol. VI, pt. i, p. 736.
37. Printed by C. H. Firth in *Scotland and the Protectorate*, p. 45 (Scot. Hist. Soc., 1899), from the Clarke MSS in Worcester College.
38. *Calendar of State Papers, Domestic*, 1654, p. 158 (London, 1880).
39. Volumes I-V of Sir John Scot's set are now in the Library of Congress; vol. V contains many corrections in the margin which were incorporated in the 1662 edition (LC5941). Robert Gordon's set of vols. I-V is in Aberdeen University Library; vol. V has a MS dedication by Gordon to the Prince of Wales, later Charles II. James Gordon's copy of vol. V is in Edinburgh University Library. Cromwell's set is in the University of Texas.
40. (*a*) Adv. MS 33.3.23 in *An Account of Writers Ancient and Modern of Scotland*, by Sir Robert Sibbald (Edinburgh, 1710). (*b*) James Maidment *Analecta Scotica*, vol. II (Edinburgh, 1837). Letter of 11th November, 1707. For Robert Gordon's will dated 4th September 1657, bequeathing all his maps and description to his son James; see *History of Scots Affairs*, vol. 1 (Spalding Club, 1841).
41. J. C. Stone, 'The preparation of the Blaeu Maps of Scotland: a further assessment', *Scot. Geog. Mag.*, vol. 86 (1970), and 'An Evaluation of the "Nidisdaile" Manuscript Map by Timothy Pont', ib., vol. 84 (1968).

Chapter 6

1. Biographical details of the French Cartographers are based on the *Biographie Universelle* and *Nouvelle Biographie Generale*.
2. Sir H. G. Fordham, 'Nicolas Sanson and his Engravers and Publishers' in *Some Notable Surveyors & Map-Makers of the 16th, 17th and 18th Centuries and their work* (Cambridge, 1929). (No confirmation has been found of the statement in the *Nouvelle Biographie Generale* (Paris, 1864), and repeated by Fordham, concerning Sanson that 'sa famille, originaire d'Ecosse'.)
3. E. G. R. Taylor, 'The Earliest Account of Triangulation', *Scot. Geog. Mag.* vol. 43 (1927).
4. Sir H. G. Fordham, 'The Cassini Family and the Triangulation and Mapping of France' in *Some Notable Surveyors* (supra). Lloyd A. Brown, *The Story of Maps* (London, 1951).

Chapter 7

1. Leo Bagrow, *History of Cartography*, revised by R. A. Skelton (London, 1964), p. 187.
2. Chr. Sandler, *Johann Baptista Homann, Matthaus Seutter und ihre Landkarten* (reprinted Amsterdam, 1963).
3. *Proc. Roy. Geog. Soc.*, vol. 1 (1879).

Chapter 8

1. *Register of the Privy Council of Scotland*, 3rd series, vol. VII, p. 109 (Edinburgh, 1915).
2. A copy of the 'Advertisement' dated 1681, printed in Edinburgh, is in several libraries.
3. *Diary of Robert Hooke, 1672-1680*, ed. by H. W. Robinson and W. Adams (London, 1935).
4. Advertisement and General Queries for the Description of Scotland by Sir Robert Sibbald, M.D., 1682, printed in *The Bannatyne Miscellany*, vol. III (Edinburgh, 1855). Sir Robert Sibbald, eminent Scottish physician and antiquary, was first Professor of Medicine in Edinburgh University and instituted the botanical garden. See DNB, vol. 52.
5. It has the text of his appointment as Geographer on 30th September 1682. On 10th April 1684 the Privy Council gave Sibbald a 'privilege' (copyright) for 19 years for his book: *Reg. Privy Council*, vol. 8, p. 432.
6. On 14th December 1682 Adair signed a bond promising to pay Thomas Gordon, merchant, £248 Scots (= £20 13s 4d sterling) by 1st February 1683 for goods supplied, but this had not been paid by 12th March 1685 (SRO Register of Deeds, Mack LVI, p. 119). £43 Scots due on 6th March 1683 had not been paid by 24th December 1684 (ib. Mack LV, p. 423). In both documents Adair is described as 'surveyor of the shires in Scotland'.
7. The references to the Privy Council in the years 1686 to 1691 are to be found in the printed *Register*, 3rd series, vols. XII (1686), XV (1690), and XVI (1691). For later years see note 12 below.
8. *Acts of the Parliaments of Scotland*, 1686, chap. 37, vol. VIII, p. 603.
9. In Rotterdam on 1st September 1687 Adair signed a commission to his wife Jean Oliphant to act as factor (agent) for him. He designated himself 'Geographer to his Sacred Majesty' (SRO Register of Deeds, DAL LXVII, p. 1279).

L

10. On 9th February 1688 Adair signed in London a bill of exchange for £12 sterling (SRO Register of Deeds, DAL LXIX, p. 935).
11. (*a*) *Memoirs of Sir Robert Sibbald 1641-1722*, ed. by F. P. Hett (London, 1932), printed from Sibbald's autobiography, NLS, MS 33.5.1. (*b*) 'Life of Robert Sibbald, written by himself,' *Analecta Scotica*, vol. 1, 1834, pp. 142-3.
12. *The Miscellany of The Bannatyne Club*, vol. II, pp. 351-88; 'Papers relating to the Geographical Description, Maps, and Charts of Scotland, by John Adair 1686-1723'; these include extracts from the unprinted Register of the Privy Council of Scotland.
13. *Acts*: 1695, *c.* 85, vol. IX, p. 491; 1698, *c.* 37, vol. X, p. 176a. *Theatrum Scotiae* (London, 1693), had 57 plates; there were several later reissues.
14. William Nicolson, *The Scottish Historical Library*, 1702, p. 22.
15. *Acts*: 1704, (i) vol. XI, p. 195a-b; (ii) 1704, *c.* 9, vol. XI, p. 203.
16. Sir Robert Sibbald, 'Adversaria'; NLS, MS Adv. 33.3.19, folio 5.
17. A. H. W. Robinson, 'Two unrecorded manuscript charts of John Adair', *Scot. Geog. Mag.*, vol. 75 (1959), p. 169.
18. Accounts of Ships at Irvine from May 1707 to 1709 from the Collector at Irvine, Patrick Royle to John Adair, H.M.'s Geographer for Scotland, 29th June 1711 (Scottish Record Office).
19. *State Papers, Domestic, Scotland*, Series II, Bundle 5, No. 11. Letter, 2nd June 1713 (Public Record Office).
20. *Calendar of Treasury Books*, vol. XXVIII (1714), pt. II, p. 170, 4th March 1713-14 (London, 1969). (A list of proposed customs' establishments in Scotland 'examined and is signed by John Adair, the Queen's Geographer in Scotland'.)
21. Letter Jean Adair to James Anderson, 2nd July 1723, in Anderson Papers, NLS, MSS Adv. 29.1.2. vol. 6, folio 254; printed in *The Miscellany of the Bannatyne Club*, vol. II. (*a*) Records of the Court of Exchequer, vol. XIV, pp. 385-6, 21st June 1723; warrant for £40. (*b*) In September 1723 Mrs Adair received £214 7s 10¾d arrears of this annuity, from the date of Adair's death to 29th September 1723, Exchequer Establishments Book 1718-28, pp. 270-82, SRO R.H. E. 224/1. Mrs Adair's name also appears in the Civil List for 1727 for £40 pension (Hist. MSS. Commn. *MSS of Lord Polwarth*, vol. V (London, 1961), p. 9).
22. Many papers were destroyed in a fire in the Exchequer in 1811 (Letter of 31st May 1920 from King's and Lord Treasurer's Remembrancer). The map of Scotland 'Nova Scotiae Tabula' was engraved by James Clark (d. 1718), at the expense of George Mossman, bookseller, but the plate was not used until printed in Paton's 1727 edition of Buchanan's *History* (letter George Paton to Richard Gough in Bodleian). Two drawings of the coasts of Scotland (Solway/Clyde and Forth) were shown to the Society of Antiquaries in London in 1724 (Gough (1780), vol. II, p. 577).

Chapter 9

1. R. A. Skelton, *County Atlases of the British Isles 1579-1703* (London, 1970), deals exhaustively with the maps of Saxton, Speed, Blome, Morden, and others. See also 'The Elizabethan Surveyors' in Sir H. G. Fordham's *Some Notable Surveyors & Map Makers* (Cambridge, 1929).

2. E. G. R. Taylor, *The Mathematical Practitioners of Tudor and Stuart England* (Cambridge, 1970).
3. William Nicolson, *The English Historical Library* (London, 1696).
4. A. W. H. Robinson, *Marine Cartography in Britain* (Leicester, 1962).
5. In the *Diary of Robert Hooke 1672-1680*, ed. by H. W. Robinson and W. Adams (London, 1935). W. Bonacker in *Kartenmacher aller Lander und Zeiten* (Stuttgart, 1966), p. 162, suggests that Moll came from Germany.
6. See illustration in A. H. W. Robinson, Two Unrecorded manuscript charts by John Adair, *Scot. Geog. Mag.*, vol. 75 (1959).
7. Clement Lempriere, draughtsman in the Drawing Room (Tower of London) Corps of Royal Engineers. He made a map in 1725 of the Roads between Inversnaid and Ft. William. Maps by Captain Clement Lempriere include Jersey 1755, Minorca 1753, Lisbon 1756.
8. The map and explanation were later included in *The True Interest of Great Britain, Ireland . . . considered*, by Sir Alexander Murray (London, 1740).
9. (*a*) Letter of 15th September 1775 from Alex Bryce to Richard Gough, MS in Gough's *British Topography*, Bodleian Library. (*b*) George Chalmers, *Caledonia*, vol. II, p. 59.
10. John Elphinstone, born 17th January 1706. Appointed Practitioner Engineer 13th March 1744; Sub-engineer 4th January 1748. (R. F. Edwards, *List of Officers of the Corps of Royal Engineers*, Chatham, 1898.) He died on 29th April 1753 (*Scots Magazine*, 1753, p. 206).
11. Robert Gough, *British Topography* (London, 1780), vol. II, pp. 586-7.
12. George Chalmers, *Caledonia* (London, 1810), vol. II, p. 58n.
13. James Dorret, (*a*) Minutes of the Burgh of Inverary, 1721-55; (*b*) SRO Saltoun MSS Boxes 411, 412, 425, 105. (Miss Mary Cosh kindly supplied these references.)
14. Richard Gough, *British Topography* (London, 1780), pp. 587-8.
15. *Méthode pour étudier la Géographie par M. l'Abbé Lenglet du Fresnoy*, 4th edn. (Paris, 1761), vol. 1, p. 415.
16. Lloyd A. Brown, *The Story of Maps* (London, 1951), chap. VII.
17. Sir George Fordham, *John Cary, Engraver, Map, Chart and Print Seller &c.*, 1754-1835 (Cambridge, 1925).
18. Aaron Arrowsmith, *Memoir relative to the construction of the Map of Scotland of 1807* (London, 1809).
19. A. H. W. Robinson (*a*) see 4 above; (*b*) *Scot. Geog. Mag.*, vol. 74 (1958).

Chapter 10

Acknowledgment is made to R. A. Skelton's article in the *Scottish Geographical Magazine* on 'The Military Survey of Scotland, 1747-55' for most of the material in this chapter.

1. J. B. Salmond, *Wade in Scotland* (Edinburgh, 1938).
2. Quoted by G. Chalmers in *Caledonia*, vol. II, p. 60n; letter dated at Newcastle, 29th December 1745.
3. Several copies of this map with the manuscript notes of Colonel Watson, Deputy Quarter Master General, showing the military posts and districts in 1749-50, are in the British Museum.
4. Aaron Arrowsmith, *Memoir relative to the construction of a Map of Scotland . . .* (London, 1809).
5. William Roy. 'An account of the measurement of a base on Hounslow Heath', *Phil. Trans.*, LXXV (1785).

6. Copy in Scottish Record Office: N. R. A. (Scot) 0077, p. 3. Dundas of Arniston, Box 19 and 20.
7. Whitworth Porter, *History of the Corps of Royal Engineers* (Chatham, 1889), vol. 1, chap. VIII.
8. Sir George Macdonald, 'General William Roy and his Military Antiquities of the Romans in North Britain', *Archaeologia* LXVIII (1917), pp. 161-228. See also DNB.
9. George Chalmers, *Caledonia*, vol. II, pp. 61-62.
10. R. A. Skelton, 'The Military Survey of Scotland 1747-55', *Scot. Geog. Mag.*, vol. 83/1 (1967).
11. R. F. Edwards, *List of Officers of the Corps of Royal Engineers*, (Chatham, 1898).
12. W. Sandby, *Thomas and Paul Sandby* (London, 1892).
13. William Roy, *The Military Antiquities of the Romans in North Britain* (London, 1793).
14. BM Map Room. K. Top XLVIII, 25-la-f.
15. R. A. Skelton, 'The Origins of the Ordnance Survey of Great Britain' *Geog. Jnl.*, vol. 128 (1962); Sir Charles Close, *The Early Years of the Ordnance Survey* (Chatham, 1926; reprinted 1969); *Report of the Select Committee on the Ordnance Survey (Scotland)* 1851 (and other Reports); *Edinburgh Review*, 1855.

Chapter 11

1. See Ian H. Adams, *Descriptive List of Plans in the Scottish Record Office*, vols. 1 and 2 (Edinburgh, 1966 and 1970).
2. Ian H. Adams, 'The Land Surveyor and his influence on the Scottish Rural Lansdcape', *Scot. Geog. Mag.*, vol. 84 (1968).
3. *Selections from the Monymusk Papers 1713-1755*, ed. by Henry Hamilton (Edinburgh, Scot. Hist. Soc., 1945).
4. *Survey of Loch Tayside, 1769*, ed. by Margaret M. McArthur (Scot. Hist. Soc., 1936).
5. *John Home's Survey of Assynt*, ed. by R. J. Adam (Edinburgh, Scot. Hist. Soc., 1960).
6. *Scottish Forfeited Estate Papers*, ed. A. H. Millar (Scot. Hist. Soc., 1909).
7. SRO Forfeited Estates Papers: Minutes of Commissioners, 1755-56 (Ref. E. 721).
8. Richard Gough, *British Topography* (1780), p. 706.
9. See J. B. Harley in *Journal of the Royal Society of Arts*, vol. CXII (1963).
10. John Strawhorn, 'An Introduction to Armstrong's Map' in *Ayrshire at the time of Burns* (Ayrshire Arch. and Nat. Hist. Soc., 1959).
11. Betty J. Chambers. 'M. J. Armstrong in Norfolk,' *Geog. Jnl.*, vol. 130 (1964), p. 427.
12. (*a*) Ian H. Adams, *John Ainslie, Map-maker* (SRO, 1971). (*b*) MS Catalogue of Drawings and Engraved Maps etc. the property of Mr Thomas Jefferys—in Royal Geographical Society. (*c*) Richard Gough, *British Topography*.
13. SRO Forfeited Estates Papers, E.P. 728/54/3(1).
14. SRO Forfeited Estates Papers E. 728/53
15. R. H. Fairclough, *Sketches of the Roads in Scotland, The Manuscript Roadbook of George Taylor* (MS).

Chapter 12

1. Peter Hill & Co.'s Catalogue in Edinburgh Public Library.
2. For biographical notes on Scottish cartographers and engravers see preceding pages.
3. Scottish Record Office 1785/86, R.H.P. 2212-6.
4. Robert Burns was a subscriber. In letters to Peter Hill: (*a*) 'I am a subscriber to Ainslie's large map of Scotland . . . when published, secure me one of the earliest impressions of the plate.' (*b*) 'I'll expect along with my trunk my Ainslie's map of Scotland.' *The Letters of Robert Burns*, ed. J. de Lancey Ferguson, vol. 1 (Oxford, 1931).
5. *Gall & Inglis, Publishers, 1810-1960*; *A History* (Edinburgh, 1960).
6. SRO CS. 245, T/1/40 and CS. 96/792.
7. *One hundred years of Map-making*: W. & A. K. Johnston Ltd. (Edinburgh, 1925).
8. *Jour. Roy. Geog. Socy.*, vol. 42 (1872), and *Proc. Roy. Geog. Soc.*, vol. 1 (1879).

Index

154

II—The Early Maps of Scotland to 1850

EXPLANATIONS

DATES. Where maps are dated, the date is given without brackets; where the date is not on the map but is on the title page of the book or atlas containing the map it is within brackets. Where an atlas has a title page with one date and one of the maps has a later date, the latter date is generally taken as the date of publication. For many maps only an approximate date is possible.

If a map contains the following features it must be of later date than:

1600	Fraserburgh
1654	Hebrides, with flat headed outline
1690	Fort William
1700	Campbeltown
1714	Inversnaid Barracks
1730	Fort Augustus, previously Killiwhimen
1748	Fort George (at Ardersier)
1776	Grantown
1801	Crinan Canal opened
1842	Edinburgh and Glasgow Railway opened

EDITIONS AND STATES. It was not intended to list in this book every edition and every state of a map, but for some of the more important maps editions are mentioned, particularly where the original plate has passed to a publisher who has removed the original name and substituted his own. To identify a map consult the index for the name appearing on the map and then examine the entries for a map of the same size and scale.

ATTRIBUTION. A map may have the names of three individuals or firms: the cartographer, the engraver, and the publisher. The same individual may often be both cartographer and engraver, or even publisher also. Mostly the cartographer's name is the one by which the map is known, but many maps are known best, or only, by the name of the engraver or of the publisher.

SIZES. The sizes given are for the printed area, measured between the outer limits of the printed border, to the nearest one-eighth of an inch, height first, width second. Sizes however may vary by up to a quarter inch, or even more, due to paper expansion or shrinkage caused by changes in humidity. As scales are expressed in inches, the sizes have been given in inches for purposes of easier comparison.

SCALES. For identification purposes the scale is given in miles per inch as measured on the scale shown on the map (m. meaning English miles and m.S. Scottish miles). Where no scale is shown on the map a scale, shown in brackets, is based on the distance between Cape Wrath and Mull of Galloway.

As the latitude and longitude of the chief points in Scotland were not correctly calculated until about 1750, the scales on the earlier maps are of little service, the distortions being often so great as to nullify the value of any scale that may be stated.

The scales on the old maps vary according to the period. The earlier maps use the scale of 48 or 50 miles to one degree. Later the English "computed" mile was put at 60 miles to a degree while the Scots remained at 48 to 50, and in Ogilby's "Britannia", 1675, the English measured mile of $69\frac{1}{2}$ miles to 1 degree was used. Adair reckoned it at 72 miles to 1 degree.

The old British mile of 2428 yards was in use in practically all the measurements and itineraries of Scotland, until the measured Turnpike Roads came into use in the middle of the eighteenth century. They were referred to as "computed" miles when the changes began. The Scottish mile of 1984 yards was called the "measured" mile.

ABBREVIATIONS

> del = delineated = drawn by
> engr = engraver
> Sc. or sculp = engraver
> edn = edition
> fl. = flourished
> in. = inch or inches
> pub. = published or publisher

LIBRARIES. The names of certain libraries are given to be of assistance to the reader and are not to be regarded as comprehensive. "All" means all those listed here. Where several atlases or books are mentioned as containing a map, the library reference means only that it has the map, either loose or in one of the atlases or books. Photocopies, now so numerous, are not listed, except in a few instances where the map is very rare.

AU	Aberdeen University	GU	Glasgow University Library
BM	British Museum	LC	Library of Congress
Bod	Bodleian Library, Oxford	MLG	Mitchell Library, Glasgow
CUL	Cambridge University Library	NLS	National Library of Scotland
EPL	Edinburgh Public Library	RGS	Royal Geographical Society
EU	Edinburgh University Library	RSGS	Royal Scottish Geographical Society

Early Maps of Britain

The earlier maps listed below are rather rudimentary in their outlines but are genuinely cartographical in their attempt to show the relation of one place to another and the use of conventional signs. They are probably only a few surviving examples of a much larger number of maps of this type. In particular, the Gough map of *c.* 1360 is thought to be one of a series of official maps out of which the early maps of the 16th century developed.

c. 1250   PARIS, MATTHEW.   Four maps of Great Britain in MSS of the 13th century.
  A.   13 × 9 in.   BM, Cotton MS Claudius D.VI.
  B.   9⅛ × 9¾ in.   Corpus Christi College, Cambridge, MS 16.
  C.   15 × 10 in.   BM, Cotton MS Julius D.VII.
  D.   14 × 9½ in.   BM, Royal MS 14 C.VII.

These maps are in manuscript chronicles written in the middle of the 13th century by Matthew Paris, monk at the Benedictine monastery of St Albans. Facsimiles in *Four Maps of Great Britain*, British Museum, 1928. Study, J. B. Mitchell, *Geogr. J.* v. 81 (1933).

c. 1360   ANON.   Map of Great Britain: the "Gough Map".
  Two MSS, vellum.   45½ × 22 in.

In Bodleian Library, MS Gough Gen. Top. 16. Most commonly known as the Gough Map, from Richard Gough who first described it in his *British Topography* (London, 1780). Facsimile, with study and list of place names by E. J. S. Parsons, Bod and RGS Lib. (Oxford, 1958).

(1477)   PTOLOMAEUS, CLAUDIUS.   Britannia Insula.   15¼ × 19.

In the *Geographia* or *Cosmographia* of Claudius Ptolomaeus, Bologna, 1477, the first printed edition of Ptolemy's maps. Numerous editions followed, and in recent years facsimiles have been published by Theatrum Orbis Terrarum, Ltd., Amsterdam, of the Bologna edition of 1477, the Ulm edition of 1482, the Strasbourg edition of 1513, the Basle edition of 1540, and Mercator's edition of 1578. These are available in many libraries.

(1513)   WALDSEEMÜLLER, MARTIN.   Tabula nova Hibernie Anglie et Scotie.
  14½ × 20.   Woodcut: a contemporary or "modern" map.

In the *Geographia* of Claudius Ptolomaeus, Strasbourg, 1513 and 1520, and on a reduced scale in later editions from 1522 to 1541.

(1520)   COPPO, PIETRO.   British Isles.
  15¼ × 21¼.   (Scale *c.* 50 m. = 1 in.)

In *De toto orbe*: Bologna, Bibl. Communale dell' Archiginnasie, MS Cod.A.117. The squarish outline of Scotland shows a slight advance on that in the portolan charts, but it is still separated from England. Reduced reproduction and description by R. Almagia, *Geogr. J.* v. 69 (1927). Study, Almagia, *Imago Mundi*, v. VII (1950). Reduced reproduction also in *Early Maps of the British Isles* by G. R. Crone (London, R.G.S. 1961).

c. 1534-1546   ANON.   Angliae Figura . . .
                 25 × 18.   Scale *c.* 23 m. = 1 in.

In BM. Cotton MS Augustus 1.i.9. This manuscript map of the British Isles contains the first extant representation of Scotland which shows a clear advance on the portolan charts and the Ptolemy maps. Reproduction in *Early Maps of the British Isles*, op. cit.

(1540)   MUNSTER, SEBASTIAN.   Anglia: nova tabula.
         10½ × 14.   No Scale.

In Munster's edition of Ptolemy's *Geographia*, published at Basle, 1540. A map of most of the British Isles (includes Scotland south of the Forth). Libraries: BM, Bod, CUL, LC, NLS.

1546   G.L.A. (Georgius Lilius Anglus).   Britanniae Insvlae . . .
         nova descriptio.
         24¼ × 30.   Scale 29 m. = 1 in.   Publ. Rome

This map by George Lily, the first of the British Isles to be engraved on copper apart from Ptolemy, contains a representation of Scotland which is a still further improvement upon the Cotton map of *c.* 1540. Reproduction and study, E. Lynam, *The Map of the British Isles of 1546*, Jenkintown, U.S.A., 1934. Reproduction also in *Early Maps of the British Isles*, op. cit. The following later versions by other engravers are known.

    1549   Antwerp.   Johannes Mollijns.   Paris Bibl. Nat.; photo BM.
    1555   London.   T. Gemini (a re-issue of the original plate).   Paris Bibl. Nat.
    1556   Rome.   A. Lafreri.   BM.
    1556   ? Rome.   I. H. S.   BM.
    1556   Venice.   Joannes Andreas Valvasso.   BM.
    1558   Rome.   Sebastian a Regibus, (or di Re), BM, Bod.
c. 1560   Venice.   Anon.   BM.
    1562   Venice.   Ferando de Berteli.   BM.
    1563   Venice.   G. F. Camocio.   BM.
    1589   Rome.   Marcus Clodius.   BM.

c. 1552   TSCHUDI, AEGIDIUS.   British Isles.   Three maps: (1) England and Scotland, 16½ × 25.   (2) England and Scotland, two sheets, 17 × 25.   (3) England, Scotland and Ireland, 13½ × 16½.

MSS in Tschudi Collection, Library of St Gallen, Switzerland. Description, and reduced reproduction of the second map, E. Heawood, *Geogr. J.* v. 81 (1933).

(1558)   HOMEM, DIOGO.   British Isles.
         14¼ × 19¼.   Scale (*c.* 70 m. = 1 in.).   BM, Add. MS.
         5415A, no. 5.

A portolan chart, but with some names from Lily 1546. Reduced reproduction in *Early Maps of the British Isles*, op. cit.

c. 1560   ANON.   L'Isola d'Inghilterra.
                5⅝ × 5⅝. (? Venice 1560). "Scotia" has 17 place names
                from Lily.
Libraries: BM.

(1564)   MERCATOR, GERARD.   Angliae, Scotiae et Hiberniae
                nova descriptio.
                35 × 50½. Scale 14½ m. = 1 in.   Publ. Duisburg.
This large and remarkable map, giving for the first time a really good outline
and as many as 600 place names, was found in the Library at Breslau in 1889
but was destroyed in 1945. There are other copies at Rome, Perugia and Paris.
Facsimile of Breslau map in 8 sheets, 12 × 17½ in., *Drei Karten von Gerard
Mercator . . . Facsimile Lichtdruck*, Berlin, 1891.   Reduced reproduction of
Scotland, 7 in. × 6 in.; *Scot. geogr. Mag.* v. 67 (1951).
Libraries: BM, Bod, MLG, NLS, RGS, RSGS, (facsimiles or photos).

1561-1566   NOWELL, LAURENCE.   A general description of
                England and Irelande with the costes adioyning.
                9 × 13.   (Scale 50 m. = 1 in.)
In BM, MS Marquess of Lansdowne. Includes Scotland as far north as Arbroath.
All the place names (*c.* 70) in Scotland appear in Nowell's larger and more
accurate maps of Scotland. (See next section.)   Reproduction in *Early Maps
of the British Isles*, op. cit.

1567   BOWYER, WILLIAM.   Map of the British Isles.
                10 × 6.   Huntington Library, San Marino, California.
MS H.M. 160, f. 140.   Photo (reduced) BM, NLS.   Possibly derived from
Mercator's map of 1564.   Bowyer was Keeper of the Public Records in the
Tower of London from 1567 to 1604; the map is among his papers but may not
be his own work.   Note by A. B. Taylor, *Scot. geogr. Mag.* v. 77 (1961).

(1570)   ORTELIUS, ABRAHAM.   Angliae, Scotiae et Hiberniae
                sive Britannicar: Insularum descriptio.
                13½ × 19½.   Scale 33 m. = 1 in.
In Ortelius's *Theatrum Orbis Terrarum*.   Based upon Mercator 1564, it appears
in subsequent editions of the *Theatrum* from 1571 to 1612.   Facsimiles of 1570
Latin and 1606 English editions by Theatrum Orbis Terrarum, Ltd., Amster-
dam, 1964 and 1968.   Reproduction in *Early Maps of the British Isles*, op. cit.
Libraries: BM, Bod, CUL, LC, MLG, NLS, RGS, RSGS.

c. 1570   ANON.   Insula Britannia.
                c. 128 × *c.* 84.   (Scale *c.* 6 m. = 1 in.) Vatican, wall map.
This decorative wall map is a variation of Lily 1546.   Reproduction and note,
R. Almagia, *Monumenta Cartographica Vaticana*, Rome 1944-45, v. IV, plate 1.
Note by A. B. Taylor in *Scot. geogr. Mag.* v. 77 (1961).

(1578)   JODE, GERARD DE.   Angliae Scotiae et Hiberniae nova
                descriptio.
                13¾ × 19½.   (Scale *c.* 40 m. = 1 in.)   Antwerp.
In De Jode's *Speculum Orbis Terrarum*, 1578 and 1593 editions.   A copy of the
Ortelius map of 1570.   Facsimile of 1578 edition, Theatrum Orbis Terrarum,
Ltd., Amsterdam, 1965.
Libraries: BM, MLG.

(1588)   ADAM, ROBERT.   Expeditiones Hispanorum in Angliam vera descriptio.
24 × 29.   Scale 40 m. = 1 in.   Augustinus Ryther eng. London.   1590.

The last of this series of maps shows the route of the defeated Spanish Armada round the north of Scotland.   This is the first map of the British Isles as a whole to show Shetland.   Reproduction in *Lord Howard of Effingham*, ed. H. Y. Thompson, Roxburghe Club, 1919.   Notes by A. M. Hind, *Engraving in England* (Cambridge, 1952), v. 1, and by A. B. Taylor, *Scot. geogr. Mag.* v. 77 (1961). Libraries: BM, Cambridge: St John's Coll. Lib. and Pepysian Lib.

Early Maps of Scotland

FIRST PERIOD 1560-1653

The first printed map of Scotland alone was published in Italy about 1560, but only one copy of this map is known. The wide distribution of engraved maps of Scotland began in 1573 when Abraham Ortelius included a separate map of Scotland in his *Theatrum Orbis Terrarum*, the atlas first published by him in 1570. This map was based on Mercator's 1564 map of the British Isles.

In 1578 Bishop John Leslie, a Scotsman resident in Rome, published two maps of Scotland, the first and smaller based on Lily's 1546 map of the British Isles, and the second and larger based on the Ortelius map of 1573.

A remarkably accurate map of the coast of Scotland, published by Nicolas de Nicolay in Paris in 1583, was said by him to be based on a manuscript map of Scotland prepared in 1540 but not now in existence.

All these maps were superseded by a new map of Scotland by Gerard Mercator in 1595, when he introduced the word "Atlas" to describe a volume of maps. This map served as the basis of all maps of Scotland during the next sixty years, including Speed's map of 1610 and Blaeu's map of 1635.

This period saw the remarkable development in cartography made by the two great publishing houses in Amsterdam, the Hondius-Janssonius firm which took over the publication of the Mercator Atlas in 1604, and Willem and Joannis Blaeu, a firm which under Joannis Blaeu expanded map production until his *Atlas Major* consisted of 12 volumes with over 600 maps.

(1457) HARDYNG, JOHN. A map of Scotland without title. 21½ × 16 in.

In *The Chronicle of John Hardyng*, BM. MS Lansdowne 204, ff. 226-227. This map is diagrammatic and decorative, the 50 places being symbolized by drawings of castles, towers, churches, and gateways. Other versions of the map are in later versions of Hardyng's *Chronicle* (BM, MS Harleian 661, and Bodleian Library, MS Selden B.10), the last reproduced in Richard Gough, *British Topography* (1780), and in *National Manuscripts of Scotland*, v. ii (1870). Hardyng spent some time in Scotland searching for documents in an attempt to prove the supremacy of England over Scotland from earliest times. His verse description of how an army might invade Scotland is printed in P. Hume Brown, *Early Travellers in Scotland* (Edinburgh, 1891). For a study of the MSS see C. L. Kingsford, "The first version of Hardyng's Chronicle", *Engl. Hist. Review*, v. 27 (1912).

1559   ANON.   Carte de la coste d'Escosse depuis Barwick jusques à Cruden faite en 1559.
$17\frac{1}{4} \times 11\frac{3}{4}$.   Scale *c*. 8 m. = 1 in.

MS (Estampes Vc 1) in the Bibliothèque Nationale, Paris.   The earliest regional map of Scotland.   Description and reduced reproduction by Marcel Destombes in "La plus ancienne carte regionale de l'Écosse", *Gazette des Beaux Arts*, 1971.

c. 1566   ANON.   Scotia: Regno di Scotia.
$10\frac{1}{2} \times 13\frac{3}{4}$.   Scale *c*. 40 m. = 1 in.

The first printed map of Scotland.   An engraved Italian map based on the Scottish part of the 1546 map of the British Isles by George Lily.   Certain differences suggest that it was not copied directly from the Lily map but from one of the derivatives, probably the one by Sebastian di Re dated 1558.   The only known copy is in the R.S.G.S.   Reproduced and described by M. C. Andrews in the *Scot. geogr. Mag.* v. 25 (1919).

c. 1561-1566   NOWELL, Laurence.   A map of Scotland, without title.
MS 2 pages, each $8 \times 5\frac{1}{2}$ in.   (Scale *c*. 35 m. = 1 in.)   See next entry.

c. 1561-1566   NOWELL, Laurence.   A map of Scotland, without title.
MS 4 pages, each $8 \times 5\frac{1}{2}$ in.   (Scale *c*. 22 m. = 1 in.)

This map, and the previous one, are on pages of a manuscript in the BM (Cotton MS Domitian A XVIII, ff. 104v-107r) by Laurence Nowell.   Note by A. B. Taylor in *Scot. geogr. mag.* v. 77 (1961).
Libraries: BM—Photos in NLS, RSGS.

(1572)   PORCACCHI, Tommaso.   Scotia.
$4\frac{1}{2} \times 5\frac{1}{2}$.   (Scale *c*. 60 m. = 1 in.)

In *L'Isole Piu Famose del Mondo*, by Tommaso Porcacchi, Venice, 1572, and later editions 1576 to 1686.
Libraries: BM, LC, NLS.

(1573)   ORTELIUS, Abraham.   Scotiae tabula.
19×14.   Scale 20 m.S. = 1 in.

In *Additamentum Theatri Orbis Terrarum* by Abraham Ortelius, Antwerp 1573, and in the numerous issues of the *Theatrum Orbis Terrarum* from 1573 up to 1612, of which there were separate editions with text in Latin, Dutch, German, French, Spanish, English and Italian.   It is based on Mercator's map of the British Isles of 1564.   Facsimile of the 1606 English edition, *The Theatre of the Whole World*, pub. by Theatrum Orbis Terrarum, Ltd., Amsterdam, 1968.
Libraries: AU, BM, Bod, CUL, LC, MLG, NLS, RGS, RSGS.

(1577)   GALLE, Philip.   Scotiae descriptio.
$3 \times 4\frac{1}{4}$ Scale *c*. 43 m.S. = 1 in.   West is at the top.   At the top is printed SCOTLAND or SCOTIA, and the page number 7.

In *Spieghel der Werelt*, by Peeter Heyns, 1577 (Antwerp), and later editions to 1603 with titles and text in Dutch, French, Latin, Italian and English.   This small atlas is generally known as the *Epitome* of Ortelius (from its title in French, Latin and English), as it contains smaller versions, engraved by Philip Galle, of the maps in the *Theatrum* of Ortelius.   See note under 1601 regarding English edition of 1602.
Libraries: BM, Bod, LC.

1578   LESLIE, Bishop JOHN.   Scotiae regni antiquissimi accurata descriptio.
11 × 7⅜.   Scale *c*. 37 miliaria = 1 in.

In *De origine, moribus, et rebus gestis Scotorum*, by John Leslie, Rome, 1578. This map is based on Lily's map of 1546, with additional place names. See next entry.
Libraries: AU, BM, Bod, EPL, EU, GU, NLS, RSGS.

1578   LESLIE, Bishop JOHN.   Scotiae regni antiquissimi nova et accurata descriptio.
18 × 21¾.   Scale *c*. 15 m. = 1 in.   (Engraved by) Natalis Bonifacius Sibenicensis, Rome, 1578.

This second map by Leslie is based on Ortelius and is larger and much better than the preceding map. Natale Bonifacio (1538-92), worked in Rome from 1575 to 1592. On a strip below the map is a dedication to James VI and the date, Rouen, 20 August 1586. Reproduction and study, R. A. Skelton, *Imago Mundi*, v. VII (1950).
Libraries: BN Paris—Photos in BM, MLG, NLS, RSGS.

c. 1580   ANON.   Scotlande.
8¾ × 11¼.   Scale *c*. 32 m. = 1 in.
MS In *The Booke of the Sea Carte* (BM Add MS 37024).

This map resembles closely Nicolay's printed map of 1583. It has fewer place names and other differences, e.g. Loch Lomond, Loch Ness and Hyrth (St Kilda), which suggest that both may be derived from an earlier map no longer in existence. Reproduction and Notes by A. B. Taylor, *Scot. geogr. Mag.* v. 77 (1961); and in *Imago Mundi*, v. XIX (1965).
Libraries: Photos in NLS, RSGS.

c. 1580   NICOLAY, NICOLAS DE.   Charte de la navigation du Royaume d'Escosse.
15¼ × 11¼.   Scale *c*. 26 m. = 1 in.

In an undated manuscript version of Nicolay's *La Navigation du Roy D'Escosse* (see next entry) in the Deutsche Staatsbibliothek, Berlin, MS Hamilton 38. A manuscript of the text only (no map) of *La Navigation*, which is in the British Museum (Harleian 3996) was probably written in 1559. Reproduction in *Imago Mundi*, v. XIX (1965).   Photo in BM, NLS.

1583   NICOLAY, NICOLAS DE.   Vraye & exacte description hydrographique des costes maritimes d'Escosse, Isles Hebrides & Orchades servant a la navigation, Par Nicolay d'Arfeville Daulphinois, premier cosmographe du Roy.
15½ × 11½.   Scale *c*. 48 m. = 1 in.

Some issues of the same plate have the title "Vraye & exacte description hydrographique des costes maritimes d'Escosse & des Isles Orchades Hebrides avec partie d'Angleterre & d'Irlande servant a la navigation Par N de Nicolay D'aulphinois Sieur d'Arfeville & de Belair . . ." In *La Navigation du Roy D'Escosse Jaques Cinquiesme du nom, autour do son Royaume, & Isles Hebrides Orchades soubz la conduicte d'Alexandre Lyndsay, excellent Pilote Escossois*, Gilles Beys, Paris 1583. (See preceding two entries.) Reproduction by J. Shearer in *Old Maps of Scotland* (Stirling, 1905.)   See 1688 for copy by John Adair.
Libraries: BM, Bod, EU, MLG, NLS.

M

(1587)   MARTINEZ, JOAN.   Iscotia.
31 × 24.   (Scale *c*. 30 m. = 1 in.)

In a manuscript atlas compiled in 1587 by Martinez, now in the Biblioteca
Nacional, Madrid, MS V.3.5. A decorative version of Ortelius 1573. Repro-
duction and note by A. B. Taylor, *Scot. geogr. Mag.* v. 77 (1961).
Photo in BM, RSGS.

c. 1590   ANON.   Scotiae nova et accurata descriptio.
15¾ × 21.   Scale 17 m. = 1 in.

This is a close copy of Leslie's larger map of 1578, so close that the XI Bishops
referred to by Leslie are copied as XL, and the Marria and Gariotha districts
of Aberdeenshire are run together as Magarriothar.
Libraries: BM—Photo in RSGS.

(1592)   NAGEL, HENRICUS.   Scotiae Tabula.
7⅜ × 10¾.   Scale *c*. 30 m.S. = 1 in.

In *Europae totius orbis terrarum* by Matthias Quad, pub. by Johann Bussemacher,
Cologne, 1592 and 1594 edns., and in *Geographisches Handbuch* by Quad, 1600
and 1608 edns. A rough copy of Ortelius's map of 1573 with Arran and the
Hebrides omitted. Reproduced in *Scot. geogr. Mag.* v. 34 (1918).
Libraries: AU, BM, Bod, EPL, GU, LC, MLG, NLS, RSGS.

(1595)   MERCATOR, GERARD.
(1)   Scotia Regnum.   13¾ × 15¾.   Scale *c*. 22 m.S. = 1 in.
(2)   Scotiae Regnum (Northern Scotland).   13¼ × 17¾.   Scale
      c. 13 m.S. = 1 in.
(3)   No title (Southern Scotland).   13⅝ × 17¾.   Scale *c*. 13
      m.S. = 1 in.

In *Atlantis Pars Altera*, Gerard Mercator; Duisberg, 1595, the third part of
his *Atlas*. Mercator issued the first part of his *Atlas* in 1585; the third part
contained the three maps listed above: Scotland on one sheet, and Scotland on a
larger scale on two sheets, Mercator's first maps of Scotland alone. The maps
show a great improvement on his map of the British Isles of 1564; a much better
outline, more accurate details of the interior, and more place names in the two-
sheet map. The maps were unchanged in numerous editions of the *Atlas*,
with text in Latin, French, Dutch, and German, up to 1635. See 1636 for later
editions. Facsimile edition by Culture et Civilisation, Brussels, n.d.
Libraries: All.

1598   LÖW, CONRAD.   Scotia Regnum.   7½ × 11.

In *Königen Buch* (etc.) by Conrad Löw, Cologne, 1598.
Libraries: LC 7783.

1598   ORTELIUS (P. M. MARCHETTI).   Scotiae.
3 × 4.   Scale *c*. 43 m.S. = 1 in.

In *Il Theatro del Mondo di Abraamo Ortelio*, by P. M. Marchetti, Brescia, 1598
and later editions published at Venice. An Italian edition of the *Epitome* of
Ortelius (see 1577 above).
Libraries: BM, Bod, LC.

(1598)   LANGENES, BARENT.   Scotia.
3¼ × 4¾.   Scale 40 m.S. = 1 in.

In *Caert-Thresoor*, by Barent Langenes, Middelburg, (1598); several later editions
were published by Cornelis Claesz, Amsterdam, with text in Dutch or French
1599 to 1609. The maps also appear in *P. Bertii Tabularum Geographicarum
Contractarum*, 1600, and later editions. (See 1616.)
Libraries: BM, LC.

1599 KEERE, PIETER VAN DEN. (Latin = Petrus Kaerius.)
  1. Scotiae pars quae incolis Stratnahern vocatur cum circumsinys, 1599. Scale 40 m.S. = 1 in.
  2. Scotiae pars orientalior in qua diversi comitatus & academia Aberdyn. Scale 20 m.S. = 1 in.
  3. Scotiae pars australissima in qua admirandus Lacus Lomondus. Scale 48 m.S. = 1 in.
  4. Scotiae pars australior in qua Edenburgum Regia, S. Andrae et Glasco archiepiscopatus. Scale 20 m.S. = 1 in.
  5. Cathnes et Orcades in. Scale 20 m. = 1 in.
  6. Hebrides insulae cum circumsinys. Scale 50 m. = 1 in.

All 3½ × 5 in. Only the first map is dated 1599; the others were probably engraved later. All six are signed "Petrus Kaerius" and all form part of a collection of 44 maps of the British Isles probably published at Amsterdam c. 1605-10 by Pieter van den Keere (1571-c. 1646). The maps were reprinted by W. J. Blaeu in his 1617 edition of Camden's *Britannia*. See 1627 for later re-issues. The maps are described in detail by R. A. Skelton in *County Atlases of the British Isles* 1579-1703, London 1970, also by J. Keunig, Pieter van den Keere, *Imago Mundi*, v. XV (1960).
Libraries: BM, Bod, CUL, NLS, RGS.

(1601) (ORTELIUS, ABRAHAM). Scotia.
  3 × 4¼. Scale c. 43 m. = 1 in.

This map engraved by the Arsenius Brothers first appeared in an edition of Ortelius's *Epitome* with Latin text by Michael Coignet issued in 1601. A French edition was issued in 1602; English in 1603; German in 1604; Latin in 1601, 1609, 1612. The 1603 English edition and the 1602 English edition of the rival issue with plates by Galle (see under 1577) have been described by R. A. Skelton as "the earliest world atlas to be published in England and the earliest world atlas with English text" (Bibliographical note to the facsimile edition of the English edition of the *Theatrum Orbis Terrarum*, Amsterdam, 1968).
Libraries: BM, LC.

c. 1605 ANON. Scotiae pars. 11 × 13.

A roughly drawn MS map based on Mercator's map of 1564 and the Ortelius map of 1570. In University Library, Copenhagen. MS AM. 22 fol. (a & b), f. 46.

(1607) HOLE, GULE (= WILLIAM). (sculp). Scotia Regnum.
  10¼ × 12⅜. (Scale c. 33 m. = 1 in.)

In *Britannia*, by William Camden (historian and antiquary, 1551-1623), London, 1607 (Latin), the first edition with maps, 1610 and 1637 (English) editions. A map based on Mercator 1595.
Libraries: All.

(1607) HONDIUS, JODOCUS.
  (1) Scotia. 5¾ × 7¼. Scale c. 50 m.S. = 1 in.
  (2) Scotiae Tabula II (Southern Scotland). 5¼ × 7⅜. Scale c. 35 m.S. = 1 in.
  (3) Scotiae Tabula III (Northern Scotland). 5⅝ × 7¼. Scale c. 31 m.S. = 1 in.

In *Atlas Minor Gerardi Mercatoris a I. Hondio*, Amsterdam (1607); and in later Latin, French and German editions up to 1621, with the name of Scotland in the appropriate language in letterpress above the map. The maps are reductions of the larger maps by Mercator (see 1595). The plates were later acquired by a

London bookseller and used in *Purchas His Pilgrimes* (William Stanley, 1625), and in *Historia Mundi, or Mercator's Atlas*, an English edition issued by Michael Sparke and Others, London, 1635, 1637 and 1639. (See *County Atlases of the British Isles*, op. cit.)
Libraries: BM, LC.

1610   SPEED, JOHN.   The Kingdome of Scotland.
          15 × 20.   Scale 19 m.S. = 1 in.

In *The Theatre of the Empire of Great Britain*, by John Speed, London, 1611. This was the first atlas of the British Isles, having 66 maps of England, Wales and Ireland, and one of Scotland. The map of Scotland based on Mercator's map of 1595 and engraved in Amsterdam (but printed in London) by Jodocus Hondius or one of his staff (with an inset "The Yles of Orknay") has in the left margin full length portraits of King James and Henry, Prince of Wales, and in the right margin, of Queen Anne and Charles Duke of York. The *Theatre* was reprinted several times; in the 1650 edition the date on the map of Scotland was altered to 1650; two years later the date was altered to 1652 and the Royal portraits were replaced by figures of a Scottish man and woman and a Highland man and woman. The imprint on the 1610 issue is John Sudbury and George Humble; then *c.* 1623 George Humble; in 1652 William Humble; 1662 Roger Rea the Elder and Younger; 1676 Thomas Bassett and Richard Chiswell. See 1670 for copy by Overton.
Libraries: All.

1616   BERTIUS, PETRUS.
   (1)   Scotia.   3¾ × 5¼.   Scale *c.* 80 m. = 1 in.   Salomon
           Rogiers caelavit.
   (2)   Scotia septentrion.   3¾ × 5¼.   Scale *c.* 48 m.S. = 1 in.
   (3)   Scotia australis.   3¾ × 5¼.   Scale *c.* 48 m.S. = 1 in.

These are new maps in the 1616 edition of *P. Bertij Tabularum Geographicarum Contractarum Libri Septen*, publ by Jodocus Hondius, Amsterdam, and also in the Latin and French editions of 1618. The maps are slightly larger than those in the earlier editions (see 1598, Langenes). They were re-issued in an edition of Camden's *Britannia* published by G. Blaeu in 1639.
Libraries: AU, BM, Bod, CUL, LC, MLG, NLS, RGS.

(1627)   KEERE, PIETER VAN DEN.
   1.   The kingdome of Scotland.   Scale *c.* 80 m. = 1 in.
   2.   The south pt. of Scotland.   Scale *c.* 21 m.S. = 1 in.
   3.   The southren parte of Scotland.   Scale *c.* 37 m.S. = 1 in.
   4.   The eastern part of Scotland.   Scale *c.* 21 m.S. = 1 in.
   5.   Part of Scotland . . . called . . . Stranauerne.   Scale *c.* 40
          m.S. = 1 in.
   6.   The iles of Hebrides wth ther borderers.   Scale *c.* 53
          m. = 1 in.
   7.   Cathanes and Orknay ins.   Scale *c.* 20 m. = 1 in.
          All 3¼ × 4¼ in.

In *England Wales Scotland and Ireland described* . . . by John Speed, 1627, (pub. G. Humble, London), and in several later editions up to 1676. No. 1 is a new map, possibly not by Van den Keere, based on Speed's map of 1610; Nos. 2 to 7 are Keere's plates (see 1599) which had been acquired by Humble, the original titles removed and new titles engraved in English. (See *County Atlases*, op. cit.)
Libraries: BM, LC.

(1628) JANSSONIUS, JOANNIS.
1. Schotia. $5\frac{5}{8} \times 7\frac{3}{4}$. Scale 40 m.S. = 1 in.
2. Scotia meridionalis. $5\frac{1}{4} \times 7\frac{3}{8}$. Scale 42 m.S. = 1 in.
3. Scotia septentrionalis. $5\frac{1}{4} \times 7\frac{3}{4}$. Scale *c.* 42 m.S. = 1 in.
In *Atlas Minor Gerardi Mercatoris* pub. by Joannis Janssonius, Amsterdam, 1628 edition, and later editions up to 1651, with Latin, French, German and Dutch text. This is a new edition of the *Atlas Minor* with new plates, engraved by Pieter van den Keere and A. Goos.
Libraries: BM, LC.

(1630) (KEERE, PIETER VAN DEN).
1. Scotia Regnum. $7\frac{1}{4} \times 10$. Scale *c.* 40 m.S. = 1 in.
2. No title (southern Scotland). $7 \times 9\frac{1}{2}$. Scale *c.* 27 m.S. = 1 in.
3. Scotiae Regnum (northern Scotland). $7\frac{1}{8} \times 9\frac{7}{8}$. Scale *c.* 27 m.S. = 1 in.
In *Gerardi Mercatoris Atlas*, Amsterodami . . Johannis Cloppenburgij, 1630 and 1636 editions with French text, 1632 edition Latin text, a new edition (the "Cloppenburg" edition) of the *Atlas Minor* (see 1628), with slightly larger plates engraved by Pieter van den Keere and published by Johannis Cloppenburg, Amsterdam. Nos. 1 and 3 are also in a 1673 edition published by J. Janssonius van Waesberge. See also 1734.
Libraries: BM, EU, LC.

c. 1630 ANON.   The Kingdome of Scotland.
$15\frac{1}{2} \times 19\frac{1}{2}$. (Scale 19 m.S. = 1 in.)
This map is based on Speed's map of 1610, with some variation in place names and without the marginal illustrations.
Libraries: BM, Admiralty, Ve.117; Photo RSGS.

(1635) BLAEU, WILLEM.   Scotia Regnum.
$14\frac{7}{8} \times 19\frac{3}{8}$. Scale *c.* 15 m.S. = 1 in.
In *Novus Atlas*, Amsterdam, apud Guiljelmum Blaeu, 1635 and later editions up to 1648, with text on reverse in Latin, German, Dutch or French. Willem Blaeu's first atlas, the *Atlantis Appendix* issued in 1630, contained a map of the British Isles; in 1635 he added "Scotia Regnum" (based on Mercator's map of 1595); then in 1654 (q.v.) this map was replaced by a new map by Robert Gordon.
Libraries: AU, BM, Bod, CUL, EPL, LC, NLS, RSGS.

(1636) HONDIUS, HENRICUS.
(1) Scotia Regnum, $13\frac{3}{4} \times 15\frac{3}{4}$; (2) Scotiae pars septentrionalis, $13\frac{7}{8} \times 17\frac{3}{4}$; (3) No title—southern Scotland, $13\frac{5}{8} \times 17\frac{3}{4}$
These are Mercator's plates of 1595 (q.v.) with Mercator's name deleted; sea shading deleted in (2) and (3); new cartouches in (1) and (2); title of (2) altered from "Scotiae Regnum"; and "Apud Henricum Hondium" engraved in (3).
In *Gerardi Mercatoris et I. Hondii, Atlas or a Geographicke description of the Regions, Countries, and Kingdomes,* (etc.), translated by Henry Hexham, pub. Amsterdam, Henry Hondius &c. 1636. Facsimile edition with introduction by R. A. Skelton, Amsterdam, Theatrum Orbis Terrarum Ltd., 1968. Nos. 2 and 3 appeared in some later editions of the *Atlas*, No. 1 was replaced in 1636 by the next map.
Libraries: AU, BM, RSGS.

(1636)   JANSSONIUS, Joannis.   Scotia Regnum.
15 × 19⅝.   Scale *c*. 15 m.S. = 1 in.

This map was first issued in an *Appendix*, with German text, to the Mercator-Hondius-Janssonius *Atlas* of 1636, and appeared in all later editions of the Atlas (i.e. up to 1662), replacing the original map of 1595. It is an almost exact copy of Blaeu's map of 1635; the title and ornamentation are identical and the differences in place names can be distinguished only by close examination. Libraries: AU, BM, Bod, CUL, EPL, MLG, NLS, RGS, RSGS.

(1644)   (HOLLAR, W.)   The north-part of England and the south-part of Scotland.
15 × 20.   Scale *c*. 6 m. = 1 in.

In *The Kingdom of England & Principality of Wales exactly described* . . . *in Six Mappes*. Known as the "Quartermaster Map". This sheet includes Scotland south of the Tay. In the first issue the map follows Speed; in the second issue, in or shortly after 1644, between 40 and 50 names were added in the Lothians. Considerably more names were added in later issues of the map. Libraries: BM., Bod., EPL, NLS.

1653   GORDON, Robert. Scotia Antiqua. See under 1654.

SECOND PERIOD 1654-1713

In 1654 Joannis Blaeu of Amsterdam published Volume 5 of his *Theatrum Orbis Terrarum, sive Atlas Novus,* containing maps of Scotland and of Scottish counties and regions based on the manuscript maps of Timothy Pont. The surviving manuscripts are now in the National Library of Scotland, along with the manuscript maps prepared by Robert Gordon of Straloch, either from the Pont originals or from his own knowledge of Scotland, for the purpose of providing Blaeu with legible drawings for engraving. The publication of this Atlas superseded all the earlier maps of Scotland, and for the next hundred years practically every cartographer used it as a basis, particularly in respect of its two most noticeable features: the curved outline of the north coast and the flat-headed, wedge-shaped outline of Lewis, which were not corrected until the surveys of Bryce and MacKenzie in the period 1744 to 1750.

(1654)   GORDON, ROBERT. (a) Scotia Regnum cum insulis adjacentibus Robertus Gordonius a Straloch descripsit. $16\frac{3}{8} \times 14\frac{1}{4}$. (b) Orcades et Shetlandicae insulae. $16\frac{5}{8} \times 7\frac{3}{8}$ together forming one plate $16\frac{5}{8} \times 21\frac{5}{8}$.
Scale *c.* 18 m. = 1 in. Dedication by Robert Gordon to the Duke of Hamilton. The map of Scotland occupies two-thirds of the sheet, the Orkney and Shetland Isles the remaining third. This is the first map to show both groups of islands. The other maps in the atlas are recorded in the County Section, in Vol. 2.

In *Theatrum Orbis Terrarum, sive Atlas Novus,* Vol. 5, by Joannis Blaeu, Amsterdam, 1654, in editions with Latin, Dutch, French or German text on the reverse; with Spanish text in 1659. The same map, with the text on the back re-set, appeared in the various editions of Blaeu's *Atlas Major (Geographiae Blavianae):* 1662, Latin text, Vol. 6; 1663, French text, Vol. 6; 1664, Dutch text, Vol. 5; 1662 on title page, but after 1664, Spanish text, Vol. 6; 1667, German text, Vol. 5. Facsimile editions: French text, Amsterdam 1967-68; without text London 1970.
These atlases contain also a second map of the same size "Scotia Antiqua qualis priscis temporibus . . . R. Gordonius a Straloch CIƆIƆCLIII", with the title in the Orkney/Shetland section. Apart from the different place names there are minor differences of cartography between "Scotia Antiqua" and "Scotia Regnum".
(See under 1693 for a close copy of this map by Philip Lea.)
Libraries: All.

(1659)   JANSSONIUS, JOANNIS = (Jan Jansson).
   1.   Extimae Scotiae pars septentrionalis in qua provinciae
        Rossia, Sutherlandia, Cathenesia, et Strath-Naverniae.
        $17\frac{1}{2} \times 20\frac{3}{4}$. Scale *c*. $4\frac{1}{2}$ m. = 1 in.
   2.   Scotiae Provinciae intra flumen Taum, et Murra fyrth
        sitae, utpote Moravia, Badenocha, Atholia, Aberdonia,
        Baneia, et Mernis. $17\frac{1}{4} \times 20\frac{3}{4}$. Scale 6 m. = 1 in.
   3.   Scotiae Provintiae inter Taum fluvium, et septentrionalis
        oras Angliae. $17\frac{1}{4} \times 21$. Scale $6\frac{1}{2}$ m. = 1 in.
   4.   Lochabria, omnesq, insulae versus occidentem sitae,
        ut Visto, Mulla aliaeque. $17\frac{1}{4} \times 21$. Scale *c*. 6 m. = 1 in.
   5.   Tabula Leogi et Haraiae ac Skiae vel Skianae insularum.
        $17\frac{1}{2} \times 20\frac{3}{4}$. Scale *c*. 5 m. = 1 in.
   6.   Lorna, Knapdalia, Cantire, Jura, Ila, Glota et Buthe
        insulae. $17\frac{1}{4} \times 21$. Scale 6 m. = 1 in.

In *Nieuwen Atlas ofte Weereldt-Beschrijvinghe* (Vol IV), Amsterdam, Joannis
Janssonius 1659. These six maps were copied by Janssonius from the maps of the
Scottish counties and regions in Vol. V of Blaeu's *Atlas Novus* of 1654, and appear in the Dutch and German editions of the Janssonius *Atlas* of 1659. They have
no imprint; at some date the map publisher Carel Allard acquired some sheets
of these six maps for his *Atlas Major*, published about 1705. After the death of
Janssonius the plates were acquired by the firm of Pieter Schenk and Gerard Valck,
who added their own name to the plates (appearing as Pet. Schenk et Ger.
Valk, or G. Valk et P. Schenk, or other variations), and sold the maps separately;
they were also included with the Schenk-Valk imprint in the *Nieuwe Atlas* published by Covens & Mortier, Amsterdam (1707-41), and in other atlases.
Libraries: All.

1665   SANSON, NICOLAS, D'ABBEVILLE.
   1.   L'Escosse Royaume en ses deux principales parties.
        $15\frac{3}{4} \times 20$. Scale 19 m. = 1 in.
   2.   L'Escosse deçà le Tay divisée en ses provinces... $15\frac{3}{4} \times 21\frac{1}{4}$.
        Scale *c*. 10 m. = 1 in.
   3.   L'Escosse delà le Tay divisée en toutes ses provinces . . .
        $15\frac{3}{4} \times 21\frac{1}{4}$. Scale *c*. 10 m. = 1 in.
   4.   Les Isles Orcadney, ou Orkney; Schetland, ou Hetland: et
        de Fero, ou Farre . . . $16\frac{7}{8} \times 21\frac{1}{2}$. Scale *c*. 10 m. = 1 in.

In *Cartes Générales de toutes les parties du monde*. Paris, 1665, and later editions.
These maps are based on the county and regional maps of Scotland in Blaeu's
Atlas Major of 1662.
Libraries: BM, Bod, EPL, EU, NLS, RGS.

c. 1670   (OVERTON, JOHN).   The Kingdome of Scotland.
        15×20 Scale *c*. 19 m.S. = 1 in.

In an atlas without title page published by John Overton (1640-1713), a London
publisher of prints and maps. This map is a copy of Speed's map of 1610,
with no imprint or date, and the title in the top left corner. It was re-issued
c. 1710 with the imprint "Printed & Sold by Henry Overton at ye white horse
without Newgate".
Libraries: Admiralty, RSGS.

(1673)   BLOME, RICHARD. A mapp of the Kingdome of Scotland, By Ric. Blome by his Ma^tys Comand.
14½ × 16.   Scale 14 m.S. = 1 in.   R. Palmer, sculp.

Dedicated to James, Duke of Monmouth. In one issue of the map the Duke is described as one of the Privy Council; in another issue as Master of the Horse and Privy Councillor. In *Britannia, or A Geographical Description of the Kingdoms of England, Scotland and Ireland* . . . by Richard Blome, London, 1673. This is one of the last of the maps using the 1595 Mercator outline.
Libraries: BM, Bod, CUL, LC, MLG, NLS, RSGS.

(1679)   GREENE, ROB. and BERRY, W. A new map of Scotland with the roads; by Rob. Greene at the Rose and Crown in Budg-Row and by W. Berry at the Globe at Chering Cross.
18⅛ × 21¼.   Scale 13⅓ m. = 1 in.   F. Lamb, sculp.

The map shows the principal roads in generalized form. The map was advertised in 1679, (*The Term Catalogues*, Vol. 1, p. 359). A re-issue with Greene's name alone appeared before 1689, as an advertisement of the map in that year was by his widow, Elizabeth Greene, (ib. Vol. II, p. 281).
Libraries: BM, Bod, MLG, RSGS.

c. 1680   WIT, F (FREDERIK) DE. Scotia Regnum divisum in partem septentrionalem et meridionalem subdivisas in comitatus. . .
22¾ × 20.   Scale 12 m. = 1 in.

In *Atlas*, Frederik de Wit (*c.* 1680 and later editions); *Atlas Terrestris*, London (J. Seller, 1680?); *Atlas Minor*, N. Visscher, Amsterdam (*c.* 1690); *Novus Totius Geographica Telluris Projectio* by Gerald Valk (1706); and in *Atlas Nouveau* by J. Covens & C. Mortier, Amsterdam (*c.* 1725). A later edition has "cum Privilegio", and gridlines.
Libraries: BM, Bod, GU, LC, MLG, NLS, RGS, RSGS.

(1683)   (MALLET, ALAIN MANESSON)
1.   Escosse.   5¾ × 3¾.   Scale *c.* 100 m. = 1 in.
2.   Royaume d'Écosse.   6 × 4½.   Scale *c.* 55 m. = 1 in.
3.   Is de Fero de Scheland, Orkney et Hebrides.   5¾ × 4¼. Not to scale; this map covers Scotland and is more a curiosity than a map.

In *Description de l'Univers*, Paris, 1683. Mallet (1630-1706) was a French engineer and geographer.
Libraries: BM, Bod, CUL, LC, RSGS.

1686   ADAIR, JOHN. A generall mappe of the wast of Scotland containing the shyres of Clydsdail Nithsdail Galloway shyres of Ayre & Renfrew.
MS 17¼ × 19¼.   Scale 4 m.S. = 1 in.   In BM. K.Top XLVIII. 43.

c. 1686   (ADAIR, JOHN). Map, without title, of the south of Scotland from the Solway to the Firth of Tay.
MS 23¼ × 18½.   Scale 4 m.S. = 1 in.   In BM. K.Top XLVIII. 42.

1687   DUVAL P(IERRE). Les isles Britaniques—le Royaume d'Escosse.
16 × 21¼.   Scale c. 35 .m = 1 in.

A large plate, having a large and ornamental cartouche, with a small map of Scotland on the left, and a list of Scottish counties or regions with the county towns on the right.
Library: NLS.

(1687)   MORDEN, ROBERT. A mapp of Scotland made by R. Gordon . . . . corrected and improved by Rob. Morden . . . London.
17⅜ × 13¾, with index of place names at sides, and list of counties at foot, the total size is 19 × 22¾. Scale 18½ m. = 1 in. The date is taken from *The Term Catalogues*, Vol. II, p. 200. (See 1695.)
Libraries: BM, Bod, NLS.

1688   ADAIR, JOHN. A true and exact hydrographical description of the sea coast and isles of Scotland, made in a Voyage round the same by that great and mighty prince James the 5th. Published at Paris by Nicolay D'aulphinois . . . 1583, and at Edinburgh by John Adair . . . Anno 1688.
15 × 11½. Scale 22 m.S. = 1 in. James Moxon, sculp.

In *The Description of the Sea Coasts and Islands of Scotland*, by John Adair, Edinburgh, 1703. Adair says that he copied Nicolay's map, (see above under date 1583), to serve until he drew a new map from his own surveys, but he never completed his surveys. Some place names have been omitted and others added. The original MS map is in NLS (MS. 1651, Board of Ordnance Collection).
    Another state of the map has the title "A True Mapp and hydrographical description of the Sea Coast and Isles of Scotland By the Navigation of the most high and mighty Prince James the 5 Anno 1538. Done at Paris by Nicolay d'aulphinois . . 1583 Renewed from a true Coppy by John Adair, Fellow of the Royal Society, Anno 1688. James Moxon, sculp."
Libraries: All.

(1688)   MORDEN, ROBERT. Scotiae nova descriptio per Robert Morden.
5⅜ × 4¾. (Scale c. 70 m. = 1 in.)

In *Geography Rectified*, 2nd edn., London 1688 (and in 3rd edn. 1693 and 4th 1700), and in *Atlas Terrestris*, London (1700?) both by Robert Morden. Also in Patrick Gordon's *Geography Anatomiz'd*, 1st edn. 1693 to 8th edn. 1719; the maps in this book have the page number in the top right hand corner.
Libraries: AU, BM, Bod, CUL, EPL, EU, LC, RGS.

1689   NOLIN, J(EAN) B(APTISTE). Le Royaume d'Escosse divisé en deux parties . . dressé par le P. Coronelli, cosmographe de la Ser^me Republ. de Venise . . . corrigé et augmenté sur les Mémoires du Sr Tillemon . . Dedié à le Prince de Galles, fils de Jacques II.
18¼ × 24. Scale c. 13 m. = 1 in.

The map has the Orkney, Shetland and Faroe Islands down the right hand side. A later edition dated 1708, dedicated to "Jacques III, roi d'Angleterre" is in *Atlas Francois*, A. H. Jaillot, Paris, 1708; in Nolin's *Atlas of the World*, n.d.; in *Recueil de Cartes Géographiques*, n.d.; and in *Atlas Général* by L. C. Desnos,

Paris, 1767-9. For Coronelli's own map of Scotland see date 1692 below. Tillemon was the pseudonym of Jean Nicolas de Tralage (d. 1699) a paris geographer who helped Coronelli.
Libraries: (1689) Bib. Nat. Paris; (1708) AU, BM, Bod, LC, NLS.

(1689?) SELLER, J(OHN).   Scotland.
$5\frac{3}{4} \times 4\frac{5}{8}$. Scale c. 60 m. = 1 in.

In *Atlas Terrestris*, London (1689); in *A New Systeme of Geography*, London, 1690; and in *Camden's Britannia Abridg'd.*, Joseph Wild, London. 1701.
Libraries: AU, BM, Bod, CUL, EPL, LC, NLS, RGS.

c. 1689 VISSCHER, NICOLAUS. Exactissima Regni Scotiae tabula tam in septentrionalem et meridionalem quam in minores earumden provincias, insulasq . . .
$22\frac{1}{4} \times 18\frac{3}{4}$. Scale c. 11 m.S. = 1 in.

In *Atlas Minor*, by Nicolaus Visscher, Amsterdam (c. 1689); *Atlas Major*, by R. & J. Ottens, Amsterdam; and with "P. Schenk, jun." added, in *Nieuwe Atlas*, by J. Covens & C. Mortier, (1705-59). A later issue of the map has a list of place names and a reference grid attached.
Libraries: AU, BM, Bod, CUL, GU, LC, NLS, RGS, RSGS.

1690   DUVAL, P. L'Escosse divisée en ses comtes ou provinces.
$18 \times 13\frac{1}{2}$. Scale c. 17 m. = 1 in.

Pierre Duval (1618-83), Géographe du Roy, was a nephew of Nicolas Sanson.
Libraries: Bibliothèque Nationale, Paris.

(1690) OVERTON, JOHN. The Kingdom of Scotland divided into the North and South parts, subdivided into Countyes . . .
$22 \times 19\frac{3}{4}$. Scale 12 m. = 1 in. Printed and sold by John Overton att the White Horse against St Sepulchres.

This map was advertised in *The Term Catalogues* (1690. Vol. II, p. 322). It is a very close copy of De Wit's map (see 1680), even to De Wit's name and title "Scotia Regnum" in the bottom left corner. John Overton, 1640-1713, printseller, London, employed Wenceslaus Hollar to copy maps.
In *A General Atlas*, by William Berry, map publisher, London.
Libraries: BM, EPL, RGS.

c. 1690 NOLIN, J(EAN) B(APTISTE). Royaume d'Écosse divisé en provinces.
$8 \times 10\frac{1}{8}$. Scale c. 40 m. = 1 in.
Libraries: RSGS.

(1692) CORONELLI, P. Cosmografia (VINCENZO MARIA).
1. Scotia: parte meridionale. $17\frac{3}{4} \times 25$. Scale 7 m.S. = 1 in.
2. Scotia: parte settentrionale. $17\frac{3}{4} \times 25$. Scale $8\frac{1}{2}$ m. = 1 in.

In *Corso Geografico Universale*, Venice 1692, (in the 1695 edition the two maps are joined together to form one sheet); in the *Atlante Veneto*, Vol. 2, 1691-6; and in *Teatro della Guerra*, Vol. 3, 1706. This two sheet map of Scotland is the old Mercator outline; the scales are inaccurate on both sheets.
V. M. Coronelli (1650-1718), was a Franciscan friar who produced numerous maps and globes, was appointed Cosmographer to the Venetian Republic, and founded in Venice the first geographical society, the Accademia Cosmografia degli Argonauti. The title page of *Corso Geografico Universale* is dated 1692, but publication was evidently delayed as one of the maps (Savoia) is dated 1693 —see *Vincenzo Coronelli*, by Ermanno Armao, Florence, 1944.
Libraries: BM, CUL, LC, NLS, RSGS.

1693   SANSON, Sr. (NICOLAS). Le Royaume d'Escosse divisé
en parties septentrionale & méridionale.   Paris, chez
H. Jaillot.
2 sheets each $17\frac{3}{8} \times 23\frac{1}{2} = 34\frac{3}{4} \times 23\frac{1}{2}$.   Scale c. 11 m. = 1 in.

In *Atlas Nouveau Contenant tous les parties du Monde*, par le Sr. Sanson: Paris,
Hubert Jaillot, Géographe du Roy, 1692-96, and later editions; in *Nouvelle
Introduction à la Géographie* par le Sr. Sanson, Paris, Hubert Jaillot, 1695;
and in *Atlas Nouveau* by Pierre (Pieter) Mortier, Amsterdam, 1696-1708. Other
issues of the map have the date 1696 or have no date.
Libraries: BM, Bod, EPL, LC, MLG, NLS, RGS, RSGS.

c. 1693   (LEA, PHILIP) (a) Scotia Regnum cum insulis adjacentibus Robertus Gordonius a Straloch descripsit.
$16\frac{5}{8} \times 14\frac{1}{4}$.   (b) Orcades et Shetlandicae, insulae. $16\frac{5}{8} \times 7\frac{3}{8}$
together forming one plate $16\frac{5}{8} \times 21\frac{5}{8}$.
Scale c. 18m. = 1 in.

This map is contained in an edition of Christopher Saxton's atlas of the counties
of England and Wales, with the addition of some new maps, including this one
of Scotland.   The map is a very close copy by Lea of Robert Gordon's Scotia
Regnum published by Blaeu in 1654, the original names being indistinguishable
from those in the Blaeu map including the Orkneys and the Shetlands and the
arms of the Duke of Hamilton, but there are several additional names in the
type-style of the Lea additions to the Saxton county maps. (Private Collection.)
(Note in Scot. Geogr. Mag. V. 87/3, 1971.)

(1695)   MORDEN, ROBT.   Scotland.
$17\frac{1}{4} \times 13\frac{3}{4}$.   Scale $18\frac{3}{4}$ m. = 1 in.

In *Camden's Britannia, Newly translated into English*: by Edmund Gibson . . .
London, 1695.   This is the map of 1687 (q.v.) with (1) a new cartouche and
shorter title, (2) prime meridian through London instead of Teneriffe, (3) some
additional place names, and (4) without lists of names at sides and foot.   See
1722, Johnston, for Gibson's 2nd edition.
Libraries: AU, BM, Bod, CUL, EU, GU, NLS, RGS, RSGS.

(1697)   ALLARD, CAROLUS (CAREL).   Novissima Regni Scotiae
septentrionalis et meridionalis tabula.
$19\frac{3}{4} \times 23\frac{1}{4}$.   Scale 16 m.S. = 1 in.

In *Atlas Minor*, Amsterdam, 1697, and in *Atlas Major*, Vol. 1 (c. 1705), both by
Carolus Allard; also in *Atlas Minor*, by A. Braakman, Amsterdam, 1706. It
was included in an *Atlas Minor*, made up and sold by Christopher Browne in
London c. 1708, with F. de Wit's name on the title page but containing maps by
various authors.   See 1740 for a re-issue of the map by Covens and Mortier.
Libraries: BM, Bod, LC, RSGS.

(1701)   MOLL, HERMANN.   Scotland.
$7\frac{1}{4} \times 7\frac{1}{4}$.   (Scale c. 50 m. = 1 in.)

In *A System of Geography*, by Hermann Moll, London, 1701 and later editions.
The 3rd edition, 1709, with the same map, has the title *The Compleat Geographer*;
also in *Atlas Manuale*, by Moll 1709.
Libraries: AU, BM, Bod, CUL, EU, NLS, RGS.

(1701)   MOLL, HERMANN.   Scotland.
$8\frac{1}{4} \times 6\frac{1}{4}$.   (Scale c. 40 m. = 1 in.)

In atlas with no title page, but "Moll" on spine.   Dated 1701 in manuscript.
Libraries: CUL.

1703 ADAIR, JOHN. See under 1688.

1705 CORONELLI, P. (VINCENZO MARIA). Le royaume d'Escosse.
18 × 23⅝. Scale 13 m.S. = 1 in.
Libraries: BM.

(1705) BROWNE, C(HRISTOPHER). North Britain or Scotland according to Gourdan improved by G. Sorocold. (sub title) A new mapp of Scotland . . . begun by appointment of Robt. Morden, finished at ye charge of C. Browne.
22¼ × 18½. Scale c. 17 m. = 1 in. J. Harris, sculp.
Dedicated to Queen Anne (1702-14). The date is taken from *The Term Catalogues*, Vol. III, p. 465, 1705: "A New Map of Scotland is now published by C. Brown at the Globe". Three issues of the map are known: (1) title as above undated; (2) with the main title restricted to "North Britain or Scotland" and dated 1708; (3) without the main title and undated. Robert Morden died 1703. Christopher Browne, d. 1712 (both map-sellers).
Libraries: AU, EPL, NLS.

c. 1705 SCHENK, PETRUS. Novissima Regni Scotiae septentrionalis et meridionalis tabula, auctore Petro Schenk.
22¾ × 19⅛. Scale 16½ m.S. = 1 in.
In *Atlas Contractus*, Petrus Schenk, Amsterdam, c. 1705.
Libraries: BM, LC, NLS, RGS, RSGS.

c. 1705 VALK, GERARD and LEONARD. Regnum Scotiae seu pars septent: Magnae Britanniae divisa in Scotiam septent: et australem . . .
19¼ × 23¼. Scale 9⅓ m.S. = 1 in.
In *Atlantis sylloge compendiosa*, G. Valck and P. Schenk, Amsterdam, 1709; and in *Nieuwe Atlas*, by Covens & Mortier (1707-41).
Libraries: BM, LC, NLS, RSGS.

(1706) LA FEUILLE, DANIEL DE. Carte nouvelle d'Écosse.
7 × 10. Scale c. 26 m.S. = 1 in.
The map is flanked by 14 views of Scottish towns and castles: Edembourg, Dundee, St Andrews, Sterling, Dunoter, Aberdeen, Glascow, Berwick, Dunkeld, Dunblane, Elgin, Mont-Rose, Inner-Ness, Perth.
In *Oorlogs Tabletten*, 1706 and *The Military Tablettes*, 1707: both Amsterdam, and later editions, some with French or Dutch titles and text. Editions from 1711 are by Paul de la Feuille.
Daniel de la Feuille, a Frenchman, settled in Amsterdam in 1683 and became an engraver and map dealer. On his death in 1709 his son Paul carried on the business until his death in 1727. A 1729 edition was published by Paul's sister Jeanne; a 1732 edition by J. Ratelband.
Libraries: BM, LC, NLS.

(1706?) FER, N(ICHOLAS) DE. Royaume d'Escosse.
14½ × 20⅛. Scale c. 14 m.S. = 1 in.
This map has no title but on the right hand side is "Table des Principaux Lieux du Royaume d'Escosse". The map is undated but the date 1706 appears on De Fer's maps of the British Isles and Ireland.
In *Atlas ou Recueil de Cartes Géographiques*, N. de Fer, Paris, 1709-28. A later edition (1746-53) was issued by his son Desbois.
Libraries: LC, MLG, NLS, RSGS.

(1706)   CORONELLI, A. P. (VINCENZO MARIA).   Scozia.
4⅞ × 7.   Scale *c*. 65 m. = 1 in.
In *Teatro della Guerra*, Vol. 3, Venice 1706
Libraries: BM.

(1707)   AA, PIETER VAN DER.   Scotia.
4⅞ × 6¼.   Scale *c*. 75 m. = 1 in.
In *Les Délices de la Grande Bretagne & de l'Irlande*, Vol. 6, by James Beeverell, publisher Pierre van der Aa, Leyden, 1707, and later editions. At the top right hand corner of the map is the page number "Pag. 1033" in the 1707 edition; "Pag. 1106" in the 1727 edition.
Libraries: AU, BM, Bod, CUL, EU, NLS, RSGS.

(1708)   (CHATELAIN, Z.).   Nouvelle carte d'Écosse.
13¼ × 12¼.   Scale 22½ m. = 1 in; with table of Scottish nobilities and index to towns, making overall size 18 × 13¾.
In *Atlas Historique*, issued by Zacharias Chatelain and Francois l'Honore, publishers in Amsterdam, in seven volumes from 1705 to 1739. On the map is "Tome 2, No. 55"; Tome II, Seconde Partie = Vol. III, issued in 1708, 1720 and 1737.
Libraries: BM, NLS, RSGS.

(1708)   MOLL, HERMAN.   The north part of Great Britain.
7 × 10.   Scale *c*. 43 m. = 1. in.
In *Fifty Six new and accurate Maps of Great Britain*. . . Begun by Mr Morden: Perfected, Corrected and Enlarg'd by Mr Moll, London, 1708. Also in *A Compleat History of Europe*, London, 1708; in *The History of the Rebellion and Civil Wars in England*, by Edward, Earl of Clarendon, 1712 and 1717 editions; and in *The Present State of Great Britain and Ireland* by Guy Miège, 1718.
Libraries: AU, BM, Bod, CUL, EPL, NLS, RGS, RSGS.

c. 1710   AA, PIETER VAN DER.
(1)   L'Écosse suivant les nouvelles observations.   8¾ × 11¾ (with frame 10½ × 15¼).   (Scale *c*. 45 m. = 1 in.)
(2)   L'Écosse meridionale.   (3) L'Écosse septentrionale.   Each 5¼ × 7⅝ (with frame 9 × 15½).   (Scale *c*. 60 m. = 1 in.)
In *L'Atlas Soulagé* etc., n.d.; in *La Galerie Agréable du Monde* (1729); in *Atlas Nouveau et Portatif*, n.d.; Map 1 is in *Le Nouveau Théâtre du Monde* 1713; and in *Nouvel Atlas* (1714); Maps 1 and 2 in *Nouveau Petit Atlas*, n.d.; all by Pieter van der Aa, Leiden. See *c*. 1730 for re-issue. About 1740 Covens & Mortier re-issued the *Nouvel Atlas* with their name substituted for Van der Aa's name on the maps.
Libraries: AU, BM, Bod, LC, NLS, RGS, RSGS.

c. 1710   HOMANN, JOHANN BAPTIST.   Magnae Britanniae pars septentrionalis qua Regnum Scotiae . . . accurata tabula ex archetypo Vischeriano desumta exhibetur imitatore.
22½ × 18¾.   Scale 11 m.S. = 1 in.
In *Atlas Novus*, by J. B. Homann, Nurnberg, n.d.; in *Grosser Atlas über die gantze Welt*, 1731 edition; *Atlas Geographicus Major*, 1759; *Bequemer Hand Atlas*, 1754-90, all by Homann's heirs. This is a very close copy of Visschers' map (see *c*. 1690).
Libraries: BM, Bod, EU, LC, NLS, RGS, RSGS.

c. 1710 NICHOLLS, SUTTON. A new map of North Britain or Scotland . . . delinea'd and engraved by Sutton Nicholls. Printed and sold by William Knight. Map 22¾ × 25½; overall size 22¾ × 36½ including table of cities and market towns on each side of map. (Scale *c.* 12½ m. = 1 in.)

This map is based on Moll's map of 1708. Roads, with mileages, are shown between centres as straight lines, the earliest instance of the application to Scotland of the method first applied by John Adams in his 1677 map of England. In a second issue with additional place names William Knight's address (the Queen's Head, Snowhill), has been added. Sutton Nicholls, a draughtsman and engraver, fl. 1687-1740. See 1778 for a re-issue by R. Marshall.
Libraries: BM (Bound in *Variae Tabulae Geographicae*, by Husson, Hague, n.d.), NLS (Newman Colln), RGS.

c. 1710 ANON. 'T Koningryk van Schotlandt in zyne Zuider en Norder deelen verdeelt.
          10⅝ × 8¼. Scale on map *c.* 10 m.S. = 1 in., very inaccurate.
Libraries: NLS.

(1713) SAVONAROLA, RAFFAELO.   Scotia.
          4¼ × 5¾. Scale *c.* 65 m. = 1 in.

In *Universus terrarum orbis scriptorum calamo delineatus*, Padua, 1713, Vol. 2, by Alphons Laser a Varea, the pseudonym of Savonarola (1646-1730), an Italian priest and geographer.
Libraries: BM, LC, RGS.

THIRD PERIOD 1714-1749

This period begins with the map published by Herman Moll in 1714. This is a definite attempt to improve the outline of Scotland and is markedly different from the Gordon-Blaeu map of 1654.

1714   MOLL, HERMAN. The north part of Great Britain called Scotland.
$23\frac{3}{4} \times 25$ for the map; $23\frac{3}{4} \times 39\frac{1}{2}$ including the views and list of market towns. Scale $12\frac{1}{2}$ m. = 1 in. Dedicated to John, Earl of Marr.

Six issues of the map are known, all dated 1714, one with no imprint, the other five with different imprints all of them beginning "Printed for H. Moll", followed by the other names associated with the printing: (1) D. Midwinter and Tho. Bowles; (2) I. Bowles and Tho. Bowles; (3) I. Bowles, T. Bowles and John King; (4) J. Bowles & Son, Tho. Bowles and John King; (5) J. Bowles, Carrington Bowles and Robt Sayer. The only road shown in the first edition is from Edinburgh, but on a late issue with imprint (5) (possibly *c.* 1760, although still dated 1714), roads have been added with the "Kings Roads", i.e. the military roads, shown by double lines. A facsimile of this last map was published in 1896, by J. Shearer, Stirling. The views on the map are Aberdeen, Edinburg Castle, Sterling Castle, Dunotyr Castle, The Bass, Channery Town in Ross, Edinburg, Glascow, St. Andrews, Sterling, and Montrose. These are small copies of illustrations in Capt. John Slezer's *Theatrum Scotiae*. George Grierson, a printer and bookseller in Dublin, made a close copy of the map but engraved the illustrations in reverse, and issued it between 1720 and 1730 with a dedication to the Lord Bishop of Kilmore and Ardagh. For Grierson's later issue, see 1746. A descriptive catalogue by Henry Stevens of all the issues of Moll's large maps is in the BM Map Room.
Libraries: Most.

1715   OVERTON, HENRY. A new and exact mapp of Scotland or North Britain described by N. Sanson . . . Translated into English at the Expence of Henry Overton of London, Mapseller. Dedicated to George, King of Great Britain, etc.
$34\frac{1}{4} \times 22\frac{3}{4}$. Scale 11 m. = 1 in. Sutton Nicholls, engr.

In the *Atlas Royal* of Herman Moll and *A Collection of Maps*, Henry Overton, London, 1706-39. This is an attempt at an exact copy of the Jaillot (1693) version of Sanson's map in outline, size and style of place names, with the addition of a view of Edinburgh Castle at the right hand side. The map was re-issued in 1745 with roads as straight double lines between towns, with title "A Map of Scotland", and views of Edinburgh and Stirling Castles. Henry Overton (fl. 1706-64), map publisher, took over in 1707 the business of his father John Overton, map and print seller. (See 1766 for re-issue by Sayer.)
Libraries: AU, BM, Bod, NLS.

1715   TAYLOR, THOMAS. The north part of Great Britain
        called Scotland.
        7¼ × 10¼. Scale 44 m. = 1 in.

In *England exactly described or a guide to travellers*, by Thomas Taylor, London
n.d. (1715 and 1716. edns.) This map is based on Moll's map of 1708 and on
Sutton Nicholl's map of 1710. Some roads are shown but not with accuracy.
Thomas Taylor (fl.· 1670-1721), map and print seller, in London.
Libraries: BM, Bod, LC, MLG, RGS, RSGS.

1718   MOLL, HERMAN. A pocket companion of ye roads of ye
        north part of Great Britain called Scotland.
        11¾ × 10¾. Scale *c*. 29 m. = 1 in. Dedicated to John Ker,
        Duke of Roxburgh.

This is a reduction of the northern part of Moll's 1717 map of Great Britain,
with the same road distances, a few main roads now in double lines, and road
distances inserted on the islands The same map, with date deleted, appeared in
Vol. III of *A Tour thro' the Whole Island of Great Britain*; By a Gentleman
(Defoe); London, 1727. See also 1727.
Libraries: BM, NLS.

(1718) WEIGEL, CHRISTOPH.   Scotia Cambdeni et Sibbaldi.
        15 × 12⅝. Scale *c*. 17 m.S. = 1 in. M. Kauffer, sculp.

In *Schul-und-Reisen-Atlas*, Nurnberg, J. D. Kohler, 1718, and in *Atlas Manualis*,
Christoph Weigel, Nurnberg, 1724. Christoph Weigel (1654-1725), engraver
and publisher in Nurnberg.
Libraries: BM, NLS, RGS.

1720   TAYLOR, THOMAS. A new mapp of Scotland or North
        Britain with considerable improvements according to the
        newest observations. Printed and Sold by Tho. Taylor,
        Mapp and Printseller, Fleet Street.
        23¼ × 39¼. Scale *c*. 12⅔ m. = 1 in.

This map has on each side a table of all the cities and market towns. It is a close
copy of Moll (1714) with roads as straight double lines between towns and
mileages. An edition dated 1731 has "Printed and Sold by Thos. Bowles . . .
and John Bowles". It was re-issued with the date 1776. Also an undated issue.
Libraries: AU, BM, Bod, EPL.

c. 1720   (DE L'ISLE, GUILLAUME).   Scozia.
        15 × 12½. Scale 17 m.S. = 1 in.

In *Atlante Novissimo*, by Girolamo Albrizzi, Venice. This map is based on
Visscher's map, but has fewer place names.
Libraries: EPL, NLS, RSGS.

1721   SENEX, (JOHN). A new map of Scotland according to
        Gordon of Straloch, revis'd & improv'd by I. Senex.
        22⅛ × 18¾. Scale 17 m. = 1 in.

In Senex's *A New General Atlas*, London, 1721. The improvements seem to be
little more than putting in Campbeltown, Port Patrick, Stranraer and Greenock.
John Senex (d. 1740), F.R.S., cartographer, engraver and publisher in London,
also issued *The English Atlas* in 1714, and a road book of England and Wales
in 1719.
Libraries: BM, Bod, EPL, EU, MLG, NLS, RGS, RSGS.

N

(1722)   JOHNSTON, ANDREW (del & sculp).
(1)   A new map of the north part of Scotland.
(2)   A new map of the south part of Scotland.
Each 14 × 18.   Scale *c*. 17 m. = 1 in.

In *Camden's Britannia*, pub. by Edmund Gibson, 2nd edn. London, 1722; and in 3rd edn. (1753) and 4th edn. (1772). (See 1695 for 1st edition.) This map is copied from Senex's map of 1721.
Libraries: BM, Bod, CUL, EPL, EU, GU, MLG, NLS, RSGS.

(1722)   (SENEX, JOHN.)   A new map of Scotland from the latest observa.
6⅛ × 7⅝.   (Scale 54 m. = 1 in.)

In *Geography Anatomiz'd or The Geographical Grammar* by Pat Gordon, 9th edition, London, 1722, and in later editions up to the 19th edition 1749. The engraver had space only for "Observa", and had to omit the "tions". At the bottom right hand corner is "front page 192". The title page mentions a new set of maps by Mr Senex.
Libraries: BM, Bod, CUL, NLS, RGS, RSGS.

(1725)   MOLL, HERMAN.   (1) Scotland divided into its shires by H. Moll, Geographer. (2) Scotia Antiqua .. R. Gordonius a Straloch.
Both 11 × 9½.   Scale *c*. 29 m. = 1 in.

In *A Set of Thirty Six New and Correct Maps of Scotland*, London, H. Moll, Tho. Bowles and John Bowles, n.d. This small atlas contains the two maps of Scotland noted above, and 34 maps of counties or districts, each about 10½ × 7½ inches, on various scales. Map (1) has few place names; no mountains are shewn. Only the names on "Scotia Antiqua" come from Gordon's map; the outline is entirely Moll's own. The atlas was re-issued in 1745 with a new title page Scotland Delineated, or Thirty Six, (etc). A facsimile of the 1725 atlas was published by Shearer, Stirling, in 1896.
Libraries: AU, BM, Bod, CUL, EPL, MLG, NLS, RSGS.

(1727)   ADAIR, JOHN.   Nova Scotiae tabula.
8 × 5¾.   Scale *c*. 58 m.S. = 1 in.   J. Clark, sculp.

In George Buchanan's *Rerum Scoticarum Historia*, 1727 edition. Clark and Adair both died in 1719 but the map (although included by Adair's widow as a printed map in a list of Adair's maps she prepared in 1723) was not published until the 1727 edition of the History.
Libraries: BM, Bod, EPL, EU, GU, NLS, RSGS.

(1727)   MOLL, HERMAN.   A new and correct map of Scotland & the isles, containing all ye cities, market towns, . . . the principal roads . . . Dedication by David Scott to Charles, Duke of Queensberry.
11¾ × 10¾.   Scale 29 m. = 1 in.

This is a Moll's map of 1718 (above). With the changed title it appeared in *The History of Scotland* by David Scott, 1727 and 1728 editions; in Moll's *Atlas Minor* 1729 and later editions, etc. A neat map of which there are many editions.
Libraries: AU, BM, Bod, CUL, EPL, EU, GU, MLG, NLS, RSGS.

c. 1729   ANON.   The north part of Great Britain called Scotland.
18 × 14.   Scale 21 m. = 1 in.

Libraries: BM.

(1730) SIBBALD, ROBERT. A map of Scotland without title.
$7\frac{3}{4} \times 5\frac{3}{4}$. Scale *c*. 63 m. = 1 in.

In *A Collection of Several Treatises in folio concerning Scotland*: (IV) The History and Description of the Sheriffdome of Linlithgow and Stirling, 1730, by Sir Robert Sibbald. Sibbald (1641-1722), a distinguished Scottish physician, botanist, antiquary and historian, was appointed Royal Geographer for Scotland in 1682.
Libraries: BM. Bod.

c. 1730 (TIELENBURG, GERRIT).
(1) L'Éscosse. $5\frac{1}{8} \times 7\frac{5}{8}$. Scale *c*. 70 m. = 1 in.
(2) L'Écosse meridionale. (3) L'Écosse septentrionale.
Each $5\frac{1}{4} \times 7\frac{5}{8}$. Scale *c*. 45 m. = 1 in.

In *Gezichten der Steeden, Gebouwen* . . . . *van Schotland en Yrland,*, Amsterdam, Gerrit Tielenburg, n.d These plates came from Van der Aa (see 1710).
Libraries: Bod.

1731 LEMPRIERE, C. A description of the highlands of Scotland: the situation of the several clans and the number of men able to bear arms, as also ye forts lately erected and roads of communication.
MS in BM 51×37. Scale $6\frac{1}{2}$ m. = 1 in.
Lempriere was a draughtsman attached to the Corps of Royal Engineers. *c*. 1715-43.

1734 COWLEY, J(OHN). A new map of North Britain with the islands thereunto belonging done from some late surveys of part of the East and West Coasts . . .
$19\frac{3}{4} \times 14\frac{1}{2}$. Scale *c*. 20 m. = 1 in. R. W. Seale, sculp.
This map, with names chiefly on the coast line, is after Moll, the only attempt to make use of the material coming to hand in the coastal surveys. Skye and the Hebrides remain as in Blaeu, but the Clyde assumes better lines.
Libraries: BM, EPL, MLG, NLS.

1734 COWLEY, JOHN. A display of the coasting lines of six several maps of North Britain.
$24\frac{1}{2} \times 20$. Scale 11 m.S. = 1 in. London.
In *The True Interest of Great Britain* . . . *Considered*, by Sir Alexander Murray, (London, 1740) along with the previous map. The map shows the various out-lines for Scotland by Gordon, Sanson, Senex, Adair, Inselin and Moll: John Cowley (fl. 1734-45), a political writer and geographer, also prepared three maps relating to Argyllshire for the same book. Charles Inselin (fl. 1700-30), French engraver, engraved a map of the British Isles in 1715.
Libraries: EPL, GU, MLG, NLS, RSGS.

(1734) COOPER, R. (sculp). The Continent of Scotland in which are marked the several shires and principal places . . .
$11\frac{7}{8} \times 7\frac{3}{4}$. Scale 22 m. = 1 in.
In *The History of Affairs of the Church and State in Scotland*, by Robert Keith, Vol. 1, Edinburgh 1734.
Libraries: BM, EU, MLG.

(1734) (DU SAUZET, HENRI). (1) Escosse, (*c.* 40 m. = 1 in.). (2) Escosse septentrionale. (3) Écosse méridionale. Each *c.* 7 × 9¾.

In *Atlas Portatif*, by Henri du Sauzet, Amsterdam, 1734. These are small plates from Mercator's Atlas Minor—see 1630.
Libraries: LC, NLS.

c. 1735 SEUTTER, (GEORG) MATTHAUS. Nova et accurata totius Regni Scotiae. 22⅝ × 19⅜. Scale 11 m.S. = 1 in. And. Silbereysen, sculp.

In *Atlas Novus*, Augustae Vindelicorum, n.d. This is a close copy of Visscher's map, but the title is quite different and there are degree lines across the sea. The "Augustae Vindel" at the end of the title is the Latin form of "Augsburg".
Libraries: BM, EPL, LC, MLG, NLS, RGS, RSGS.

c. 1740 COVENS, JOHANNES and MORTIER, CORNELIS. Novissima Regni Scotiae . . . . tabula. 19¾ × 23. Scale 12 m. = 1 in.

This is Allard's map of (1697) with his name removed, and Covens and Mortier's names substituted.
Libraries: BM, Bod, EPL.

c. 1740 COVENS, JOHANNES and MORTIER, CORNELIS. L'Écosse suivant les nouvelles observations. 8¾ × 11¾. Scale *c.* 45 m. = 1 in.

In *Nouvel Atlas*, Covens & Mortier, (*c.* 1740) Amsterdam. This is Van der Aa's map (see 1713), with his name removed and Covens and Mortier substituted.
Libraries: BM, LC.

(1742) (COWLEY, J.). A Map of Scotland divided into its counties . . . 5¼ × 4¼. (Scale *c.* 75 m. = 1 in.)

In *A New and Easy Introduction to the Study of Geography*, by J. Cowley, London, 1742.
Libraries: BM, Bod, CUL, NLS, RGS.

1744 BRYCE, (REV.) ALEXR. A map of the north coast of Britain from Row Stoir of Assynt to Wick in Caithness. 27½ × 19. Scale 3⅓ m. = 1 in. R. Cooper, engr.

This map covers only the north coast of Scotland and the adjoining parts of the east and west coasts; its importance is that it was based on a detailed survey and showed that Cape Wrath, and not Faro Head, was the N.W. extremity of Scotland, thus correcting an error which had persisted for nearly a century.
Libraries: BM, Bod, NLS, RSGS.

(1744) SEALE, R. W. (del & sculp). A map of the Kingdome of Scotland from the latest and best observations for Mr Tindal's continuation of Mr Rapin's history. 19¼ × 15½. Scale 19 m. = 1 in.

In *The History of England* by Mr Rapin de Thoyras, London, Vol. III, 1744 and 1751 editions. Seale, cartographer and engraver in London, fl. 1732-75, engraved maps for several publications.
Libraries: Most.

(1744?) TIRION, ISAAK. Nieuwe kaart van't noordergedeelte van Grootbritannie behelzende het koningryk Schotland. $12\frac{1}{2} \times 14\frac{1}{2}$. Scale $27\frac{1}{2}$ m. = 1 in.

In *Nieuwe en Beknopte Hand-Atlas*, Isaak Tirion, Amsterdam, 1744 and later editions; and in *Hedendaagsche Historie op Tegenwoordige Staat van Groot Britannie*, by T. Salmon, Amsterdam, 1755. A map of Great Britain in the Atlas is dated 1743. Isaak Tirion (1705-65) bookseller and publisher in Amsterdam, issued atlases of maps which were based on the work of De L'Isle, Moll, and other cartographers.
Libraries: BM, EPL, MLG, NLS, RGS, RSGS.

1745   ELPHINSTONE, JOHN. A new & correct Mercator's map of North Britain. Published by And. Millar, 6th March 1745. $26\frac{1}{2} \times 21$. (Scale $13\frac{1}{3}$ m. = 1 in.) T. Kitchin, sculp.

This map marks a great step in advance in the mapping of Scotland, for although the Hebrides and Skye remain as in Blaeu's Atlas, the mainland is much more accurate except for the inability to put the lochs from Inverness to Fort William in a straight line. It was published only two months before the "1745", and was used apparently by both armies in their movements. There are two issues of this map, although both bear the same date. The first does not show Culloden; the second has Culloden inserted, as well as a 30 fathom line in the sea above the Bell Rock. The BM Map Room has one of the first issue with certain main roads and military roads coloured, and four of the second issue, two with the Highland military roads marked and two with the posts where troops were stationed (1750 and n.d.).
Libraries: BM, Bod, EPL, NLS, RGS, RSGS.

1746   BOWEN, EMAN(UEL). A new & accurate map of Scotland or North Britain . . . exhibiting the Kings Roads, etc. Dedicated to William Duke of Cumberland by Thos. Bakewell . . . Map & Print Seller, London. $20\frac{3}{4} \times 22\frac{3}{4}$. Scale 16 m. = 1 in.

A second title "A New Map of Scotland or North Britain" is printed along the top of the sheet. In addition to the date 1746, some copies have an additional imprint at top left: "Published Feb. 24th 1745" the old style dating for Feb. 1746. The battle of Falkirk (17 Jan 1746) is marked. The map is covered with double straight line roads or distances with computed miles marked, all taken from Sutton Nicholls (*c.* 1710), and Taylor (1720). The Kings Roads are shown by dotted double lines with a table of these and their mileages at the top.
Libraries: BM, Bod.

1746   ELPHINSTONE, JOHN. A new map of North Britain. Four sheets = 57×42. Scale 7 m. = 1 in.

This map has been revised from Edgar's Surveys of Stirling, Perth and Inverness, and shows a plan of Culloden, lists of the clans for and against the Government, and views of the castles at Edinburgh, Dumbarton, Stirling and Blackness, and of the Corrieyairack Road.
Libraries: MS in BM. Photostat in EPL and RSGS.

1746   LE ROUGE, GEORGES LOUIS. L'Écosse suivant les nouvelles observations publiés à Londres en 1735 par Bowles.
21¾ × 19. Scale 10 m. = 1 in.

In *Atlas Général*, Paris, chez le Sr. Le Rouge, n.d. A French map acknowledged to be copied from Bowles. Le Rouge (fl. 1741-78), was a military engineer who produced several plans and fortifications and held the appointment of "Ingénieur-Géographe du Roy" to Louis XV.
Libraries: BM, LC, NLS, RGS, RSGS.

1746   PATERSON, G. and W.   Scotland.
5¼ × 4⅞. Scale *c.* 62 m. = 1 in.

In "A Description of the Chanonry of Old Aberdeen", by William Orem in *Bibliotheca Topographica Britannica*, Vol. 5, London, 1782.
Libraries: AU, BM, Bod, CUL, NLS.

c. 1746   GRIERSON, GEORGE. To the . . . . Duke of Cumberland this new map of Scotland . . . with the roads and distances mark'd down (is dedicated).
23¼ × 25. Including views at the sides and table of market towns at the foot 29¼ × 39. Scale *c.* 12½ m. = 1 in.

In *The World Described or a new and correct Sett of Maps* by George Grierson, Dublin, n.d.
This is an almost exact copy of Moll's map of 1714, with only a few minor differences. It has the same eleven views, but all in reverse. The road system is taken from Sutton Nicholls (see 1710), with some minor omissions. The dedication to the Duke of Cumberland and the insertion of "Culloden" date the map as 1746 or later. In Grierson's first issue of the map it had Moll's original title (see 1714) and was dedicated to the Lord Bishop of Kilmore and Ardagh; for his second issue Grierson altered the title and dedication and inserted "Culloden 1746". Grierson was a printer and bookseller in Dublin from *c.* 1715 to *c.* 1753 who copied several maps by Moll and others. Arrowsmith in his *Memoir* (see under d. 1807) says "Grierson about the same time (1745) published a two sheet map of little value".
Libraries: RGS.

(1747)   BOWEN, EMANL. A new and accurate map of Scotland compiled from surveys and the most approved maps and charts.
12½ × 8¾. Scale *c.* 38 m. = 1 in.

In *A Complete System of Geography*, London, 1744-47.
Libraries: BM, CUL, LC, NLS, RGS, RSGS.

(1747)   BOWEN, EMAN(UEL). A new & accurate map of Scotland or North Britain drawn from surveys and most approved maps and charts . . . with several improvements not to be found in any other map extant.
17 × 13⅞. Scale 20 m. = 1 in.

In *A Complete System of Geography*, London 1744-47 and other editions: also in Bowen's *A Complete Atlas*, London, 1752. The map shows Culloden 1746.
Libraries: AU, BM, Bod, CUL, EPL, LC, MLG, NLS, RGS, RSGS.

(1748) (LE ROUGE, GEORGE LOUIS). Le Royaume d'Écosse divisé en ses parties méridionale et septentrionale. $10\frac{1}{2} \times 8$. Scale c. 35 m. = 1 in.

In *Atlas Nouveau Portatif*, Paris, chez le Sr. Desnos, 1748, and later editions. Libraries: LC, NLS, RGS, RSGS.

1748 ROBERT DE VAUGONDY, (GILLES). Royaume d'Écosse divisé en provinces. $6\frac{3}{8} \times 7\frac{3}{4}$. Scale c. 50 m. = 1 in.

In *Atlas portatif* (*supplement*), M. Robert, Paris, 1748-49. Gilles Robert de Vaugondy (1686-1766), and his son and successor Didier, were both in turn appointed "Géographe du Roi". Libraries: LC, RSGS.

1749 KITCHIN, T(HOMAS). Scotland drawn from the latest surveys. $7\frac{1}{4} \times 5\frac{5}{8}$. Scale 41 m. = 1 in.

In *Geographia Scotiae*, a pocket atlas of Scotland with 32 small maps of the counties each about $5\frac{3}{4} \times 6\frac{1}{2}$ in. (with some double page maps), by "T. Kitchin, Gr." (= Geographer) (six maps have no name). The map is little more than a pocket version of Elphinstone's map of 1745 of which it is a fairly close copy. A second edition was issued in 1756. This volume is sometimes bound as part of T. Osborne's *Geographia Magnae Britanniae*. Libraries: AU, BM, Bod, CUL, EU, MLG, NLS, RSGS.

(1749) JEFFERYS, T. (sculp). Scotland. $7\frac{1}{4} \times 7\frac{3}{4}$. Scale c. 41 m. = 1 in.

In *A New Geographical and Historical Grammar* by Thomas Salmon, London, 1749, and editions up to 1758. T. Salmon (1679-1769) travelled extensively in Europe and in 1739-40 accompanied Anson on his voyage round the world. He wrote several historical and geographical works, the most successful being his *Grammar*, first published in 1749, with new editions up to 1786. Libraries: BM, Bod, EU, GU.

FOURTH PERIOD 1750-1807

One result of the Jacobite movement of 1745 was the discovery that no reliable maps of the Highlands were available and so the Military Survey—the precursor of the Ordnance Survey—was undertaken in 1747. Although completed in 1755 the drawings were not made available to map publishers until 1805.

In 1750 a greatly improved map of Scotland was produced by James Dorret, who was in the employment of the Duke of Argyll. Dorret's map was the basis of practically every map of Scotland for the next forty years until John Ainslie in 1789 published a map which incorporated the west coast surveys of Murdoch Mackenzie and the new county surveys which made their appearance from 1763 onwards. Finally, in this period, came the map of Scotland by John Stockdale, on the scale of $3\frac{1}{2}$ miles to an inch, the largest map of Scotland published before the Ordnance Survey work in the later 19th century.

1750   DORRET, JAMES. A general map of Scotland and islands thereto belonging, from new surveys, the shires properly divided & subdivided, the forts lately erected & roads of communication or Military Ways...
4 sheets $35\frac{1}{2} \times 23\frac{3}{4}$ plus 2 sheets $35\frac{1}{2} \times 5\frac{3}{4} = 71 \times 53$. Scale 4 m. = 1 in.

For the first time a really good outline becomes available. Skye and Islay are not well done, and the Great Glen from Inverness to Fort William has too much of a curve, but taken as a whole, the map is an immense improvement on anything that preceded it. The size of the copper plates on which the maps were engraved is remarkable; there are four large sheets and a narrow strip of the Outer Hebrides necessary to complete the map when mounted. There was a reduced edition in 1751, and another in 1761.
Libraries: BM, Bod, EPL, GU, NLS, RGS, RSGS.

c. 1750   ANON.   Scotland.
$7\frac{1}{8} \times 7\frac{3}{4}$. Scale *c.* 40 m. = 1 in.

In *The Abridgement or Summarie of the Scots Chronicle* by John Monipennie, Glasgow, *c.* 1750.
Libraries: NLS.

c. 1750   BICKHAM, GEORGE (engr). A map of the north part of Great Britain called Scotland.
$6 \times 5\frac{1}{2}$. (Scale *c.* 70 m. = 1 in.)

In *The British Monarchy* by G. Bickham, 1743-54. The map is on the lower half of a page and the title is on the upper half. George Bickham (Senior) (1684-1758), an engraver and author of many books on penmanship. *The*

188

British Monarchy contains bird's-eye views of the counties of England, some by Bickham, senior, and some by George Bickham, junior (fl. 1735-57). Facsimile edition pub. 1967.
Libraries: BM, Bod, CUL, EPL, NLS, RSGS.

1751   DORRET, JAMES (del & sculp). A correct map of Scotland from new surveys. April 30th 1751.
        30 × 24. Scale 10 m. = 1 in.
Libraries: BM, CUL, EPL, NLS, RSGS.

1751   ROBERT (DE VAUGONDY, GILLES). Le Royaume d'Écosse divisé en shires ou comtés par le Sr. Robert.
        $19\frac{1}{4} \times 22\frac{1}{2}$. Scale *c.* 11 m.S. = 1 in.
In *Atlas Universel* par Robert, Géographe, et par Robert de Vaugondy, son fils, Paris, (1752), and later editions. A re-issue of the map still dated 1751 has many town names re-engraved in larger letters. A later edition of the map has the date deleted. Other copies are known with the title "L'Écosse divisée en Shires ou Comtés". See 1778.
Libraries: BM, CUL, EU, GU, LC, MLG, NLS, RSGS.

(1753) (EULER, L.)   Tabula geographica Scotiae.
        15 × 12. Scale 19 m.S. = 1 in. In bottom right-hand corner "Schottland".
In *Atlas geographicus omnes orbis terrarum regiones*, Berlin, 1753, also in 1756 and 1760 edns. Leonhard Euler (1707-83), a German Swiss mathematician and cartographer; editor of Atlas of Russia, St Petersburg, 1745; for long a member of L'Acadèmie des Sciences in St Petersburg and died there.
Libraries: AU, LC, NLS.

(1754) BOWEN, EMAN. An accurate map of Scotland or Nth. Britain drawn from the best authorities.
        $6\frac{7}{8} \times 8\frac{3}{4}$. Scale *c.* 50 m. = 1 in.
In *Geography Anatomiz'd* by Pat Gordon, M.A., F.R.S., 20th edn., London, 1754. For maps in earlier editions see 1722, John Senex.
Libraries: AU, BM, Bod, NLS.

1754-5 (PALAIRET, JEAN). (1) le. Carte d'Écosse 1754. (2) 2e. Carte d'Écosse 1755.
        Each $20\frac{3}{4} \times 22\frac{1}{4}$. Scale $15\frac{1}{3}$ m. = 1 in. Map 1 has the names only of counties and rivers; map 2 has the principal towns added.
In Jean Palairet's *Atlas Méthodique*; J. Nourse & P. Vaillant, London 1755. Jean (also John) Palairet (1697-1774), agent in London of the French States General and French teacher to the children of George II, wrote a *Nouvelle Introduction à la Géographie Moderne* in 3 vols., London 1754-5, and other works.
Libraries: BM, GU, LC, RGS.

(1755) The Military Survey of Scotland 1747-55, comprising the following manuscript maps all in the British Museum Map Room. The map is commonly known as the "Roy Map", from William Roy, who was engaged on it throughout.
1.   The original drawing/protraction of Northern Scotland north of Edinburgh and Glasgow, with parts of the Lothians, Peeblesshire and Lanarkshire, in 84 rolls; on a scale

of 1 inch to 1000 yards and oriented to magnetic north.
BM. Ref. K.Top. XLVIII 25a.

2. A complete map of the Scottish mainland consisting of (*a*)
a "fair copy" of the original drawing of Northern Scotland
(1 above), combined with (*b*) the original protraction of
Southern Scotland (for which no "fair copy" was made),
in 38 sheets of unequal size. The scale is 1 inch to 1000
yards: the map is oriented to magnetic north. This is
the principal map. According to Arrowsmith "In the
fair copy of the North of Scotland the mountains and
ground appear shaded in a capital style by the pencil of
Mr Paul Sandby, subsequently so much celebrated as a
landscape draftsman. The outlines were drawn and other
particulars were inserted under the care of (Colonel)
Watson by sundry assistants." The draughtsmanship of
Southern Scotland is not quite up to the standard of the
"fair copy" of Northern Scotland.
BM. Ref. K.Top XLVIII 25-1b, c. Photocopies in EU,
NLS, RSGS and elsewhere.

3. A reduction from (2) on one quarter the scale, i.e. 1 inch
to 4000 yards; oriented to magnetic north; in a single roll,
10 feet by 7 feet. This map is unfinished, the topography
being completed but only a few place names inserted. It
is a careful copy of the larger map, e.g. with plantations
and field boundaries corresponding exactly with the
original. Drawn by Paul Sandby.
BM. Ref. K.Top XLVIII 25-1d.

4. A reduction from (3) on three-eighths of its scale, i.e. 1 inch
to 6 miles; oriented to magnetic north; in two rolls.
Drawn by Thomas Chamberlain in the Ordnance Office
in the Tower of London between 1787 and 1790, but
uncompleted.
BM. Ref. K.Top XLVIII 25-1f.

5. Another reduction of (2) on the same scale as (3), i.e.
1 inch to 4000 yards; a completed map in 21 sheets,
oriented to true north. The authorship is unknown; the
style of drawing and lettering are different from map 3.
The workmanship is excellent, although in making this
copy the draughtsman has not followed the original with
absolute fidelity in all the details of fields, etc. Towns,
villages and hamlets are coloured red; water pale blue.
BM. Ref. K.Top XLVIII 25-1e. Photocopy RSGS.

1757 BELLIN, J. N. Carte Réduite des Isles Brittaniques.
(1)   Troisième feuille. Partie méridionale de l'Écosse.
(2)   Quatrième feuille. Partie septentrionale de l'Écosse.
Each sheet $22 \times 34\frac{1}{4}$. (Scale *c*. 11 m. = 1 in.)
The whole map consists of five sheets of which two cover Scotland. Bellin's
name is on sheet 1. In Bellin's *Hydrographie Françoise*, 1756-65, Paris.
Libraries: BM, Bod, CUL, LC, NLS, RSGS.

(1757) BELLIN, J. N. Écosse.
7¼ × 5½. Scale *c*. 65 m. = 1 in.
In *Essai géographique sur les Isles Brittaniques*, by M. Bellin, Paris, 1757.
Libraries: BM, Bod, CUL, EU, NLS.

(1758) (BOWEN, EMANUEL). Scotland.
Drawn and engraved by J. Gibson. Revised, corrected
and improved by Eman. Bowmen, London.
3¾ × 2½. Scale *c*. 107 m. = 1 in.
In *Atlas Minimus*, by Eman. Bowen; London, 1758. Also in later editions up
to 1798.
Libraries: BM, Bod, CUL, LC, RGS.

(1758) PHINN, T. (sculp). A new and accurate map of Scotland,
drawn from surveys and the most approved maps and
charts.
15 × 12. Scale 21 m. = 1 in.
In *Scots Magazine*, Edinburgh, May 1758. This map shows the routes of armies
in 1745 and 1746 and the route of Prince Charles's journey after the Battle of
Culloden. Thomas Phinn, engraver in Edinburgh, fl. 1746-60.
Libraries: BM, Bod, CUL, EPL, EU, NLS.

(1759) EXPILLY, (JEAN JOSEPH). L'Écosse.
6 × 4½. Scale *c*. 58 m. = 1 in.
In *Description Historique-Géographique des Isles Britanniques*, by M. l'Abbé
Expilly, Paris, 1759. Abbé Expilly (1719-93), French traveller and geographer,
was the author of *La Cosmographie* 1749; *La Topographie de l'Univers* 1758;
Le Géographe Manuel 1757, and other works.
Libraries: BM, Bod.

(1759) PRINALD (sculp). A new map of Scotland or North
Britain.
11¾ × 7¾. Scale *c*. 40 m. = 1 in.
In *A New Geographical Dictionary*, London, 1759, and in *Atlas to Rider's History
of England*, 1764.
Libraries: BM, NLS.

(1760) PHINN, T. (engr). A new map of Scotland.
7⅛ × 7¾. (Including views of Edinburgh and Stirling
Castles 7⅛ × 13). Scale 40 m. = 1 in.
In *A History of the Whole Realm of Scotland*, 1760.
Libraries: NLS.

1761 DORRET, JAMES (Land Surveyor). An accurate map of
Scotland drawn from all the particular surveys hitherto
published with many additional improvements.
22¼ × 20⅜. Scale 14 m. = 1 in. Printed for and sold by
Robt. Sayer.
In *The Large English Atlas* by Emanuel Bowen, Thomas Kitchin and others,
1787 edn. This is the third of Dorret's maps of Scotland—(1) the "General
Map" of 1750 and (2) "A Correct Map" 1751. Some copies of the 1761 map
have no date.
Libraries: BM, CUL, EPL, EU, LC, MLG, NLS, RGS, RSGS.

(1761)   KITCHIN, T. (sculp). A map of Scotland; at top: Écosse.
4 × 4¾. Scale *c.* 75 m. = 1 in.
In *A New General and Universal Atlas* by Andrew Dury, London, 1761 and 1770. Andrew Dury, surveyor, engraver and map publisher, fl. 1742-78.
Libraries: BM, Bod, RGS.

1762   KITCHIN, (T). A new and accurate map of Scotland for Busching's Geography.
11 × 8¾. Scale 32 m. = 1 in.
In *A New System of Geography* by A. F. Busching, Vol. III, London, 1762.
Libraries: AU, BM, GU, NLS.

1762   ROBERT DE VAUGONDY, (GILLES).   L'Écosse.
9½ × 8¾. Scale 32 m. = 1 in. Arrivet inv. et sculp., E. Dussy, engr.
In *Nouvel Atlas Portatif,* par le S. Robert de Vaugondy, Paris, 1762, and later editions.
Libraries: BM, LC, NLS, RGS.

(1763)   (BOWEN, EMANUEL). A map of North Britain or Scotland from the newest surveys & observations.
21¾ × 19. Scale 15 m. = 1 in.
In *The Large English Atlas* by Emanuel Bowen, Thomas Kitchin and others, 1763 and 1785 editions. Printed for Thos. Bowles, John Bowles & Son, & Robt. Sayer, London (1763); Printed for Robt. Wilkinson, Carington Bowles, and Robt. Sayer (1785). Also in *A General Atlas,* 1769 and 1774: Printed for John Bowles, Carington Bowles and Robt. Sayer.
Libraries: AU, BM, Bod, CUL, MLG, RGS, RSGS.

1764   (DORRET). A new and accurate map of Scotland with the roads . . . . from Mr Dorret's late map of Scotland. Printed for and sold by Robt. Sayer . . and Andrew Dury 1764.
13¾ × 12½ Scale 22½ m. = 1 in. There is an issue dated 1770.
Libraries: BM, Bod, NLS, RSGS.

(1764)   BELLIN, J. N.   Carte de l'Écosse.
8 × 6¼. Scale *c.* 50 m. = 1 in.
In *Le Petit Atlas Maritime,* Paris, 1764.
Libraries: BM, Bod, EU, LC, RGS.

1765   BRION DE LA TOUR, LOUIS. L'Écosse dressée conformement aux observations astronomiques et aux itinéraires.
9⅛ × 10¼ (with text panels 11⅛ × 18⅞). Scale 25 m.S. = 1 in.
In *Atlas Général, Civil, Ecclésiastique, et Militaire,* par M. Brion, Paris, 1766. The 1790 edition of map in *Atlas Général et Élémentaire* par le Sr. Desnos, Nouvelle Edition, Paris, 1786, has "L'Écosse: Par M. Brion et publié par S. Desnos, 1790". Also later editions. Louis Brion de la Tour, French engineer, and "Géographe du Roy", fl. *c.* 1765-1823; he produced the *Atlas Général,* several small atlases and numerous geographical works.
Libraries: BM, Bod, LC, MLG, NLS, RSGS.

(1765)   KITCHIN, Thos.   Scotland from the best authorities.
          10½ × 7⅛.   Scale 30 m.S. = 1 in.
In *A New System of Geography*, by D. Fenning and J. Collyer, Vol. II, London, 1765 and later editions (uncoloured); and (with coloured county borders and at top "Vol. II, p. 598"), in *Universal Geography*, by John Payne, London, 1791.
Libraries: AU, BM, Bod, CUL, EU, GU, NLS, RGS.

c. 1765   LOTTER, Tobias Conrad.   Nova et accurata totius
          Regni Scotiae delineatio.
          22¾ × 19½.   Scale 11 m.S. = 1 in.   And. Silbereysen,
          sculp.
This is Seutter's map (see 1735), with his name replaced by his successor, Lotter.
Libraries: EPL, NLS, RSGS.

(1765?)   ANON.   A new & accurate map of Scotland divided into
          shires drawn from a late survey.
          13⅜ × 12.   Scale *c*. 23 m. = 1 in.
Libraries: BM, Bod, RSGS.

1766   SHERIFF, Charles.   Scotland.
          7½ × 8.   Scale *c*. 50 m. = 1 in.
Libraries: MS Map in RSGS.

(1766)   SAYER, Robert.   A new and exact mapp of Scotland
          or North Britain described by N. Sanson—Translated into
          English at the expence of Robert Sayer.
          33¼ × 22¾.   Scale 11 m. (9 m.S.) = 1 in.   Sutton Nicholls,
          sculp.
This is the 1715 plate of the same title, now considerably worn, with Overton's name replaced by Robert Sayer; the date 1715 is still visible. Roads have been added as double lines more or less straight, with a road shown direct from Fort William over the mountains to Cape Wrath. The map was advertised in Sayer's Catalogue of 1766; a later issue was published by Laurie and Whittle on 12th May 1794. Robert Sayer (1725-94) map publisher in London; was succeeded by Laurie & Whittle (see 1799).
Libraries: NLS (1794).

1767   PALMER, (William) (sculp).   A new and accurate map of
          Scotland divided into shires from the most authentick
          surveys.
          17¼ × 15⅞.   Scale 18⅓ m. = 1 in.
In *A General History of Scotland*, by William Guthrie, London, 1767.
Libraries: AU, BM, CUL, EPL, EU, NLS.

(1767)   GAVIN, H. (engr).   Scotland with a list of the royal
          burroughs and other principal towns.
          7 × 7¾ (8⅞ × 7¾ with list of towns).   Sc. 43 m. = 1 in.
In *A New Geographical and Historical Grammar* by Mr. (Thomas) Salmon, Edinr. 10th edn. 1767. Some copies of this edition have the map with no engraver's name.
Libraries: AU, BM, CUL, NLS.

(1767)   KITCHIN, T. (sculp).   Scotland from the best authorities.
          7 × 7¾.   Scale *c*. 49 m. = 1 in.
In *A New Collection of Voyages*, Vol. VII, London, J. Knox, 1767.
Libraries: CUL, RGS.

(1769)   JEFFERYS, T.   (sculp).   Scotland.
          $7 \times 7\frac{3}{4}$.   Scale 43 m. = 1 in.

In *A New Geographical and Historical Grammar* by Thomas Salmon, 1769 edn.
The map is almost identical with the 1767 map. Also in *The New Universal
Geographical Grammar* by Thomas Salmon, 1782 edn.
Libraries: BM.

1770   PHILIPPE, Mr.   L'Écosse.
         $10\frac{1}{2} \times 15$.   Scale *c*. 22 m.S. = 1 in.   Moithey, del et sculp.
         Hérault, scrip.

M. Philippe is described on the map as Censeur Royal de l'Académie d'Angers
and professor of history.
Libraries: RSGS.

(1770)   LODGE, J.   (sculp).   A new and correct map of Scotland
          from the most accurate surveys.
          $12 \times 11\frac{1}{4}$ Scale *c*. 26 m. = 1 in.

In *A New History of Scotland* by John Belfour, London, 1770.
Libraries: AU, BM, Bod, EPL, EU, GU, NLS.

c. 1770   BOWEN, T.   A new & accurate map of that part of
           Great Britain called Scotland.
           $12\frac{5}{8} \times 8\frac{5}{8}$.   Scale *c*. 34 m. = 1 in.   Engraved for the *Com-
           plete English Traveller*.

Thomas Bowen (d. 1790), engraver and map seller, son of Emanuel Bowen
engraved maps for Taylor & Skinner's *Survey of the Roads of North Britain* and
other publications.
Libraries: MLG.

1771   BONNE, (RIGOBERT).   Carte du Royaume d'Écosse.
         $11\frac{7}{8} \times 16\frac{5}{8}$.   Scale *c*. 28 m.S. = 1 in.   Arrivet, sculp, Paris.

In *Atlas Moderne ou Collection de Cartes*: Lattre, Paris; (1771-83). Bonne
(1729-95), French hydrographer and cartographer, issued an *Atlas Maritime*
in 1762, *Petit Neptune Anglais* in 1763, *Atlas Portatif c.* 1785, etc. The map was
re-issued with the date 1787.
Libraries: BM, LC, NLS, RSGS.

(1771)   KITCHIN, THOS.   Scotland with the roads from the latest
          surveys. At top: Engraved for Guthrie's *New Geographical
          Grammar*.
          $14\frac{1}{2} \times 13\frac{1}{4}$.   Scale *c*. 24 m. = 1 in.

In *A New Geographical Historical and Commercial Grammar* by William Guthrie,
2nd edn., Edinburgh, 1771. Also in *A New System of Modern Geography*, by
William Guthrie, London, 1782. See also 1785. William Guthrie, born at
Brechin and educated at Aberdeen University, settled in London in 1730.
In 1767 he published a *History of Scotland* in 10 vols. His Geographical
Grammar went through 24 editions.
Libraries: AU, BM, Bod, CUL, EU, GU.

(1771)   KITCHIN, THOMAS.   Scotland from the best authorities.
          $7 \times 7\frac{3}{4}$.   Scale 49 m. = 1 in.

In *A New Geographical, Historical and Commercial Grammar*, by W. Guthrie,
London, 3rd edn., 1771, 4th & 5th edns; in *The New Universal Geographical
Grammar* by T. Salmon, continued by J. Tytler, Edinburgh, 1778; and in
Grammar and Present States of Kingdoms of This World, by W. Guthrie, London,
1777.
Libraries: AU, BM, CUL, NLS.

1773   KITCHIN, THOMAS. North Britain or Scotland divided into its counties corrected from the best surveys & astronomical observations.

26¼ × 21. Scale 12½ m. = 1 in. Printed for the Author.

In *A New General Atlas*, by W. Faden. Another edition of the map is dated 1778 and has "Printed for W. Faden". Another re-issue is dated 1790.
Libraries: BM, EPL, LC, MLG, NLS, RGS, RSGS.

(1773)   (KITCHIN, THOMAS). A new and complete map of Scotland and islands thereto belonging from actual surveys.

4 sheets each 23½ × 19¾ or 2 sheets each 23½ × 39½. Scale 7¼ m. = 1 in.

There were various issues of this map; with illustrations of sailing vessels and without them; with or without a scale. Later issues had different titles—see Bowles, 1782 and 1806. This is one of the earliest maps showing light lines following the coast lines, in place of the horizontal lines that hitherto had been customary.

(1) In *A General Atlas or Description at large of the Whole Universe*, by Thomas Kitchin, Senior & Others, published by Robert Sayer and Thomas Jefferys, 1773, the map has the imprint "Printed for Robt. Sayer . . and Carington Bowles". (2) In *A General Atlas describing the Whole Universe*, by Thomas Kitchin, Senior and others, printed for Robert Sayer, 1773, the map has no imprint. Some 15 editions of this *Atlas* were published, first by Sayer, then Sayer and Bennett, and from 1795 by R. Laurie and J. Whittle, with new maps of Scotland in 1782 (Armstrong), 1790 (Campbell), and 1810 (Enouy).
Libraries: All.

(1773)   (KITCHIN, THOMAS). Scotland from the surveys made by order of the late Duke of Cumberland. Improved from the large map of Mr Dorret.

2 sheets each 23½ × 39¾. Scale 7¼ m. = 1 in.

This seems to be the map which was advertised by Robert Sayer in his 1766 Catalogue as "A new and correct map of Scotland, made under the directions, and by order of, his late Royal Highness the Duke of Cumberland . . ."
Libraries: Not located.

1774   DUNN, SAMUEL. Scotland and its islands or the north part of Great Britain divided into shires.

18¾ × 13½. Scale *c*. 23½ m. = 1 in.

In *A New Atlas of the Mundane System*, by Samuel Dunn, London, Pub. R. Sayer, 1774, and later editions. The 1788 and 1796 editions have the same map with the date altered to 1786. Another edition of the map is dated 1794. Also in *The Royal English Atlas* by Emanuel Bowen and Thomas Kitchin, London, 1780 edition.
Libraries: AU, BM, Bod, LC, RGS, RSGS.

1774   ROY, Gmo. (General WILLIAM). Mappa Britanniae septentrionalis faciei Romanae.

23⅞ × 18½. Scale 18½ m. = 1 in. J. Cheevers, sculp.

In *The Military Antiquities of the Romans in North Britain* by William Roy, London, 1793. A map of Roman Scotland, drawn by Roy on the basis of the Military Survey (see 1755), with the Hebrides largely taken from Dorret's map of 1750 and place names based on Bertram's map attributed to Richard of Cirencester. The map in *Military Antiquities* has "Published . . . April 23rd, 1793"; another issue (possibly a proof issued before the book) lacks Roy's name and has no dates; the dated map has three Roman sites added. The map is one of the early examples of the new style of soft etched hill shading so different from the pimple or turtle style shading.

Reproduction, reduction, in R. A. Skelton, "The Military Survey of Scotland 1747-1755", *Scot. geogr. Mag.* v. 83 (1967).

Libraries; AU, BM, Bod, CUL, EPL, EU, GU, MLG, NLS, RSGS.

1775   ARMSTRONG, Captain (ANDREW). A new map of Scotland with the distances on the post & other roads in measured miles laid down from actual surveys . . . 22 × 17⅛. (Scale *c.* 16 m. = 1 in.) Printed for and Sold by Carington Bowles . . . London. Pub. Nov. 9th 1775.

At the top tables of distances are given from Edinburgh and from Inverness. Roads are shown as double lines with mileage; only a few rivers are shown, no mountains; and not many place names.

Libraries: BM, Bod, EPL, LC, NLS, RSGS.

1775   ARMSTRONG, Captain (ANDREW). Bowles's new pocket map of Scotland with the distances on the post and other roads in measured miles. Nov. 9th 1775. 21¾ × 17¼. (Scale *c.* 15 m. = 1 in.)

In *Bowles's Universal Atlas*, by John Palairet, London; Carington Bowles (1775-80).

Libraries: BM, EPL, LC, NLS.

(1775)   (PALAIRET, JOHN).   Scotland. 17 × 21. Scale *c.* 24 m. = 1 in.

In *An Elementary and Methodical Atlas* by John Palairet, 2nd edn. 1775, London. Libraries: BM, NLS.

1776   TAYLOR, GEO. and SKINNER, ANDW. A general map of the roads of Scotland made out from actual surveys, taken 1775. Publish'd . . . March 20th 1776. 14 × 12⅝. Scale *c.* 23 m. = 1 in. Pyle, sculp.

In *Taylor & Skinner's Survey and Maps of the Roads of North Britain or Scotland*, London, 1776. Also in *The Traveller's Pocket Book, or an Abstract of Taylor & Skinner's Survey of the Roads of Scotland*, London, 1776. See 1792.

Libraries: AU, BM, Bod, EPL, NLS, RSGS, SRO.

1776   ZATTA, ANTONIO.   Il Regno di Scozia. 11¾ × 15½. (Scale *c.* 40 m. = 1 in.)

Map E.1. in *Atlante Novissimo*, Tomo 1, Venice, 1779. (See 1779 infra.) Antonia Zatta, cartographer and publisher in Venice, fl. 1757-97.

Libraries: BM, LC, NLS, RSGS.

1777   (ARMSTRONG, MOSTYN JOHN).
(1)   A map of the counties of North Britain. 8 × 6. Scale 57 m. = 1 in.
(2)   Road map of Scotland. 7½ × 5½. Scale *c.* 47 m. = 1 in. H. Ashby, engr.

Maps 1 and 2 in *A Scotch Atlas*, by Mostyn John Armstrong, 1777. Other editions 1787 and 1794.

Libraries: AU, BM, Bod, CUL, EPL, EU, LC, NLS, RGS, RSGS.

1777   BAYLY, J. (sculp). A map of Scotland the Hebrides and
        part of England adapted to Mr Pennant's tours.
        23⅝ × 17⅞. (Scale *c.* 20 m. = 1 in.) May 1st 1777.
In *A Tour of Scotland in 1769* and *A Tour in Scotland and Voyage to the Hebrides*,
1772 by Thomas Pennant, London, 1777 edns. Also in 1790 edition.
Libraries: All.

1778   AINSLIE, JOHN. This map of the country round Edin-
        burgh. (A map covering a large part of east & central
        Scotland.)
        23 × 22¾. Scale 4 m. = 1 in. Later issues 1779, 1801 and
        1812.
Libraries: BM, Bod, NLS, RGS, RSGS.

1778   FADEN, WM. North Britain or Scotland divided into its
        counties.
        26 × 21. Scale 12½ m. = 1 in. Pub. Dec. 1st 1778.
In *A General Atlas*, by W. Faden. A re-issue of Kitchin's map of 1773. A later
issue dated 1790.
Libraries: BM, NLS.

1778   MARSHALL, R. A new map/mapp of North Britain or
        Scotland.
        22½ × 25¼. 22½ × 36¼ including table of cities and market
        towns. (Scale *c.* 16 m. = 1 in.)
This is a re-issue of the map by Sutton Nicholls (see 1710).
Libraries: RSGS.

1778   ROBERT, (DE VAUGONDY). L'Écosse divisée en
        shires ou comtés . . . à Venise par P. Santini.
        19⅛ × 22⅜. Scale 11 m.S. = 1 in.
This edition published by Santini in Venice is Robert's 1751 map, entirely re-
engraved with some changes in place names, e.g., Dumfries-Sh in place of
Nitisdale Sh., and a new cartouche.
Libraries: NLS, RSGS.

(1778) PALMER, (WILLIAM) (engr). A new and accurate map
        of Scotland from the latest observations.
        7¼ × 7⅞. Scale *c.* 50 m. = 1 in.
In *A Tour through the island of Great Britain* by Daniel Defoe, vol. IV, 8th
edn. 1778.
Libraries: BM, Bod, CUL, RGS.

1779   ZATTA, ANTONIO. (1) La Scozia meridionale. (2) La
        Scozia settentrionale.
        Each 12 × 15¾. Scale *c.* 12 m.S. = 1 in. G. Zuliana (inc);
        G. Pitteri (scr).
Maps EII and EIII in *Atlante Novissimo*, Tomo 1 (see 1776). All three maps
appear with later dates.
Libraries: BM, LC, NLS.

    O

(1779)   KITCHIN, T.   Scotland drawn from the best authorities.
          $7\frac{1}{2} \times 9$.   Scale 47 m. = 1 in.

In *A New Geographical, Historical and Commercial Grammar*, by W. Guthrie,
6th edn. 1779; and later edns.   In the 10th edn. 1787 the map has a new title
omitting "drawn", and Kitchin's name.
Libraries: BM, Bod, NLS.

1780   GAVIN, H.   (sculp).   Scotland from the best authorities.
          $7\frac{1}{4} \times 7\frac{1}{2}$.   Scale c. 43 m. = 1 in.

In *The Town and County Almanack*, 1780.
Libraries: Bod.

(1780)   (PORTE, ABBÉ JOSEPH DE LA).   Carte du Royaume
          d'Écosse.
          $7 \times 8\frac{1}{2}$.   Scale c. 36 m.S. = 1 in.

Plate 13 of *Atlas Moderne Portatif*, Paris, 1780; also 1786.   De la Porte (1713-79),
French cartographer, published also an *Atlas ou Collection de Cartes géo-
graphiques*, 1787, and was author of the first 26 volumes of *Le Voyageur Français*.
Libraries: BM, RGS.

1781   CARY, JOHN.   A map of Scotland.
          $7 \times 6\frac{1}{2}$.   Scale c. 55 m. = 1 in.
Libraries: MLG.

1782   KNOX, J.   A commercial map of Scotland with the roads,
          stages and distances brought down to 1782.
          $28\frac{1}{2} \times 21\frac{3}{4}$.   (Scale c. 12 m. = 1 in.)

In *A View of the British Empire*, by John Knox, 1784.   A great many paragraphs
engraved on the map deal with Scotland's history, products, manufactures,
fisheries, proposed canals, etc. This is based on Dorret's outline but the detail
is not so exact; roads and distances are shown clearly.   There were several
editions each brought down to date—1784, 1788, 1791.
Libraries: BM, CUL, EPL, NLS, RSGS.

1782   LIZARS, D. (sculp).   Map of Scotland with the principal
          roads.
          $10 \times 7\frac{1}{2}$.   Scale c. 35 m. = 1 in.
In *The Universal Scots Almanack*.
Libraries: Bod, EU, NLS.

1782   BOWLES, CARINGTON.   Bowles's new pocket map of
          Scotland laid down from the original survey of James
          Dorret, geographer: with the addition of new roads.
          May 20th, 1782.
          $21\frac{3}{4} \times 20\frac{1}{4}$.   Scale 14 m. = 1 in.

In *Bowles's Universal Atlas*, by John Palairet, London.   This is a close copy of
Dorret's map of 1761. Another edition of the map is dated 1791.   A 1795
edition of the map (pub. by Bowles & Carver) is called "Bowles's New One-
Sheet Map"; another issue is undated.
Libraries: BM, Bod, NLS (Newman Colln.), RSGS.

1782   BOWLES, CARINGTON. Bowles's new and accurate map
        of Scotland . . . . from the original survey of James Dorret,
        geographer; with the addition of new roads (and other
        improvements).
        47 × 39½. Scale 7¼ m. = 1 in. Carington Bowles, London,
        1782.
Libraries: AU.

1782   ARMSTRONG, MARCUS. A new map of Scotland or
        North Britain wherein all the post and other public roads
        are correctly delineated . . . Pub. April 17th 1782.
        4 sheets each 24½ × 20¾ = 49 × 41½. Scale c. 7½ m. = 1 in.
Maps 8 and 9 in *A General Atlas describing the whole Universe*, by Thomas
Kitchin, Snr. & Others, pub. by R. Sayer and J. Bennett, London, 1782. This
map is interesting in its road data. Nothing is known of Marcus Armstrong,
who styles himself Geographer. See 1790 (Campbell) for a re-issue.
Libraries: AU, BM, CUL, LC, MLG, NLS (Newman Colln.), RGS, RSGS.

1782   STACKHOUSE, T.   Present Scotland.
        15⅛ × 14¾. Scale 24 m. = 1 in. S. J. Neele, engr.
In *An Universal Atlas*, by T. Stackhouse, London, 1783; and later editions.
(5th edition 1798.) In some editions the map is undated. Thomas Stackhouse,
cartographer and publisher, 1706-84.
Libraries: BM, Bod, NLS.

(1782) ANON. A new and correct map of Scotland drawn from
        the latest surveys of that part of Great Britain.
        11⅞ × 8⅝. Scale 33 m. = 1 in.
In *The New and Universal System of Geography* by George H. Millar, London,
1782; in *The New Comprehensive and Complete History of England* by Edward
Barnard, London, 1782; and in *A New and Complete Collection of Voyages
and Travels* by J. H. Moore, London, n.d., each map having the title of the book
at the top. The map was also issued without a book title.
Libraries: AU, BM, Bod, CUL, GU, NLS, RGS.

(1782) ANON.   Scotland.
        7 × 7¾. Scale c. 42 m. = 1 in.
In *A New Universal Geographical Grammar*, by T. Salmon, revised by J. Tytler,
2nd edn., Edinburgh 1782.
Libraries: BM, RGS.

1783   AINSLIE, JOHN. Ainslie's travelling map of Scotland
        shewing the distances from one stage to another. J.
        Ainslie, St Andrew's Street, Newtown, Edinburgh, Nov.
        1783.
        23¼ × 21¼. Scale 14 m. = 1 in.
A later edition is dated 1789; another is undated. In the N and NW all the dotted
roads and other distances are taken from M. Armstrong's map of 1782. A
notice on the map states: "Estates accurately Survey'd and Neatly Plann'd
Drawings Copied diminished or enlarged and Engraving expeditiously executed
by John Ainslie".
Libraries: MLG, NLS, RSGS.

1783   ANDREWS, JOHN. Andrews' new and accurate travelling map of the roads of Scotland.
        30 × 20½. (Scale *c.* 14 m. = 1 in.) W. Haydon, engr.
Distances on roads are shown. Two dates of publication appear on the map: Nov. 28th 1782 and Feb. 4th 1783. John Andrews (fl. 1766-1809) land surveyor and geographer, London.
Libraries: CUL, NLS (Newman Colln.).

1784   HARRISON & CO.   A new map of Scotland.
        9¾ × 8⅝. Scale *c.* 45 m. = 1 in.
In *The Geographical Magazine* by William F. Martyn, Vol. 2, 1785.
Libraries: BM, Bod, CUL, EU, NLS, RGS.

1784   LODGE, JOHN (sculp). A map of Scotland with the roads.
        14¼ × 12½. Scale 22½ m. = 1 in.
In *The Political Magazine*, 1784, vol. 7, p. 285. Re-issued in 1795 with imprint and engraver's name erased. John Lodge, engraver, fl. 1754-94.
Libraries: BM, Bod, CUL.

(1784) KITCHIN, T. Scotland divided into its counties from the latest surveys.
        14¾ × 13½. Scale 25 m. = 1 in. Alex. Hogg, publisher.
In *The New British Traveller*, by G. A. Walpoole, 1784.
Libraries: BM, EPL, MLG, RSGS.

1785   ANON.   Carte d'Écosse et des Isles Hebrides.
        16¼ × 15¾. Scale 21 m. = 1 in.
In *Voyages aux Montagnes d'Écosse*, Genève, 1785.
Libraries: NLS.

1785   (KITCHIN, T.) Scotland with the principal roads from the best authorities: (at top: Engraved for Guthrie's New System of Geography). 1st Jan. 1785.
        14½ × 13¼. Scale *c.* 24 m. = 1 in.
In *The Atlas to Guthrie's System of Geography* (1785). This map is the 1771 Kitchin Map with Kitchin's name removed.
Libraries: BM, Bod, LC, NLS.

1785   BELL, A. (engr). A new map of Scotland: The Hebrides and western coasts . . . from the best authorities.
        18¾ × 13¼. (with text 18½ × 15½). Scale 22 m. = 1 in.
In *An Account of the Present State of the Hebrides and Western Coasts of Scotland* 1785, by James Anderson, Edinburgh, 1785. Andrew Bell (1726-1809) was the co-founder and original joint proprietor of the *Encyclopaedia Britannica*.
Libraries: BM, Bod, CUL, EU, NLS, RSGS.

1786   CONDER, T. (sculp).
   1.   A new map of the southern part of Scotland.
         9 × 12½. Scale 13 m. = 1 in.
   2.   A new map of the middle part of Scotland.
         8¾ × 13. Scale *c.* 15 m. = 1 in.
   3.   A new map of the counties of Orkney, Caithness, Sutherland, Ross & Cromarty; (scale *c.* 14 m. = 1 in.); The Orkney isles; The Shetland isles (scale *c.* 16½ m. = 1 in.); together, 8 × 12¾.

4. A new map of the Western Isles of Scotland (scale *c.*
    19 m. = 1 in.); A new and correct map of the counties
    of Argyle, Bute and Dumbarton (scale *c.* 15 m. = 1 in.);
    together, 8½ × 13.

In *Historical Descriptions of New and Elegant Picturesque Views of the Antiquities
of England and Wales* by Henry Boswell. Alexr. Hogg, Publisher, London, 1786.
T. Conder, cartographer and engraver, fl. 1775-1801.
Libraries: BM, Bod, CUL, EU, GU, NLS, RSGS.

1787   HAYWOOD, JAMES. A new map of Scotland divided into
        counties. October 1st 1787.
        16¼ × 14¾. Scale *c.* 21 m. = 1 in. S. J. Neele, sculp.

In *A School Atlas*, by John Harrison, London, 1791.
Libraries: BM, LC, RSGS.

1787   HARRISON, J. (pub.). Map of Scotland from the latest
        discoveries. May 23rd 1787.
        13½ × 11½. Scale 23 m. = 1 in.

Libraries: RSGS.

1787   SCHRAEMBL, F. A. Karte von Scotland verfasst von
        Herrn J. Dorret Neuherausgegeben . . .
        21¾ × 20¼. Scale 14 m. = 1 in. J. Stenger, engr.

In *Grand Atlas Universel*, 1786-94; *Allgemeiner Grosser Atlas* 1800, both P. J.
Schalbacher, Wien, 1800. Franz Anton Schraembl (1751-1803), cartographer
and map publisher in Vienna.
Libraries: BM, LC, NLS, RGS, RSGS.

(1787) BONNE, (RIGOBERT).   Carte de l'Écosse.
        13¾ × 9⅛. Scale *c.* 31 m. = 1 in. Hérisson, del: André,
        sculp.

In *Atlas Encyclopédique*, M. Bonne, Paris, 1787.
Libraries: EU, RGS, RSGS.

1789   AINSLIE, JOHN. Scotland drawn and engraved from a
        series of angles and astronomical observations.
        9 sheets each 23¼ × 21¼ = 70 × 64. Scale 4 m. = 1 in.

This map is dated 1788 at top and foot, but below the title has "Published
Jan. 1st 1789 by John & James Ainslie, St Andrew's Street, Newtown, Edinburgh,
& William Faden, Charing Cross, London". Dedicated to the Right Honble.
Henry Dundas.
   There were several issues of this map: (1) Printed & Sold by John & James
Ainslie, Booksellers & Stationers, St Andrew's Street, Newtown, Edinburgh,
and William Faden, Geographer to the King, Charing Cross, London. Pub-
lished Jany 1st 1789 by John & James Ainslie (etc.). (2) Printed and Sold by the
Proprietor Thomas Brown, North Bridge Street, Edinburgh and William Faden
(etc.) Published . . . . With Improvements till 1800 by Thomas Brown, North
Bridge Street. (3) Second edition. Brought down to 1825 by John Ainslie,
Land Surveyor, Edinburgh. Published by D. Lizars, 61 Princes Street, and
James Gardner, London. (4) Scotland on Nine Imperial Sheets by the late
John Ainslie Corrected to 1834. (5) Later edition to 11th edition "with improve-
ments till 1840".
   After the first edition substantial alterations were made in the Counties of
Angus and Kirkcudbright, and to a lesser extent in the County of Renfrew,
as a result of Ainslie's own surveys of Angus in 1794 and of Kirkcudbright and

Renfrew in 1796. Revision was also made of North Uist, following a survey by Reid in 1802, and of Harris and South Uist, after surveys by Ainslie and William Bald respectively in 1805. Various roads were also added throughout, and now appeared in Islay, Jura, and Mull, in addition to Harris and Uist.

Each of the nine sheets forming the map was dated, all originally 1789. This was altered to 1800 for the second issue by Thomas Brown, and there were at least two issues of this date: (1) from the original plates unaltered; (2) with the alterations described above, some of which must have been made after 1805 when the Harris and South Uist surveys were available. Complete maps are also found with some sheets dated 1789 and others 1800.
Libraries: Most.

1789   HATCHETT (sculp).   A new map of Scotland.
        $9\frac{7}{8} \times 8\frac{1}{4}$. Scale 34 m. = 1 in.

In *A History of England* by Alexander Bicknell, London, 1794.
Libraries: BM, MLG, NLS.

(1789)   BEUGO, J(OHN).   Scotland with the roads from the latest surveys.
         $14\frac{1}{8} \times 12\frac{7}{8}$. Scale 25 m. = 1 in.

In *A New Geographical Grammar* by William Gordon, Edinburgh, 1789.
Libraries: BM, NLS.

(1789)   CARY, JOHN.   A new and correct map of (1) the south part of Scotland. (2) the north part of Scotland.
         2 sheets $15 \times 20\frac{1}{2}$ and $16\frac{1}{2} \times 21\frac{1}{4}$. Scale *c.* 12 m. = 1 in.

In *Britannia* by William Camden, translated by Richard Gough, London, 1789. Also in the 1806 edition of Camden, where the maps are dated 1805. The same maps were also issued in John Cary's *New British Atlas*, published by John Stockdale, Piccadilly, 1805.
Libraries: AU, BM, Bod, CUL, EPL, EU, GU, NLS, RGS, RSGS.

(1789)   CARY, J(OHN) (sculp).   A map of Scotland.
         $7\frac{1}{8} \times 6\frac{1}{4}$. (Scale *c.* 55 m. = 1 in.)

In *The Traveller's Companion: or New Itinerary of England & Wales, with Part of Scotland* by Thomas Pride and Philip Luckcombe, London, 1789.
Libraries: AU, BM, CUL, NLS, RGS.

(1789)   REILLY, FRANZ, J. J. VON
  (1)   Das Königreich Scotland. $11\frac{1}{4} \times 8\frac{1}{2}$. Scale 27 m.S. = 1 in.
         Ignaz Albrecht, engr.
  (2)   Des Königreichs Scotland südlicher Theil.
         $7\frac{7}{8} \times 10\frac{1}{2}$. Scale 18 m.S. = 1 in.
  (3)   Des Königreichs Scotland nördlicher Theil.
         $8\frac{1}{2} \times 10\frac{3}{4}$. Scale *c.* 18 m.S. = 1 in.

In *Schauplatz der Funf Theile der Welt*, Maps Nos. 86-88 (Vol. 1), Wien, 1789-91. Franz Johann Joseph von Reilly (1766-1820), publisher, Vienna. Editions of the *Schauplatz* appeared in 3 to 6 volumes, with up to 886 plates.
Libraries: BM, LC, NLS, RSGS.

1790   AINSLIE, JOHN.   Scotland.
        $10\frac{3}{4} \times 9\frac{3}{4}$. Scale *c.* 29 m. = 1 in.

In *Scotland Delineated* (by Robert Heron), Edinr. 1791.
Libraries: BM, Bod, CUL, EPL, GU, NLS, RSGS.

1790   CAMPBELL, Lieutenant (ROBERT). A new and correct map of Scotland or North Britain with all the post and military roads, divisions . . . (etc). Printed for Robert Sayer, 10th Jany. 1790.
4 sheets each $24\frac{1}{2} \times 20\frac{5}{8}$ or in 2 sheets each $24\frac{1}{2} \times 41\frac{1}{2}$ = $49 \times 41\frac{3}{4}$. Scale $7\frac{1}{2}$ m. = 1 in. Re-issued by Laurie & Whittle with date 12 May 1794.

In *A General Atlas* by T. Kitchin, London, 1790 edition; in *A New Universal Atlas*, by Thomas Kitchin, Senr. & Others, London, 1796 (1794 map); and in later editions of both.

This map (and the next one) are re-issues by Sayer of old plates in his possession. This one is Marcus Armstrong's map of 1782, with extensive revision and reworking of the four plates, the N.W. coast slightly revised and the Western Isles entirely redrawn except for the north part of Lewis. Some roads have been added (based on Ainslie's map of 1789) and some redrawn: it has a new cartouche and new title. Lieut. Campbell is unknown.
Libraries: Most.

1790   CAMPBELL, Lieutenant (ROBERT). A new map of Scotland or North Britain drawn from the most approved surveys . . . . Pub. by Robert Sayer, 12th May 1790.
$22\frac{1}{4} \times 20\frac{3}{8}$. Scale *c*. 14 m. = 1 in.

In *A General Atlas* by Robert Sayer. The same map dated 1794 is in *A New and Elegant Imperial Sheet Atlas* by Robert Laurie & James Whittle, London, 1798.

This map is printed from the original plate of Dorret's map of 1761, with a complete change of title and cartouche, new scale, many roads added, many place names re-engraved at a larger size; and the west coast of Lewis and Harris revised from Mackenzie's survey. See 1794.
Libraries: BM, Bod, CUL, LC, MLG, NLS, RSGS.

c. 1790   BARBIÉ DU BOCAGE, J. D.   L'Écosse avec ses isles.
$17\frac{1}{8} \times 10\frac{1}{2}$. Scale *c*. 26 m. = 1 in. Dien, scripsit.

Jean Denis Barbié du Bocage (1760-1825), French geographer, was one of the founders of the Geographical Society of Paris.
Libraries: RSGS.

c. 1790   (BARLOW, JAMES). The north part of Great Britain called Scotland.
$17\frac{1}{2} \times 14\frac{1}{4}$. Scale *c*. 22 m. = 1 in.

This is an oval-shaped map in a rectangular frame, having in each corner of the rectangle one large and two small circles containing a description of Scotland. The British Museum copy is in an atlas of maps of the same style with the map of Sweden and Norway inscribed "Ja. Barlow, Sculpt". The map of England is virtually an exact copy of S. Parker's England & Wales (*c*. 1728) even to the circles, and the map of Scotland has also the appearance of early 18th century. Barlow engraved plans for Thos. Telford in 1803.
Libraries: BM, CUL.

c. 1790   BROWN, THOMAS. A new & accurate travelling map of Scotland with the distances marked between each stage in measured miles.
$21\frac{3}{4} \times 17\frac{1}{4}$. Scale $10\frac{1}{2}$ m.S. = 1 in. McIntyre, sculp.

Pub. by Thomas Brown, Bookseller, Edinburgh, and John Brown Glasgow. A later edition has mountains and many more place names.
Libraries: AU, BM, CUL, EPL.

c. 1790   STEWART and MEIKLE & J. MURDOCH (Publishers, Glasgow). A map of Scotland with the roads.
19¼ × 16½. Scale 15½ m. = 1 in.
Libraries: RSGS.

1791   HOOPER, S. (Publisher). An index map to the antiquities of Scotland.
17¾ × 14⅞. Scale 19 m. = 1 in.
In *The Antiquities of Scotland* by Francis Grose, London, 1797.
Libraries: BM, Bod, CUL, EPL, EU, GU, NLS, RSGS.

(1791)   CARY, J. (engr).   The contour of Scotland.
18½ × 16¾. Scale *c.* 16 m. = 1 in.
In *Prospects and Observations on a Tour in England and Scotland*, by Thomas Newte, London, 1791.
Libraries: AU, BM, Bod, CUL, EPL, EU, GU, NLS.

(1791)   KITCHIN, T.   Scotland.
In *Universal Geography*, by John Payne, London, 1791.
Libraries: AU, BM, EU, GU, NLS.

1792   AINSLIE, JOHN (Land Surveyor).   Scotland.
18⅝ × 17⅜ (with table of distances from Edinburgh 23 × 17⅜).
Scale *c.* 16 m. = 1 in.
Published . . Sept. 1st 1792 and sold by James Ainslie, St Andrew's Street, Edinburgh, etc.
Libraries: BM, CUL, MLG, RSGS.

1792   KINCAID, ALEX. Scotland with the roads & post towns.
10⅜ × 9½. Scale *c.* 30 m. = 1 in. T. Conder, sculp.
In *A New Geographical, Commercial and Historical Grammar*, by Alex Kincaid, 2nd edn. Edinburgh, 1792.
Libraries: BM, NLS.

1792   PYLE (sculp). A general map of the roads of Scotland. Edinburgh.
11¾ × 13. Scale *c.* 23 m. = 1 in.
This is Taylor & Skinner's "General Map" of 1776, used by W. Gordon and R. N. Cheyne for their *Traveller's Directory through Scotland*. A second issue in 1798 has "Engraved for R. Gordon, No. 30 Parlt. Close, Edinburgh".
Libraries: EPL, NLS.

(1792)   (NEELE, S. J. (engr)).   Scotland.
4¾ × 5¼. (Scale *c.* 75 m. = 1 in.)
In *The Youth's General Introduction to Guthrie's Geography*, by W. Perks, London, 1792 and 1793 editions. Samuel John Neele (1758-1824), engraved numerous maps of Scotland.
Libraries: AU, BM, GU, NLS.

1794   CARY, JOHN. (Engr). Cary's new map of England & Wales, with part of Scotland.
Each sheet 10 × 8. Scale 5 m. = 1 in.
This map is on 81 sheets of which 13 cover Southern Scotland up to St Andrews/ Inveraray. This appears to be the first map with the meridian of Greenwich. Later revised issues appeared from 1816 to 1834.
Libraries: BM, Bod, CUL, NLS, RSGS.

1794   LAURIE, R. H. and WHITTLE, JAMES. A new and exact
        mapp of Scotland or North Britain.
        33¼ × 22¾. A re-issue of Sayer's map of 1766 (q.v.).
Libraries: NLS.

1794   WILKINSON, ROB'T. A new and accurate map of
        Scotland from the latest surveys. Jan. 1st 1794.
        11⅜ × 8⅝. Scale 30 m. = 1 in.
In *A General Atlas*, by Robt. Wilkinson, London, 1794 and 1800 edns. and in
View of the Principal Towns, Castles, Abbeys, etc., in Scotland, publ by R.
Wilkinson, 1797.
Libraries: AU, BM, LC, NLS, RSGS.

(1794) RUSSELL, J. (del & sculp). Scotland from the best
        authorities.
        7½ × 8¾. Scale 47 m. = 1 in.
In *A New Geographical, Historical and Commercial Grammar*, William Guthrie,
14th edn., London, 1794, up to 21st edn. 1808; the later issues without Russell's
name.
Libraries: AU, BM, Bod, CUL, GU.

c. 1794 ANON. A new and accurate map of Scotland from the
        latest surveys.
        10⅝ × 8½. Scale 31 m. = 1 in.
Libraries: NLS.

1795   CASSINI, GIO, M. (engr).
        (1) La parte meridionale della Scozia. (2) La parte setten-
        trionale della Scozia.
        Each 13¼ × 18½. Scale 12 m.S. = 1 in.
In *Nuova atlante geografico universale delineato*, Vol. II, Rome, 1792-1801.
Giovanni Maria Cassini, engraver in Rome, fl. 1788-1805.
Libraries: LC, NLS, RSGS.

1795   MORRISON & SON, R. (Publishers). A new map of
        Scotland from the best authorities.
        10¼ × 9¼. Scale *c.* 31 m. = 1 in. R. Morrison & Son,
        Booksellers, Perth.
In *A New and Complete System of Universal Geography*, (Anon), Edinburgh,
1796, and in *The Modern Gazetteer*, by Alex. Aitchison, Perth, 1798.
Libraries: AU, NLS, RSGS.

(1795) (CAREY, M.) Scotland with the principal roads from
        the best authorities.
        14⅜ × 11. Scale *c.* 24 m. = 1 in.
In *The General Atlas* for Carey's edition of Guthrie's Geography, Philadelphia,
Mathew Carey, 1795, and later editions up to 1818. Mathew Carey (1760-1839),
atlas publisher in Philadelphia.
Libraries: BM, LC.

(1795) CLEGG, JOHN.   Scotland.

In *Elements of Geography*, by John Clegg, Liverpool, 1795.
Libraries: AU, BM.

c. 1795   BROWN, THOMAS (Publisher).   A new and correct map of Scotland reduced from Mr Ainslie's nine sheet map.
4 sheets each $24 \times 20\frac{1}{2}$.   Scale $7\frac{1}{2}$ m. = 1 in.

Although this map professes to be reduced from Ainslie's nine-sheet map, it is very carelessly done. The date of this map is difficult to fix, as it does not appear in Brown's list of maps for sale.
Libraries: RSGS.

1797   LAURIE & WHITTLE.   A new map of Scotland for ladies needlework.
$16\frac{3}{4} \times 14\frac{1}{4}$.   Scale 24 m. = 1 in.

Libraries: RSGS.

1797   MENZIES, J. (sculp).   Map of Scotland with the roads.
$10\frac{1}{8} \times 9\frac{1}{8}$.   (Scale *c.* 30 m. = 1 in.)

In *Scotland Described* by Robert Heron, 1797, 1799 and 1806 edns.
Libraries: AU, BM, Bod, CUL, EPL, EU, GU, NLS.

(1797)   BELL, A. (sculp).   Scotland.
$7 \times 7\frac{5}{8}$.   Scale 53 m. = 1 in.

In *Encyclopaedia Britannica*, 3rd edn. 1797.
Libraries: BM, Bod, CUL, EU, MLG.

(1797)   KINCAID, A.   Scotland with the roads & post towns.
$10\frac{1}{8} \times 8\frac{3}{4}$.   Scale *c.* 31 m. = 1 in.   J. Menzies, sculp.

In *A New Geographical Historical and Commercial Grammar*, 3rd edn. Alex. Kincaid, Edinburgh 1799 and later edns.
Libraries: BM, NLS, RSGS.

(1797)   NEELE, (S. J.) (sculp).   Scotland.

In *Atlas to Crutwell's Gazetteer*, J. Robinson, London, 1797, 1799 and 1808.
Libraries: BM, Bod, GU, NLS, RGS, RSGS.

1798   FADEN, WILLIAM.   Scotland or North Britain.
$4\frac{3}{4} \times 4$.   Scale 77 m. = 1 in.   W. Palmer, sculp.

In *Atlas Minimum Universalis*, London, Wm. Faden, 1798.
Libraries: BM.

1798   NEELE, (S. J.) (sculp).   Scotland.
$8 \times 9\frac{1}{8}$.   Scale *c.* 50 m. = 1 in.   Pub. by E. Newbery.

In *The British Tourist* by William Mavor, London, 1800.
Libraries: AU, BM, Bod, EPL, EU, NLS, RGS.

(1798)   (CHANLAIRE, P. G.)   Isles Britanniques—Quatrième carte: Écosse.
$12\frac{3}{4} \times 17\frac{7}{8}$.   Scale *c.* 34 m. = 1 in.   André, scrip. P. F. Tardieu, sculp.

In *Atlas Élémentaire de Géographie*, and in *Atlas Universel de Géographie*, both by E. Mentelle and P. G. Chanlaire, Paris, An. VI (1798). Pierre Gabriel Chanlaire (1758-1817), Paris geographer, published several atlases in association with Edmé Mentelle (1730-1815), also a geographer.
Libraries: BM, LC, NLS, RSGS.

(1798)   MENZIES, J. (sculp).   A new travelling map of Scotland divided into counties & parishes with the roads.
2 sheets each $10 \times 13\frac{1}{4} = 20 \times 13\frac{1}{4}$. Scale $10\frac{1}{2}$ m. = 1 in.

In *The Traveller's Guide*, by J. Fairbairn, Edinburgh, 1798, and later editions up to the 4th (1808).
Libraries: BM, Bod, NLS, RSGS.

(1798)   WALKER, (JOHN).   Scotland: Engraved for Walker's Geography.
$7\frac{1}{2} \times 8\frac{1}{2}$. Scale 50 m. = 1 in.

In *The Universal Gazetteer* by John Walker, 2nd edn. London, 1798, and later editions. John Walker (1759-1830), of Cockermouth; in 1788 published *Elements of Geography*. In 1799 he graduated M.D. at Leyden.
Libraries: AU, BM, Bod, CUL.

1799   LAURIE & WHITTLE.   A general map of Scotland distinguishing the Lowland Highland and intermediate districts.
$21\frac{1}{2} \times 18$. (Scale *c.* 14 m. = 1 in.) Luke Hansard, printers, London.

In Appendix P to *Report of the House of Commons respecting the Distilleries in Scotland*. Parliamentary Papers: Vol. XI. Reports from Committees 1782-99. Robert Laurie (*c.* 1755-1836) and James Whittle (*c.* 1757-1818) in partnership succeeded in 1794 to the business of Robert Sayer (1725-94), map and chart publisher.
Libraries: BM, NLS, RSGS.

1799   RUSSELL, J. (engr).   Scotland drawn from the best authorities.
$18\frac{1}{8} \times 15\frac{3}{4}$. Scale *c.* 21 m. = 1 in.

In *The Atlas to Guthrie's System of Geography*, London, 1800 and 1808. Later editions have the same map dated 1801 and 1811; also undated.
Libraries: BM, Bod, CUL, LC, NLS, RGS, RSGS.

1799   ANON.   A map of Scotland with the roads engraved for Heron's Tour.
$19\frac{1}{4} \times 16\frac{1}{2}$. Scale 15 m. = 1 in.

In *Observations made in a Journey through the Western Counties of Scotland*, by Robert Heron, Perth, 1799 edition.
Libraries: BM, CUL, EPL, EU, GU, RGS.

(1799)   (BERTHOLON).   Carte du Royaume d'Écosse.
$7 \times 8\frac{5}{8}$. Scale *c.* 36 m. = 1 in.

In *Atlas Moderne Portatif* par le Citoyen Bertholon, Paris, 1799.
Libraries: RGS.

(1799)   KIRKWOOD (sculp).   Outline of Scotland with the principal roads.
$13\frac{1}{4} \times 9\frac{5}{8}$. Scale 25 m. = 1 in.

In *Scotland Delineated* by Robert Heron, 2nd edn., 1799.
Libraries: BM, Bod, EPL, NLS.

(1799)   RUSSELL, (J. C.)   A general view of the roads of Scotland.
          6 × 7½. (Scale *c.* 50 m. = 1 in.)
In *A New and Accurate Description of all the Direct and Principal Cross Roads
in Great Britain,* by Daniel Paterson.   12th edn; 1799, and 13th edn. 1803.
Libraries: BM, EU, NLS.

1800   NEELE, S. J. (sculp).   Scotland engraved for Dr Garnett's
          Tour.
          18½ × 13¾.   (Scale *c.* 20 m. = 1 in.) Cadell & Davies,
          Strand.
In *Observations on a Tour through the Highlands . . .* by T. Garnett, M.D.,
London, 1800.
Libraries: AU, BM, Bod, CUL, EPL, EU, GU, NLS, RGS.

1800   STOCKDALE, J.   Scotland.
          14¾ × 13.   Scale 25 m. = 1 in.
Libraries: CUL.

(1800)   MENZIES, J. (sculp).   Map of Scotland engraved for the
          outline of the Mineralogy of the Scottish Isles.
          17⅝ × 16½.   Scale 16½ m. = 1 in.
In *Mineralogy of the Scottish Isles,* Edinburgh 1800, and in *Mineralogical Travels
through . . Scotland,* 1813, both by R. Jameson. Libraries: BM, NLS.

(1800?)   (SHARMAN, J.)   Scotland.
          8¾ × 6½.   Scale 42 m. = 1 in.
Libraries: LC, NLS, RGS.

c. 1800 AINSLIE, JOHN (Geographer).   The Environs of Edin-
          burgh, Haddington, Dunse, Kelso, Jedburgh, Hawick,
          Selkirk, Peebles, Langholm and Annan . . . making a
          complete map of the South East District of Scotland . . .
          Sold by Thomas Brown, Ed.
          48 × 32.   Scale 2 m. = 1 in.
The map has a table of distances between the towns.   One edition has the pro-
posed railway between Kelso and Berwick.   An 1812 edition was issued by
Thos. Brown, and a later edition by W. & A. K. Johnston and others.
Libraries: NLS.

c. 1800 BLONDEAU (sculp).   Écosse.
          7½ × 8⅝.   Scale *c.* 49 m. = 1 in.
Libraries: RSGS.

c. 1800 NEELE, S. J. (sculp).   Scotland.
          9½ × 5⅝.   Scale 37 m. = 1 in.
In *The Modern Royal Atlas,* pub. by G. Miller Dunbar.
Libraries: NLS.

c. 1800 ANON.   Écosse.
          10 × 8.   (Scale *c.* 35 m. = 1 in.)
Libraries: MLG, RSGS.

1801   CARY, JOHN (engr). A new map of Scotland, from the latest authorities.
         4 sheets each $17\frac{1}{2} \times 19\frac{7}{8}$ or 2 sheets each $17\frac{1}{2} \times 39\frac{3}{4}$. Scale 8 m. = 1 in. London.

A map of Scotland, which first appears in the *Cary's New Universal Atlas* of 1808; the map is dated August 1st 1801. In the atlas of 1808 the four sheets are indexed as:

"7, 8, Scotland, Southern Part"
"9, 10,   —   Northern Part"

Later editions of the atlas appeared in 1811, 1813, 1819, 1824 and 1828, with maps dated 1811 et seq.
Libraries: BM, Bod, EPL, GU, MLG, NLS, RGS, RSGS.

1801   LAURIE, ROBERT and WHITTLE, JAMES. Scotland or North Britain.
         $9\frac{3}{4} \times 7\frac{7}{8}$. Scale 37 m. = 1 in. Jones & Smith, sculp.

In *A New and Elegant General Atlas*, Laurie & Whittle, 1802.
Libraries: BM, LC.

1801   NEELE (sculp). Map of the roads of Scotland.
         $11\frac{3}{4} \times 9\frac{1}{4}$. (Scale 32 m. = 1 in.)

In *A Tour through the whole island of Great Britain*, Vol. VI, by Rev. C. Crutwell, 1801.
Libraries: BM, NLS.

(1801)   BROWN, THO. A new and accurate map of Scotland with the roads.
         $13\frac{3}{8} \times 11\frac{1}{2}$. Scale *c.* 19 m. = 1 in. Gavin & Son, sculp.

In *A General Atlas* (1801) and in *Atlas of Scotland being a New Set of County Maps*, n.d., both by Thomas Brown, Edinburgh.
Libraries: BM, CUL, LC, NLS, RSGS.

(1801)   NEELE, S. J. (engr). General map of Scotland except the three northern counties.
         7×10. Scale *c.* 25 m. = 1 in.

In *Remarks on Local Scenery and Manners in Scotland*, by John Stoddart, London, 1801.
Libraries: AU, Bod, CUL, EPL, EU, GU, NLS.

1802   ARROWSMITH, (AARON). Scotland.
         $10\frac{1}{4} \times 8\frac{1}{8}$. Scale *c.* 35 m. = 1 in. Lowry, sculp.

In *Modern Geography* by John Pinkerton, and in *Atlas to Pinkerton's Modern Geography*, both Cadell & Davies, London, 1802.
Libraries: AU, BM, Bod, CUL, EU, GU, LC, NLS.

1802   COOKE, JOHN (engr). Scotland.
         Circular map, $5\frac{1}{2}$ in. diameter. (Scale *c.* 70 m. = 1 in.)

In *The Universal Atlas*, London, 1802.
Libraries: Bod.

(1802)   NEELE, S. J. (sculp). Map of Scotland with the line of separation between the highlands & lowlands.
         $9\frac{1}{4} \times 8\frac{1}{4}$. (Scale *c.* 30 m. = 1 in.)

In *A History of the Rebellion in the Year 1745*, by John Home, London, 1802.
Libraries: AU, BM, Bod, CUL, EPL, EU, NLS.

1803   ENOUY, JOSEPH. A new map of Scotland compiled
          from actual surveys . . . . .
          $24\frac{5}{8} \times 19\frac{1}{4}$. Scale *c.* 14 m. = 1 in. Joseph Bye, engr.
"An improved edition, with the new roads", is dated 1807 in Kitchin's *General
Atlas*, R. Laurie & J. Whittle, London, 1810.
Libraries: AU, BM, CUL, EPL, LC, NLS, RGS, RSGS.

1803   TELFORD, T. and DOWNIE, M. Road map of Scotland.
          $24\frac{3}{4} \times 21$. Scale *c.* 12 m. = 1 in. J. Barlow, engr.
With the *Survey and Report of the Coasts and Central Highlands of Scotland*,
by T. Telford, 1803. See also Reports 1 and 2 of the Parliamentary Commissioners, 1804-5. The same map, without the names of Telford and Downie,
with 31 intended roads shown, and with the title "Map of the Intended Roads
& Bridges in the Highlands . . .", was issued with the first *Report of the Commissioners for the Highland Roads and Bridges* in 1804; and dated 1805, with
additional roads, in their Second Report.
Libraries: BM, Bod, CUL, EPL, NLS, RSGS.

1803   (ADAMS, JOHN).   Scotland.
          $6\frac{3}{8} \times 8$. (Scale *c.* 70 m. = 1 in.)
In *The Young Lady's and Gentleman's Atlas* by J. Adams, London, 1805.
Libraries: BM.

1803   RICHARDSON, THOS. (Land Surveyor). New travelling
          map of Scotland shewing the principal direct & cross
          roads with the distances.
          $25 \times 21\frac{3}{4}$. Scale $11\frac{1}{4}$ m. = 1 in. Deane, sculp, Glasgow.
Libraries: BM.

(1803)   IVORY, T. (engr).   Scotland.
          $19\frac{1}{4} \times 16\frac{1}{2}$. Scale 15 m. = 1 in.
In *The Gazetteer of Scotland*, pub. by W. Chalmers, Dundee, 1803, and 2nd
edn. 1806.
Libraries: AU, Bod, CUL, EPL, GU, NLS, RSGS.

(1803)   NEELE, S. J. (engr).   Scotland.
          $9\frac{1}{4} \times 7\frac{3}{4}$. (Scale *c.* 32 m. = 1 in.)
In *A Letter to the Rt. Hon. C. Abbot containing an Inquiry into . . . . extension of
the fisheries*, by Robert Fraser, London, 1803.
Libraries: BM, Bod, EU, GU, NLS.

(1803)   RUSSELL, J. C. (del & sculp).   Scotland.
          $8\frac{5}{8} \times 7\frac{3}{4}$. Scale *c.* 40 m. = 1 in.
In *The School Atlas*, by Richard Phillipps (1803).
Libraries: BM.

(1803)   WALLIS, JAMES. A new and accurate map of Scotland.
          $9\frac{3}{4} \times 8\frac{1}{8}$. Scale *c.* 30 m. = 1 in.
In *Wallis's Pocket Itinerary*, London, 1803.
Libraries: BM.

1804   KIRKWOOD, J. & SONS (engrs).   Scotland.
          $13\frac{1}{8} \times 10\frac{3}{8}$. Scale 26 m. = 1 in.
Libraries: Bod, NLS, RSGS.

1804   KIRKWOOD, J. & SONS. This map of Scotland
        constructed and engraved from the best authorities.
        27¼ × 22. (Scale *c*. 11 m. = 1 in.) Published by J.
        Kirkwood & Sons, Edinburgh, and W. Faden, London.

Later editions 1810 and 1812. On the reverse or cover "Kirkwood & Sons'
Travelling Map of Scotland". The map shows the routes of Pennant, Dr
Garnett, Lettice, and Campbell. It also shows the "Distillery Line", distilleries
north or north-west of the line paying a lower rate of duty on spirits than those
in the lowlands.
Libraries: AU, BM, Bod, CUL, EPL, EU, GU, MLG, NLS.

1804   PATTESON, Rev. EDWARD. Scotland ancient and
        modern.
        10 × 8. Scale 35 m. = 1in. Jones & Smith, sculp.

In *A General and Classical Atlas*, 1804 and 1825 editions. There are two maps,
one with only rivers and county boundaries, the second with towns and mountains
added.
Libraries: BM, RGS.

1804   STIELER, AUGUST. Charte von Scotland.
        17½ × 21. Scale 22m. = 1 in.

In *Allgemeiner Hand-Atlas der ganzen Erde*; A. C. Gaspari, Geographisches
Institut, Weimar (1804-11). A later (1821) edition has the same map dated 1817.
Libraries: BM, LC, RSGS.

1804   ANON. Map of Scotland from the best authorities.
        10 × 7⅝. Scale *c*. 36 m. = 1 in.

In *A System of Geography*, W. & D. Brownlie, Booksellers, Glasgow, 1805.
Libraries: NLS, RSGS.

(1805) DASSAUVILLE, W. (sculp). Scotland with the principal
        roads.
        13½ × 9¾. Scale 25 m. = 1 in.

In *The Scotch Itinerary*, by J. Duncan, 1805 edn.
Libraries: BM, Bod, CUL, EPL, EU, GU, NLS.

1806   BOWLES, CARRINGTON. Bowles's new four-sheet map of
        Scotland comprehending all the cities, boroughs, market
        and sea-port towns, (etc.) 2nd June 1806.
        47 × 39½. Scale 7¼ m. = 1 in. Bowles & Carver, London.
        This is the 1782 map with a new title.

Libraries: BM.

1806   BROWN, T. (Publisher). A travelling map of Scotland
        including all the new and intended roads, bridges, &
        canals.
        2 sheets each 15½ × 23½, or joined 30¼ × 23½. (Scale *c*.
        11 m. = 1 in.). Paton, scrip; D. Lizars, sculp.

A later issue, undated, was published by William Swinton, successor to T.
Brown.
Libraries: BM, CUL, EPL, NLS, RSGS.

1806   BYE, J. (engr). A new map of Scotland with the Caledonian
         Canal.
         $9\frac{1}{2} \times 7\frac{3}{4}$. Scale *c*. 38 m. = 1 in.

In *Travels in Scotland*, by Rev. James Hall, London, J. Johnson, 1807.
Libraries: AU, BM, Bod, CUL, EPL, EU, GU, NLS, RSGS.

1806   SCOTT, R. (engr). Map of intended roads and bridges in
         the Highlands of Scotland (a map of Scotland north of
         Glasgow).
         $8\frac{1}{4} \times 8\frac{1}{2}$. (Scale *c*. 35 m. = 1 in). In *Scots Magazine*, 1806.
Libraries: BM, EPL, MLG.

1806   STOCKDALE, JOHN. Map of Scotland from the latest
         surveys. Pub. 1st Jan. 1806.
         12 sheets each $24 \times 26\frac{1}{2}$ (total 92×79 in.).

This map, the largest scale map of Scotland published before the one inch
Ordnance Survey, is singularly irregular in quality. In part it is very detailed,
with many place names and roads evidently based on existing county maps;
other parts have relatively few place names or roads where no detailed county
maps were available. Hill shading is very pronounced in general, but very
inadequate in Perthshire. The map is less crowded with detail than Arrowsmith's
map of 1807. The map was afterwards issued by Wallis, after Stockdale's death
in 1814. See 1816.
Libraries: Bod, CUL, EPL, GU, NLS, RGS, RSGS.

(1806?)   AINSLIE, JOHN.   Scotland.
         $10\frac{3}{4} \times 9\frac{3}{4}$. Scale 28 m. = 1 in.

In *Gazetteer of Scotland*, 2nd edn., 1806.
Libraries: AU, Bod, CUL, EPL, NLS.

1807   FADEN, WILLIAM. A map of Scotland drawn chiefly
         from the topographical surveys of Mr John Ainslie and
         from those of the late General Roy, etc. Published June
         4th, 1807.
         2 sheets $21\frac{1}{2} \times 36\frac{1}{2} = 43 \times 36\frac{1}{2}$. Scale 7 m. = 1 in.

The main roads are shown more clearly than in Stockdale's map and the hill
shading is better. The British Museum has proofs at various stages. A 2nd
edition was issued in 1820 and 1829 and there were later editions by James
Wyld, successor to Faden (see 1832).
Libraries: BM, CUL, EPL, MLG, NLS, RSGS.

1807   WILKINSON, R.   Scotland.
         $11\frac{1}{4} \times 8\frac{3}{4}$. (Scale *c*. 30 m. = 1 in.) B. Smith, sculp.

In *Wilkinson's General Atlas of the World*, 2nd edn. London, 1809.
Libraries: BM, NLS.

(1807)   ANON.   Scotland with the roads.
         $9\frac{7}{8} \times 8\frac{3}{4}$. (Scale *c*. 30 m. = 1 in.)

In *The New Picture of Scotland*, pub. J. Morison, Perth, 1807.
Libraries: EPL.

FIFTH PERIOD 1807-1850

The years 1806 and 1807 saw the completion of three large scale maps of Scotland—Stockdale's map, scale 3½ miles to an inch, and Faden's map, scale 7 miles to an inch, but neither of these could equal the map issued by Aaron Arrowsmith in 1807, scale 4 miles to an inch.

So much was the outline of Scotland standardized by this map, that for the next fifty years there was practically no change in the outline, and the innumerable maps that appeared were based on Arrowsmith's map (some on Faden's map), with a few changes in some of them from new charts or from the county maps, which improved the details and showed the changes of the turnpike roads hardly noticeable in the general maps of the country.

It is impracticable to catalogue all the maps of Scotland published in small atlases, guide books, geographical textbooks and travel books in this period, and so other small maps may be met with which are not in the following list.

1807   ARROWSMITH, Aaron. Map of Scotland constructed from original materials obtained under the authority of the Parliamentary Commissioners for making roads and building bridges in the Highlands of Scotland.
4 sheets each 35½ × 28. Scale 4 m. = 1 in. Published by A Arrowsmith, London, June 25th 1807. Re-issues: 1810 and by G. F. Cruchley in 1840, 1841, 1849.

In this map of Scotland, Arrowsmith has spared no pains to produce a map that would have an accuracy in detail new to the period, and setting a far higher standard of exactitude than had been the custom to expect. In some minor details Arrowsmith does not appear to have secured the latest information, but the better map can easily be found by comparing it with Stockdale's map (1806), which occasionally was more correct. Neele, who engraved Stockdale's map, was also the engraver employed on a number of Scottish maps, and evidently was in possession of, and no doubt made use of, some later maps than those used by Arrowsmith. A *Memoir* published by Arrowsmith in 1809 describes the inception and preparation of the map.
Libraries: Most.

1807   ARROWSMITH, A(aron). Map of Scotland from original materials obtained by the Parliamentary Commissioners for Highland roads and bridges and exhibiting the intended roads and bridges.
23½ × 19¾. Scale *c.* 12 m. = 1 in.

In *The Third Report of the Commissioners for making Roads and building Bridges in the Highlands of Scotland.* The same map (with the title altered to "exhibiting

the Roads and Bridges made, contracted for, or under consideration, 1809"), appears in the *Fourth Report*, 1809. The *Fifth Report*, 1811, has a map from a new plate very closely copied from the original with revisions and additions; it was re-issued in 1813 (*Sixth Report*) and 1815 (*Seventh Report*). In the *Eighth Report*, 1817, the map was again a new plate, a close copy of the previous one, but with small differences; this plate with extensive revisions, deletions and additions appear in the *Ninth Report*, 1821.
Libraries: AU, BM, Bod, CUL, EPL, MLG, NLS, RGS, RSGS.

1807   ARROWSMITH, AARON. Map of Scotland from original materials obtained by the Parliamentary Commissioners for Highland roads and bridges and exhibiting the intended roads and bridges.
11¼ × 9.   Scale *c*. 25 m. = 1 in.   E. Jones, engr.

In *The Literary Panorama*, Vol. III, 1807, and in *Sketch of a Tour in the Highlands of Scotland* (Larkin), 1819.
Libraries: BM, NLS.

1808   COOPER, (H). (del & sculp).   Scotland.
2 sheets each 7¼ × 8¼.   Scale 29 m. = 1 in.

Plates XLII and XLIII in *A Topographical Dictionary of the United Kingdom*, by Benjamin Pitts Capper, published by R. Phillips, London.   Also in later editions 1813 and (with map dated 1824), in 1825, 1826 and 1829.
Libraries: BM, Bod, CUL, EU, GU, NLS, RGS.

1808   KIRKWOOD & SON (engr.) Scotland: engraved for the 2nd edn. of Scotch Itinerary, 11 April 1808.
13 × 10⅜.   Scale 26 m. = 1 in.

In *The Scotch Itinerary* by James Duncan, 2nd edn., Glasgow, 1808.
Libraries: BM, Bod, EPL, EU, GU, NLS.

1808   LAURIE, ROBT. and WHITTLE, JAS. Scotland.
13¾ × 9½.   Scale *c*. 31 m. = 1 in.
Libraries: NLS, RSGS.

1808   LIZARS, D. (engr). Scotland with the great roads and canals.
19 × 15.   Scale 19 m. = 1 in.   Edinburgh.
Libraries: NLS, RSGS.

1808   SMITH, CHARLES.   Scotland.
14⅛ × 10½.   Scale 24 m. = 1 in.   B. Smith, sculp.

In *Smith's New General Atlas* by C. Smith & Co. London, 1808 and later editions. In the 1808 *Atlas* the map has no roads; in the 1809 *Atlas* the map is still dated 1808 but roads and more mountains have been added and other minor alterations made.   The 1826 *Atlas* has the same map with the date deleted.   Charles Smith, engraver and map publisher, London, fl. 1800-52.
Libraries: BM, Bod, NLS, RSGS.

(1808)   ANON. A new and accurate map of Scotland from the latest surveys.
10¾ × 8½.   Scale *c*. 30 m. = 1 in.

In *A General Description of Scotland*, by G. A. Cooke, London, 1808.
Libraries: BM, NLS, RSGS.

1809   CARY, J. Cary's new sheet map of Scotland from the latest authorities.
$30\frac{1}{4} \times 24\frac{1}{4}$. Scale 11 m. = 1 in. London. Several later editions were published up to 1837.
Libraries: BM, CUL, MLG, NLS, RGS, RSGS.

1809   COOPER, (H). (del et sculp). Scotland drawn and engraved for Playfair's Geography.
$22\frac{1}{4} \times 18\frac{1}{4}$. Scale 16 m. = 1 in.
In *A New General Atlas*, by Principal James Playfair, and in *Atlas to Playfair's Geography*, both London, 1814, and later editions. In the 1839 issue, "Revised and Corrected to the present time by William Pyper", the title is "SCOTLAND"; roads have been added and an illustration of Fingal's Cave. The map also appears in Playfair's *A Geographical and Statistical Description of Scotland*, Edinburgh, 1819, with "engraved for Dr. *Playfair's Statistical Account*". James Playfair (1738-1819), born in Perthshire, minister of the Church, appointed Principal of St Andrews University in 1800, also wrote *A System of Geography Ancient and Modern*, 6 vols. H. Cooper, engr., fl. 1806-23.
Libraries: AU, BM, EPL, EU, GU, LC, NLS, RGS, RSGS.

1809   NEELE, S. J. (sculp).   Scotland.
$10\frac{1}{4} \times 7\frac{3}{4}$. Scale *c.* 35 m. = 1 in.
In *A New Royal Atlas* (Companion to the New Geographical Grammar by the Rev. John Evans), London, 1809.
Libraries: AU, CUL.

1809   STOCKDALE, JOHN.   Scotland.
$18\frac{7}{8} \times 13\frac{1}{2}$. (Scale *c.* 20 m. = 1 in.) S. I. Neele, engr. London.
Libraries: Bod.

1809   ANON.   Charte von Schottland.
$16\frac{1}{2} \times 12$. (Scale *c.* 28 m. = 1 in.) Geographisches Institut, Weimar.
Libraries: BM.

1810   ROWE, ROBERT. A new map of Scotland describing all the direct and principal cross roads, etc.
$25\frac{1}{4} \times 20\frac{1}{2}$. Scale *c.* 17 m. = 1 in.
A later issue is dated 1818. Robert Rowe (*c.* 1775-1843), geographer, engraver and publisher in London.
Libraries: CUL, NLS.

1810   ANON.   Charte von Schottland.
$17\frac{1}{2} \times 20\frac{1}{2}$. Scale 22 m. = 1 in.
In *Allgemeiner Hand-Atlas der ganzen Erde*, Wien, 1807-15.
Libraries: BM.

(1810) MITCHELL, E. (sculp).   Scotland.
10×8. (Scale *c.* 35 m. = 1 in.)
In *Encyclopaedia Britannica*, 4th edition, 1810.
Libraries: AU, BM, Bod, CUL, EU, NLS.

(1810) RUSSELL, J. C. (Exec.)   Scotland.
$8\frac{1}{2} \times 7\frac{1}{4}$. (Scale *c.* 42 m. = 1 in.)
In *Ostell's New General Atlas*, London, 1810.
Libraries: BM.

c. 1810   WALKER, (JOHN).   Scotland.
8⅜ × 7¼.   Scale 40 m. = 1 in.

In *Walker's New Atlas.*
Libraries: RSGS.

1811   MENZIES, J. & G. (engr).   A travelling map of Scotland
copied from a map accompanying the Reports of a Parliamentary Commission for making roads in the Highlands of
Scotland.
22¼ × 15¼.   Scale 12½ m. = 1 in.

In *Traveller's Guide through Scotland and its Islands* (Edinburgh, John Thomson
& Son), 5th edn. 1811, and 6th edn. 1814, but with mountains and hills added.
In 7th edn. 1818, the map is dated 1813 with a few minor alterations; in the
8th edn. 1824, and 9th edn. 1828, with date omitted. The 1813 issue also appears
in *An Account of the Principal Pleasure Tours,* 1819; and later editions to 1834.
Libraries: AU, BM, EPL, NLS, RSGS.

1811   PINKERTON, JOHN.   Scotland—Northern part.   1812
Scotland—Southern part.
Each 20½ × 27⅜.   Scale 8¼ m. = 1 in.   Drawn under the
direction of Mr Pinkerton by L. Hebert; S. I. Neele,
sculp.

In *A Modern Atlas* by John Pinkerton, London, 1815. This *Atlas* was issued in
parts between 1809 and 1814.   John Pinkerton (1758-1826), Scottish historian,
was author of a *History of Scotland,* 2 vols; *Modern Geography,* 2 vols; *A
General Collection of Voyages and Travels,* 17 vols. and other works.   See
"John Pinkerton: An Armchair Geographer of the early Nineteenth Century",
by O. F. G. Sitwell, *Geogr. J.* v. 138 (1972).
Libraries: Most.

1811   RUSSELL, J.   Scotland drawn from the best authorities.
18¼ × 15¾.   Scale 20 m. = 1 in.   London, 1811.

In *A New System of Modern Geography,* by Wm. Guthrie, 1811 edn.
Libraries: NLS, RSGS.

1811   WILKINSON, ROBT. (Pub.).   Scotland.
24¼ × 20⅛.   Scale 15½ m. = 1 in.   June 4th 1811.

In *A General Atlas* by Robert Wilkinson, 1802 (1811 issue).   Later issues of the
map by Wm. Darton dated 1825 and 1826.
Libraries: BM.

(1811)   ARROWSMITH, AARON.   Écosse.   14 × 11.

In *Nouvel atlas universel-portatif de géographie ancienne & moderne,* Paris, H.
Langlois, 1811.
Libraries: LC 6030.

1812   PHILLIPS, R. & CO.   Scotland.
11 × 8¾.   Scale 32 m. = 1 in.   Cooper, Execut; R. Phillips,
London, 1812.

In *An Atlas for Schools* by the Rev. J. Goldsmith, London, 1813.   Rev. J.
Goldsmith was the pseudonym of Sir Richard Phillips (1767-1840) sheriff of
London 1807, an author and publisher of numerous works.
Libraries: AU, BM, RGS.

1812   PENNY, R. (engr).   Scotland.
        7½ × 8⅞.   Scale 45 m. = 1 in.
In *A Compendious System of Modern Geography* by Thomas Myers, London, 1812.
Libraries: BM.

1812   Walker's geographical tour through Scotland.
        18½ × 14¾.   Scale *c.* 13 m. = 1 in.   London: Published March 9th 1812 by Wm. Darton.
A rough map with routes numbered 1 to 205.
Libraries: NLS.

(1812) HARRISON, SAM (sculp).   Scotland.
        10½ × 8⅞.   Scale *c.* 41 m. = 1 in.
In *A New and Elegant General Atlas*, by Fielding Lucas, Baltimore, (1812). Fielding Lucas (1781-1845), American cartographer and publisher, published several atlases from *c.* 1812 onwards.
Libraries: BM.

(1812) LUFFMAN, J. (geogr).   Scotland.
        9¼ × 7¾.   (Scale *c.* 31 m. = 1 in.)
In *Atlas of the World*, 1812.   John Luffman, London, geographer and engraver, fl. 1776-1820.
Libraries: BM.

(1812) TARDIEU, J. B. (engr).   Écosse.
        12¾ × 8¾.   Scale 42 m. = 1 in.   Écrit par Giraldon.
In *Atlas Complet* . . . de M. Malte-Brun, Paris, 1812.
Libraries: NLS.

(1812) (WILKINSON, ROBERT).   Scotland with the principal roads from the best authorities.
        14⅛ × 13⅛.   Scale 24 m. = 1 in.
In *Wilkinson's General Atlas of the World*, 2nd edn. 1809 (1812 issue).
Libraries: BM.

1813   AINSLIE, JOHN.   Scotland with its islands: drawn from the topographical surveys of John Ainslie; pub. by Wm. Faden.
        30 × 21.   Scale 11 m. = 1 in.
In *A General Atlas*, by Wm. Faden, London, 1821.   For later editions published by J. Wyld (successor to Faden), see 1840.
Libraries: BM, CUL, LC, RGS.

1813   ASPIN, J.   Scotland drawn from the best authorities . . . for the illustration of Lavoisne's Atlas . . .
        13½ × 12¼.   Scale 25 m. = 1 in.   J. Walker, sculp.
Also headed "Geographical and Statistical Map of Scotland", with text 16 × 19¾ in.   In *A Complete Genealogical . . . Geographical Atlas*, by C. V. Lavoisne, pub. by J. Barfield, London, 1814 and later editions.   An American edition of the *Atlas* pub. by M. Carey & Son, Philadelphia, has the map engraved by J. Yeager.
Libraries: BM, EPL, LC, MLG, NLS, RGS, RSGS.

1813   CARY, JOHN.   Scotland. $11\frac{1}{2} \times 9\frac{1}{4}$.

In *Cary's New Universal Atlas*, 4to. London, 1813. This atlas has the same title as the atlas of 1808, but it is smaller in size. Second edition 1817.
Libraries: Bod, RGS.

1813   DELAMARCHE, Fx.   Écosse.
        $10 \times 11\frac{1}{4}$.   Scale 37 m. = 1 in.
Libraries: NLS.

1813   NEELE, (S. J.).   Scotland.
        $17\frac{1}{8} \times 11\frac{7}{8}$.   Scale 20 m. = 1 in.   Pub. by S. & G. Neele, Strand, Jan. 1st, 1813.
Libraries: NLS.

1813   ANON.   Scotland from the best authorities.
        $8\frac{3}{4} \times 7\frac{3}{8}$.   (Scale *c.* 40 m. = 1 in.)

In *An Atlas to Guthrie's Geographical Grammar*, London, 1815.
Libraries: RGS.

1813   ANON.   Scotland containing the post roads.
        $33 \times 23\frac{3}{4}$.   (Scale *c.* $9\frac{1}{2}$ m. = 1 in.)

MS map in Public Record Office, London (MPD 110). This map shows the roads travelled daily by mail coaches, horse post, foot runner, etc. Reproduction in *Three Centuries of Scottish Posts*, by A. R. B. Haldane, Edinburgh, 1971.

(1813)   CARY, JOHN.   Scotland.
        $9 \times 7\frac{5}{8}$.   (Scale *c.* 40 m. = 1 in.)

In *A New Elementary Atlas*, London, 1813; re-issued in 1818.
Libraries: BM, RGS.

1814   ARROWSMITH, A(ARON) (sculp).   Map of Scotland containing a sketch of the Military Roads, also of those since made by means of . . . Act of 1803.
        $11\frac{3}{4} \times 7\frac{1}{2}$.   Scale 25 m. = 1 in.

In *Papers relating to the Military Roads in Scotland . . . and Highland Roads . . . presented to Parliament . . .* 1814.
Libraries: BM, NLS, RSGS.

1814   DARTON, WILLIAM (engr).   A new map of Scotland from the latest authorities.
        $11\frac{1}{4} \times 9\frac{1}{4}$.   Scale *c.* 34 m. = 1 in.   London: William Darton.
Libraries: EPL.

1814   WILKINSON, ROBERT.   Scotland.
        $11\frac{1}{2} \times 8\frac{3}{4}$.   Scale *c.* 29 m. = 1 in.   J. Archer, (sculp).

In *Wilkinson's General Atlas*, 2nd edition, 1809 (1816 issue).
Libraries: BM, RGS, RSGS.

1814   WHITTLE, JAS. and LAURIE, R. H.   Scotland, antiently Alba.
        $31 \times 23\frac{1}{2}$.   Scale 10 m. = 1 in.

Re-issued in 1823 by Richard H. Laurie.   (Robert Laurie retired in 1812; his son Richard then became a partner; Whittle died in 1818.)
Libraries: AU, BM, NLS, RSGS.

(1814)   (SINCLAIR, Sir JOHN).   Scotland in 9 divisions.
        $9\frac{1}{4} \times 7\frac{1}{8}$. (Scale c. 40 m. = 1 in.)

In *General Report of the Agricultural State . . . of Scotland*, by Sir John Sinclair, Edinburgh, 1814. John Sinclair (1754-1835), a noted agriculturist in Caithness, organized the first Statistical Account of Scotland published in 1791-99.
Libraries: AU, BM, Bod, EPL, EU, GU, NLS, RSGS.

1815   THOMSON, JOHN.   Scotland.
        $23\frac{1}{2} \times 19\frac{7}{8}$. Scale c. 13 m. = 1 in. Drawn & engr. by Hewitt. April 1st 1815.

Plate 11 in *A New General Atlas* by John Thomson & Co., Edinburgh, 1817. Also in slip-case labelled "A New Travelling Map of Scotland . . . Constructed from Mr Arrowsmith's celebrated Map . . . (etc.)"; this has an engraved five column itinerary on each side. For 2nd edition of *Atlas* see 1821.
Libraries: BM, Bod, CUL, EPL, EU, NLS, RSGS.

c. 1815   ANON.   Scotland.
        $10\frac{3}{4} \times 9$. Scale 30 m. = 1 in.

In *A New General Atlas of the World* (c. 1815).
Libraries: Bod.

1816   MENZIES (sculp).   Scotland with the principal roads.
        $13\frac{1}{4} \times 9\frac{1}{4}$. Scale 26 m. = 1 in.

In *The Itinerary of Scotland*, 1816 edn.
Libraries: NLS.

(1816)   WALLIS, JAS.   Map of Scotland from the latest surveys.
        12 sheets each $24 \times 26\frac{1}{2} = 93 \times 78$. Scale $3\frac{1}{2}$ m. = 1 in. London.

This is a re-issue of Stockdale's map of 1806. James Wallis, engraver, fl. 1810-20, also published several small atlases of English and Welsh counties.
Libraries: RGS, RSGS.

1816   ANON.   Scotland divided into separate shires with the great roads and canals.
        $19\frac{1}{4} \times 15\frac{7}{8}$. Scale 19 m. = 1 in.

In *The Scotch Itinerary* by James Duncan, 3rd edn. 1816.
Libraries: BM, NLS.

1817   ARROWSMITH, A.   Scotland.
        $9\frac{3}{4} \times 8$. Scale c. 31 m. = 1 in. Sy Hall, engr.

In *A New General Atlas* by A. Arrowsmith, pub. by A. Constable & Co., Edinburgh, 1817.
Libraries: BM, Bod, RGS.

1817   KIRKWOOD & SONS (engr).   Scotland.
        $13 \times 10\frac{3}{8}$. Scale c. 26 m. = 1 in.

In *A Topographical Dictionary of Scotland* by David Webster, Edinburgh, 1817, and later editions.
Libraries: BM, Bod, CUL, EPL, EU, GU, NLS, RGS, RSGS.

(1817)   DAVISON, W. (sculp).   Scotland.
          10 × 8.   (Scale *c*. 35 m. = 1 in.)
In *Encyclopaedia Britannica*, plate 477, 5th edn., 1817.
Libraries: AU, BM, Bod, CUL, EU.

(1817)   EWING.   Scotland.
          9⅝ × 7¼.   (Scale *c*. 36 m. = 1 in.)   Oliver & Boyd, pub.
          Edinburgh.
In *Ewing's New General Atlas*, n.d. but advertised in the *Scotsman*, May 1817;
later edition *c*. 1842.
Libraries: BM, NLS.

(1818)   WALLIS, (JAMES).   Scotland.
          9½ × 7¼.   Scale 37 m. = 1 in.
In *A New and Complete System of Universal Geography*, London 1818.
Libraries: Bod.

1819   SMITH, (sculp).   Scotland.
          9½ × 7¾.   Scale 31 m. = 1 in.
In *A Geographical Historical and Commercial Grammar* by William Guthrie,
23rd edn., London, 1819.
Libraries: BM, EU, NLS.

(1819)   BRADLEY, J.   Scotland.
          7 × 8.   Scale *c*. 53 m. = 1 in.
In Bradley's *Universal Atlas*, London, 1819.
Libraries: AU, BM.

(1819)   WYLD, (J).   Scotland.
          11¾ × 8¾.   Scale *c*. 28 m. = 1 in.   Hewitt, engr.
In *A General Atlas*, by J. Wyld. Pub. by John Thomson & Co., Edinburgh,
1819 and later editions.
Libraries: BM, LC, NLS, RSGS.

1820   LIZARS, W. & D.   A new travelling map of Scotland with
          the distance in miles.
          19¾ × 15¾.   (Scale 16 m. = 1 in.)
In Duncan's *Itinerary of Scotland*, 4th edn. 1820, 5th edn. 1823, 6th edn. 1827,
without change.   In 7th edn. (undated) the title is "Lumsden & Son's New
Travelling Map"; it has several additions to the roads.
Libraries: BM, Bod, EPL, GU, NLS, RSGS.

1820   NEELE & SON (engr).   Scotland.
          5⅜ × 4½.   Scale 62 m. = 1 in.   R. Phillips & Co., Pub.,
          London.
Libraries: MLG.

c. 1820 HILL, PETER & CO.   Travelling map of Scotland, with
          the distances on the great roads.   W. H. Lizars, engr.
          Edinburgh n.d.
This is a volume of 53 sectional maps, each 5¼ × 4, Scale 7 m. = 1 in., with an
index map of Scotland, 6¾ × 5¼.   See 1825 for re-issue by Oliver & Boyd.
Libraries: BM, EPL.

(1820)   PIGOT, J. (engr).   A new map of Scotland.
         16 × 12¾. Scale 24 m. = 1 in.
In *The Commercial Directory of Scotland*, etc., J. Pigot & Co., Manchester, 1820.
Libraries: RSGS.

(1820)   (ROSSI, LUIGI).   Scozia.
         7 × 8¾. Scale 50 m. = 1 in.
In *Nuovo Atlante di Geografia Universale*, Luigi Rossi, Milano, 1820. Luigi Rossi (1764-1824), Italian cartographer and map publisher.
Libraries: BM.

c. 1820 CLERK, T. (engr).   Scotland.
         19¼ × 15¾. Scale c. 16 m. = 1 in.
T. Clerk, engraver in Edinburgh (fl. 1810-35), engraved maps for Thomson's *General Atlas*, Thomson's *Atlas of Scotland*, and plans of towns for Wood's *Town Atlas*.
Libraries: NLS (Photostat).

c. 1820 ANON.   Scotland.
         15⅝ × 9¾. Scale c. 24½ m. = 1 in.
In *Views in Scotland*, by J. Mitchell.
Libraries: AU.

1821   AINSLIE, JOHN.   Map of the environs of Glasgow, Paisley, Ayr, Lanark, Sanquhar, Wigtown, (etc.).
         4 sheets each 24¾ × 16⅛. Scale 2 m. = 1 in. T. Clerk, engr.
Libraries: RSGS.

1821   KIRKWOODS (sculp).   Scotland.
         13½ × 10¾. Scale c. 22 m. = 1 in.
Edinburgh: Published by Waugh & Innes and Kirkwood & Son, 1821.
Libraries: RSGS.

1821   THOMSON, JOHN.   Northern Part of/Southern Part of Scotland.
         2 sheets each 19¾ × 23½. Scale 9½ m. = 1 in. Hewitt, sculp.
Plates 11 (1) and (2) in *A New General Atlas*, by John Thomson & Co., Edinburgh, 2nd edn. 1821; also in 1828 and 1829 edns. Also in slip-case labelled "A New Travelling Map of Scotland with the latest improvements". Edinburgh, Published by John Thomson & Co., (etc.) . . . 1824, and later issues.
Libraries: BM, EPL, EU, LC, NLS, RSGS.

c. 1821 SWINTON, WILLIAM. Scotland. Published by William Swinton, successor to Mr Thomas Brown, Edinburgh.
         20 × 32. (Scale c. 12 m. = 1 in.) Thomas Brown died 1820.
Libraries: CUL.

1822   PEAT, ALEXR. & CO. (Pub., Edinburgh).   A general map of the roads of Scotland.
         14 × 12⅝. Scale c. 23 m. = 1 in. Pyle, sculp.
This is a re-issue of Taylor and Skinner's map of 1776, now showing mountains and canals. See 1792.
Libraries: RSGS.

(1822)   LIZARS, W. H. (del. & sculp).   Map of the Highlands of Scotland denoting the districts or countries inhabited by the Highland clans.
22½ × 18¾. (Scale *c.* 13 m. = 1 in.)

In *Sketches of the character, manners and present state of the Highlanders of Scotland*, by David Stewart, Edinburgh 1822 and 1825 edns.
Libraries: BM, EU, NLS.

1823   HALL, SIDY. (del & engr).   Scotland.
9¼ × 7⅛. Scale *c.* 36 m. = 1 in.

In Walker's *Universal Atlas*, C. & J. Rivington, London, 1823 edn. Sidney Hall, *c.* 1818-60 cartographer and engraver, London, engraved several maps of Scotland.
Libraries: BM, LC.

1823   LAURIE, RICHD. HOLMES. Scotland: Published 1st Feby. 1823: London.
31 × 23½. Scale 9½ m. = 1 in.

An "improved edition" is dated 1833, another (with some railways added) 1844.
Libraries: BM, NLS, RSGS.

(1823)   HALL, SIDY. (sculp).   Scotland.
9⅞ × 7⅝. Scale *c.* 35 m. = 1 in.

Plate CCCCLXXVII in *Encyclopaedia Britannica*, Vol. 18, 6th edn. 1823.
Libraries: BM.

1824   STIELER, ADOLF.   Schotland mit der nordlichen Spitze von England.
13½ × 11¼. Scale *c.* 30 m. = 1 in.

In *Hand-Atlas* by Adolf Stieler, Gotha, J. Perthes 1834. For 2nd edition see 1837. Adolf Stieler (1755-1836), distinguished German geographer and cartographer, published (with collaborators) several atlases and a map of Germany in 85 sheets.
Libraries: BM, LC, RGS.

(1824)   FINLEY, A(NTHONY).   Scotland.
11¼ × 8½. Scale 29 m. = 1 in. Young & Delleker, sculp.

In *A New General Atlas*, A. Finley, Philadelphia, 1824; and later editions.
Libraries: BM, Bod, LG.

1825   ARROWSMITH, A. & A.   Scotland.
12 × 8¾. Scale 26½ m. = 1 in. London.

In *Outlines of the World* by Aaron Arrowsmith, London, 1825. Another edition 1828. Another edition of the map has "Re-Published Jan. 1, 1845, by G. F. Cruchley, Mapseller, London".
Libraries: BM, Bod, LC, RGS.

1825   PIGOT & CO. Pigot & Co's. new map of Scotland.
26¾ × 20¼. Scale *c.* 13 m. = 1 in. London.

In *Pigot & Co's New Commercial Directory of Scotland* for 1825-26. Later issues dated 1837 and 1840, "with the latest improvements" in Pigot & Co's. *British Atlas*, 1839, 1840 and 1844 editions. See 1845.
Libraries: BM, EPL, EU, MLG, NLS.

(1825)   HALL, SIDY. (engr).   Scotland.
          $9\frac{3}{4} \times 7\frac{1}{2}$. Scale 36 m. = 1 in. Pub. by Longmans, Hurst, etc.

In *An Atlas of Modern Geography* by Samuel Butler, London, 1825. Also 1829 and 1831 editions.
Libraries: BM, Bod, RGS.

(1825)   LIZARS (sculp).   Scotland: engraved for the Scottish Tourist.
          $17 \times 13\frac{1}{4}$. (Scale *c*. $17\frac{1}{2}$ m. = 1 in.)
In *The Scottish Tourist and Itinerary*, Edinburgh, 1825, 1827 and 1830 edns.
Libraries: BM, Bod, CUL, NLS, RSGS.

(1825)   LIZARS, W. H. (sculp).   Tourist's Guide to the picturesque scenery of Scotland.
          $17 \times 13\frac{1}{2}$. Scale *c*. 7 m. = 1 in.
A map of Central Scotland. In *The Scottish Tourist and Itinerary*, by William Rhind, Edinburgh, 1825 and later edns.
Libraries: BM, Bod, CUL, NLS, RSGS.

c. 1825 DASSAUVILLE, WM (drawn & engr).   Scotland.
          $14\frac{1}{4} \times 10\frac{3}{4}$. Scale 25 m. = 1 in. Pub. by Oliver & Boyd.
Libraries: BM, MLG.

c. 1825 Oliver and Boyd's travelling map of Scotland with the distances on the great roads.
          A volume of 53 small maps, each $5\frac{3}{8} \times 4$ (Scale 7 m. = 1 in.) covering Scotland with an "Index Map", $6\frac{7}{8} \times 5\frac{1}{8}$.
This is a re-issue by Oliver & Boyd, with a new title page of the volume originally published by P. Hill & Co. (See 1820.)
Libraries: NLS, RSGS.

c. 1825 SCOTT, R. (engr).   Scotland.
          $13\frac{3}{4} \times 11\frac{1}{2}$. Scale *c*. 23 m. = 1 in. Glasgow: Khull Blackie & Co.
Libraries: MLG, NLS.

c. 1825 ANON.   Scotland.
          $22\frac{7}{8} \times 17\frac{1}{4}$. Scale *c*. 16 m. = 1 in.
Shows county boundaries and table of distances from Edinburgh and Glasgow.
On cover "Travelling Map of Scotland".
Libraries: BM, EPL.

1826   WILKINSON, ROBERT.   Scotland.
          $24\frac{1}{4} \times 20\frac{1}{8}$ Scale $15\frac{1}{2}$ m. = 1 in. Dated 1825, republished with additions and corrections by William Darton, 1826.
In *A General Atlas*, London, Robert Wilkinson (1802 on title page).
Libraries: BM

c. 1826 LIZARS, D.   Scotland.
          2 sheets each $16\frac{1}{4} \times 20\frac{1}{4}$. (Scale *c*. $11\frac{1}{2}$ m. = 1 in.)
In *The Edinburgh Geographical and Historical Atlas*, pub. by Daniel Lizars, *c*. 1826; later editions pub. by J. Hamilton *c*. 1831, and as *Lizars' Edinburgh Geographical General Atlas*, by W. H. Lizars (1840).
Libraries: BM, Bod, EU, NLS, RGS.

1827   LOTHIAN, JOHN.   Scotland.
         $9\frac{3}{4} \times 7\frac{1}{2}$.   Scale 33 m. = 1 in.

In *Lothian's County Atlas of Scotland*, Edinburgh, 1827; later editions 1830, 1835 and 1838.

This small Atlas of Scotland was intended to be ready in 1826, and an engraved title with that date was prepared, but the last maps were not ready until March 1827 and the preface is dated 1827. The dates were several times altered on the maps, and as they were sold separately in neat cases, most copies of the complete atlas have varying dates all through. The editions seem to be 1827, 1829, 1830, 1835 and 1838. The maps are well drawn and as a work of reference it is one of the best portable atlases of Scotland. It was re-issued by A. & C. Black in 1848. The review in the *Scotsman*, that appeared when it was published, stated that it was "much superior to anything of the kind of the size and price now to be had". A set of historical maps was issued in 1829; this has the same map of Scotland but with the title "Modern Scotland".
Libraries: BM, Bod, CUL, EPL, MLG, NLS, RGS, RSGS.

1827   NEELE, JAS. & JOSIAH (sculp).   Scotland.
         $9\frac{1}{2} \times 7\frac{3}{8}$.   Scale *c*. 31 m. = 1 in.

In *A Geographical, Historical and Commercial Grammar* by William Guthrie, 24th edn. 1827.
Libraries: BM, EPL.

1827   PASS, J. (sculp).   Scotland.
         $9\frac{3}{4} \times 7\frac{3}{4}$.   Scale *c*. 37 m. = 1 in.

In *Encyclopaedia Londoninensis*.
Libraries: BM, RSGS.

(1827)   LIZARS, W. H. (del & engr).   Scotland.
         $9\frac{3}{4} \times 7\frac{5}{8}$.   (Scale 36 m. = 1 in.)

In *Encyclopaedia Edinensis*, vol. 3, Edinburgh, 1827.
Libraries: BM, NLS.

(1827)   VANDERMAELEN, P. M. G.   Partie de l'Angleterre.
         $19 \times 22\frac{7}{8}$.   (Scale *c*. 25 m. = 1 in.)

In *Atlas Universel*, Bruxelles, 1827. Philippe Vandermaelen (1795-1869), Belgian cartographer.
Libraries: BM, Bod, GU, RGS.

1828   HALL, SIDNEY.   Scotland.
         $20 \times 16\frac{1}{4}$.   Scale 16 m. = 1 in.   Published by Longmans, Rees etc.   London, 1828

In *A New General Atlas* by Sidney Hall, London, 1830. The 1849 Atlas has this map with railways up to date.
Libraries: BM, Bod, MLG, RGS, RSGS.

1829   LOTHIAN, JOHN.   Scotland.
         $13\frac{1}{2} \times 11\frac{1}{2}$.   Scale 19 m. = 1 in.   Edinburgh, 12th May 1829.   On cover: Travelling map of Scotland.

Libraries: RSGS.

(1829)   NEELE, J. & J. (sculp).   A new travelling map of Scotland.
         $14\frac{1}{4} \times 11\frac{1}{2}$.   Scale 22 m. = 1 in.   Pub. by S. Leigh, London.

In *Leigh's New Pocket Road-Book of Scotland* 1829. Also 1836, 1839 and 1840 editions.
Libraries: BM, CUL, EPL, EU, GU, RGS.

(1829) TEESDALE, HENRY and CO. Scotland.
$25\frac{1}{4} \times 20\frac{1}{2}$. Scale $17\frac{1}{2}$ m. = 1 in.

In *New British Atlas*, by Henry Teesdale & Co., London, 1829. Later editions 1830, 1831, 1832, 1833, 1835 and 1840. Teesdale, map publishers from *c.* 1828 to 1857, published two atlases of English counties.
Libraries: BM, MLG, NLS.

1830 MURRAY, T. L. Scotland.
27×18. Scale 16 m. = 1 in. Hoare & Reeves, sculp.

In *An Atlas of the English Counties divided into Hundreds* . . . . London n.d. Another edition with map dated 1831.
Libraries: EPL, MLG, NLS, RGS.

1830 STARLING, THOMAS (del & engr). Scotland.
$5\frac{1}{2} \times 3\frac{1}{2}$. Scale *c.* 70 m. = 1 in. London.

In *Geographical Annual*, London, 1830, and later editions.
Libraries: BM.

(1830) ARROWSMITH, A. & S. Scotland.
$9\frac{1}{4} \times 8$. Scale $38\frac{1}{2}$ m. = 1 in.

In *An Atlas of Modern Geography*, by A. Arrowsmith, 1830 edn.
Libraries: BM, RGS.

c. 1830 GARDNER, W. R. (del & engr). New and improved map of Scotland including its islands.
$29\frac{1}{4} \times 24\frac{1}{8}$. Scale $10\frac{1}{2}$ m. = 1 in. London, Wm. Darton, Map & Print Seller.

Libraries: BM, CUL, NLS (Newman Colln.), RSGS.

(1830?) FENNER (engr). Scotland.
$5\frac{5}{8} \times 4\frac{1}{2}$. Scale 64 m. = 1 in.

In *Fenner's Pocket Atlas*, London (1830?).
Libraries: BM, RGS.

1831 DOWER, JOHN (del & engr). Scotland.
$16\frac{1}{4} \times 13\frac{1}{4}$. Scale 20 m. = 1 in.

In *A New General Atlas of the World* by John Dower; H. Teesdale & Co., London, 1831. Later editions 1835, 1838, 1842, 1845, and undated.
Libraries: BM, Bod, EU, GU, LC, RGS, RSGS.

1831 HALL, SIDNEY (engr). Scotland.
$14\frac{3}{8} \times 9\frac{5}{8}$. Scale 27 m. = 1 in.

In *A Topographical Dictionary of Great Britain and Ireland*, by John Gorton, London, 1833; in *A New British Atlas* by Sidney Hall, 1833 and later editions; in *A Travelling County Atlas*, by Sidney Hall, 1842 and later edns.; and in *A New County Atlas*, by S. Hall, 1847.
Libraries: BM, Bod, CUL, NLS, RGS, RSGS.

(1831?) DOWER, J. (del & engr). Scotland.
$10\frac{1}{4} \times 8\frac{1}{4}$. Scale 32 m. = 1 in. London: William Orr.
Libraries: RSGS.

1832   CARY, JOHN. Cary's improved map of England and
         Wales, with a considerable portion of Scotland.
         65 sheets each 19¾ × 25. Scale 2 m. = 1 in. of which
         sheets 56, 57, 60-65 cover southern Scotland up to Cupar-
         Inveraray. The completed map is dated 1832, but the
         individual sheets for southern Scotland have various dates
         from 1827 and 1830.
Libraries: BM, Bod, CUL, MLG, RSGS.

1832   CLERK, T. (engr).   Scotland.
         20¼ × 16½. Scale 16 m. = 1 in.
In *The Gazetteer of Scotland*, by W. & R. Chambers, Edinburgh 1832 and 1833
editions. Another issue of the map is undated.
Libraries: EPL, EU, NLS, RSGS.

1832   MALTE-BRUN, CONRAD. Écosse: entièrement revu et
         corrigé par M. J. J. N. Huot.
         11¾ × 8¾. Scale 33 m. = 1 in. Thierry, engr.
In *Atlas complet du précis de la géographie universelle de Malte-Brun.* Bruxelles,
1837. Conrad Malte-Brun (1775-1826), was joint author with E. Mentelle of
Geographie Mathématique physique et politique in 16 vols., and *Précis de la
Geographie universelle* in 8 vols. The latter was translated into English and
widely used.
Libraries: EU, BM, LC, RGS.

1832   WYLD, Js. A map of Scotland drawn chiefly from the
         topographical surveys of Mr John Ainslie . . . showing
         the great and cross roads . . .
         42 × 37. Scale 7 m. = 1 in. Published by Js. Wyld,
         Successor to Mr. Faden.
This is Faden's map of 1807 revised, with the addition of new canals, etc.
Several later editions.
Libraries: MLG, RSGS.

(1832)   ARROWSMITH, A. Ecclesiastical map of Scotland
         showing the boundary of the synods and presbyteries and
         the site of each parish church.
         20⅞ × 16¾. Scale c. 13 m. = 1 in. Pub. by Peter Brown,
         Edinburgh. W. H. Lizars, engr.
In *The Clergy of the Kirk of Scotland*, Edinburgh, 1832.
Libraries: BM, Bod, MLG, NLS.

(1832)   MURPHY, W. (engr). Scotland: engraved for the Scottish
         Tourist.
         17 × 13¼. (Scale 17½ m. = 1 in.)
In *The Scottish Tourist and Itinerary*, 4th to 6th edns., Edinburgh, 1832, 1834,
1836. In the 8th edn. 1842, without Murphy's name, with some railways added.
In the 9th edn. (1845) with title changed to "Geological Map of Scotland".
Murphy carried on business in Edinburgh as engraver and copper plate printer
from c. 1826 to c. 1853.
Libraries: BM, NLS, RSGS.

(1832) MURPHY, W. (drawn & engraved). An outlined map of Scotland exhibiting the . . . counties.
$6\frac{5}{8} \times 4\frac{3}{4}$. (Scale *c.* 65 m. = 1 in.)

In *Pocket County Atlas of Scotland*; published by Alex. Macredie, Edinburgh, consisting of 33 plates of county maps on different scales. Undated, but the owner has written 12 July 1832 in manuscript on NLS copy.
Libraries: CUL, EPL, NLS.

(1832) (THOMSON, JOHN). Index map to the atlas of Scotland.
$19\frac{1}{4} \times 13\frac{3}{4}$. Scale $18\frac{1}{2}$ m. = 1 in.

In *Atlas of Scotland*, by John Thomson & Co., Edinburgh, 1832. At first the maps were issued to subscribers in counties on publication, wrapped in a thin printed sheet, those for Linlithgow, Stirling, Edinburgh, Berwick, Peebles, and Kirkcudbright being issued in 1820-21. The last were Inverness and Nairn. Butterworth, Clerk, Dassauville, Hall, Hewitt, Menzies, Moffat, and Neele were employed in engraving the fifty-eight plates. The venture brought Thomson to bankruptcy in 1831, but the Atlas was completed and published in 1832. The plates were sold to W. & A. K. Johnston, who re-issued the Atlas in 1855, with their own name in place of Thomson's.
Libraries: Most.

c. 1832 SCOTT, R. (engr).   Scotland.
10×8. Scale *c.* 31 m. = 1 in.

In *Atlas to Bell's Geography*. Pub. by Arch. Fullarton & Co., Glasgow.
Libraries: RSGS.

1834 ARMSTRONG, Captain. Bowles's new one-sheet map of Scotland. Endorsed in MS: sketch diagram of the principal triangles of Scotland and its islands by Hastings T. Murphy, Lieut. R.E., 9th Jany. 1834.
Libraries: Public Record Office, London (MPH 43/13).

1834 ARROWSMITH, J.   Scotland.
$23\frac{1}{2} \times 19\frac{3}{8}$. Scale 12 m. = 1 in.

In *Guide to the Highlands and Islands of Scotland* by George and Peter Anderson, London, 1834, and in *The London Atlas of Universal Geography*, John Arrowsmith, London, 1835, and later editions.
Libraries: BM, Bod, CUL, EPL, EU, LC, NLS, RGS, RSGS.

1834 WALKER, J. &. C. (sculp). Scotland, in three parts.
(1) $11 \times 15\frac{1}{2}$, (2) $13\frac{1}{4} \times 16$, (3) $15 \times 12\frac{3}{4}$. Scale *c.* $12\frac{1}{2}$ m. = 1 in. Baldwin & Cradock, London, 1834.

In *Maps (or General Atlas) of the Society for the Diffusion of Useful Knowledge*; vol. 1, London, 1844. In the 1845 and 1849 editions the maps are dated 1841 and the imprint altered to Charles Knight & Co. Also issued in 1834 in slip-case labelled "Scotland in Three Parts with a Plan of Edinburgh".
Libraries: BM, LC, NLS (Newman Colln.), RSGS.

(1834) LIZARS, W. H. (del & engr). Tourist's guide to the picturesque scenery of Scotland.
$17\frac{1}{8} \times 13\frac{1}{4}$. Scale 10 m. = 1 in.

In *The Scottish Tourist and Itinerary*, 5th edn. 1834. This map, covering a substantial part of Scotland (from Ayr and Hawick to Loch Maree and Banff, and from Loch Alsh to Aberdeen) replaced in the 5th edition, 1834, of *The Scottish Tourist and Itinerary*, an earlier map of the same title engraved by Lizars. It appeared in later editions to the 9th, 1845, with the addition of new railways.
Libraries: BM, EPL, NLS, RSGS.

(1834)   (PINNOCK, W.)   Scotland.
           9 × 6½.   Scale 40 m. = 1 in.
In *The Guide to Knowledge*, ed. by W. Pinnock, London, 1834.
Libraries: Bod.

(1834)   TARDIEU, AMBROISE.   Écosse.
           10⅞ × 8¾.   Scale *c*. 31 m. = 1 in.
In *Itinéraire et Souvenirs d'Angleterre et d'Écosse* by M. Ducos, vol. 3, Paris,
1834. The volume includes another map "Écosse occidentale et Hebrides
mèridionales", 10⅜ × 10¾.
Libraries: BM, NLS.

c. 1835   LOTHIAN, J.   Scotland.
            13¾ × 10¾.   Scale 18 m. = 1 in.
In *The New Edinburgh General Atlas* . . . revised . . . by J. Lothian, Edinburgh,
c. 1835.
Libraries: Bod.

(1836)   TANNER, HENRY SCHENCK.   Scotland.
           11 × 9.   Scale *c*. 30 m. = 1 in.   J. & W. W. Warr, engrs.
In *A New Universal Atlas* by Henry S. Tanner, Philadelphia, 1836. Later
editions 1839, 1843, and 1844. Re-issued in 1846 and later by S. A. Mitchell.
H. S. Tanner (1786-1858), cartographer in Philadelphia.
Libraries: BM, LC, NLS.

1837   BELL, ALLAN & CO.   Scotland.
           13¾ × 11½.   Scale *c*. 23 m. = 1 in.
In *A New General Atlas of the World*, London, 1837-38.
Libraries: LC.

1837   CRUCHLEY, G. F.   Scotland.
           25 × 19½.   Scale *c*. 12 m. = 1 in.   London.
Later issue dated 1842. George Frederick Cruchley (fl. 1823-76), map seller,
engraver and globe maker, London, successor to John Cary.
Libraries: BM.

1837   STARLING, THOMAS. (del & engr).   A map of Scotland.
           16 × 12.   Scale 20 m. = 1 in.   Pub.: George Virtue,
           London.
In *Scotland Illustrated* by William Beattie, M.D., London, 1838, with date 1837,
and as "Carte physique et routière de l'Écosse" in French edition, *L'Écosse
Pittoresque*. Also with date 1839.
Libraries: BM, Bod, CUL, EPL, EU, NLS, RSGS.

1837   STULPNAGEL, F. VON.   Schotland.
           12 × 13⅞.   Scale 30 m. = 1 in.   Ad. Gottschalck, sculp.
In *Hand-Atlas*, by Adolf Stieler, Gotha, 2nd edn. 1837, 3rd edn. 1842. The 4th
edn. 1847, has the same map and below the date 1837 has "Revidirt 1845".
Stulpnagel (1781-1865), German cartographer.
Libraries: BM, NLS.

(1837)   SCOTT, R. (engr).   A map of Scotland distinguishing
           particularly the districts or countries inhabited by the
           Highland clans. Pub. by Arch Fullarton & Co., Glasgow.
           17 × 14. (Scale *c*. 17½ m. = 1 in.)
In *A History of the Highlands*, by James Browne, 1837 edn.
Libraries: BM, EU, NLS.

(1837) WRIGHT, A. (del & engr). Scotland.
$8\frac{1}{4} \times 6\frac{3}{8}$. (Scale c. 42 m. = 1 in.) Published by Oliver & Boyd, Edinburgh.

In *An Introductory Atlas of Modern Geography*, by Alexander Reid, Edinburgh, 1837 and 1848 edns. Also in his *A School Atlas of Modern Geography*, 1848, and 1855 edns. and in *A Cyclopaedia of Commerce*, by William Waterston. Alexander Reid, LL.D., was headmaster of Edinburgh Institution.
Libraries: BM, Bod, NLS.

1838 KNOX, JAMES. Map of Scotland. Engraved partly by J. Bartholomew and partly by W. & A. K. Johnston. Pub. Edinburgh: John Anderson and William Hunter. $19 \times 15\frac{1}{4}$. Scale 16 m. = 1 in.
Libraries: NLS.

1838 MARMOCCHI, F. C. (1) La Scozia meridionale. (2) Parte settentrionale della Scozia.
Each $8\frac{3}{4} \times 12\frac{1}{8}$. Scale 18 m.S. = 1 in.
In *Atlante di Geografia Universale*, F. C. Marmocchi, Florence, 1840.
Libraries: BM.

(1838) BLACKWOOD, WILLIAM and SONS. Scotland.
$17\frac{3}{4} \times 14\frac{3}{8}$. Scale 17 m. = 1 in. Drawn & Eng. by W. H. Lizars.

In *The New Statistical Account of Scotland*, Vol. 1, 1845, and in *Blackwood's County Atlas of Scotland*. The Atlas contains 31 separate maps of the Counties and Islands, $7\frac{1}{8} \times 9\frac{1}{2}$, on scales between 4 m. and 11 m. per inch. Editions of the Atlas appeared in 1838, 1839, 1847, 1848, and 1853.
Libraries: All.

(1838) TELFORD, THOMAS. Map of Scotland, shewing the Highland roads and bridges made . . .
$16\frac{1}{4} \times 13\frac{1}{8}$. Scale 18 m. = 1 in.
In *Atlas to the Life of Thomas Telford*, London, 1838.
Libraries: BM, Bod, CUL, EU, GU, NLS.

(1838) ANON. Map of the circulation of letters in Scotland.
$19\frac{1}{2} \times 15\frac{1}{2}$. (Scale $14\frac{1}{2}$ m. = 1 in.)
In *British Parliamentary Papers 1837-8*, XX, part 1. Reproduction in *Three Centuries of Scottish Posts* by A. R. B. Haldane, Edinburgh, 1971.
Libraries: BM, Bod, CUL, NLS.

(1839) DARTON, WM. and SON. New & improved map of Scotland including its islands.
$29\frac{1}{4} \times 24\frac{1}{8}$. Scale c. 11 m. = 1 in. London.
This is Gardner's map of c. 1830 with railways added, etc.
Libraries: BM.

(1839) HALL, S(IDNEY) (engr). Scotland, Northern Part: Southern Part; also Part I and Part II.
2 sheets each $9\frac{3}{4} \times 14\frac{1}{2}$; = $19\frac{1}{2} \times 14\frac{1}{2}$. Scale 18 m. = 1 in.
In *Black's Economical Tourist of Scotland*, A. & C. Black, Edinburgh, 1839; in *Black's General Atlas*, 1840 and 1841 editions; in *Black's County Atlas of Scotland*, 1848; in *Encyclopaedia Britannica*, 7th edn. 1842; in *Black's Picturesque*

Q

Tourist of Scotland, 1840, and later editions; in the *Guide to the Highlands & Islands of Scotland*, by G. & P. Anderson, 1842 edn.; and separately published in cover labelled Black's Travelling Map of Scotland.
Libraries: All.

1840   WYLD, James.   Scotland with its islands drawn from the topographical surveys by James Wyld.
$30 \times 21\frac{1}{4}$.   Scale 11 m. = 1 in.

Plate 11 of *A New General Atlas of Modern Geography*, by J. Wyld, London, 1840.   Later editions of map dated 1842, 1843, 1846, and undated.
Libraries: BM, LC, NLS, RSGS.

1840   ANON.   Scotland engraved for the Pocket Gazetteer.
$16\frac{3}{4} \times 13$.   (Scale *c.* 17 m. = 1 in.)

In *An Enlarged Gazetteer of Scotland*, by J. P. Lawson, Edinburgh, 1841.
Libraries: EPL, NLS, RSGS.

(1840)   DARTON, WILLIAM and SON.   Scotland.
$9\frac{5}{8} \times 7\frac{1}{2}$.   Scale *c.* 37 m. = 1 in.

In *Peter Parley's Atlas of Modern Maps*, London, 1840.
Libraries: BM, Bod, NLS.

c. 1840   FINDLAY, Alexr. (del & engr).   Scotland.
$9\frac{3}{4} \times 7\frac{1}{2}$.   Scale 34 m. = 1 in.   Pub. by Thomas Kelly, London.

Libraries: RSGS.

1841   CRUCHLEY, G. F. (engr).   Scotland.
$18\frac{1}{4} \times 13\frac{3}{4}$.   Scale $18\frac{1}{4}$ m. = 1 in.

In Cruchley's *General Atlas*, London, 1843, and later editions.
Libraries: BM, Bod, RSGS.

1841   WALKER, J. & C. (sculp).   Scotland.
$15\frac{1}{2} \times 12\frac{1}{2}$.   Scale 19 m. = 1 in.   Baldwin & Craddock. (pub.)

In *Maps of the Society for the Diffusion of Useful Knowledge*, Vol. 1, Chapman & Hall, London, 1844.   In some 1844 copies and in later editions the imprint is Charles Knight & Co.
Libraries: BM, Bod, CUL, EPL, EU, GU, LC, NLS, RSGS.

(1842)   ARROWSMITH, J.   Scotland.
$6\frac{3}{4} \times 5\frac{1}{2}$.   Scale 40 m. = 1 in.

In *An Atlas of Modern Geography* by Aaron Arrowsmith, London, 1842 edn.
Libraries: BM.

(1842)   BROWN, J. (del & engr).   Scotland, exhibiting the principal roads, railways, rivers, canals . . .
$20\frac{1}{2} \times 16\frac{1}{8}$.   Scale 15 m. = 1 in.

In *The Descriptive Atlas of Scotland* by J. P. Lawson, Edinburgh, 1842.
Libraries: NLS.

(1842)   HALL, Sidy.   Scotland.
$9\frac{1}{2} \times 7\frac{1}{2}$.   Scale 35 m. = 1 in.

In *An Atlas of Modern Geography* by Samuel Butler, 1842 edn.
Libraries: BM, Bod.

(1842)   WALKER, J. and C. (sculp).   Scotland.
          15¾ × 13.   Scale 20 m. = 1 in.
In *The Topographical Statistical and Historical Gazetteer*, 1842 and later edns.,
and in J. & C. Walker's *This British Atlas*, London 1845 and later editions.
Libraries: BM, Bod, EPL, EU, NLS.

(1842)   WYLD, JAMES.   Scotland.
          9⅝ × 7⅝.   Scale 35 m. = 1 in.   Stockley, sculp.
In *An Atlas of Modern Geography* by James Wyld, London, 1842.
Libraries: BM, NLS.

(1842)   WYLD, J.   Scotland.
          10¾ × 8⅞.   Scale 30½ m. = 1 in.   Stockley, sculp.
In *An Atlas of the World*, James Wyld, London, 1842 and 1849.
Libraries: BM.

c. 1842 JOHNSTON, W. & A. K.   New road map of Scotland
          with the distances from Edinburgh and from port to port.
          38½ × 23½.   Scale 9½m. = 1 in.   Edinburgh.
On the cover "Johnston's Road Map of Scotland".   Railways are listed with
the date when opened—last date 1841.   A later issue is dated 1848.
Libraries: NLS (Newman Colln.), RGS.

1842?   HAGEN, T.   Scotland.
          26¼ × 23¼.   (Scale *c.* 11 m. = 1 in.)
A crude map described on the cover as an "Instructive Travelling Map . . for
Games".
Libraries: BM, Bod, CUL.

1843   JOHNSTON, A. K.   Scotland.
          23½ × 19½.   Scale *c.* 12½ m. = 1 in.   W. & A. K. Johnston,
          engrs.
Plate 5 of the *National Atlas of Historical, Commercial and Political Geography*,
Edinburgh, 1843.   Later editions 1845, 1846, 1850.   Also issued as Johnston's
Travelling Map of Scotland.
Libraries: BM, Bod, CUL, EPL, EU, GU, LC, NLS, RSGS.

(1843)   HALL, SIDY. (del & engr).   Scotland.
          10¼ × 8½.   Scale *c.* 35 m. = 1 in.
In *A Modern Atlas* by Alexander G. Findlay, London, T. Tegg, 1843.   A. G.
Findlay (1812-75), geographer and publisher, took over the business of Laurie
& Whittle in 1838.
Libraries: BM, Bod, NLS.

(1843)   LIZARS, W. H. (engr).   Scotland . . . constructed under
          the direction of James Findlay, Inspector of Letter
          Carriers . . . General Post Office, Edinburgh.
          16¾ × 12⅞.   Scale *c.* 15 m. = 1 in.
In *Directory of Gentlemen's Seats, etc. in Scotland*, Edinburgh, 1843.
Libraries: Bod, EPL, EU, NLS, RSGS.

(1843)   LODGE, J. (sculp).   Scotland.
          8¾ × 7¼.   Scale *c.* 43 m. = 1 in.
In *A General Atlas for the use of Schools*, by John Adams, London, 1843.
Libraries: BM, Bod.

(1844)   ARCHER, J. (del & engr).   Scotland.
$11\frac{1}{8} \times 9$. Scale 29 m. = 1 in.

In *The College Atlas* by James Gilbert, London, 1844, and in Gilbert's *Modern Atlas of the World*, n.d. John W. Archer (1808-64), engraver in London, noted for his collection of drawings of London antiquities.
Libraries: BM, Bod, RGS, RSGS.

(1844)   HALL, S. (engr).   Scotland.
2 sheets $16 \times 22\frac{1}{4}$ or one sheet $32 \times 22\frac{1}{4}$. Scale 10 m. = 1 in.

In *Black's General Atlas* by A. & C. Black, Edinburgh, 1844 and later editions and in *Guide to the Highlands and Islands of Scotland*, by G. and P. Anderson, 1847 and 1851 edns. Also dissected and folded into sections as Black's New Travelling Map of Scotland.
Libraries: BM, Bod, EPL, EU, NLS, RGS.

(1844)   (LOTHIAN).   Scotland.
$13\frac{7}{8} \times 10\frac{7}{8}$. Scale *c.* 19 m. = 1 in.

In *The Scottish Tourist's Steam-Boat Pocket Guide*, 1844 edn.
Libraries: NLS, RSGS.

1845   BETTS, JOHN.   Bett's new map of Scotland.
2 sheets each 15×25. Scale $9\frac{2}{3}$ m. = 1 in.

Title is on southern sheet; on the north sheet is "The Northern Part of Scotland". In *Betts' Family Atlas*, London (1844-47). Also later editions of the map on one sheet, undated.
Libraries: BM, Bod, CUL, EPL, NLS, RGS, RSGS.

1845   SLATER, I.   I. Slater's new map of Scotland with the latest improvements.
$26\frac{1}{2} \times 20\frac{1}{2}$. Scale *c.* 13 m. = 1 in.

A re-issue of Pigot's map of 1825 (q.v.) by Isaac Slater, Manchester, who renamed the atlas I. Slater's *New British Atlas*.
Libraries: BM, Bod, NLS.

(1845)   GELLATLY, J. (del & engr).   Scotland.
$10\frac{1}{4} \times 8\frac{1}{4}$. Scale 30 m. = 1 in.

In *Atlas of Ancient and Modern Geography*, Edinburgh, 1845, and in *Chambers's Atlas for the People*, 1846, both W. & R. Chambers. J. Gellatly, engraver and lithographer, in West Register Street, later George Street, Edinburgh.
Libraries: BM, Bod, GU, NLS, RSGS.

1846   MITCHELL, S. A. See 1836 TANNER.

(1846)   CARRINGTON, F. A. A map of Scotland divided into counties, shewing the principal roads, railways, rivers, canals, etc.
6 sheets each $26\frac{1}{4} \times 25$ or 3 sheets each $26\frac{1}{4} \times 50$. Scale 5 m. = 1 in. J. Dower, engr.

The edition of 6 sheets forms the "Supplementary Volume" to *A Topographical Dictionary of Scotland*, by Samuel Lewis, London, 1846; for this reason the date 1846 is generally assigned to the map, but the RGS copy of 3 sheets is dated in manuscript 1842 on each of the sheets. Also folded and stamped on covers "Lewis's Map of Scotland". Later editions of the map 1849 to 1861.
Libraries: BM, Bod, CUL, EPL, EU, GU, LC, NLS, RGS.

(1846)   (LOTHIAN, J.)   Scotland.
         15¼ × 12½.   Scale 19 m. = 1 in.
In *The People's Atlas*: Revised by J. Lothian: Published by James Macleod, Glasgow, and others, 1846.
Libraries: BM, Bod.

1847   ARROWSMITH, S(AMUEL).   Map of Scotland constructed for the use of the National Schools of Ireland.
         62½ × 47½.   Scale 5¼ m. = 1 in.
Libraries: BM.

1847   SHARPE, (JOHN).   Scotland.
         16¼ × 12½.   Scale 18 m. = 1 in.   J. Wilson Lowry, engr.
In *Sharpe's Corresponding Atlas*, London, 1849.
Libraries: BM, Bod, LC, NLS, RSGS.

(1848)   BECKER, F. P. & CO. (engrs).   Scotland.
         11½ × 9½.   Scale *c*. 29 m. = 1 in.
In *The Universal Atlas of Modern Geography*, London, 1848, and in *Becker's Omnigraph Atlas of Modern Geography*, London, n.d.
Libraries: BM, Bod, NLS.

(1848)   SWANSTON, G. H. (engr).   Map distinguishing particularly the districts or countries inhabited by the Highland clans.
         20½ × 16⅛.   (Scale 14½ m. = 1 in.)
In *A History of the Highlands*, by James Browne, 1848 edn.
Libraries: NLS.

1850   COWPERTHWAIT, THOMAS & CO.   Scotland.
         12 × 9¾.   Scale *c*. 31 m. = 1 in.   Cowperthwait, publisher in Philadelphia.
Libraries: RSGS.

(1850)   ADLARD, ALFRED. (del & engr).   Scotland.
         10¾ × 8½.   Scale *c*. 31 m. = 1 in.
In *Adlard's Vignette Modern Atlas*, London, 1849/50.
Libraries: BM, Bod.

(1850)   DOWER, J. (del & engr).   Scotland.
         10¼ × 8¼.   Scale 32 m. = 1 in.
In *A Descriptive Atlas* by the Rev. Thomas Milner, London, 1850.
Libraries: BM, Bod, CUL, GU, NLS, RSGS.

c. 1850 (LIZARS, W. H.).   Scotland.
         9¾ × 8.   (Scale *c*. 36 m. = 1 in.).
In *A Modern and Ancient General Atlas*, by W. H. Lizars, Edinburgh, n.d.
Libraries: BM.

c. 1850 LOWRY, J. W.   Scotland.
         11¼ × 8⅝.   Scale 33 m. = 1 in.   Chapman & Hall, London.
Libraries: RSGS.

c. 1850   MURPHY, W. (del & engr).   Scotland.
            5 × 4.   Scale 64 m. = 1 in.

In Atlas, no title page, pub. by Myles Macphail, Edinburgh; n.d.   Macphail took over the business of Alex. Macredie, (see 1832), booksellers and publishers, 11 South St David St., in 1843/4.
Libraries: BM.

1862   BLACK, A. and C.   Black's new large map of Scotland.
            12 sheets each 18½ × 19¼.   Scale 4 m. = 1 in.   Drawn and
            Engraved by J. Bartholomew.

This excellent and finely engraved map was the most popular map of Scotland prior to the completion of the 1 inch Ordnance Survey about 1887.   The map was also issued in atlas form as "Black's New Atlas of Scotland".
Libraries: Bod, NLS, RSGS.

Index to Maps of Scotland

(m. = Scale in miles per inch)

Bertholon
  1799   36 m.
Bertius, Petrus
  1598   40 m.
  1616   80 m.
Betts, John
  1845   9⅔ m.
Beugo, John
  1789   25 m.
Bickham, George
  1750   70 m.
Black, A. & C.
  1839   18 m.
  1844   10 m.
  1862   4 m.
Blackwood, W. & Sons
  1838   17 m.
Blaeu, Joannis
  1653   18 m.
  1654   18 m.
Blaeu, Willem
  1635   15 m.
Blome, Richard
  1673   14 m.
Blondeau
  1800   49 m.
Bonne, Rigobert
  1771   28 m.
  1788   31 m.
Bowen, Emanuel
  1746   16 m.
  1747   38 m.
  1747   20 m.
  1754   41 m.
  1758   107 m.
  1763   15 m.
Bowen Thomas
  1770   34 m.
Bowles, Carington
  1775   15 m.
  1782   14 m.
  1782   7¼ m.
  1806   7¼ m.
Bowyer, William
  1567   — m.
Bradley, J.
  1819   53 m.
Brion de la Tour, Louis
  1765   25 m.
Brown, J.
  1842   15 m.
Brown, Thomas
  1790   10½ m.
  1795   7½ m.

1801   19 m.
1806   11 m.
Browne, Christopher
  1705   17 m.
Bryce, Alexander
  1744   3⅓ m.
Butler, Samuel
  1824   36 m.
Bye, Joseph
  1803   14⅓ m.
  1806   38 m.

Camden, William
  1607   33 m.
Campbell, Lt. Robert
  1790   7½ m.
  1790   14 m.
Capper, Benjamin J.
  1808   29 m.
Carey, Mathew
  1795   24 m.
Carrington, F. A.
  1846   5 m.
Cary, John
  1781   55 m.
  1789   12 m.
  1789   55 m.
  1791   16 m.
  1794   5 m.
  1801   8 m.
  1809   11 m.
  1813   40 m.
  1832   2 m.
Cassini, Gio. M.
  1795   12 m.
Chanlaire, P. G.
  1798   34 m.
Chatelain, Z.
  1708   22½ m.
Cheevers, J.
  1774   18½ m.
Claesz, Cornelis
  1598   40 m.
Clark, J.
  1726   4½ m.
  1727   58 m.
Clegg, John
  1795   — m.
Clerk, T.
  1820   16 m.
  1832   16 m.
Cloppenburg, Johannis
  1630   40 m.
  1630   27 m.

Gibson, John
 1758 107 m.
Goldsmith, J.
 1812 32 m.
Gordon, Robert
 1653 18 m.
 1654 18 m.
Greene, Rob.
 1679 13⅓ m.
Grierson, George
 1746 12½ m.

Hagen, T.
 1842 11 m.
Hall, Sydney
 1817 31 m.
 1823 36 m.
 1823 35 m.
 1824 36 m.
 1828 16 m.
 1831 27 m.
 1839 18 m.
 1842 17½ m.
 1842 35 m.
 1843 35 m.
 1844 10 m.
Hardyng, John
 1457 — m.
Harrison & Co.
 1784 45 m.
Harrison, J.
 1787 23 m.
Harrison, Sam
 1812 41 m.
Hatchett
 1789 34 m.
Haydon, W.
 1783 14 m.
Haywood, James
 1787 21 m.
Hebert, L.
 1811 8¼ m.
Hewitt
 1815 13 m.
 1819 28 m.
 1821 9½ m.
Heyns, Peeter
 1577 44 m.
Hill, Peter
 1820 7 m.
Hole, William
 1607 33 m.
Hollar, W.
 1644 6 m.

Homann, Johann Baptist
 1710 11 m.
Homen, Diego
 1558 70 m.
Hondius, Henricus
 1636 22 m.
 1636 13 m.
Hondius, Jodocus
 1607 50 m.
 1607 35 m.
Hooper, S.
 1791 19 m.

Ivory, T.
 1803 15 m.

Jaillot, A. H.
 1693 11 m.
Janssonius, Joannis
 1628 40 m.
 1636 15 m.
 1659 — m.
Jefferys, Thomas
 1749 41 m.
 1769 43 m.
Jode, Cornelius de
 1578 40 m.
Johnston, Andrew
 1722 17 m.
Johnston, W. & A. K.
 1838 16 m.
 1842 9½ m.
 1843 12½ m.

Keere, Pieter van den
 1599 40 m.
 1627 80 m.
 1630 40 m.
Kincaid, A.
 1792 30 m.
 1797 31 m.
Kirkwood, Robert and James
 1799 25 m.
 1804 11 m.
 1808 26 m.
 1817 26 m.
 1821 22 m.
Kitchin, Thomas
 1745 13⅓ m.
 1749 41 m.
 1761 75 m.
 1762 32 m.
 1765 30 m.
 1767 49 m.

Mitchell, E.
1810   35 m.
Mitchell, S.
1846   30 m.
Moll, Herman
1701   50 m.
1701   40 m.
1708   43 m.
1714   12½ m.
1718   29 m.
1725   29 m.
1727   29 m.
Morden, Robert
1687   18½ m.
1688   70 m.
1695   18¾ m.
1705   14⅓ m.
Morrison & Son, R.
1795   31 m.
Moxom, James
1688   22 m.
Munster, Sebastian
1540   —
Murphy, H. T.
1834   14 m.
Murphy, W.
1832   17½ m.
1832   65 m.
1850   64 m.
Murray, T. L.
1830   16 m.

Nagel, Henricus
1592   30 m.
Neele, James & Joseph
1827   31 m.
1829   22 m.
Neele, S. J.
1782   24 m.
1787   21 m.
1792   75 m.
1797   24 m.
1798   50 m.
1800   20 m.
1800   37 m.
1801   32 m.
1801   25 m.
1802   30 m.
1803   32 m.
1806   3½ m.
1809   35 m.
1809   20 m.
1811   8¼ m.

1813   20 m.
1820   62 m.
Nicholls, Sutton
1710   12½ m.
1715   11 m.
1766   11 m.
Nicolay, Nicolas de
1580   26 m.
1580   32 m.
1583   48 m.
Nolin, Jean Baptiste
1689   13 m.
1690   40 m.
Nowell, Laurence
1566   50 m.
1566   35 m.
1566   22 m.

Oliver & Boyd
1825   7 m.
Ortelius, Abraham
1570   33 m.
1573   20 m.
1577   44 m.
1598   43 m.
1601   43 m.
Overton, Henry
1715   11 m.
Overton, John
1670   19 m.
1690   — m.

Palairet, John
1754   15⅓ m.
1755   15⅓ m.
1775   24 m.
Palmer, William
1767   18¾ m.
1778   50 m.
1798   77 m.
Paris, Matthew
1250   — m.
Pass, J.
1827   37 m.
Paterson, G. and W.
1746   62 m.
Patteson, Rev. Edward
1804   35 m.
Payne, J.
1791   — m.
Peat, Alexr.
1822   23m.

Smith, B.
1807　30 m.
1808　24 m.
1819　31 m.
Smith, Charles
1808　24 m.
Speed, John
1610　19 m.
1627　80 m.
1630　19 m.
Stackhouse, T.
1782　24 m.
Starling, Thomas
1830　70 m.
1837　20 m.
Stewart, Meikle & Murdoch
1790　15½ m.
Stieler, Adolf
1824　30 m.
1837　30 m.
Stieler, August
1804　22 m.
Stockdale, John
1800　25 m.
1806　3½ m.
1809　20 m.
Stulpnagel, F. von
1837　30 m.
Swanston, G. H.
1848　14½ m.
Swinton, William
1806　11 m.
1821　12 m.

Tanner, Henry Schenck
1836　30 m.
Tardieu, Ambroise
1834　31 m.
Tardieu, P. F.
1798　34 m.
1812　42 m.
Taylor, George and
Skinner, Andrew
1776　23 m.
1792　23 m.
Taylor, Thomas
1715　44 m.
1720　12⅔ m.
Teesdale, Henry
1829　17½ m.
Telford, Thomas
1803　12 m.
1838　18 m.

Thomson, John
1815　13 m.
1821　9½ m.
1832　18½ m.
Tielenburg, Gerrit
1730　70 m.
1730　45 m.
Tirion Isaak
1744　27½ m.
Tschudi, Aegidius
1552　— m.

Valk, Gerard and Leonard
1705　9½ m.
Vandermaelen, P. M. G.
1827　25 m.
Visscher, Nicolaus
1689　11 m.

Waldseemüller, Martin
1513　— m.
Walker, J. and C.
1834　12½ m.
1841　19 m.
1842　20 m.
Walker, John
1798　50 m.
1810　40 m.
Wallis, James
1803　30 m.
1816　3½ m.
1818　37 m.
Weigel, Christoph
1718　17 m.
Weiland, Carl Ferdinand
1844　— m.
Whittle, See Laurie & Whittle
Wilkinson, Robert
1794　30 m.
1807　30 m.
1811　15½ m.
1812　24 m.
1814　29 m.
1826　15½ m.
Wit, Frederick de
1680　12 m.
Wright, A.
1837　42 m.
Wyld, James
1819　28 m.
1832　7 m.
1840　11 m.

Printed in Great Britain
by T. & A. CONSTABLE LTD., Hopetoun Street.
Printers to the University of Edinburgh